"And are we yet alive?"

A History of the Northwest Texas Conference of the United Methodist Church

"And are we yet alive?"

A History of the Northwest Texas Conference of the United Methodist Church

by

David J. Murrah, Ph.D.

Foreword
by
Bishop D. Max Whitfield

State House Press

Buffalo Gap, Texas

Library of Congress Cataloging-in-Publication Data

Murrah, David J.
"And are we yet alive?": a history of the Northwest Texas Conference of the United Methodist Church / by David J. Murrah; foreword by D. Max Whitfield.
p. cm.
Includes bibliographical references and index.
ISBN 978-1-933337-35-7 (alk. paper)
1. United Methodist Church (U.S.). Northwest Texas Conference--History. 2. Texas, West--Church history. I. Title.

BX8382.2.M87 2009
287'.67645--dc22

2009001593

State House Press
P.O. Box 818
Buffalo Gap, TX 79508
(325) 572-3974
www.mcwhiney.org/press

Distributed by Texas A&M University Press Consortium
(800) 826-8911
www.tamu.edu/upress

Printed in the United States of America

ISBN 978-1-933337-35-7

Book designed by Rosenbohm Graphic Design

Contents

Maps and Illustrations

Foreword

The Northwest Texas Conference of the United Methodist Church originated from the western expansion of the United States. People moved into the vast prairies and ranchland of West Texas seeking a new life with new opportunities, and Methodism mirrored the population's migration. Pastors saw themselves as missionaries and evangelists. They encountered the isolation, dangers, and physical elements assured of God's presence and confident of the apostle Paul's affirmation: "For to me, living is Christ and dying is gain" (Phil. 1:21). They joined in partnership with laity, enabling new converts to grow in grace and move toward Christian perfection.

The division of labor that occurred in 1910 to establish two annual conferences from the original Northwest Texas Conference, establishing a Central Texas Conference and a new Northwest Texas Conference, enabled Methodism to continue its rapid expansion. The primary motivations propelling individuals and families to leave behind previous relationships and confidently face an unknown future were their love for God and their love for their neighbors. The salvation of souls and the expansion of God's kingdom demanded that they make hard decisions and consciously follow the leading of the Holy Spirit.

We can learn much from the Methodist pioneers of Northwest Texas. Some had a passion to reach people. They exhibited great courage by taking on a vast territory; they went by horseback, buggy, and bicycle and on foot and even swam flooded rivers to ensure that the gospel would be preached. Some sacrificed any hope of wealth, and to a large extent their families, to answer God's call. Many labored with full expectation of the Holy Spirit's work: as Cal C. Wright wrote of those days, "We were in tune with God. The witness of the Spirit continued with us. Methodism grew mightily."

The motivation of pastors and laity at the beginning of the twenty-first century obligates the present Northwest Texas Conference to engage a new frontier with a bold, new direction. It is not a frontier of unsettled land with few established communities, but rather a frontier where residents no longer consider the Christian faith as a vital part of their families and communities. Fewer youth and young adults know the Christian story, and some congregations feel their primary responsibility is to care for the present members of their community of faith. The salvation of souls and the expansion of God's kingdom require pastors and laity to learn from the history of those who established this conference and to tackle the new frontier with the passion demonstrated by our Lord Jesus for every resident within its bounds. The stories and experiences of those who established and led this conference for the past 100 years should drive the present pastoral and lay leadership to advance like a mighty army into a new century of evangelism and service.

I highly commend this book to anyone interested in the western expansion of Methodism and those particularly interested in the communities and congregations in the Northwest Texas Conference of the United Methodist Church. Dr. David J. Murrah has captured the historical facts and the Christian spirit that produced and sustained these disciples and that continue to propel them into a new frontier. This history recalls the past, reveals the present reality, and guides the church toward a remarkable future.

D. Max Whitfield
Resident Bishop of the Northwest Texas/New Mexico Area
August 2008

Preface

In 2010, the Northwest Texas Conference of the United Methodist Church will celebrate its one hundredth anniversary. However, at its birth in 1910, the conference began with twice as many congregations as it has today—nearly 200 strong churches and another 200 part-time "schoolhouse" churches—within its charge. Thus, its history really reaches back to the 1870s, when a handful of dedicated preachers determined to carry the gospel to wherever the people were on the northern and western Texas frontier.

The forerunner of the Northwest Texas Conference, which was also known by the same name, stretched northwestward from Georgetown and Waco, and by the early 1900s was the state's largest geographically and numerically. As a result of its size and growth, the General Conference in 1910 divided this vast territory into the Central Texas Conference and a new Northwest Texas Conference. The former was already urbanized and settled; the latter was a region that was still in the process of conquering the frontier.

The new Northwest Texas Conference rose to the challenge, and for nearly forty years it grew rapidly. But in the mid-1960s, the growth of Methodism in the conference and the nation reached its zenith and then started a gradual decline that continues to this day. Although this study celebrates the tremendous achievements of the Northwest Texas Conference in bringing salvation and civility to its vast territory, it also examines the challenge of decline and the conference's efforts to find renewal and revival.

Charles Wesley's great hymn "And Are We Yet Alive?" is the traditional call to worship at conference assemblies. The question is more relevant now than ever before as United Methodists throughout the Northwest Texas Conference and the nation face the challenges of a changing society and world. Methodists have always drawn strength from one another, thanks to the historic connectional system; today, more than ever, they need to face the future with the hope of Wesley's words:

What troubles have we seen,
What mighty conflicts past,
Fightings without, and fears within,
Since we assembled last!

But out of all the Lord
Hath brought us by His love;
And still He doth His help afford,
And hides our life above.[1]

I want to express my appreciation to Bishop Max Whitfield and the conference office for support of this project, and especially to my longtime friend Rev. Eddie Allsup, who recently retired as conference director. His successor, Rev. Ava Berry, also provided valuable insight and suggestions, and Karla Abernethy-Thetford and Rosemary Prumer of the conference office provided valuable photo and publicity support. Thanks also to Dr. Garry Nall and the members of the conference's Archives and History Commission for selecting me for this project and for being so very helpful in its production. Several members of the commission took time to proof the manuscript, including Cleo Morrison, Donna Porter, Pat Williamson, Pauline Gwyn, Betty Carr, and Lynn Guy. Christena Stephens also gave valuable assistance in critiquing chapters. Thanks also to Texas Tech history professor Paul Carlson, and former McMurry University professors Rob Sledge and Robert Monk for sharing materials and offering very helpful suggestions. Garry and Annette Nall were also most gracious in proofreading, providing leads, and giving warm hospitality while I was researching in Amarillo.

Dozens of other people—too many to mention here—granted me interviews and provided resource material. Their contributions are cited in the endnotes. But I would be remiss in not mentioning Rex and Letha Mauldin of Abilene, who gave wonderful counsel and opened their home to me for many days while I researched at the conference archives. I am also deeply indebted to the late Darris Egger for his interest in this project, and for the wonderful historical legacy he left through his several books dealing with conference history.

I am especially grateful to Pat Williamson, the archivist for the Northwest Texas Conference archives. Not only did she make herself available for every visit I made to the archives, but she answered every inquiry I made by phone and e-mail, spending hours locating and scanning material. I also want to thank Joe Specht,former director of the Jay-Rollins Library at McMurry, for his willingness to open the archives in Pat's absence and for his considerable support of its mission during his tenure. Without the archives and its rich trove of conference history, this book would not have been possible. I am also appreciative of my wife, Ann, who once again became an "author's widow" for nearly three years as she tolerated my countless hours at the computer.

David J. Murrah
Rockport, Texas
August 2008

Chapter 1

"What Mighty Conflicts Past"

They came from across the plains—by rail, by buggy, by horseback, by automobile—to join together in worship and work. In so doing, they inaugurated the newest of the Methodist conferences in the Methodist Episcopal Church, South.

The place was Clarendon, in the heart of the Texas Panhandle. It was November 1910. For Thomas Hanks, pastor at Texline's Methodist Church in the far northwest corner of the Panhandle, the trip to conference was an easy half-day train ride of 110 miles, all on the Fort Worth & Denver line. For J. G. Miller, pastor at Vernon on the east side of the new conference, the trip was similarly easy—a 116-mile trip on the same railroad. B. F. Gassaway's trip from Higgins in the northeastern Panhandle meant a 130-mile ride on the Santa Fe to Amarillo, a short transfer between depots, and then a 60-mile trip to Clarendon.

For many others, however, the trip was much longer. Pastors in the southern part of the conference from Midland on the west to Abilene and Baird on the east would have to ride the Texas & Pacific train to Fort Worth and then catch the FW&D to Clarendon. For Midland pastor

R. B. McSwain, it meant a trip of nearly 600 miles by rail—a two-day trip. Still others, such as J. D. May at Fluvanna or R. J. McElrath of Lamesa, had buggy trips of sixty miles or more just to reach a railroad. By 1910, the scattered pastors across the sparsely settled South Plains would travel to the new railhead at Lubbock, where they could get a direct connection to Amarillo, and then on the FW&D to Clarendon. And some, unable to afford the rail rates, chose to ride horseback or go by buggy.

Regardless of the trip's difficulty, approximately 200 gathered in the new sanctuary on that brisk November day at Clarendon's Methodist Church. After the opening hymn, "Jesus, Lover of My Soul," the congregation joined together to repeat Charles Wesley's question in the hymn that had been used at Methodist conferences for more than 100 years: "And Are We Yet Alive?"

If an answer had been demanded, it would have been: "Yes, we are!" Excited to be a part of the first annual session of the new Northwest Texas Annual Conference, and elated because they were part of one of the fastest-growing areas in the United States, the delegates rejoiced when they heard the report that during 1910, the conference had seen "8,900 conversions, 9,000 additions to the church, 17 new parsonages and 25 new churches built."[1] At the end of 1910, the new conference posted its membership at 35,099 in 415 churches and preaching points, with 189 churches housed in their own buildings.

The new conference was in the position to grow rapidly. During the first ten years of the twentieth century, the population of its region had tripled, growing at a rate of more than 23,000 a year; with new railroads being built daily, the Panhandle-Plains clearly was in the midst of a boom. What a great opportunity for these mission-minded Methodists!

In the exuberance of the moment—the newness of Clarendon's sanctuary, the growth of the region, and the new conference—onlookers may not have fully appreciated the fifty-year-old foundation already present. Many in 1910 perhaps did not know that the establishment of a new conference for the Panhandle-Plains region was the fulfillment of a twenty-year dream. Also, the new rail age of 1910, which provided safe and fast transportation for many conference attendees, overshadowed the memories of the years when Methodist preachers covered circuits of 300 miles or more in Northwest Texas, all on horseback.

The pioneers of the region had for decades traveled great and difficult distances to attend the annual conference meetings of the old Northwest Texas Conference, a region that at one time had encompassed nearly half of the state. Several had labored alone on the frontier in the cause of Christ under the worst of conditions, becoming greatly discouraged when drought virtually wiped out years of labor when farmers abandoned homesteads in the 1880s and '90s to move back east. Thus, to understand the modern Northwest Texas Conference, born with relative ease in 1910, it is necessary to examine the difficult labor pangs that preceded its birth.

Methodism comes to Texas

Methodism came to America around 1760 as a lay movement, twenty-two years after John and Charles Wesley began an evangelical awakening in England. In 1744, the first annual Methodist conference was held in England. In 1784, Thomas Coke, acting on authority from John Wesley, began organizing the Methodist Episcopal Church in America; at the famous Christmas Conference in Baltimore, Maryland, he and Francis Asbury were elected as superintendents, or bishops, of the new church. In 1792, the church held its first quadrennial General Conference at Baltimore; at the second, in 1796, it organized itself into six annual conferences, including an "open-ended" Western Conference.[2]

In 1803, while traveling across the Appalachians into Tennessee, Asbury marveled that there were "four or five hundred [emigrants] crossing the rude hills while we were." He estimated that there must have been 400,000 to 500,000 such travelers migrating west every year and thus wrote, "We must take care to send preachers after these people."[3]

Send they did. In 1814, Tennessee preacher William Stevenson traveled a wide circuit across sparsely settled Arkansas, preaching wherever he could find people. He returned in 1815 and crossed the Red River into Texas (then under the control of Spain), where he found a few trappers and traders—or as he noted, "a settlement of Americans in the bounds of the Province of Texas. Here I formed a Methodist Society in the same year."[4] Stevenson was not only the first Methodist preacher to work in Texas but also the first Protestant to hold services within the bounds of the future state.

Stevenson's work bore fruit. Described by his bishop as an "excellent preacher," Stevenson preached God's love and mercy and, as Methodist historian Walter Vernon noted, "had no sympathy with narrow and exclusive denominations that created divisions among Christians." Thus, Stevenson set the tone for Texas Methodism, to reflect the fruit of God's spirit, "love, joy, peace, long suffering, gentleness, meekness, [and] temperance."[5]

After Stephen F. Austin's initial colonization of Texas under grants from Spanish and, later, Mexican authorities, Methodism was not allowed to be openly proclaimed, as Roman Catholicism was to be the official religion of Mexican Texas. But Henry Stephenson (a colleague of William Stevenson) and William's grandson James Stevenson and several others secretly preached in homes where possible. In 1832, the first camp meeting was held in Sabine County in deep East Texas. When Mexican authorities did not show any formal opposition, preaching became more public in that part of the province.[6] In 1833, James Stevenson helped to establish McMahan's Chapel, near San Augustine, which became the oldest continuing congregation in Texas.[7] In 1834, the new Mississippi Conference created a Texas mission and appointed Henry Stephenson to head the work.[8]

The outbreak of the Texas Revolution and the subsequent victory of the Texans over the Mexican army at San Jacinto served to open the door for formal mission work. While the General Conference of 1836 was in session at Cincinnati, Ohio, news of the Texas victory reached the floor. The excitement of the moment yielded immediate results when a prominent preacher, former college president, and delegate, Dr. Martin Ruter, volunteered to go to Texas as a missionary.[9] During the next two years, Ruter traveled more than 2,200 miles through the new Republic of Texas; in April 1838, he reported that he had located twenty societies with 325 members scattered across the frontier. Sadly, Ruter died within a month of his report, and two of his lieutenants fell seriously ill. However, new preachers came from Tennessee to give the work a boost, and by 1839, the Texas mission listed 797 members, including forty-three of color.[10]

The new Clarendon Methodist Episcopal Church, South, in 1910, site of the first Annual Northwest Texas Conference.

In May 1840, the General Conference recognized the progress and split Texas off from the Mississippi Conference, creating the Texas Conference to serve the vast region. At its first meeting in late December 1840, only nine members and six probationers were in attendance. Presiding Bishop Beverly Waugh was not discouraged, likening the gathering to the small group at the Christmas Conference in Baltimore fifty-six years before that led to the organization of Methodism in America. "Our [Texas] conference continued in session four days," he recalled. "Several sinners were converts to God . . . the appointments of eighteen preachers were announced, and the conference closed full of good feeling."[11]

In the mid-1840s, national political events profoundly affected Texas Methodism. First, the 1844 General Conference of the Methodist Episcopal Church divided the Texas Conference along the Trinity River into two conferences, Eastern Texas and Texas.[12] Second, debates about slavery polarized the General Conference; Southern delegates withdrew after the conference and adopted a Plan of Separation. In 1845, the

Southern conferences, including the two Texas conferences, voted to join the new denomination: the Methodist Episcopal Church, South.[13] At the time of separation, the two Texas conferences had approximately 5,000 white and 1,000 colored members.[14] Also, in 1845, the Republic of Texas came to an end as Texas entered the Union. The annexation by the United States led directly to war with Mexico beginning in 1846.

After the war's end in 1848, Texas entered into a period of relative peace and prosperity, and Methodism began to grow rapidly. By this time, the circuit-rider system had adapted well to the Texas frontier. By 1859, the state's Methodists had increased their membership six-fold to nearly 39,000 and added a third conference, the Rio Grande Mission Conference, which served all of Texas south and west of San Antonio. By 1860, the Methodists were the largest denomination in the state, and the church's newspaper, *The Texas Wesleyan Banner*, forerunner to the *United Methodist Reporter*, had the largest circulation of any newspaper in Texas.[15]

The Civil War impacts Texas Methodism

Sadly, the peace and prosperity of the 1850s gave way to the violence and hardships of the 1860s as the United States fought its Civil War, completely disrupting Methodist work. Dozens of Methodist preachers enlisted in the armies, with most of those from Texas going into Confederate service. Because the U.S. Army had abandoned the Texas frontier, which before the war had been relatively free from Indian attacks, settlers in northern and western Texas were forced to move east in order to find protection in the more settled areas. Moreover, no bishops were able to come to Texas for annual conferences from 1862 through 1865.[16] As a result, Texas Methodist church membership fell almost 50 percent, property fell into disrepair or was lost altogether, and funds dried up.[17] The Civil War did far more damage to the national Methodist Episcopal Church, South, than it did to the Texas conferences. Total membership across the South fell by two-thirds, and many church buildings were destroyed or badly damaged. Also, the denomination's missions, publishing, and educational programs were severely disrupted.[18] Moreover, some Northern Methodist leaders criticized their Southern co-religionists for supporting slavery. One bishop called the Southerners "rebel Methodists" and "came into the South, bearing an order from the Secretary of War authorizing him to fill Southern Methodist pulpits with preachers from his own church."[19] Still another Northern bishop noted that the South was "crude in character and backward in development."[20]

Such action and criticism, however, only served to regenerate the ME Church, South. Delegates to the Fifth General Conference in April 1866 (there had been no General Conference in 1862) gathered in New Orleans and stayed into early May. Delegates elected four new bishops, including Enoch M. Marvin, a Missourian who had moved to Texas during the war. More important, they laid down a foundation of reform and reorganization that would eventually serve to spark tremendous growth in the ME Church, South. They dropped the rule for required attendance at class meetings and did away with the six-month probationary membership period. Pastoral terms were increased from two to four years. The holding of district conferences was also recommended to the annual conferences, as was the inclusion of lay representatives in the councils of the church.[21]

In spite of the church's numerical losses, the 1866 General Conference anticipated future growth and created a framework for the addition of more conferences in Texas. Subsequently, the large Eastern Texas Conference divided into two conferences, with the northern part taking the name of the Trinity Conference (later changed to North Texas). The Rio Grande Conference became the West Texas Conference, later to be named the Southwest Texas Conference in 1939. And, the Texas Conference was divided between Georgetown and Austin, with the largely unsettled northern portion given the name of the Northwest Texas Conference.[22]

Beginnings of the first Northwest Texas Conference

At the time of its creation in 1866, the Northwest Texas Conference had a sparse population that lived along a line stretching from Georgetown on the south, to Waco and to Corsicana to the northeast, and to Fort Worth on the north. Its western boundary followed the "road from San Antonio to Fort Mason; thence due north to the Colorado River; thence up said river to the Big Spring [now Big Spring]; thence due north to the State line" at top of the Texas Panhandle.[23] Thus, the conference included the mostly unsettled portion of the western half of North Texas as well as the entire eastern half of the Panhandle, which at that time was largely unexplored. In reality, the conference's western boundary coincided with the line of settlement, or frontier, and in 1866 that line stretched from Llano northeastward to Palo Pinto northwest of Fort Worth.[24]

Expansion of the new conference into its vast frontier region was totally dependent upon the condition of the frontier itself, and in 1866, the frontier was a dangerous place. The greatest threat to settlers and itinerant ministers was from Indian raids. Prior to the Civil War, the federal government had established a line of forts across the northwestern Texas frontier, stretching from Fort McKavett, located northwest of present-day Junction, to Fort Belknap, northwest of Graham in Young County. With the outbreak of the war, the U.S. military abandoned the forts. During the war, the state of Texas placed troops on the frontier, but with a 300-mile line to cover, safety could not be guaranteed. At the end of the war and with the collapse of state government, the frontier troops melted away, and the line was totally unprotected. As a result, the frontier continued to "roll back" to the east by a hundred miles or more, especially in North Texas.[25] Indian attacks occurred as far south as Mason and San Saba. By October 1866, raiders had killed 78 people in 14 frontier counties.[26]

Although Texas had suffered during the war, the state saw few military conflicts and thus hardly any battle destruction. The Deep South fared differently—farms and plantations lay in ruins. As a result, Texas offered the promise of a fresh beginning, and a new migration began almost immediately as yeoman farmers pushed the cotton kingdom deeper into Texas. The newcomers helped to bolster Methodism. Thus, when delegates to the first annual session of the new Northwest Texas Conference gathered in Waxahachie on September 26, 1866, there was a spirit of great optimism in the air. The war was over, and it was time for a fresh start. And the General Conference had given the new conference an area that stretched more than 600 miles from its southern boundary north of Austin all the way to the top of the Panhandle!

Twenty members of the Northwest Texas Conference's ordained clergy were in attendance, and they reported a membership of 3,950 whites, 520 colored, and 242 baptisms for the year, including 141 infant

The Northwest Texas and other conferences of Texas, Methodist Episcopal Church, South, 1866-1886 (Adapted from Walter N. Vernon, et.al., *The Methodist Excitement in Texas*).

baptisms.[27] The conference included thirty-two "effective" or ordained clergy and eighty-five local preachers, located in four districts, with eight "charges" in each district.[28] Among others, the conference ordained Davis Medlock, "a Colored man" as deacon.[29] It also established six standing committees: Candidates on Trial, Public Worship, Education, Books and Periodicals, Sabbath Schools, and Domestic Missions. Among the reports given, the Education Committee chairman boldly stated that "we regard the fostering, supervision, and promotion of educational interests as an indispensable part of our vocation as a church."[30] This initiative would prove to be an important facet of the conference's future.

One of the attendees of the first Northwest Texas Conference was frontier preacher Peter Gravis, who had been dodging Indians and working virtually without pay. He knew of the great challenge that faced the new conference and described it this way: "This little Spartan band of thirty-two heroes went forth in the name of God, to combat error, sin and poverty, combined with the danger of losing life at the hands of a merciless savage, against whom they had no protection, but the eternal promise."[31]

Gravis, who would later become famous in Northwest Texas Conference annals, worked out of Stephenville and points north and west, to include the farthest reach of the northwest frontier along the Brazos valley at Palo Pinto. His missions were scattered over a 180-mile circuit. In his memoirs, he noted that 1868 was particularly difficult and bleak:

> The Indians in ten-fold fury ranged over the country, day and night, stealing our property and killing our citizens, capturing our children and raping our women. The frontier was defenceless [sic], all the arms having been arrested by the Federals . . . . Added to this state of things, men began to handle horses and cattle without authority, and as the civil arm was paralyzed, mobs sprung up and men were hung to trees by night and no clue to the perpetrators.[32]

In spite of the difficulty of the situation, Gravis continued his work and in the summer of 1868 had a "grand revival" at his westernmost outpost, Palo Pinto: "The revival began at one of my quarterly meetings, and as the Presiding Elder, Brother [James M.] Johnson, could not remain with me, I called on Brother [George] Webb Slaughter, Missionary Baptist, who came to my assistance. We preached turn about and divided the converts. I got about forty-five out of the seventy-five. The whole town was stirred, and the hardest sinners converted."[33]

In time, the frontier situation began to improve. In 1867, the U.S. government began re-establishing outposts on the Texas frontier, which in turn helped to gradually restore order over a seven-year period. The new forts stretched from Fort Davis, in far West Texas, northeastward to Fort Richardson, at Jacksboro. As the frontier quieted, settlers began to re-occupy abandoned farms and ranches, and some even began to push farther into Northwest Texas. By the early 1870s, soldiers and settlers were occupying the southeastern part of the region that was to become the modern Northwest Texas Conference, and Methodist preachers were not far behind.

The Northwest Texas mission frontier

Prior to the Civil War, a few hardy families had settled in Shackelford County north and west of present-day Albany. Even though they were on the cusp of the frontier, the ranchers received protection from, and had a ready market for their cattle at, near-by Camp Cooper. With the abandonment of the post in 1861, the settlers, including John C. Lynch and his family, "forted up" to provide for protection. After the war, with the 1867 establishment of Fort Griffin north of present-day Albany, a community called Fort Griffin, or Hidetown, began to take root. This little outpost served as a marketplace for the nearby fort and eventually became a supply point for buffalo hunters who were beginning to venture west into the rolling and high plains area. Also, the Western Cattle Trail also passed through the area, bringing cowboys, saloons, and dance hall girls to the community. By 1870, the area around Fort Griffin boasted a population of 455.[34] Otherwise, in the rest of the vast area that was to become the modern Northwest Texas Conference, there was not a single person listed in the 1870 census.

Meanwhile, within four years of its founding, the Northwest Texas Conference had recouped membership loss from the war for its area and began to expand as the region's population increased. By 1871, the conference's membership had more than doubled from its 1866 total, with 10,000 members in 54 churches or circuits. Baptisms totaled nearly 20 percent of its membership, with more than 1,800.[35] But Methodist Church leadership, such as Bishop George F. Pierce, recognized that to reach into the isolated areas, "robust, fearless, [and] self-denying men" would be needed. In September 1873, Pierce issued a unusual call for preachers to serve the vast Northwest Texas frontier: "The dainty, the timid, have no business here. The rides are long, the fare plain—the exposure in wind and weather very great, often severe—pay scanty . . . . Who will volunteer?"[36]

One who answered the bishop's call was Levi Collins, who had turned forty-six when he was licensed to preach in 1873. On his first assignment, he went straight to the mission field of the Northwest Texas Conference with work at Eastland and Fort Griffin. At Fort Griffin, he found a warm welcome in the large stone home of rancher John Lynch. There, Collins preached perhaps the first Methodist sermon in what would become the modern Northwest Texas Conference. He also preached to the people who would become the first church of that vast region.[37]

No doubt, Rev. Collins' work was challenging. The town of Fort Griffin was widely known as a lawless place, and its reputation was well deserved. At one time or another, it served as the home of notorious characters such as Lottie Deno, Mollie McCabe, Pat Garrett, Doc Holiday, Wyatt Earp, John Wesley Hardin, and John Selman.[38] Perhaps because of the town's reputation, Collins initially held his services at the Lynch ranch, arriving on Saturday and staying until Monday. According to one historian, "people for miles around attended the services and Mrs. Lynch served dinner for all . . . ."[39] His work did not go unrewarded; by 1875, the Fort Griffin Mission reported forty-eight members, one profession of faith, and an enrollment of twelve in Sabbath School.[40] Later, services were held in the community opera house. In the summer, Collins and other Methodist pastors joined with Baptists in holding camp meetings from ten days to two weeks long.[41]

Significant events in 1874–5 signaled an approaching end to the Texas frontier. For more than 150 years, Comanche and Kiowa bands had provided a formidable barrier to their prime hunting grounds, the southern Great Plains of the United States. But in 1874, the U.S. Army—in a prolonged campaign known as the Red River War—successfully forced the Comanches and their allies to permanent reservations in Oklahoma. Second, widespread exploration of the region by the military in 1875 revealed the plains to be an ideal range for cattle once the vast buffalo herds were cleared. Thus, from Dodge City, Fort Griffin, and other gateways, buffalo hunters poured into the region to harvest hides from the shaggy beasts. By 1877, they had done their job, leaving the high plains vacant for enterprising cattlemen and adventurous farmers. All that was lacking was a railroad to provide easy market access.

At the end of Reconstruction in Texas in 1875, the state was beginning to enjoy a new prosperity, especially in farming and ranching. Construction of railroads, essential for agricultural production, had by 1876 linked Houston to Dallas and Texarkana to Fort Worth.[42] Construction on the Texas & Pacific line that was to link Fort Worth and El Paso halted in 1876 because of a national depression and financial trouble. However, in anticipation of the railroad's arrival, farmers and ranchers accelerated their invasion of the Northwest Texas frontier and rapidly pushed the line of settlement north and west. By 1876, ranchers and farmers had moved into southern Callahan County, where two communities, Callahan City and Belle Plain, were established.[43] Taylor County, to the immediate west, also began to grow. And, in accordance with Francis Asbury's wishes, Methodists were quick to "send preachers after these people."[44] The mission frontier of the Northwest Texas Conference had begun a steady march westward.

Chapter 2

"Preserved by Power Divine"

In the mid-1870s, although the threat of Indian raids had subsided, the Northwest Texas frontier was still a dangerous place. Even as the military was rounding up the various bands of Comanche and Kiowa at the close of the Red River War in 1874, buffalo hunters were plunging into the plains, and behind them came skinners, cowboys, rustlers, saloons, and prostitutes. Law and order had not yet arrived, and thus the region was perhaps more dangerous than ever before. Yet Methodist circuit riders, showing an unequaled bravery, did not hesitate to plunge into the field.

Three routes of expansion: Course 1

Methodism's push into Northwest Texas proceeded along three courses, two of which were sponsored by the ME Church, South, and the third by the Northern-based ME Church. Levi Collins, who had taken the work to Fort Griffin, headed the first course. Ever extending his circuit westward, Collins at the 1877 annual conference was appointed to the Belle Plain Mission. [1] Belle Plain, located six miles southeast of present-day Baird, immediately thrived and would soon host the first

Methodist college within the bounds of the modern Northwest Texas Conference. Collins also ranged into southern Taylor County County, where he probably organized churches at Buffalo Gap and Jim Ned in 1878 (later called the Rogers Church near present-day Lawn).[2]

Meanwhile, laymen and local preachers seized the opportunity to forward the Methodist cause. M. M. Norris, an early settler in Mulberry Canyon southwest of Abilene (site of the future home of the Conference Camp Butman), built a brush arbor around 1879 and shared preaching duties with a Methodist circuit rider, probably H. C. Tramel, who served the Clear Fork (perhaps Phantom Hill) Mission northeast of Abilene. By 1879, the Taylor Mission, which included scattered churches in southern Taylor County, reported a membership of seventy. [3] Other mission points listed in the 1879 *Conference Journal* included Belle Plain, Phantom Hill, Reynolds (which probably should be "Runnels," in present-day Runnels County), and Nolan.[4] By 1880, these missions, along with the one at Buffalo Gap, accounted for 293 members, a reflection of just how fast the region had grown even without the benefit of a railroad.[5]

By 1880, the Northwest Texas Conference, in only 13 years, had grown more than 500 percent from its founding and boasted a membership of nearly 28,000, making it the largest conference in Texas geographically and numerically as well.[6] The conference also reported 3,603 prospective members "received by trial, 2,204 by letter, 1,557 adult baptisms, and 158 expulsions.[7] On the mission field, the western side of the conference, growth had been substantial enough to form the Belle Plain District, comprising eight circuits and missions. The "Noland" Mission was the farthest west, in Nolan County, and was pastored by none other than Levi Collins.[8]

The second route of expansion

At the same time that the conference created the Belle Plain District in 1880, it decided to form a second new district, the Panhandle District, even though only three small missions existed in the designated area. It was perhaps the greatest leap of faith that the conference ever attempted. For the task of trying to bring the gospel to an area larger than New England, the conference chose a veteran of the Civil War and the frontier, fifty-two-year-old Peter W. Gravis, to be the presiding elder. Gravis accepted the challenge.[9] His instructions were to "take the towns first"; the only problem was that there were no towns![10]

During the next several months, Gravis, (accompanied sometimes by his daughter Maggie, and other times by a young pastor, James Taylor Hosmer,) made remarkable and adventurous journeys by buggy deep into Northwest Texas—accounts that Gravis recorded in his classic book, *Twenty-five Years on the Outside Row of the Northwest Texas Conference*. The most ambitious trip was to Mobeetie and Clarendon. Mobeetie, with the nearby Fort Elliott, was a town even rougher than Fort Griffin. Gravis carefully recorded the trip in letters that he sent back home. It is useful to outline the details of the trip here, because in spite of seeming failure, in reality it firmly planted Methodism across Northwest Texas. It also revealed the difficulties that itinerant preachers faced, as well as their fears, faithlessness, and faithfulness.

Gravis began the work of the Panhandle District in February, 1881, setting out from his home in Comanche in a buggy pulled by two horses, bound for Seymour. It was a trip of 160 miles just to get to the beginning point.[11] There he met with Jeremiah Farmer and Hosmer, two young pastors ready to go into the field. Farmer had been assigned to the Wichita Mission in Wichita County. (Later in the year, it was discovered that the county was within the bounds of the North Texas Conference.) Hosmer, who was designated to pastor the Hardeman Mission in Hardeman County, had grown up in Alabama, where he had been licensed to preach in 1874 at age twenty-six.[12] He was thirty-two when he set out with Gravis for Hardeman County, and like Gravis, he would become legendary in Texas Methodism.

Interestingly, the 1881 *Conference Journal* lists "P. Tacket" to supply the Seymour Mission. However, no Tacket is ever mentioned in Gravis's notes. In all likelihood, "P. Tacket" was in reality Pleasant Tackitt, the rather famous Methodist frontier circuit rider and missionary to the Indians, who had moved to Parker County in 1856 and to Young County near Fort Belknap in 1858.[13] At age seventy-eight, Tackitt probably realized he was too old to make the monthly trips from Fort Belknap up to Seymour and withdrew from the assignment.[14]

Farmer had formed the Seymour Mission in the spring of 1880, and by November 1880 a church had been organized with 12 charter members.[15] After holding the regular quarterly conference for the mission, Gravis, with his daughter Maggie and young Hosmer, set out for a sixty-mile trip to Hosmer's farthest outpost: Pease City, located four miles north of present-day Crowell in Foard County.[16] Apparently Hosmer had previously preached there in 1880, probably in the city's only building, a rock post office. There they held the first quarterly conference for the Hardeman Mission.[17]

From Pease City, Gravis went east to Vernon, where Hosmer had also established a preaching point the year before. Gravis recorded his inhospitable visit there: "We stayed all night with a man named Chowning. That night the cowboys robbed me of two revolvers, my overcoat, gloves, stake-rope, and my daughter Maggie's sack."[18] Undeterred, Gravis and Maggie apparently returned home to Comanche safely and prepared for a second trip in the spring. Their February trip covered approximately 450 miles.

On Monday, May 9, 1881, Gravis and his daughter again set out from Comanche and covered the same route to Seymour and Vernon. His notes reveal his optimistic view of the new country as he described how that they got lost and had to seek special shelter for the night:

> Night came on and we were welcomed by Sprawls and Bowers who each keep a hotel by the side of the road. They have a wide fame among Western travelers. Their mansions are large, with liberal ventilation. They are carpeted with grass, with colors to suit the seasons. The roof is the starry skies and the moon is the lamp for both establishments. . . . Brother Sprawls . . . kindly pointed us to a spreading live oak, which seemed to extend its fraternal arms to receive us.[19]

After arriving in Seymour, Gravis held the second quarterly conference for the mission; Pastor Farmer's report showed eighteen additions since the last quarterly meeting. On Sunday, probably May 15, two more were added to the church. Gravis and Maggie remained in the area until Thursday, May 19, intending to be in Vernon by Sunday. However, heavy spring rains delayed their advance. At the Wichita River crossing about 18 miles north of Seymour, near present-day Lake Kemp, they found the river flooded. They spent the night with "Brother Long," whose home was one of the preaching points on the Seymour mission. On Friday, they followed the Western cattle trail north and progressed fifteen more miles but found Beaver Creek flooded and with "two or three" large cattle herds backed up trying to cross the swollen stream. They spent the afternoon and evening watching cowboys driving more than 3,000 head across the creek.

The next morning, Gravis was awakened by the sound of cowboys driving still another herd across the creek. He and Maggie rushed to break camp in an effort to cross the stream ahead of the cattle, but they were too late. The herd got to the crossing first, and they had no choice but to wait until the last of the cattle had crossed. Gravis described his attempted crossing in detail:

> By the time the rear cattle were entering the stream I drove up to the crossing. What an ugly sight. Muddy water and slippery banks, and with all, dreadfully steep. As the last cow made her exit from the stream, I drove down into the "muck" water, but I did not come "straightway out of the water," [a biblical allusion] for when I reached the opposite bank I found it so steep and slippery that my horses could not stand up and pull us out.[20]

Both Gravis and Maggie jumped into the muck, but before they could try to get the horses and the buggy out, a trail drover hailed them from behind and sent two of his cowboys to the rescue. After they had pulled the buggy out and up the ravine, the drover helped them cross another bad crossing at Little Beaver Creek. From there, Gravis and Maggie raced on to Vernon in time for an 11 a. m. Saturday service. "I found Brother J. T. Hasmer [Hosmer] at his post, very jubilant over his success since my last visit to his work. He had succeeded in organizing a church and Sunday School at Vernon."[21] There were seven in attendance, counting Hosmer and Gravis and Maggie (who sat in the buggy at the door because she was covered with mud). In the afternoon, Gravis held the first quarterly conference ever held in Wilbarger County.

Going Up the Trail to Mobeetie

The adventure had only begun. After making arrangements to leave Maggie at Vernon with their host family, Gravis and Hosmer headed north on June 20, following the Western cattle trail. An eleven-mile trip brought them to the famous Doan's Store, located a mile south of the crossing at the Red River into Indian Territory. At Doan's, the preachers were well received by Johnathan Doan, a "Quaker and a Mason."[22] The next morning, they arrived at what drovers called "the jumping-off place"—the river crossing. At that point, the Red River Valley is low and flat, but the riverbed sprawled nearly a mile across.[23] Depending on the season, most of the bed would have been dry sand, but as horses and buggy approached the main channel, quicksand was a major concern.

Gravis knew the peril. "I tell you . . . it was a fearful jump," he wrote a few days later: ". . . I clucked to my old faithful itinerant horses, and they began the leap. I did not close my eyes or hold my breath, but observed everything that came within the range of my vision. Thirty minutes by the watch! What a jump!" Once on the other side, he reflected upon the significance of the crossing: "When I reached the landing, I was out of the "pan" [handle], and in the Indian Territory, and 120 miles from Mobeetie, the point to which I started."[24]

Depending on one's point of view, Gravis and Hosmer were either in Greer County, Texas, or the federally controlled Indian Territory. At the time, both Texas and the federal government claimed the region between the South Fork and North Fork of the Red River, a situation caused by the lack of knowledge of the region when the boundary between Spanish Texas and the United States was fixed in 1819.[25] Although Gravis referred to the area as the "Indian Nation," he and other Texas Methodists considered the area as a part of the Northwest Texas Conference; eight years later, Hosmer would return to establish a church at Martha (now Oklahoma) and pastor at Mangum and Frazier.[26]

In all likelihood, the preachers continued to follow the Western cattle trail through the Indian Territory, "seeing no sign of civilization through the nation, except for a stage stand." At the stage stand (probably near present-day Sayre, Oklahoma), where they must have spent the night, Gravis and Hosmer heard tales—"many hard things"—about Mobeetie. The gossip, which they had already heard in Seymour, gave them second thoughts about continuing their journey.[27] Nevertheless, they continued—turning westward, probably following a military road—and once again entered Texas directly into the Panhandle, passing through the future town of Wheeler. On Friday, June 24, the preachers camped just east of Mobeetie, expecting to reach the town the next morning.

Rev. Peter W. Gravis

Before they could break camp, two ranch cowboys came riding by; as was the custom, the preachers invited them for breakfast, but they took care not to reveal their profession. Gravis recalled how the conversation with one of the cowboys caused him some alarm about going into Mobeetie:

> Both had been on a tear the day before, and still had with them the insignia of their rank—a bottle of whiskey. They were very communicative and gave profuse accounts of Mobeetie . . . . One told us of an incident, which occurred a few days before. While he was relating it, I caught myself catching my breath. For sport a man went around among the groups . . . and five saloons, saying, "Boys, there will be preaching at the courthouse to-night." "Who?" shouted several voices. "He's a d_ _n fool," shouted two or three, "he'd never get out alive. . . ." This, and similar reports caused me to regret the loss of time and expenditure of money to visit the place.[28]

In all likelihood, the two cowboys recognized that Gravis and Hosmer were preachers and were simply goading them with a story. The preachers, not accustomed to such West Texas mores, did not catch on.

However, the episode did not shake Gravis' faith completely. In spite of his fear, he decided to at least drive into town to "see how it goes." On that Saturday, Mobeetie was a bustling place; lots of people

Rev. James Taylor Hosmer

were in town. Already a county seat, Mobeetie had a population of 200 or more. The main street "was jammed with various businesses, including livery stables, wagon yards, a barbershop, a drugstore, a Chinese laundry, a blacksmith shop, two hotels, and boarding houses," in addition to five saloons, "all in full blast."[29] Soldiers from nearby Fort Elliott, buffalo hunters, and cowboys from surrounding ranches patronized the saloons and houses of prostitution.

Gravis parked the buggy on the main street but would not leave it unguarded. He stayed in it and dispatched Hosmer to make necessary purchases of supplies. As was typical in any rural West Texas community then (and, for that matter, now), strangers in town invited questions and stares. "Them's fine horses," Gravis overheard someone say, and he immediately feared that they would be "scalp[ed] and robbed." Instead of identifying themselves as preachers, the two slipped on through town and decided to head for safer ground in Clarendon.

However, Gravis's conscience, or perhaps the prodding of the Holy Spirit, would not let them proceed for much more than a mile. There they stopped for lunch and then kept a careful eye on the road back to town. They slipped off the main road, camped in some heavy brush, and tethered the horses with chains, and soon their courage returned. The next morning was Sunday; Gravis, acting like the presiding elder that he was, dispatched Hosmer back into town "on a reconnoitering expedition." Hosmer left about 9 a. m. and by late afternoon had not returned. Gravis feared that some ill had befallen his companion.

However, he soon saw the young preacher striding up the road, "his face all aglow with success." Gravis carefully recalled Hosmer's explanation of his delay:

> "Oh," said he, "It's a better place than we thought it was. I got one subscriber for the [Texas Christian] Advocate. They found out that we are Methodist preachers and wanted to know why we did not stop and preach for them. The hotel keeper invited me home with him and gave me a good dinner."

Gravis, perhaps feeling guilty for being so fearful, and perhaps jealous that his young colleague had gotten a good home-cooked meal, sharply replied: "That's clever, but your long absence aroused my fears very much. I thought they had captured my spy." However, emboldened by the news, Gravis announced that they would go back into town in the morning and "plant our banner and publish our terms of amnesty. I must preach in Mobeetie."

Hosmer, also perhaps feeling guilty because they did not preach on Sunday, protested and insisted that they press on to Clarendon. Gravis overruled him with tongue-in-cheek humor: "as I was Commander-in-Chief of all the forces in the Panhandle, I told him we would spend one more day, if not the week, in Mobeetie."[30]

On Monday, the preachers stormed the town and won it without a fight. The hotel operator who had graciously hosted Hosmer the day before offered them free lodging for the week if they would stay. They visited through the town and scheduled a preaching service for that night: June 27, 1881. According to Gravis, "we were the first itinerant preachers to visit this place." The ME, South gospel had finally been preached in the Panhandle. Gravis was overwhelmed with the community's conduct: "I never saw a more orderly congregation, or a more appreciative people anywhere," he reported.[31]

By now, both Gravis and Hosmer must have felt that the long journey had been worth the effort. They set a date for a "protracted meeting" in September; on Tuesday, they were ready to move on and headed for Clarendon, some sixty miles to the southwest. Although Mobeetie had been their primary destination, they must have felt that since they were fairly close to Clarendon, they should drive over and learn more about the community about which they had heard so much, a place founded by Northern Methodists. After their fearful experience at the wild outpost of Mobeetie, Hosmer and Gravis looked forward to visiting with fellow Methodist brethren in Clarendon where they expected to be welcome with open arms. What a shock it must have been to Gravis and Hosmer when they arrived at Clarendon or "Saint's Roost," and found out that they had no welcome at all!

The third route of Methodist expansion

As previously mentioned, Levi Collins had led the Methodist incursion into the southern part of the Northwest Texas mission field; Peter Gravis and James Hosmer led the second course on the northern side. The third wave, however, came at the hands of the Methodist Episcopal Church—Northern Methodists! What were these people doing in Clarendon in the first place?

The founder of Clarendon, Rev. Lewis Henry Carhart, was an unusual character for his day: he was a Methodist preacher, and he was rich—or at least his wife was. Born in 1833 in New York, he received degrees in theology from Northwestern University and its prestigious Garrett Biblical Institute before serving in the Union Army during the Civil War. In 1866, he joined the Arkansas Conference of the ME Church and by 1877 had become pastor at Sherman, Texas.

While there, he learned that he could purchase land in the Panhandle for as little as 64 cents per acre if he provided the survey. His dream was to establish a colony of Methodists where saloons would be banned. At the same time, he could sell land to prospective colonists. By 1878, he had hired the survey of 343 sections and chose a town site he named Clarendon, —perhaps for his wife, Clara, whose family probably provided money for the venture. Carhart promoted the colony widely and soon attracted settlers from the North and East, including seven retired Methodist ministers.[32] By 1880, the pioneers had built a small church, for which Carhart purchased a large cast bell to call the faithful to worship.[33]

When Gravis and Hosmer arrived in Clarendon on June 30, 1881, they promptly announced (in contrast to their Mobeetie encounter) that they were ministers of the ME Church, South. "I expected something like a paternal reception from the brethren . . . ," Gravis recalled with some chagrin, "but when I announced that myself as a minister of the ME Church, South, I imagined I saw some manifestations of hostil-

Clarendon founder Rev. Lewis H. Carhart provided this bell in 1880 for the Methodist Episcopal Church at Clarendon. It now hangs in the bell tower at the Lakeview UMC in Dalhart. Photo courtesy Davy Mitchell, Lubbock.

ity towards us. We were not invited to preach, or even stay with them for the night."[34] Obviously, the Northern Methodists had no interest in helping Gravis and Hosmer evangelize the Panhandle.

Disgusted, Gravis and Hosmer camped near the little town, and Gravis spent the evening writing the letters that recorded for posterity their Mobeetie and Clarendon adventure. "Well, everyone to their own liking;" Gravis wrote to a friend, "as the old woman said when she kissed the cow; which, fraternally speaking, she had a perfect right to do, especially if the cow belonged to her."[35]

The next day, Gravis and Hosmer started back east. Their return route took them through settled ranch country along the route that, perhaps unknown to them, would become the future route of the Fort Worth & Denver railroad. Taking their time, they may have visited ranches and farms along the way before "jumping off the handle back into the pan" into Hardeman County, reaching there on July 20 and rejoining Gravis's daughter. They had been gone for one month and had made a 350-mile loop into the Indian Territory and the Texas Panhandle.

Apparently, Gravis returned home to Comanche, but he was back on the field by late September to hold the fourth quarterly meeting at Vernon for the Hardeman Mission outpost. The results were disappointing, to say the least, as apparently no one showed up for the presiding elder's visit. And in spite of Hosmer's report that the mission was "in healthy condition," Gravis noted that the receipts for the year totaled $11.50.[36] Gravis then proceeded to Seymour for the fourth quarterly conference there on the first Sunday in October before returning to Comanche.

After spending months on the road and traveling nearly a thousand miles, Gravis took heart that he and his preachers had done the best they could. "Our work has been mainly to gather in and organize our membership, which we found scattered over this sparsely settled country. . . . We have advanced from one society of seven members to four societies with fifty-one members." However, with other parts of the conference growing rapidly, Gravis and Hosmer must have been bitterly disappointed, and especially after the conference met in November 1881. At that time, the conference decided to discontinue the Panhandle District "because the missionary treasury was empty."[37] Gravis was reassigned to Church Extension, but Hosmer remained on the field, and the Seymour Mission was placed in the Eastland District.[38]

The work of Hosmer and Gravis during that summer of`1881 did not go in vain. It laid the groundwork for dozens of churches in the future Northwest Texas Conference. While both would live to see two major railroads reach into Northwest Texas, neither would live to the full fruition of their work. Gravis superannuated in 1882 but returned in 1887 to preach for a year at Stephenville, where he lived in a parsonage for the first and only time in his career. He continued to preach at camp meetings and quarterly conferences into the 1890s. He died in Zephyr in January 1902 at the age of seventy-four.[39]

James Hosmer worked the same area for the rest of his ministry; at Seymour, he had a mission circuit that covered thirty-four preaching points. He began Methodist work at Margaret (1885), Chillicothe (1886), Childress (1887), Medicine Mound (1888)), and Goodlett (1888). He also returned to Clarendon in 1887 and established the foundation for a new Methodist church that was founded the following year.[40] Even more important, he returned to saloon-filled Mobeetie and began the church there, where in 1893 evangelist Abe Mulkey would preach one of the greatest revivals in the history of Texas, resulting in more than 300 conversions.[41]

After moving to Greer County in the Indian Territory, Hosmer was superannuated in 1892 because of illness. His eleven years of exposure to the ever-changing West Texas weather took a heavy toll, and he died August 4, 1893, only forty-four years old. According to his obituary in the 1893 conference journal, Hosmer "literally sacrificed himself upon the altar of the church."[42] His work helped to create an expression that circulated on the plains during periods of bitterly cold weather: "there is nothing out today but crows and Methodist preachers."[43]

The railroad invades West Texas

While Gravis and Hosmer were making their way by buggy deep into Northwest Texas, shining new rails were being laid across the region to the south. In fact, April 1, 1880, marked a new beginning for the Northwest Texas Conference, for on that day the Texas & Pacific Railroad began extending its line from Fort Worth into the heart of West Texas. This meant that the region's sparse population of 12,000 would soon begin to increase. It also meant that farmers and ranchers would have access to cheaper goods as well as a way to get their products to market. What it meant for Methodist work was that there would soon be towns where new churches could be started. But the presence of a railroad did not mean that the circuit-rider preachers would be able to give up their horses and buggies to make their rounds. Passenger rates were five cents per mile; thus, a trip from Fort Worth to the new city of Abilene would cost a preacher $7.50—a week's wages or more.[44]

Where the railroad went, new towns appeared almost overnight, and the few scattered settlements missed by the railroad went into immediate decline. This was due in part to the influence of several wealthy Taylor County ranchers who persuaded the T&P to shift its route to northern Taylor County and thereby bypass Buffalo Gap, the area's largest town. As a result, by late 1880, when the T&P had reached into the bounds of the future Northwest Texas Conference in Callahan County, it bypassed the established towns of Callahan City and Belle

First railroads in Northwest Texas, 1890.

Plain. Meanwhile, along the railroad, the towns of Catclaw (later Putnam) and Vickery (later Baird) were quickly established.[45]

By January 1881, the railroad had reached the future site of Abilene. With the backing of the railroad as well as the local ranchers who manipulated the shift of the line to the north, promoters proclaimed Abilene to be the "Future Great City of West Texas" and set a date for the sale of town lots. Hundreds arrived early to set up businesses, and by early March, Presbyterians were already having services.[46] On March 15 and 16, 1881, promoters sold over 300 lots.[47]

By mid-April, the line had reached as far west as Colorado City, causing a brief population rush there. It continued on west rapidly and linked with the Southern Pacific in far West Texas at Sierra Blanca. The railroad's completion not only provided rail service to West Texas but also made the region a part of a transcontinental link. The region was poised to grow rapidly.

With a foothold already established in the Abilene area by Levi Collins and others, Methodists moved rapidly to get churches in the new railroad towns. In the fall of 1881, the Northwest Texas Conference appointed additional preachers to the Belle Plain District to serve new churches already started or planned for Abilene, Merkel, Sweetwater, and Colorado City.[48] No matter that Presbyterians organized the first church in the new town of Abilene—the Methodists were not far behind, and in the fall of 1881 they held services that led to the establishment of the First Methodist Church of Abilene.

Within weeks of the formation of the Abilene church, Collins and Robert F. Dunn were preaching in the new town of Sweetwater. Dunn rented a room above a saloon in which to hold services where he preached his first sermon[49] One night a bunch of drunk cowboys shot holes through the ceiling and interrupted the service. Undaunted, on the next meeting night, Dunn preached in the saloon.[50] He organized the First Methodist Church of Sweetwater in the fall of 1881, and by the end of the next year, the church had built a sanctuary and a parsonage.[51]

As settlers progressed into West Texas, Methodists, Baptists, and Presbyterians were at the forefront of church establishment. O. F. Rogers, a Presbyterian, preached the first sermon in Colorado City in 1881, also in a saloon, but there the proprietor of the Lone Wolf bar had the decency to cover the liquor bottles. Collins organized the Methodist church in Colorado City in 1882, but whether it or the Baptist church was the first established there has long been a matter of dispute.[52]

The Northwest Texas Conference, already the largest of the Texas conferences, with more than 30,000 members, continued to push its borders west. As noted by the Committee on the State of the Church for 1881, the conference rejoiced "to learn that our beloved Methodism has lost none of its characteristic feature of aggressiveness to supply sparsely settlements with the Ministry of Christ and carrying the Gospel into regions beyond."[53] By the end of 1881, missions and churches within the bounds of the future Northwest Texas Conference reported 553 members.[54] Among the missions, the Pecan, Buffalo Gap, Jim Ned and Lytle Gap missions, with nearly 400 members combined, served as anchors for initial Methodist work until the towns along the railroad grew enough to assume the load.[55]

The arid region west of Sweetwater initially was not as attractive to prospective farmers. Also, the big ranches controlled by the Cowden, Merchant, Slaughter, and Scharbauer families and others slowed the advancing settlement line. As a result, Methodist work along the T&P developed more slowly after 1881. For example, work in Big Spring did not start until either late 1882 or 1883, and in Midland in 1885.[56] However, churches near the rail line grew as settlers moved in; by 1885, the Abilene District had nearly tripled in membership to more than 1,400 members.[57]

Away from the railroad, church plantings were slower. In the area north of the T&P, five churches were established along the old military road that ran east to west and where ranchers and former buffalo hunters had settled in the 1870s. Anson's church began in 1882 with seventeen members. Farther west, early settlers in the trading post town of Snyder started a Methodist church in 1883, a year before Scurry County was organized. Also in 1883, the church at Throckmorton was established along with a mission point at Dickens in 1884. Preaching also began at Haskell in November 1884 and the church was organized the following year.[58] The church at Moran was also organized in 1885.

Ranchers took the lead both in organizing Knox County and a Methodist Church church in Benjamin in 1886. W. E. Caperton, pastor of the Seymour mission circuit, made the thirty-two-mile trek to establish the new church. Its founding provided a congregation in the last county in the tier that lay below the Red River. By the end of 1886, the Methodist frontier in Northwest Texas stretched along a curved line that stretched south and west from Hardeman County on the north to Midland. Only two Methodist outposts lay beyond that line: the church at Mobeetie, where Gravis and Hosmer had labored in 1881, and a mission at Dickens. Otherwise, forty-seven largely unsettled counties, mostly in the Panhandle, had no churches in an area as large as the already settled area of the Northwest Texas Conference.

The second attempt to take the Panhandle

As previously noted, in 1881, the Northwest Texas Conference had sent Peter Gravis into the Panhandle in an effort to have churches in place for the expected rush of settlers that would come with the planned

Fort Worth & Denver railroad. However, its construction was much slower than that of the T&P. The FW&D extended only from Fort Worth to Wichita Falls by the fall of 1882, and to Chillicothe in 1886. Its lack of progress slowed the advance of settlers and churches into the region.

Drought also delayed settlement of the region. Just as the FW&D finally reached the southeastern edge of the Panhandle, a two-year drought in 1886–87 burned up crops and pastures, precipitating a major drop in cattle prices. Farmers and ranchers suffered, and so did the preachers. At the 1886 annual conference, a pastor reported that "the unprecedented drought prevailing throughout the northwestern portion of our conference territory . . . has left the missionaries in a manner destitute."[59] The next year, another pastor reported that he had "gone hungry to bed one hundred nights this year. I have left one extremity of my work and rode to the other in search of one meal of nourishing food. I have heard children ask with pinched faces, 'Are we to have meat for dinner today?'"[60]

Despite the gloomy report, 1887 marked the beginning of a renewed advance of Methodism into the Panhandle. By the end of the year, the FW&D had doubled its mileage, passing through the future site of Amarillo as it reached the Canadian River just south of Tascosa. Along its route, towns and churches rapidly appeared. Methodist churches or missions were established near or along the line in Crowell, Childress, Claude, and Lakeview (Hall County) in 1887 and in Clarendon and Childress in 1888. The Claude church holds the distinction of being organized within its own building, already free of debt.[61]

Meanwhile, the Santa Fe railroad began its invasion of the Panhandle from Kansas in late 1886, and by 1888 it had reached the center of the Panhandle at Panhandle City.[62] At the same time, promoters built a fifteen-mile line south from Panhandle to link the Santa Fe with the FW&D, hoping that the connection would make Panhandle City the coming great city of the Plains. But it would be Amarillo, sitting on the edge of the great cattle country to the north and west, that ultimately became the crossroads of the region.[63]

As a result of the new rail lines, the 1888 Northwest Texas Conference created a second district for the frontier area, the Vernon District. Like the old 1881 Panhandle District, the new Vernon district's size was challenging. It stretched nearly 200 miles from Seymour to the new missions and preaching points at Cataline in Hemphill County, to the west to coming churches at Amarillo and then south to Estacado in eastern Lubbock County. The Vernon church was the only station; other missions and circuits included Seymour, Benjamin, Mangum (in Greer County, Oklahoma), Clarendon, Childress, Margaret, Throckmorton, and Farmer.[64] The pastor at Mobeetie,, Rev. J. T. Bloodworth, walked twice a month fifteen miles east to preach at Cataline (which later became Allison).[65] By 1888, circuit riders had organized churches at Lipscomb and Timms City, both in Lipscomb County, north of the Canadian River—perhaps in response to Northern Methodists, who had been holding services in the new town of Canadian.[66]

Meanwhile, Bloodworth had expanded his circuit by preaching near the future town of Amarillo at the Frying Pan Ranch headquarters, probably in the summer of 1887.[67] In the spring of 1888, Isaac Mills, pastor of the new Clarendon mission, preached in Amarillo and then returned in November of that year to formally organize a church, with the assistance of the presiding elder of the Vernon District, Jerome Harralson.[68] Within twenty years, the Amarillo church was the largest in the conference. In October 1889, Mills and Harralson organized a church in the new community of Canyon City, south of Amarillo, holding the organizational service in the town's first store. [69]

As the Fort Worth & Denver completed its line across the Panhandle, settlers rapidly moved into the Panhandle and central South Plains and began to organize counties and churches. The opening of the Panhandle for settlement signaled a new era in church development for the ME Church, South. Of the sixty-seven counties in the current Northwest Texas Conference, only six had been settled and organized before 1880, and all of these lay on the conference's southeastern edge, except for Wheeler County. From 1881 to 1886, an additional eighteen counties were organized, most of which adjoined one of the new rail lines. But from 1887 to 1892, twenty-six additional Panhandle counties were organized and settled. During that same five-year period, the number of new churches tripled as seventy-one new preaching points were established. [70] Of these, nearly half were founded during 1889–90. As one county historian noted, "By the time the settler was unloaded and cozy in his modest cabin, a Methodist circuit rider was knocking on the door."[71]

The circuit riders did their job well, going into the most far-flung areas. One of the remotest outposts was at Benjamin, where mission work began in 1884 and the church organized in 1886. When the church began raising money for a building, one lady took the matter into her own hands. According to J. T. Griswold, "Sister Weatherly wrote a letter to every governor in the United States and to every congressman, and senator in the nation," asking for a donation to build a church. Reportedly, a large majority of the politicians responded generously.[72]

In 1889, circuit riders began to preach in Collingsworth County and organized a mission at Wellington in 1890.[73] The first Methodist service in Stonewall County was also in 1889, and a church was organized at the county seat of Rayner. By the end of the year, the Stonewall circuit boasted 126 members at four missions, with 106 professions of faith.[74] Also, by 1890, churches had been established in Crosby County at Farmer, near present-day Cone, and at Emma, which shared a pastor with the church at Estacado[75]

Recognizing the significance of the region's growth, the annual conference chose to meet at Abilene in 1890, marking the first time that a church within the present bounds of the Northwest Texas Conference had been asked to host the meeting.

Reaching the Llano Estacado

One of the last areas in the United States to be settled was the waterless and treeless Llano Estacado, the South Plains of Texas. Hale County was seventy-five miles away from a rail depot, and Lubbock County was more than 100. By the early 1880s, the area was controlled by big ranches that utilized the new technology of barbed wire and windmills to take advantage of the vast pastures. But even cowboys needed the gospel, and preachers and circuit riders began to make their way to the scattered rural communities that served the region.

A Northern Methodist took the lead in Hale County in 1883. Retired preacher Horatio Graves from New York planned to establish a Methodist colony similar to what Rev. Lewis Henry Carhart had done at Clarendon. Graves purchased four sections of land in central Hale

County and in 1884 established a post office that he named Epworth in honor of John Wesley's birthplace.[76] He started a Sunday School in a small schoolhouse and held services there.

Meanwhile, another settler in 1888 had established the nearby town of Plainview, which quickly became a supply center for a wide region. When the county was organized in July 1888, Plainview defeated rivals Hale City and Epworth to become the county seat, and Southern Methodists took the lead. In the fall of 1888, the ME, South pastor of the Estacado Mission, John B. Hawkins, organized Plainview's First Methodist Church.[77] The next year, in 1889, Plainview's new pastor (and pastor of the Epworth Circuit), R. M. Morris, organized what later became the Hale Center ME Church, South which first met at Graves' Epworth schoolhouse. Morris also organized another Hale County church in 1893 that would become Lakeview.[78]

Morris also met with thireen Lubbock settlers in 1892, perhaps in the new Lubbock County jail, to organize what would become in time the largest church in the Northwest Texas Conference.[79] One of Lubbock's first Sunday School teachers was a young man named James Winford Hunt, who grew up in the Quaker community of Estacado. As a young man, he became publisher of the short-lived Epworth *Chronicle* and formed a Christian Endeavor Society for young people.[80] He later moved to Lubbock, where he taught a Sunday School class attended by all faiths. In time, Hunt would surrender to the ministry and become one of the Northwest Texas Conference's most influential members and founder of McMurry College. [81]

To divide or not to divide

By the end of 1892, the population of the Panhandle-South Plains area had increased six-fold from only 12,000 in 1880 to 75,000. Approximately 7,500, or 10 percent, were Methodists. At the annual conference at the end of 1892, preachers reported that Methodists now had churches or preaching points in nearly every settled county of Northwest Texas. During the year, in addition to Lubbock, new churches had been organized at Gail, Matador, Paducah, Roscoe, Truscott, and near present-day Turkey. Meanwhile, the Northwest Texas Conference's membership totaled 54,000, reflecting a 100 percent increase since 1880.[82] The conference also comprised nearly 40 percent of the state's membership. Pleased with such reports, the conference debated whether it should divide its vast territory.

Discussion about division had surfaced several times in previous years, usually just prior to the meeting of the General Conference. In 1879, the Northwest Texas Conference Committee on Boundaries considered division but took no action.[83] In 1881, the Corsicana District asked for division, but without success.[84] However, the Committee on Boundaries agreed to allow the counties along its southeastern border (Leon, Freestone, Limestone, Robertson, Falls, and Milam) to be transferred to the Texas Conference.[85]

At the 1892 conference, the bishop appointed a Committee on Division; its chairman, Samuel Wright, delivered an eloquent but less than modest report that praised the work of the Methodist pioneers in Northwest Texas:

> Even the railroads, those iron deities that metamorphose parched plains into paradises, did not, could not with their resistless force plunge into our great panhandle country until Gravis and Hosmer and Farmer had gone before and beckoned the Methodist hosts to follow after into the goodly land. Who, so much as the Methodists, have spread themselves along these lines of railroad, and by patient industry have conquered the soil and forced it to deliver up its hidden treasures? Who have built the cities with their colleges and schools, their elevators and mills, their banks and boards of trade?[86]

Wright noted that some conference members were impatient and called for immediate division; others wanted to delay it by a few years, and still others sadly deplored division so as to not to sever "the relations of love and harmony and usefulness, which have for so many years existed among us."[87] Those calling for delay won the debate, and the committee recommended that division be initiated in 1893.

However, 1893 was not kind to Northwest Texas. Drought and a national depression took a heavy toll on the region. Up until the late 1880s, rainfall on the plains was abundant; the central Panhandle received

Famed Texas Methodist evangelist Abe Mulkey. Photo courtesy Methodist Children's Home, Waco, Texas.

an average of 36 inches for 1884 and 1885.[88] After those wet years, rainfall began to gravitate toward what today would be considered "normal," but to the region's new ranchers and farmers, it seemed that an extended drought had begun. The year 1893 was a real drought year; the Abilene area, which had received approximately 24 inches per year from 1886 to 1892, caught only 16 inches for 1893.[89] Farther west, Colorado City saw only 8 ½ inches.[90]

The drought was devastating to ranchers, farmers, and Methodism in Northwest Texas. "In some sectors, whole congregations of Methodists have been disbanded," the Committee on Division reported to the 1893 annual conference, "and whole circuits and missions have lost their identity." The Abilene District's membership declined by 10 percent, marking the first time that the mission territory of Northwest Texas had seen a decrease. Because of the drought, the conference determined not to ask for division.[91]

The drought may have also spurred Methodists in the Panhandle to seek "showers of blessings" in another way. By the 1890s, summer camp-meeting revivals had become common among the rural communities. The first camp meeting within the bounds of the future conference may have been one that Methodist preacher John A. Wallace held at Albany in 1881.[92] As churches of all faiths were established, it was common for several denominations to meet together. One young man in the new town of Anson described an 1890s joint camp meeting held by the Baptist, Presbyterian, Christian, and Methodist churches under a brush arbor: "We had a great revival. Seventy-nine people were converted and joined the different churches. There's not a sinner left in Anson!"[93]

In 1893, however, revivals became something different from camp meetings when Corsicana's Abe Mulkey came to the Panhandle in late winter and staged a series of meetings. Mulkey had been a successful merchant but began preaching after being licensed by the Methodist church in 1885.[94] He was an immediate success. A Fort Worth revival netted 200 conversions, and soon he was much in demand. Mulkey developed an entertaining style of folksy, animated sermons punctuated with what the editor of a north Texas newspaper described as "acrobatic, double-back action."[95]

Mulkey's Panhandle tour began in Childress in February 1893. He arrived on the train to find six-foot snow drifts. Undaunted, he held a ten-day revival there. After a visit to the ranch of a relative near Quanah, Mulkey moved on to Clarendon, where "we found the enemy in battle array"—perhaps referring to a snowstorm, or to critics who opposed his method of preaching. After a ten-day meeting there, Mulkey reported that "many were led captive and crossed the line and joined the Lord's host."[96]

At the close of the Clarendon revival, Mulkey rested for two days at the nearby "palatial home" of the famed rancher Charles Goodnight. Mulkey enjoyed seeing Goodnight's "park," where "wild buffalo, deer, stags and antelope" grazed. From the Goodnight home, Mulkey caught the train to Amarillo, arriving March 1 to a wonderful reception. "Even all the business houses closed doors and suspended business," Mulkey recalled, "and God wonderfully routed the enemy. We were able to convert scores for our side."[97] While in Amarillo, Mulkey was taken to Palo Duro Canyon, where he walked down and found "a wall of ice a foot thick behind the falls."

Mulkey closed out his Panhandle tour with a buggy trip to the historic "inland town" of Mobeetie, where he followed the footsteps of Gravis and Hosmer. Mulkey said only that it was "a gracious meeting." In his summary on his trip through the plains country, Mulkey must have gained a new appreciation for the pioneer circuit riders who had preceded him: "It was a long hard rough work through the plains and we were surely tired. In this we learned the lesson of endurance as good soldiers and we received blessings that we could not have received under other circumstances. The Sweets always attend the Bitter."[98]

The drought was indeed bitter, but the reward was sweeter. Although the Abilene District's membership had declined by 10 percent, it was up by more than a hundred in the Vernon District, where Mulkey had preached several revivals. At the end of the year, Methodists rejoiced at the 1893 Northwest Texas annual conference when it was announced that there had been 18,000 conversions and 4,573 adult baptisms for the year, which more than offset the losses due to the drought: "Fifteen thousand [have been] added to our Church, with a net increase of 5,334, which is greatly in excess of any previous report."[99]

And the church survived because God called workers "unto the harvest." While still a student in Alabama, J. T. Griswold felt a call to preach on the Northwest Texas frontier. Shortly after receiving his license to preach, he recalled that "an impression came over me to 'go to Northwest Texas to preach' ":

> I hesitated not but promptly said, "That I will do." As I began to talk Northwest Texas among my colleagues at college, they would say, "You are crazy, boy! That is nothing but a desert. There are no people out there, and why throw away your life? You will either starve to death or freeze to death."[100]

Although he came near to freezing, Griswold would prove his colleagues wrong and would be a major force in seeing the "desert" bloom with churches.

CHAPTER 3

"Glory and Thanks to Jesus Give"

In 1892, Ed Wallace was in his mid-twenties, newly married and fresh out of school. He had joined the Northwest Texas Conference in 1891 and was first assigned to Hogtown (later known as Desdemona) in Eastland County, the oldest settlement in North Texas west of the Brazos.[1] Ed was happy at Hogtown, and assumed he would be returned to that comfortable place as conference approached.

The conference met at Waco in 1892. As was typical at the time, the bishop read the new appointments just before adjournment. Like all the other preachers, Wallace waited with nervous anticipation. Soon he heard the bishop say "Hogtown"—but it was assigned to someone else! A few minutes later, he heard his own name assigned to places he had never heard of: "Briscoe and Floyd."

Wallace was pleased, thinking that he had been "elevated" to two half-station communities, and he sought out the former pastor for clarification. Wallace never forgot the conversation: "Floyd and Briscoe *counties,*" the preacher said "in a tone indicating that he thought any fool ought to know that . . . . You will be the only preacher in the two counties—you will have exclusive control of the territory—thirty-five by seventy miles." [2] The circuit would require more than a hundred miles of traveling to 14 preaching points. Only then did Wallace realize that he had indeed been "elevated"—by several hundred feet to the high plains of Northwest Texas.

Wallace's assignment was indicative of the ministerial challenges in Northwest Texas: long distances to cover in often trying weather. Although his presiding elder provided some relief in his second year by assigning Floyd County to someone else, the elder added preaching points in Swisher, Hall, Armstrong and Motley counties to Wallace's circuit and wryly remarked, "There are other points you are expected to look after." Wallace's new charge would require a circuit of 300 miles.[3]

Wallace accepted the challenge and came to love the plains. "This is a fine country," he prophetically noted, "and perhaps some day may be the garden spot of Texas. It is possible that irrigation will be simplified and improved, and the power for raising the inexhaustible water supply to the surface will be perfected."[4] Wallace's vision for the plains was decades away, and the region remained dependent upon favorable weather to stimulate future growth.

At the time, church growth was directly tied to favorable weather. Although rainfall was adequate in 1894, the region was slow to recover from the effects of the drought of 1893. From 1885 to 1892, the new areas of Northwest Texas averaged more than ten new congregations a year; however, in 1893, only one congregation was established within the bounds of the future Northwest Texas Conference: at Gilliland in north central Knox County. Although the Flomot Church in Motley County does trace its origin to 1893, it was founded as a Cumberland Presbyterian church and did not enter the Northwest Texas Conference until 1903. [5]

Growth brings a new district

In spite of slow growth, the conference in 1894 created the Clarendon District in the Panhandle, carving it out of the Vernon District's area. The new district included twelve missions and circuits stretching from Kirkland in southeastern Childress County westward to Lubbock, and then north to include all of the settled area of the Panhandle.[6]

However, the move did little to foster new church growth, as the nation struggled with an economic depression. Only three churches were founded in 1894: two in established county seat towns at Canadian and Miami, and at Dunn in Scurry County. The following year, only Dumont and Estelline were added. And, in 1896, two additional churches were started in the most remote region of the Panhandle, at Channing and Ochiltree (later moved to Perryton). In the older, settled areas, new churches appeared at Kirkland and Caps (near Abilene) in 1896, and three more in 1897 at Putnam in Callahan County, and Westover and Round Timber in Baylor County.

It is significant to note conference statistics for 1897. By the end of the year, the entire old Northwest Texas Conference reported a total membership of 67,819, a figure comparable to the present membership of the modern Northwest Texas Conference. In 1897, the conference included 206 charges that included 747 churches or "societies." Of the 747 churches, 383 had buildings and 184 had parsonages. For the year, these churches had 6,089 infant and adult baptisms, and averaged 33,270 in 545 Sunday Schools.[7] Thus, the church was averaging nearly one baptism for every ten members.

The year 1898 marked the twenty-fifth anniversary of the founding of the first church within the bounds of the future Northwest Texas Conference. During that time three districts and fifty charges had been established, but the area had only eight full time churches or "stations," and all but one were located on the low rolling plains, which included Abilene, Colorado City, Vernon, Quanah, Childress, Seymour, and Clarendon. On the high plains, onlyAmarillo had a full time church.

New church starts accelerated in 1898, but only on the rolling plains. Of the twenty-nine Methodist congregations organized from in 1898 through 1900, all but two were located in the rolling plains. Four of these, Loraine, Trent, Clyde, and Stamford were in towns on a railroad. By 1900, the sixty-six-county region of the future Northwest Texas Conference boasted a population of 103,894, a growth of nearly 100 percent since 1890. However, 87 percent of the population was located in thirty-four counties of the rolling plains and along the Texas & Pacific railroad. Only 16,479 lived in the remaining thirty-two counties of the South Plains and Panhandle, and of those, fourteen counties had less than 200 people each. Big ranches—Slaughter, XIT, Matador, JA, Francklyn, Turkey Track—still controlled much of the area on the high plains and were keeping settlers out of their pastures.

A new wave of railroads

A new boom was imminent. The Texas Legislature helped tremendously the prospect for growth in the Panhandle when in 1895 it passed the Four-Section Act. This legislation provided that settlers could claim up to four sections of land and purchase it for as little as one dollar per acre, with only eighty dollars down.[8] The law required for settlers to actually live on the land and make improvements. Meanwhile, the nation by 1898 was in full recovery from the economic depression that had plagued the country following the Panic of 1893. Railroad construction resumed and locomotive whistles soon signaled that renewed colonization of the high plains was underway.

As prospective settlers began to return to the plains, the railroads resumed their interest in the region. In 1898, a group of New Mexico ranchers began building a line from Amarillo southwest, to run to the Texas-New Mexico border where it would continue on to the Pecos Valley and Roswell.[9] By March 1, 1899, the line opened service; however, since several big ranches still dominated the region through which it passed, initially, only the Methodist Church in the new town of Hereford was established in 1899 along the line.[10] In 1900, the Texas Central Railroad completed an extension of its line from Albany to Stamford, which prompted a boom in the rolling plains area.[11] And, in 1901, the Rock Island railroad began a line that cut across the northwestern part of the Panhandle and intersected with the Fort Worth & Denver to create a potential boom town at Dalhart.

Closing "the outside row."

For many years, Methodist preachers referred to the counties farthest removed from the settled areas as "the outside row." By 1900,"the outside row" for the Northwest Texas Conference was the tier of counties on the far west side of the Panhandle and the top two rows of coun-

Rev. W. B. McKeown and his wife Amelia, pioneers of the upper Texas Panhandle, 1890. Both served McMurry College in its formative years in the 1920s. Photo courtesy Boyd McKeown.

ties across the top of the region.These eighteen counties represented the Conference's—as well as Texas'—last frontier.

The taking of the upper Panhandle for Methodism fell into the reluctant hands of W. B. McKeown. From 1899 to 1900, McKeown served as president of the Methodist-affiliated Clarendon College. In the summer of 1900, the Presiding Elder asked him to take the church at Channing and do a survey of the upper Panhandle. At the time, the only churches in the counties north of the Canadian River were Channing and Hartley on the west and Higgins and Lipscomb on the east, and a small church in southern Ochiltree County.

McKeown recalled the challenge he faced: "I settled on four counties to organize the work in them and take others until I had all under the supervision of the Church. I would spend a week in a county and preach on Sunday, giving such encouragement and help as I thought would help . . . ." For this work, he selected the isolated counties of Sherman, Moore, Hansford, and Ochiltree. "I could not rent a house, or even a room, in all that territory," he later recalled. [12]

In September 1900, McKeown set out to survey his four counties and called from ranch to ranch. On one Sunday, he was supposed to be at Coldwater, the remote county seat of Sherman County.[13] Coldwater had been established when cowboys working for rancher William B. Slaughter organized Sherman County. But, McKeown got lost on the endless plains and wandered about until nearly 4 in the afternoon. "Soon a small object in the distance gradually grew into a building—the courthouse—the very place I had been trying to reach since 8 o'clock that morning. Imagine, if you can, my amazement to find the people still there, expecting the preacher to come.[14] The faith demonstrated by the folk at Coldwater reflected both their devotion to preaching as well as a patient tolerance for newcomers to the plains.

McKeown was pleased with the response he received and thus recommended to his Presiding Elder that a new mission be formed and that a new preacher be appointed at Annual Conference. Thinking his work was done, McKeown prepared to take an appointment down state and was surprised when the PE asked him to take the new Coldwater Mission. McKeown immediately wrote the PE, saying he could not accept, due to the hardships of the work. But after a sleepless night, he accepted after asking himself, "Can I afford to recommend for another a work which, because of its hardships, I will not take myself? Is this the spirit of our holy Christianity? Such an act [of rejection] is cowardly."[15]

McKeown's acceptance of the Coldwater Mission made an immediate impact on the Northwest Texas last frontier. From Channing, he rode the train to Texline, where he preached regularly. Then, in June 1901, he paid a call on the new town of Dalhart that had sprung up at the intersection of the Fort Worth & Denver line and the new Rock Island line just arrived from the northeast. It was a rough place: in spite of spending a night when "seven men were knocked down that night and robbed," McKeown stayed in town to organize the Methodist Church, with seven members.[16]

To the east of Dalhart, at the new town of Stratford, McKeown encountered still a different element. He scheduled a revival for late July 1901; the saloon promoters countered by planning to stage a footrace to attract gamblers, offering a $1,000 prize![17] McKeown was incensed at the waste of money. While the race promoters were laying out the track, he and other new settlers prepared an arbor for the revival, and began the meeting on the night before the race. "I talked to the earnest little group of the trial on Mount Carmel and reminded them that Elijah's God is ours," McKeown recalled. "They prayed, met again on the following morning, prayed some more, and then again during the race."

After the afternoon service, McKeown's curiosity got the best of him and he made his way to the railroad station to learn "how the race came out." "It went off," the station agent said wryly, "the whole thing blew up; they fell out among themselves; I never saw such a gun play in my life; it looked like everyone would be killed. They finally decided to call off the whole thing, pulled down their stake of $1,000, the Missouri crowd left on the train a few minutes ago and the others have all gone home!"[18]

Happily, the little band of Christians at Stratford continued their meeting with McKeown, and, at its end, sixty people were in attendance and pledged $600 towards a new church building. At the same time McKeown organized a Sunday School and started the building program. The new church became the first Methodist building north of the Canadian River.[19] As Panhandle historian Laura V. Hamner recorded, "Stratford started well, having church, school, good people. Through the years, the town has maintained the standards set on a hot July day in 1901 when one faction of citizens met to run a race . . . and the other faction met to pray . . . ."[20]

McKeown did not limit his ministry to Channing, Texline and Stratford. Once a month, he made a long trip to the little community of Hansford, located on Palo Duro Creek, six miles west of present-day Spearman, where he organized the first church in the county in July 1901. The church later relocated to Spearman. He also preached at Ochiltree, a church which later moved to Perryton. And, in August 1901, after a "protracted meeting," he organized a church at Dumas.[21]

Although he only stayed on the mission field three years, McKeown had closed the northern Panhandle frontier, primarily due to the dedication of his devoted wife Amelia. As he later recalled, "While working there, it cost us about $250.00 a year above all we received from the charge and the Mission Board. To stay, [my] wife went in to the school room (as soon as there was a school), kept house, without any assistance, not even a husband, and with her wages we stayed our time out."[22] Among her trials, Amelia McKeown kept a small home in Channing without the benefit of women friends, faced down a band of Kiowa Indians passing through the country, battled a prairie fire, taught school, moved to Stratford, and celebrated the first public Christmas in Sherman County, all in 1901.[23]

In his brief stay in the upper Panhandle, McKeown organized or pastored churches at Channing, Hartley, Dumas, Dalhart, Stratford, Spurlock, Middlewell and Hansford.[24] He later said he traveled more than twenty-five thousand miles in his buggy, and an additional two thousand miles by train.

While McKeown labored in the "outside row," George Fort brought organized Methodism to Gray County, last in the upper Panhandle to see the advance of Methodist work. Even though the railroad had arrived there in 1888, no towns were established. Religion was brought to the scattered ranch families once a year as all denominations gathered for a summer camp meeting. A Methodist circuit rider named Brockman first preached in the area in the 1880s, and then the Methodist pastor at Clarendon came for the summer camp meetings. Even after the first school house was built in 1896 near the little community of Lefors, services were held only once a year.[25] Finally, in 1901 and 1902, the Rock Island constructed a line westward from Oklahoma passing through the southern end of Gray County, and McLean and Alanreed were established. In late 1902 Rev. Fort organized both churches. The McLean church was the first of any denomination in Gray County.[26]

The South Plains Frontier

As the mission work of McKeown and Fort closed the Methodist frontier in the upper Panhandle, the only church frontier left in the Conference was the still unsettled counties of the western South Plains. Thus the "outside row" shifted to the western South Plains, a 150-mile corridor that ran from Parmer County south to Andrews and Martin counties. This region lacked for settlers because it was under complete control of big ranches. Moreover, its sandy soil was not as attractive for farming as were other areas of the region. The land required more water than did the north plains of Texas, and thus drought often sent many settlers back east. One observer reported that, in 1900, "There were men who had been on these claims from two to ten years who . . . concluded that this country was not worth fooling with. They loaded their wives and children on their wagons, tied the cows thereto, called the dogs, and tacked notes on their dugout doors saying, 'You may have it! We are going back to where it rains!'" [27]

However, events in Heaven and Austin soon prompted a new land boom on the South Plains. First, God provided the water. Abundant rainfall, which always has been essential for quality life on the plains, fell generously beginning in 1900. Abilene received thirty-two inches of rain in 1900, six inches above average. In Scurry County, abundant rainfall began in late fall of 1905, followed by a heavy snow that stayed on the ground well past Christmas. As a result, in the spring, the South Plains turned into a garden as wheat, grain and cotton crops flourished.[28] From 1900 through 1908, Abilene's average was approximately 26 inches per year, but in 1905, 1906, and 1908, rainfall measured nearly thirty inches or more.[29]

And, in Austin, the Texas Supreme Court in 1902 broke the control that ranchers had over state-owned land in the Panhandle and South Plains by stopping the practice of "lapse-leasing," wherein ranchers would cancel and then renew a lease without allowing the land to come on the market. The ruling prompted "land rushes" in several counties as ranchers and farmers battled on the steps of various courthouses to see who could file on the land first. Finally, in May 1905, the Legislature revised the state's land laws again to allow for sale to the highest bidder.[30] The end result was that, by 1905, thousands of acres of ranch land was thrown open for settlement. Prospective settlers waited in line in Big Spring for as long as six weeks when choice pieces of land were released.

A renewed demand for land, driven by rising commodity prices and an impending new railroad boom postured the Northwest Texas area for rapid growth. Land promoters described the semi-arid South Plains as "the land of bright promise."[31] In 1907, the Hereford newspaper, the Hereford Brand, published a poem that expressed the nature of the land promotion and boom:

To the Panhandle country, my friend why not go?
Where the winters are mild with seldom deep snow . . . .

Where the people are prosperous and live at their ease,
Enjoy a climate that's free from disease.
Pure air and pure water with bright sunny skies,
One glance at this country will open your eyes . . . .

Where land is now cheap, but not so will remain,
as thousands are going on the home seekers' train . . . .

My friends take advice secure a good thing,
A home in the Panhandle is fit for a king,
But while you can, you will find out in time,
The truth simply stated in this little rhyme.[32]

New settlers poured into the Panhandle-Plains at more than six thousand per year and the Methodist Church was hard pressed to reach them all, but its servants made a valiant effort, moving into the most isolated areas of the South Plains. The Methodist Church at Tahoka was organized in the spring of 1903; work expanded to Moore's Draw in 1905 after a big revival.[33] Then, in 1904, the Tahoka pastor, J. O. Gore, rode his bicycle from Tahoka to the little village of Chicago in Dawson County and organized a church there. In 1905, the town site of Lamesa, located two miles south of Chicago, won a hotly-contested county seat election, and soon the whole town of Chicago moved to Lamesa where the first Methodist church building was constructed in 1907.[34] The Lamesa circuit alone included seven other preaching points Pride, Mullins, Sparenburg, Five Mile, Higginbotham, Cooksey, Sunset, and Lou.

"The call from all directions was for more schools, more churches, and more preachers", reported J. T. Griswold. "Our old Northwest Texas Conference was taxed to the limit to care, in a measure, for the situation." [35] To meet the demand, the Conference in 1904 created the Colorado District in the area of the western South Plains that had the newest settlements, appointing Griswold as presiding elder. During his tenure, Griswold witnessed firsthand the transformation of the plains from a "desert to a lovely oasis:" "Lubbock's old plank walks had given way to cement walks; Plainview, the beautiful, was more beautiful; and the Amarillo regions had made astonishing growth . . ." he recalled. "It is unbelievable how quickly Lamesa sprang into a nice town." [36]

After 1904, the work within the bounds of present Northwest Texas Conference grew rapidly. During 1904, nine new churches were established; twenty-three in 1905, twenty-two in 1906; and an additional seventeen in 1907. Of these seventy-one churches, forty were in the Panhandle and South Plains. The rapid growth prompted further action by the Conference. In 1906 it created the Plainview District, the fourth for the Panhandle-Plains area, carving it out of the Colorado and Vernon districts. In 1907, the Conference met in Amarillo and reported a membership of nearly 90,000 for the entire Conference area. [37] At the end of 1908, its membership had reached 98,006 and reported for the year 6,363 baptisms and 607 church buildings. To accommodate the growth, the Conference in 1908 added the Stamford District, taking churches from the Vernon, Colorado, and Abilene districts.[38]

Renewed attempts to divide the Conference

Because it was geographically the largest conference in the state, and by 1900, the largest numerically, the Northwest Texas Conference became a target for division and for territory raiding by other conferences. By 1900, its membership totaled nearly as much as the other three Texas conferences combined.[39] At the 1900 conference at Georgetown, the Vernon District petitioned the Conference calling for division just to the west of Fort Worth, which would have split off Weatherford, Abilene, Vernon and Clarendon districts as well as the western part of the Fort Worth District. But a majority on the Committee on Conference Boundaries opposed the move, citing "the predominant sentiment

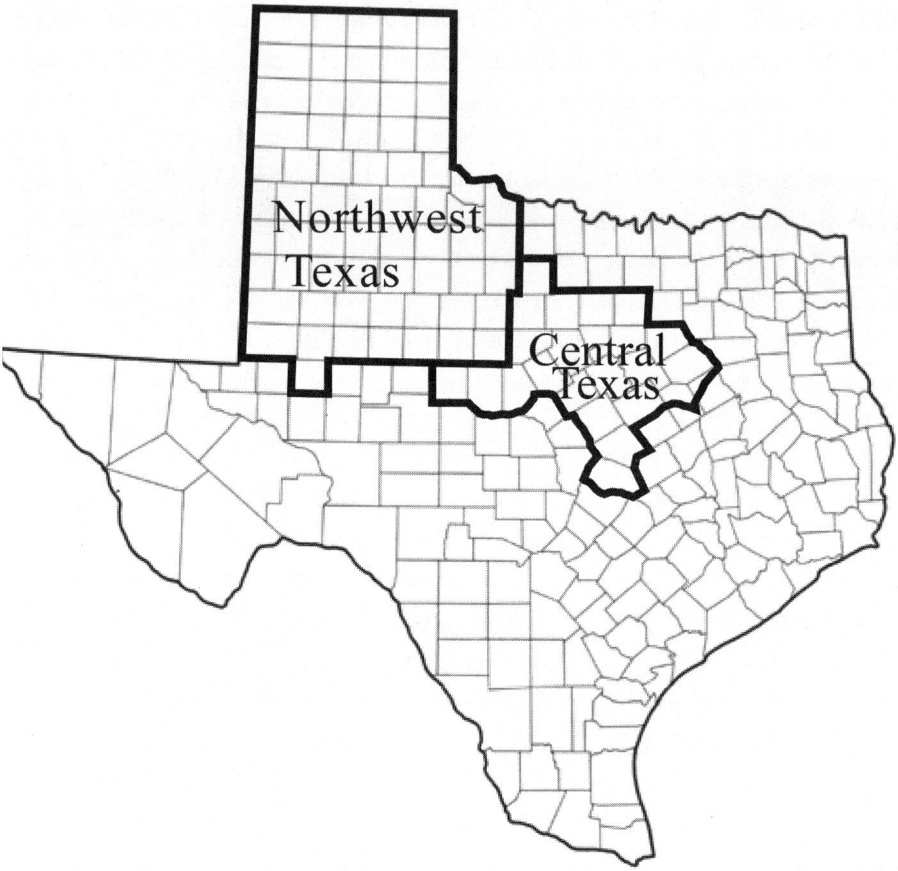

1910 Division of Northwest Texas Conference into the new Northwest Texas and Central Texas conferences

in the territory proposed for the new Conference is decidedly against such a measure." [40]

A minority report was also presented, calling for the establishment of a committee to study "a line of division as shall be just and equitable . . . ." [41] A strong debate over the minority report went for three days, but the Conference finally rejected the minority report by a vote of eighty-eight for and 114 against. [42]

The other conferences, especially the sparsely settled West Texas Conference, kept pressuring the General Conference for a piece of Northwest Texas. In 1902, the General Conference, meeting in Dallas (the first time ever in Texas), rejected major division but did grant to the West Texas Conference the counties of Burnet, Lampasas, , and Mills, and the western portion of Williamson County.[43] Separation of this territory did not sit well with the Northwest Texas Conference. Moreover, when the West Texas Conference petitioned the 1906 General Conference to transfer Brown and Coleman counties to its territory, Northwest Texas reacted strongly with its own petition, which asked that the counties lost in 1902 be restored to Northwest Texas: "We are surprised and pained at the action of the majority of the West Texas Conference . . . ," the Committee on Boundaries noted, and it called to "again make [the] Colorado River the dividing line, which is a natural boundary and was an established line between the two conferences from 1882 to 1902."[44]

As rapid growth continued, the division question arose again at the 1908 Northwest Texas Conference in Waco. One committee presented a resolution asking that the Northwest Texas Conference consult with the West Texas Conference to address the boundaries between the two. However, Horace Bishop, presiding elder for the Corsicana District, presented a substitute resolution that called for leaders to establish a "line for the equitable division of the Northwest Texas Conference, arrange all the preliminaries for such division, and prepare a Memorial to the General Conference, requesting that the Northwest Texas Conference be divided into two strong conferences."[45]

The time for division was right, and perhaps was aided by conference planners who set the 1907 conference at Amarillo and the 1908 one in Waco, more than 400 miles apart, forcing participants to travel long distances each year. Regardless, in 1908, the conference initiated division by a vote of 162–107 and forwarded the request to the General Conference to be considered at its 1910 meeting.

On November 10, 1909, the conference convened in Stamford in what was anticipated to be the last meeting of the original Northwest Texas Conference. By then, the conference had grown to sixteen districts and numbered 282 preachers, with an additional thirty-seven on trial. The conference reported for the year a membership of 105,956, a growth of 7 percent from the previous year. The conference also experienced 1,959 infant and 5,925 adult baptisms for the year.[46]

The highlight of the 1909 conference was the presentation of the Special Committee on Division. This committee, composed of sixteen lay and sixteen clergy members, recommended a division line that somewhat followed a natural geographic feature: the line that separated the Cross Timbers region from the rolling plains to the west. The line was to follow the west lines of Young, Stephens, and Eastland counties and then turn west along the north line of Brown County to the Colorado River.[47]

The committee also recommended that the two new conferences be named the Central Texas and the Northwest Texas conferences, and that the archives of the old Northwest Texas Conference be placed with the Central Texas Conference. Thus, even though the new Northwest Texas Conference would retain the historic name, it became the "new kid on the block," as the older portion of the former conference was to retain the records of the old conference.

The members of the 1909 Northwest Texas Conference approved the committee's report on division and the draft memorial for the General Conference unanimously. In anticipation that the General Conference would approve the division, the last act of the old Northwest Texas Conference was to designate Waxahachie as the site for the first meeting of the new Central Texas Conference in 1910, and Clarendon as the site for the new Northwest Texas Conference.[48]

As the members departed from Stamford, they must have known that division was soon to be a reality. The huge Northwest Texas Conference, with sixteen districts, needed to be divided. The proposed division would give the majority of districts and members to the new Central Texas Conference, but it would also give the new Northwest Texas Conference about two-thirds of the old conference, a territory that was growing rapidly. In a sense, it was a separation of the old from the new, the former being the older established churches in Central Texas and the latter the booming area of the Panhandle-South Plains.

Interestingly, as indicated by Table 1 below, the six districts of the proposed new conference would get only 30 percent of the members but 34 percent of the preachers. This difference was probably due to the larger number of missions in the new Northwest Texas area. Additionally during the last year of the old conference, the districts of the new area accounted for 33 and 34 percent of adult baptisms and professions of faith respectively, and a whopping 60 percent of the conference's infant baptisms, reflecting that the new settlements were populated with younger couples producing large families.

Table 1.

District	Local preachers	Professions of Faith	Adults baptized	Infants baptized	1909 Total membership
Vernon	17	730	452	145	6,716
Clarendon	20	546	332	132	5,316
Abilene	19	401	228	56	5,581
Colorado	20	654	334	103	4,749
Plainview	22	441	213	107	3,903
Stamford	44	830	406	147	5,897
Totals	**142**	**3,602**	**1,965**	**690**	**32,162**[49]
Total for all of old Northwest Texas Conference 1909	418	10,529	5,925	1,031	105,956
% of Variation	34	34	33	66	30

A new conference for Northwest Texas

The 1910 General Conference, meeting in May in Asheville, North Carolina, approved the division without debate, and the new Northwest Texas Conference was born. Attending from the Northwest Texas Conference were nine clergy and nine lay delegates. Of the clergy, three were from the soon-to-be new conference: Presiding Elder J. T. Griswold of the Stamford District; Jerome Duncan, president of Stamford College; and Presiding Elder G. S. Hardy of the Plainview District. These, along with President H. A. Boaz of Fort Worth Polytechnic

College (later Texas Wesleyan University), played significant roles in the conference's work and its peaceful division. Lay delegates from the area of the new conference included prominent Northwest Texans G. A. F. Parker of Hereford, C. M. Pattillo of Stamford, and E. B. Bynum of Abilene.[50]

With the blessing of the General Conference, delegates to the first session of the new Northwest Texas Conference gathered on Wednesday, November 9, 1910, in Clarendon. They sang with great exuberance, "And Are We Yet Alive?"[51] The forty-four-year history of the old Northwest Texas Conference, and the labors of hundreds of itinerant missionaries within the bounds of the new conference since the 1870s, all pointed to that glorious day in Clarendon as the delegates assembled in the local church's brand-new sanctuary. A local legend says that the bishop came in one door just as the carpenters were exiting through another! Indeed, the conference session was the first meeting to be held in the new building. "A handsomer structure is not to be found," declared the editor of the *Texas Christian Advocate*: "It is almost a four square building with a central dome. It has a large auditorium with the Sunday School chapel back of it and still in front of the pulpit."[52] According to the editor, the church would seat 1,500. Before the close of the historic conference, every seat was needed.

James Atkins, who had been elected a bishop in 1906, presided over the opening session. [53] John M. Barcus, who had served as secretary of the old Northwest Texas Conference for twenty years, was asked to call the roll.[54] Atkins preached the opening sermon, choosing for his text Luke 10: 1–24: "the harvest indeed is plenteous, but the laborers are few." In the afternoon, the conference gave way to the first religious service in Clarendon's beautiful new edifice. "The business houses closed, the schools adjourned, and the Bishop and cabinet were mostly present to participate in the hour of worship," reported *Texas* the *Advocate.* Another service followed that night.

The historic meeting continued on Thursday, carefully following the requirements set forth in Methodist church law as published in the *Discipline.* Each presiding elder from the conference's six districts reported on their work; all had glowing reports except for the Colorado District. Its presiding elder, Simeon Shaw told the conference the severe drought in his section was taking its toll: "He spoke most feelingly of the heroism of his preachers who in the face of the poverty and self-denial so bravely stood by the work," reported the *Advocate.* "Many counties lost half their population, but the splendid service [of the district's preachers] resulted in a net gain of membership."

Bishop James Atkins, first bishop of the modern Northwest Texas Conference (1910-1913)

In all, membership for the six districts increased by 3,812 to a total 35,099—an increase of nearly 11 percent.[55] There were twenty-five new churches, bringing the total number of "societies" in the conference to 364. More than half (189) had buildings; the rest were housed in schoolhouses or homes. The increase in membership meant that one out of every ten people living in the bounds of the new conference was on the roll of a Methodist church.

On Friday and Saturday, the conference continued with routine business. Every one of the 130 preachers was called to stand before the bishop and report on his year's work. At each presentation, the conference was given the opportunity to question the character of its ministers, as the *Discipline* required. Usually, the reports were all favorable; however, when the name of Plainview, Presiding Elder G. S. Hardy was called, one of his preachers, S. R. Twitty, "arose and preferred charges against him for mal-administration."[56] On the following day, Twitty's name was called, and Hardy told the bishop that there were charges against Twitty and that a committee had recommended a trial. Twitty then tried to withdraw his charge against Hardy, but the bishop had heard enough and responded by appointing a trial committee to hear the accusations against Twitty.

Early the next morning, the trial committee met in the Donley County Courthouse to hear the charges against Twitty. The proceeding ended in minutes: "The Chair ruled that the specifications, if proven, would not sustain the charge and the case was dismissed."[57] Whether the incident caused hard feelings is unknown; the next day, Twitty asked for an appointment to attend school at Yale University, and the conference approved his request.[58]

In spite of the short rift, the conference moved along harmoniously, culminating in an emotional day on Sunday. At the "Love Feast" that morning, dozens testified, including "Martha A. Rogers, "one of the saints of the frontier." A lifelong Methodist, the sixty-eight-year-old "Grandma" Rogers inspired the large crowd to shouts. "It reminded me of the good old times," noted the editor of the *Advocate.* At the 11 a. m. service, the bishop preached to a packed house of "perhaps 2,000" and later ordained the first class of elders. These included Marcus Beavers, John McCarley, Victor Trammell, Leslie Robeson, and O. P. Clark. Clark. Clark would remain a member of the conference until his death in 1979 at age ninety-seven.[59]

On Sunday night, the bishop read the appointments and announced the creation of three new districts (Amarillo, Hamlin, and Big Spring), which made nine districts for the new conference. One hundred forty-four preachers were appointed to fill the pulpits of more than 400 churches and preaching points. On Monday morning, all headed for home to move or to begin anew at their respective appointments. It was indeed a new day for Northwest Texas, which, at long last, had a conference of its very own.

Chapter 4

"Then let us make our boast Of His redeeming power"

People of the Texas high plains today are quite sensitive to outsiders' perspectives about their wind-swept region, and they felt no differently at the birth of the new Northwest Texas Conference. In 1911, Rev. O. P. Kiker, Presiding Elder for the Amarillo District, reported to the General Conference's Board of Church Extension that those who had predicted the region would never be settled were completely wrong: "Against this prophecy the people went and homes were builded [*sic*] and schools and churches . . . . The tide swept on and the opening fields yielded to the plow and the hoe," he wrote. "Then a more sturdy type climbed the cap-rock and stood to view the limitless spread of the Llano Estacado, or staked plains."[1]

Kiker noted that the plains was becoming "a realm where cities, factories, farms, dairies, orchards, and vast irrigation schemes tell the story

Constructed in 1902, the Channing church was organized in 1896 and remains as one of the oldest Methodist congregations north of the Canadian River. Photo by author.

of a wonderful civilization with a more abundant prospect." At the same time, he pointed out that the region presented a three-fold challenge to Methodism. First, the new settlers of Northwest Texas demanded quality and big plans. "Our citizens are broad-minded seeing matters in a large way," he noted. "They project and enjoy great enterprises. Their endeavors are best inspired with a broad proposition. They deal frankly and in the open. They require much from a church and school standpoint."

Second, he indicated that many of the new Panhandle Methodists, especially in the Amarillo area, were from the "Northern Church:" "We are not taking care of them as we should. This tide is coming in so fast that we find the necessity for establishing new charges in the interim. We need more men and even more money. It would be a very wise church policy . . . to enter well this country and hold it rather than spend money later defending it or even trying to redeem it from other influences."[2]

Third, he noted that the area north of the Canadian River, which he asserted was "the best portion of the plains country," had just begun to be colonized. "By all means," he concluded, "we should fully cover all this territory and do it now." In summary, Kiker's assessment well reflected the challenge faced by the church leadership; however, it did not give enough credit to the way the church had already covered the territory through its legendary circuit-riding system.

City vs. rural churches

Today, 76 percent of the population of the Northwest Texas Conference lives in the five urban counties of Lubbock, Midland, Potter, Randall, and Taylor, and the Methodist churches therein account for approximately 50 percent of the conference's membership. In 1910, only 17 percent of the area's population lived in those same counties, and their Methodist churches comprised only 12 percent of the conference membership. Thus, the great majority of Methodist churches in 1910 were where the people were: in the country.[3]

Thanks to the circuit riders, the new Northwest Texas Conference's greatest strength was its rural membership. In 1910, the conference included 415 "societies" served by 148 pastoral charges.[4] Only forty-seven of the 415 were single-church charges. The remaining 368 societies were a part of multiple-church circuits that averaged 3.6 churches per pastor.[5] Only 190 of the churches reported having "houses of worship"; the remaining 225 churches were probably housed in rural schoolhouses or homes.

The majority of the smaller churches and circuits were located in rural communities or the countryside and accounted for the majority of the total membership. The Kirkland Circuit in Childress County was

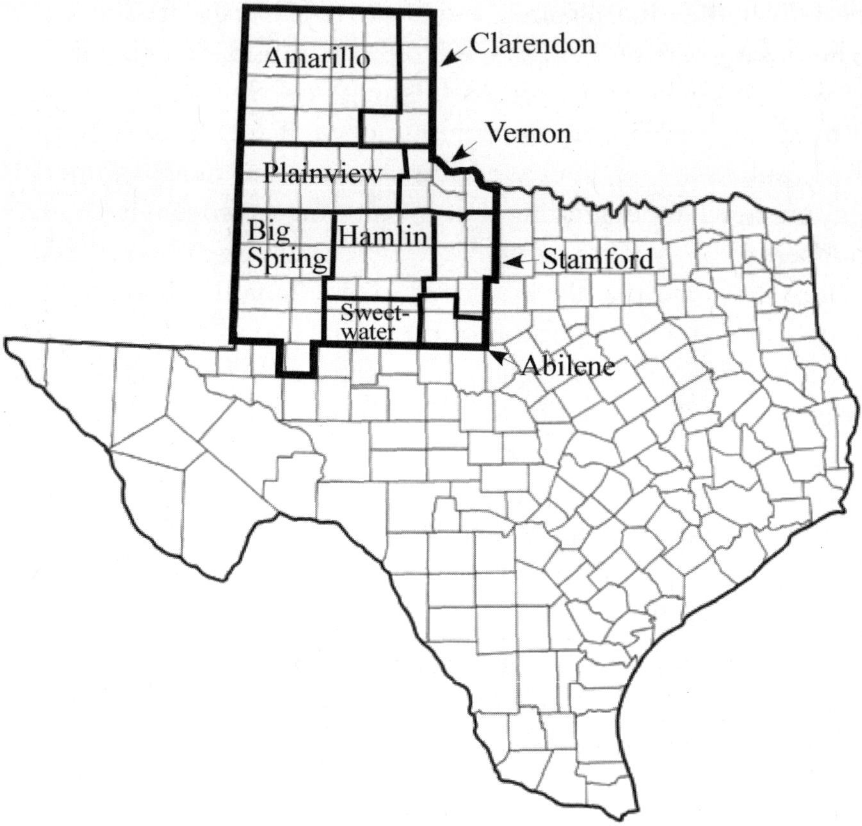

The nine districts of the Northwest Texas Conference, 1912.

the largest rural charge, with seven societies. It had a membership of 508 and ranked ninth among all the charges! Other large rural or small -town circuits in 1910 included Merkel (493), Clyde (425), Vera Circuit (423), Tye Circuit (399), Childress Mission Circuit (392), Blackwell (391), Dunn Circuit (379), and Ovalo Circuit (375). The top sixteen rural circuits held 17 percent of the overall conference membership.

Although the conference's country churches were scattered over the entire region, the majority were located in the older settled areas in the southeastern part of the area. The Vernon District had several large rural churches and circuits, including Kirkland, Quail, Estelline, Spring Creek, Tolbert, Margaret, and Vera, all of which had more than 225 members. Also, circuits surrounding Childress, Chillicothe, Vernon, and Wellington averaged nearly 300 members each.[6] In the Abilene district, the two largest circuits were Merkel and Clyde, both larger than either of the two Abilene churches.

In the new urban communities, the top fifteen city churches held only 22 percent of the conference's membership. (In 2006, the top fifteen churches held 42 percent of the conference membership.[7]) The forty-seven single-church charges, including the top fifteen, reported 14,673 members, or 42 percent of the total membership, with the majority located in county seat towns. Amarillo's church (now Polk Street), was the conference's largest, with 907 members, followed by Stamford St. John (790), Clarendon (743), Childress (580), Vernon (now First) (576), Quanah (575), Plainview (now First) (563), Haskell (550), and Big Spring (now First) (543).

Stamford St. John was the largest church not located in a county-seat town, followed by nearby Hamlin and Munday churches. All three were in new rapidly-growing new railroad towns; Hamlin even had three rail lines.[8]

The districts

The composition of the new conference's nine districts varied. Fewer settlers lived in the western part of the area, so it was difficult to create an equal balance among them in size and strength. For example, the new Amarillo District covered the entire upper Panhandle, but the Hamlin and Stamford district headquarters were located only 18 miles apart, both in Jones County and neither a county seat town.[9] In spite of the size difference, the bishop created a fairly equitable balance in membership. Four districts—Amarillo, Clarendon, Plainview, and Vernon—had equal assessments for the year, each with 13.2 percent. The Abilene and Stamford districts were required to raise 11 percent of the conference budget, while the Hamlin and Colorado districts were responsible for 9 percent. The Big Spring district's District's assessment was 6 percent.[10]

In 1911, the Colorado District became the Sweetwater District and remained in existence with the eight others until a new district alignment was announced at the 1917 annual conference. By that time, many new churches had been established in the South Plains area surrounding

Five years after its creation, the Northwest Texas Annual Conference returned to Clarendon, the site of its 1910 organization, where an enterprising photographer captured this scene. Photo courtesy Jay Gage and First United Methodist Church, Clarendon.

Lubbock, prompting the bishop to create a Lubbock District to replace the Big Spring District. In 1918, the Hamlin District was discontinued, leaving the conference with eight districts.[11] These changes remained in effect until 1930.

The role of the Sunday School and evangelism

With nine districts and many well-established circuits, the Northwest Texas Conference took the gospel to virtually every corner of the vast region it served. At the heart of the conference's success was its emphasis on Sunday Schools. Texas Methodists embraced wholeheartedly the national Sunday School movement that brought great improvements in literature and programs after 1900.[12] In Northwest Texas, the Sunday School served as an effective tool to provide widely scattered rural communities with religious training on a weekly basis in the absence of a circuit-riding preacher.

As a result, the Northwest Texas Conference became a leader in Sunday School attendance. In 1909, before the division of the old conference into two, enrollment ran 72 percent of total church membership; in the districts that would make up the new Northwest Texas Conference, enrollment was 77 percent compared to total membership.[13] Moreover, with Sunday School advocate James Atkins as its bishop, the new conference became the model for Sunday School enrollment. In 1910, it reported that 258 of the 415 churches had Sunday Schools totaling nearly 28,000 students, or 80 percent of the conference membership.[14] In 1912, Sunday School enrollment stood at 83 percent relative to total membership, and by 1916 rose to 87 percent, the highest ever before or since.[15]

With its strong Sunday School program, the Northwest Texas Conference was positioned for continued steady growth in the years ahead.

However, conference leaders were concerned that the majority of its churches had no houses of worship. In 1911, J. H. Chambless appealed to the readers of the *Texas Christian Advocate* to increase giving to church extension funds:

> We have 415 societies in the Northwest Texas Conference and only 189 houses of worship. . . . How are we to carry on our Sunday school, to say nothing of other departments of Church work, in school houses when others are using the same houses just as we are? We must go to work to house these congregations. To do this we must have money.[16]

Evangelism was another hallmark of the early days of the Northwest Texas Conference. Revivals were held every summer and usually with great results. At Wellington in 1909, John Smith, owner of the local pool hall, was converted and closed his place of business at the end of a great revival there under a Rev. Tooley.[17] In 1910, the presiding elders reported that 8,900 conversions for the year (one for every four members), as well as 2,345 adult baptisms, 1 (one for every 15 fifteen members).[18] According to one longtime conference preacher, C. G. Williams, "most older converts" chose to be immersed and were baptized at community baptisms at a pasture tank or pond.[19]

Drought, war, and influenza

However, dynamic evangelism could not negate the effect of drought on church membership. Primarily due to a devastating dry spell that began in 1910, the conference's dynamic annual growth of 7 to 10 percent that characterized the first decade of the century slowed dramatically. In 1911, membership grew by only 341 to a total of 34,991, and in 1912 dropped slightly.[20] Ironically, during the drought, Sunday School enrollment and new churches both increased. By the end of 1912, the conference recorded its largest number of churches ever: 453.[21]

The impact of the drought was short-lived. The outbreak of World War I in Europe in 1914 and the return of abundant rainfall recharged the West Texas boom. The war created new markets for cotton and wheat and hastened the transition of the region from ranching to farming.[22] The rainfall rate nearly doubled in some areas.[23] Cotton farmers made great profits in 1915, prompting a renewed demand for cotton acreage on the South Plains.[24] Farmers once again poured into the area, allowing the Northwest Texas Conference to reap its own harvest with steady (but not dramatic) growth. By the end of 1915, the conference had added forty-five Sunday Schools and increased church membership by more than 2,000, to 36,711.[25]

Nevertheless, dry weather returned to the southern plains with a vengeance in 1917, creating one of the region's worst droughts ever. Abilene saw only about 1.5 inches of rain during the crucial crop-growing months of June and July.[26] Lubbock received only 5.5 inches from January to September and only 8.73 inches for the year.[27] As a result, many farmers made no crops and once again abandoned their farms. The drought continued into the winter and spring of 1918. The weather only worsened when a severe cold snap killed thousands of cattle weakened by the extended drought, causing more losses throughout the plains.[28]

Adding to these devastations was a Spanish influenza epidemic that hit the entire country in the fall of 1918, causing death and wreaking havoc on family and church life. Nationally, the outbreak, the worst in American history, claimed more than 500,000 lives.[29] September 22 was declared a "churchless" Sunday in Throckmorton, and public gatherings were forbidden.[30] Crowell's church disbanded its Sunday School for "many" Sundays.[31] At Hedley, Cal C. Wright, who had just returned from serving in the Army as a chaplain in Kentucky, found himself acting as the community "doctor, nurse, preacher, and undertaker" during the epidemic.[32] In October, Lubbock's mayor ordered the closing of schools, movie theaters, and churches for an extended period.[33]

Lubbock's ban on public meetings directly impacted the annual session of the Northwest Texas Conference, as it was scheduled to meet there in early November 1918. Because most of the delegates were scheduled to stay in homes, conference leaders presumed they would have to cancel or postpone. However, the Abilene District District's presiding elder, Rev. O. F. Sensabaugh, and one of his pastors, J. W.

Hunt at Abilene St. Paul's, with only three-days notice, offered to host the conference at Abilene, even though that city's leaders were somewhat reluctant. Sensabaugh recalled: "The city fathers allowed us only three days' stay with no special city rallies."[34] At the time, the conference normally stretched over five days.

The shortened session, which met November 6–8, recorded probably the greatest number of absentees in conference history; twenty-four of the thirty-six designated lay delegates did not attend. Of the sixteen delegates from four districts in the Panhandle and South Plains, only two made the trip. However, fifty-four of the eighty-three clergy members did attend, rushing through their committee work and reports in record time.[35]

The flu pandemic did not affect Northwest Texas as much as it did urban areas, but church growth still suffered a major blow. "The war and the drouth conditions have hampered the work, both materially and spiritually," O. P. Clark reported in the 1918 *Journal*. "The people have allowed their depressed condition to be reflected in their spiritual lives."[36] The two droughts of the teens cut new church plantings in half, from fifteen per year to seven.[37] By the end of 1918, church membership in the conference had sustained its largest single-year drop: 9 percent, to 37,782. Although the drought ended in the fall of 1918, it would take two full years for the region—and the church—to recover. Conference membership remained level for 1919 and later surged to 1917 levels by the end of 1920, with 41,680 adherents.[38]

A larger role for women

Prior to 1918 in the Methodist Church, South, women had no representation, even though they were a major force in the day-to-day work of the congregations. The practice only mirrored national political practice; in 1918, none of the Southern states except Texas allowed women to vote in political elections. However, a national women's suffrage movement was gaining strength, and in the midst of the movement, the ME, South, General Conference approved legislation in 1918 granting laity rights to women, provided that 75 percent of the delegates to the annual conferences did the same. These voters—all men—approved the measure by a combined vote of 4,280–157.[39]

One of the leaders in the national Methodist movement—the Women's Laity League—was Lena Elva Hyder Rollins, daughter of one of the Northwest Texas Conference's early Abilene ministers, J. A. Hyder.[40] Her role perhaps influenced the Northwest Texas Conference vote at its influenza-shortened meeting in Abilene; the delegates voted for women's laity rights by a vote of 95–0.[41] The following year, in 1919, four of the eight districts responded by electing to the annual conference its first female lay delegates. The Clarendon District sent two: Mrs. T. C. Delaney of Memphis and Mrs. J. C. Wells of Lakeview. The Sweetwater District also elected two, Mrs. J. G. Merritt of Colorado City, and Mrs. C. C. Higgins of Snyder. The Lubbock and Plainview Districts sent one each: Mrs. W. E. Lyon of Lubbock, and Mrs. W. M. Lane of Floydada. The other fifty-eight lay delegates were men.[42] Although acceptance of women's participation was slow in coming, the Northwest Texas Conference did elect Lena Hyder Rollins as one of its delegates to the 1922 General Conference, the first one at which women were eligible to serve. It also designated Mrs. W. B. (Amelia) McKeown as an alternate delegate.[43]

Revival fires burn the plains

As the conference celebrated its ten-year anniversary in 1920, it could point proudly to a 39 percent increase in membership in spite of the droughts. Three churches reported at least 1,000 adherents (Amarillo Polk Street, Clarendon, and Plainview). In addition, preachers had established sixty-four new congregations during the decade, but there was a net decrease in total churches from a decade-high 453 in 1912 to 404 in 1920.[44] Nearly half of the new churches were located in the South Plains cotton country surrounding the Lubbock area.

At the November 1919 annual conference in Lubbock, the new bishop, W. F. McMurry, introduced Dr. George R. Stuart from Birmingham, Alabama, who preached several stirring sermons on evangelism. One morning service attracted "a great audience and the speaker stirred every heart," reported the *Journal*. "Amid singing and old time shouting, a great handshaking service was held at the close."[45]

The impact of Stuart's preaching had a far-reaching effect. Apparently McMurry required his presiding elders to report evangelistic activity in detail, as evidenced by rare revival statistics, which appear in the 1921 conference *Journal*. For the year, the presiding elders reported that nearly every church in their districts held a revival, and a few held more than one. Of the 383 churches, 367 held revivals and reported an unprecedented 9,452 conversions for the year.[46] Although not every conversion led to church membership, the conference did record nearly 4,800 additions on professions of faith, more than doubling the previous year.[47]

The last great railroad boom in Texas also spurred new growth of the conference in the 1920s, mostly on the South Plains. Settlers began moving into the former ranch country west of Lubbock and helped to close the final "outside row" of counties. As quickly as new towns were founded, Methodist circuit riders were on hand to establish new churches at Ropesville in 1921 and Levelland, Morton, and Bledsoe in 1924.[48] As in many communities, the Morton church first met in the school, later in the new courthouse, and, after Baptists built a church with only a dirt floor, used their building, affectionately known as 'the Mule Barn."[49]

Optimism, like the mood of the nation in the Roaring '20s, now abounded at every annual conference, and the mood was infectious. One pastor recalled attending his first conference at Plainview in 1923. "In those days every preacher made his report on the Conference floor. The reports were interesting, but I began to suspect even then, that some of the reports were blown up to make a poor year sound pretty good."[50] But the years were good: in 1925, conference contributions topped $1 million for the first time, and the following year the conference confidently purchased 315 acres in Ceta Canyon near Palo Duro Canyon for a campground site.[51]

Conference membership increased steadily from 1921 through 1927, averaging 6 percent per year, topping 60,000 by the end of 1927.[52] During the same period, forty-two new churches were started, twenty-five of which were on the South Plains surrounding Lubbock. The Borger oil boom in 1926 stimulated growth in the upper Panhandle, leading to the founding of churches in Borger and Phillips in 1926 and Stinnett in 1927, which became the last county seat town in the conference to have a Methodist church.

Meanwhile, the little city of Lubbock, with a population of only 7,000 in 1923, saw its future change immediately with its selection as the home for the coveted new Texas Technological College. The state's choice of Lubbock instead of rival sister city Amarillo or thirty-four other communities that vied for the school sent shock waves through the region and set into motion events that would impact the very existence of the Northwest Texas Conference's fledgling colleges. To understand these events, a background review of the conference's college efforts is necessary.

Northwest Texas support for Methodist colleges

Methodists were the first to establish a college in frontier Northwest Texas. Led by pioneer preacher J. T . L. Annis and L. F. Miller, the Belle Plain District of the Northwest Texas Conference established the region's first college in 1881 at Belle Plain in Callahan County south of Baird.[53] Noted for its music curriculum, Belle Plain College functioned as both a public school and college, and enrollment grew to 122 by the mid-1880s. However, the town of Belle Plain began to lose residents after the county seat was moved to Baird in 1883. Enrollment declined rapidly after the state improved support for county schools, and poor weather in 1886 and 1887 hurt the local economy. The college finally closed because of bankruptcy in 1892.[54]

Meanwhile, the Northwest Texas Conference in 1891 established Polytechnic College in Fort Worth (which later would become Texas Wesleyan University), to which some West Texans sent their children.[55] The conference also supported Southwestern University in Georgetown, Texas. Established in 1873, Southwestern by 1906 had become one of the largest Methodist colleges in the nation, with 322 enrolled for college courses.[56]

A new Methodist university for Texas

A long-held dream of a major Methodist university for Texas got caught in the midst of a growing rivalry between Fort Worth and Dallas. As early as 1906, Polytechnic President Hiram A. Boaz and Southwestern's President Robert S. Hyer had privately discussed the possibility of moving Southwestern to North Texas in order to take advantage of a larger population base. Hyer, however, favored Dallas.[57] In 1910, Boaz wrote to Hyer, proposing that Southwestern move to Fort Worth to merge with Polytechnic. Somehow the letter became public and set off a firestorm.[58] Ardent Southwesterners opposed the idea of relocation; Dallas supporters, who had already been courted by Hyer, quickly formed a committee to try to lure the college to Dallas.

Meanwhile, Dallas Mayor Stephen Hay, seized the initiative and met in Little Rock, Arkansas, with Wallace Buttrick, an official of the Methodist General Education Board. Buttrick agreed to work toward moving Southwestern or help start a new university at Dallas, if the city could raise $300,000 and provide land.

The controversy played out in the editorial pages of state newspapers throughout 1910. Southwestern University supporters who opposed relocation subsequently won over the college's trustees, who declined Dallas's offer. At the same time, recognizing that he was fighting a losing battle, Boaz also withdrew his plan to merge Polytechnic with Southwestern.[59] However, Polytechnic then faced a new threat: the possibility of a new Methodist college in Dallas. Was North Texas big enough for two Methodist schools so close together? James Atkins, the bishop of the new Northwest Texas Conference, suggested that the Texas conferences create a statewide education commission to resolve the question.[60]

By the time the state's annual conferences met in the fall of 1910, most of the details of a resolution to the conflict had been worked out. The new Northwest Texas Conference joined others to approve a resolution that would create a statewide commission and empowered it "to accept or reject the proposition submitted by the City of Dallas or such as may be submitted by any other city of Texas."[61]

Dallas college promoters persisted. In the spring of 1911, the new Methodist Education Commission accepted Dallas's offer of 662.5 acres and $300,000, and named the school Southern Methodist University (SMU). In addition, it silenced two potential critics by electing Southwestern's Hyer as president and Polytechnic's Hiram Boaz as vice president of the new institution. On Thanksgiving Day 1912, Northwest Texas Conference Bishop James Atkins, and Bishop E. D. Mouzon, who would become its bishop in 1916, laid the cornerstone for Dallas Hall, the new administration building for SMU. In September 1915, the new university opened with more than 700 students.[62]

While SMU was being established, Polytechnic College, at the recommendation of the Methodist Education Commission, changed its name in 1914 to Texas Woman's College. Its ownership also passed from the exclusive hands of the Northwest Texas and Central Texas conferences to all five of the "English-speaking" conferences of Texas. In 1934, the school was renamed to Texas Wesleyan College and became coeducational.[63]

New colleges for Northwest Texas: Clarendon and Seth Ward

Meanwhile, in Northwest Texas, the saga of the Methodist colleges played out in somewhat unusual fashion. As the Panhandle's population increased, new colleges began to appear. In 1898, the Northwest Texas Conference established Clarendon College as a junior college after local residents offered the conference land and a multi-story brick building.[64] By 1900, the school had eight teachers and 109 students. In December 1903, the Clarendon College Cowboys played the first interscholastic football game in game in the Panhandle, defeating the nearby Goodnight Academy, 16–10. By 1916, Clarendon College boasted the largest junior college enrollment in the South.[65]

At Plainview, members of the Holiness Association, or Nazarene Church, founded Central Plains Holiness College in 1907. Initially well-funded, this new school was housed in an imposing four-story building with twenty-seven rooms. In addition, two large frame buildings served as boys' and girls' dormitories.[66] Even though its enrollment was more than 200 in 1909, the Holiness Association found the task of running the school too difficult and in late 1909 sold it to the Plainview District of the Northwest Texas Conference for $32,000.[67]

Methodists renamed the school in honor of the first native-born Texas bishop of the ME Church, South, Seth Ward, who had died the previous year in Japan.[68] Organized as a two-year coeducational college designed to prepare students to enter Southwestern University, the new Seth Ward College fielded football, basketball, and baseball teams and became a natural rival of the new Wayland Baptist College,

Clarendon College, Clarendon, Texas

Seth Ward College,
Plainview, Texas

also located in Plainview. Enrollment at Seth Ward averaged more than 200 from 1913 through 1915.[69]

Unfortunately, two fires soon brought tragedy to the little college. The men's dormitory burned in 1914, and before it could be rebuilt, a second fire in March 1916 destroyed the huge main building as well as the girls' dormitory. Unable to secure $50,000 in funding to rebuild, the school's trustees voted to close the college at the end of the 1916 spring term.[70]

Stamford College

Fire also played key roles in the short history of another Northwest Texas college. In 1906, the presiding elders of the Colorado and Abilene districts, J. T. Griswold and John H. Morris, began advocating the establishment of a religious college in central West Texas. They formed a committee from the two districts, which selected Stamford as the site after receiving a large gift of land and $67,000 from the local Swenson family of Stamford.[71] Probably because of the family's connection to New York, a New York City architect was hired to design the campus and main building. The result was, in the archi-

Stamford College,
Stamford, Texas

tect's words, "a massive and imposing structure of gray limestone, quarried within twenty miles of Stamford. Its five stories, including the basement and tower, contain a floor area of approximately 42,500 square feet."[72] With the handsome new building and two dormitories, built at a total cost of $140,000, the new school appeared headed for permanence.[73]

Opened as the Stamford Collegiate Institute in September 1907, the school had after two years an enrollment of more than 300 and changed its name to Stamford College.[74] But as drought conditions settled over West Texas in the years after 1910, enrollment dropped and debt increased sharply. The worsening situation attracted the attention of Abilene pastor James Winford Hunt. Once a newspaper editor and publisher in Lubbock and Plainview, Hunt had been licensed to the ministry in 1903 and pastored at Channing, Dalhart, and Snyder before moving to St. Paul's in Abilene.[75] Already a noted orator and champion of temperance and education, Hunt took a special interest in the struggling college and, in June 1916, left his pastorate to assume control of the school.

By the fall of 1916, the conference's Education Committee reported that Hunt was "putting new life into it [the college] through things material and things mental and things moral and things spiritual."[76] But Hunt's hard work and leadership could not prevent destruction from drought, war, and fire.

The hard drought of 1917, coupled with the United States' entry into World War I, took its toll on college enrollment and fund-raising efforts.[77] In April 1918, fire destroyed the college's main building, and with it the dream for Stamford College.[78] The school closed at the end of the spring semester.

The fire-born tragedies at Plainview and Stamford left Clarendon College as the only college in the Northwest Texas Conference. In 1919, it reported an enrollment of 370 and the fact that it could not accommodate all of its applicants.[79] Rev. Hunt, who was reappointed to St. Paul in Abilene in 1918, took this information to heart and seized the opportunity to fulfill his dream for a college for the south end of the conference.

The beginning of McMurry

National events helped Hunt's vision. Out of the Atlanta General Conference in 1918 came the "Christian Education Movement," an ambitious plan to raise millions of dollars for support of Southern Methodist and Emory universities. In December 1919, the education campaign commission also designated "tentative apportionments" to smaller colleges.[80] Soon after this action, Hunt preached to his congregation a sermon titled "Methodists' Opportunities in West Texas" and told of his vision for a school in Abilene.

Hunt approached the Abilene Chamber of Commerce but found no immediate support.[81] He also continued to work through the conference's Board of Education; a week before it was to meet in Abilene on March 19, 1920, he apparently arranged for the local Lions Club to feature a program on the possibility of a Methodist college for Abilene. The city's newspaper gave the program a front-page headline.[82]

The publicity probably prompted the community of Stamford to try to regain its Methodist college. At the meeting of the Northwest Texas Conference's Board of Education on March 19, both Stamford and Abilene delegates presented proposals. Stamford offered a new $100,000 administration building and two dormitories, to be situated on the twenty-acre site of Stamford College. Its delegation politely noted that Abilene already had two church-related schools: Abilene Christian (affiliated with the Churches of Christ) and Simmons College (Baptist). But Abilene countered with a handsome proposal, offering $350,000 and twenty-five acres of land (later increased to thirty-two), as well as free water and a streetcar connection to the main part of town. J. W. Hunt

Rev. James W. Hunt, founder of McMurry College, pictured at his desk in 1925. Photo from the 1925 The Totem, the McMurry College yearbook, courtesy Pat Williamson.

promoted the Abilene site, noting that it provided a more central location. The Board of Education concurred and sent its recommendation to the annual conference.[83]

At the 1920 annual conference, the Board of Education presented its formal recommendation for placing the school at Abilene. However, it required both the deed to the proposed thirty-two acres as well as "$300,000 in cash or such equivalent" to be delivered by April 1, 1921 (later extended to April 4).[84] And in a bold move, the board also recommended to the conference that it "withdraw as a patronizing Conference from Southwestern University at Georgetown, Texas, and from Texas Woman's College, Fort Worth, Texas." This recommendation signaled the board's intent to focus the conference's resources on Southern Methodist, Clarendon, and the new school at Abilene. The board also recommended that Hunt be appointed "commissioner" of the new college.[85]

Apparently well-orchestrated by Hunt's careful planning, events moved rapidly. The two Abilene churches, St. Paul and First, pledged to raise $200,000, and the Abilene Chamber of Commerce committed to raise $100,000. Meanwhile, four Abilene residents—Henry Sayles Jr., a Presbyterian, Ed Hughes, an Episcopalian, K. K. Leggett, a Baptist, and J. M. Cunningham, a Methodist—donated a forty-two-acre tract in south Abilene for the school. Throughout the fund-raising campaign, such ecumenical support continued, as the presidents of Abilene Christian College and Simmons College gave contributions and strong endorsements. In dramatic fashion, donors gave the final $12,000 on April 4, 1921, the last day of the deadline.[86]

McMurry College, Abilene, Texas 1923 Photo from Fane Downs and Rob Sledge, eds., *Pride of Our Western Prairies: McMurry College, 1923-1988.*

The next day, the Board of Education met in Abilene, heard the reports of the church and Chamber of Commerce fund-raising campaigns, and after "thorough discussion" accepted Abilene's offer and committed to build the new college. "The committee appointed by the Methodist church in Abilene and the city . . . was one of the nicest committees I have ever dealt with," recalled Board Chairman J. T. Griswold. "They were courteous, frank, clear, patient; and above all else, they showed a deep earnestness for the school and its great success. There was not a moment of confusion or wrangle during the entire procedure."[87] The board also "promised that "this Conference would raise in its educational campaign $150,000," an amount that had been specified by the 1918 General Conference for a new junior college in Northwest Texas as a part of the $13 million national campaign.[88]

The board also made two other recommendations to the annual conference: that the new school be named in honor of Bishop W. F. McMurry, and that its president be J. W. Hunt.[89] In October 1921, the Northwest Texas Conference met in Amarillo; on October 8, it approved without dissent the board's recommendations for the new college. On September 29, 1923, McMurry College opened as a four-year academy (including a two-year junior college curriculum) in a new, beautiful three-story brick building and a girls' dormitory, named Hunt Hall. Nearby rooming houses were leased for men's residences. Nearly 200 students enrolled on opening day.[90] It was a day of rejoicing for Hunt and the Northwest Texas Conference.

The rise and fall of the University of Amarillo

With two colleges, Clarendon and McMurry, within its bounds by 1923, the Northwest Texas Conference seemed to have worked out its educational needs in a satisfactory manner. However, in 1923, both schools offered only junior college curriculums, and the school leaders knew that in order to attract funding from the General Conference, they needed to upgrade their schools to four-year colleges. The Northwest Texas Conference concurred in November 1923 and committed to endowment campaigns for both schools.[91] McMurry acted promptly, adding upper-level classes in each of its first two years, and was accredited as a "first-class" institution by the Texas Association of Colleges in 1926.[92]

However, Clarendon College found itself caught in a location struggle. For many years, local residents had heard rumors that their college was going to be moved to a larger town. In an effort to prevent such a move, in 1924 residents formed the Citizens Senior College Committee to raise funds to elevate the school to senior college status.[93] As a result, Clarendon College added its third year of work in 1924 and received recognition as a four-year accredited school in 1925.[94]

But the effort only made Clarendon College even more attractive for relocation. Amarillo residents, after being stung on their failed bid to land Texas Tech, decided to go after the little Methodist school as a foundation for a larger school in their city.[95] In May 1924, George Shearer, the presiding elder of the Amarillo District and a member of the Northwest Texas Conference's Board of Education, arranged for the board to meet publicly with Amarillo residents to discuss a Methodist college for the city. Included were McMurry President J. W. Hunt and Clarendon President George Slover. The meeting seemingly went well and set into motion the development of a major offer to the conference: the creation of the University of Amarillo.[96]

In 1925, wealthy cattleman Lee Bivins was elected mayor of Amarillo, and he soon offered land and $50,000 to attract a Methodist school. Clarendon College was the target. In November 1926, the conference's Board of Education recommended that the conference appoint a twenty-six-member special Location Commission "to look carefully into the matter of the permanent location of Clarendon College." This provoked considerable opposition from the Clarendon community, including the college's now-president emeritus, Slover , and Clarendon College Board member (and perhaps chairman) R. E. Porter. However, the college's new president, R. E. L. Morgan, "made a plea for confidence in Clarendon College and for a decision that would settle, for all time, the location of the College, and requested the appointment of the Commission." The conference concurred by a majority vote and appointed the special commission.[97]

The commission's creation caused considerable controversy throughout the Panhandle. Shortly after the conference, Morgan appealed to local residents to be patient and to "continue their loyal support of Clarendon College; otherwise there will be an irreparable injury done to the institution."[98] Phoebe K. Warner, a noted writer from the town of Claude, wrote: "To remove it [from Clarendon to Amarillo] would erase all the patriotic devotion that has made the school possible. Why move everything to Amarillo just because it is a little larger. . . . To Clarendon it is a real child of love; to Amarillo it would be a stepchild."[99] The Clarendon College trustees noted that they believed "that a permanent endowment of from $250,000 to $500,000" could be raised in Clarendon, provided that the school remain there.[100]

Even in Amarillo, there was opposition to moving the Clarendon school. Amarillo's Board of City Development announced in February 1927 that it would "give no aid nor comfort" to the effort to move the college: "the Board of City Development is not going to move a hand to build Amarillo up by tearing down other towns."[101] Delayed by a smallpox outbreak in Amarillo, the Location Commission finally met on March 1, 1927. In spite of the strong opposition, the commission surprisingly voted to move Clarendon College to Amarillo by a 17–1 vote.

Shortly after the decision, Morgan sadly noted that the college would close at the end of the 1927 summer session. [102] He also resigned and made plans to move to Amarillo to establish the university there.[103] In May 1927, Clarendon College graduated its first—and last—senior class. However, the college's closure proved to be premature. Negotiations between the conference and Amarillo moved too slowly to have a campus available by the fall of 1927.

On August 29, 1927, the commission met again, considered "several offers made by Amarillo citizens," and quickly determined that the best offer was from Mayor Bivins, who promised 700 acres and a $200,000 administration building, free and clear of debt. The offer stipulated that 280 acres would be immediately sold to raise money for two $150,000 dormitories, as well as for endowment, and that the city of Amarillo would furnish a hard-surfaced road, sewer, light, and gas connections to the campus.[104] The offer seemed too good to be true, but the commission accepted Mayor Bivins'Bivins's proposal and recommended that the 1927 annual conference commit to establish in Amarillo a "modern, Standard 'A' Grade Senior College" and to raise $500,000 for endowment.[105] In November 1927, the conference approved the proposal.

Meanwhile, Clarendon was determined to keep a college. Its leaders decided in the spring of 1927 to acquire the Methodist campus and convert the facility to a publicly supported municipal junior college. As a result, the conference sold the property to the local school district for $42,000.[106] Clarendon College became a secular school when it reopened in 1928 as a publicly supported junior college.[107]

With the Clarendon College question settled, the only thing that remained was for Amarillo to raise $200,000 in order to build a university there. But in 1927, declining rainfall and falling commodity prices signaled a downturn in agricultural prosperity.[108] Perhaps also distracted by the oil boom that had hit the upper Panhandle in the Borger area, Amarillo residents could not replicate what Abilene had done for McMurry: to raise $200,000 in less than two months.

In November 1928, the Methodist Conference Board of Education tried to spur the Amarillo courtship by offering a commendation to Bivins and the city of Amarillo because they had "striven earnestly for more than a year, but have been unable to fully meet the terms of the contract." At the same time, the board recommended that the conference postpone any fundraising for the proposed university until after the completion of "the projected campaign for the endowment of McMurry College is completed." However, to show good faith on its part and in an effort to keep the Amarillo door open, the conference also recommended that the bishop appoint George Slover as president of the unfounded Amarillo college "and to authorize him to represent the Conference in the further consideration of the proposition."[109]

However, Amarillo residents had learned a lesson from Clarendon. In the spring of 1929, Amarillo legislators succeeded in passing in Austin a bill to create public junior college districts. Gov. Daniel J. Moody signed the bill on April 2, 1929, and three months later, Amarillo voters approved the district. The new junior college, the first created under the new bill, opened in September 1929.[110] Apparently Methodist leaders failed to understand the significance of Amarillo's action: in November, the Methodist Board of Education still held out for a deal, stating that "we desire Amarillo to know whenever she is ready . . . the Church is ready to cooperate in the movement."[111] But that would be the last mention of a Methodist church college for Amarillo or anywhere else in the Northwest Texas Conference; the coming Great Depression saw to that.

Fundamentalists attack Methodist colleges

Competition for church schools was not the only problem that Methodism faced during the 1920s. Its new colleges found themselves embroiled in the "fundamentalism" versus "modernism" controversy.

Those who generally advocated a literal interpretation of the Bible and those who were prompted by scientific literary criticism of the Bible squared off in public and private debates.[112] The controversy caught national attention during Tennessee's famous 1925 John Scopes "monkey" trial, which pitted fundamentalist politician William Jennings Bryan against Scopes's agnostic lawyer, Clarence Darrow.[113] In Northwest Texas, the dispute primarily concerned what was being taught in Methodist colleges, prompted by fundamentalist attacks on the writing and teaching of SMU professor John A. Rice.

Rice's 1920 book, *The Old Testament in the Life of Today*, caught the wrath of the literalists who opposed Rice's endorsement of modern criticism that said, among other things, "the first six books of the Old Testament had been written by several authors . . . and then edited into final form much later by temple scribes." His statements played right into the hands of conservatives, and a "storm" hit the pages of the *Texas Christian Advocate* in April 1921, primarily consisting of letters from readers demanding Rice's removal from SMU. Within a month, the beleaguered professor resigned.[114]

His departure was welcomed by many in the Northwest Texas Conference. Its Board of Education drafted a strongly worded resolution that lauded good scholarship as long as it did not question the "divine origin" of Scripture. It called for "allegiance to the Bible as the inspired Word of God" and for Methodist leaders not to use anyone who questions "the fundamentals of our faith" or who cannot "accept the verity of the Scripture in their entirety."[115] The resolution passed unopposed.[116]

The fundamentalist-modernist issue did not go away easily. Fanned by fundamentalist Baptist leader J. Frank Norris of Fort Worth and W. E. Hawkins, Jr., a young Methodist preacher in the Central Texas Conference, charges of heresy continued, most of it focused on SMU and Texas Woman's College. Norris spoke in Abilene, where he "packed" the City Auditorium: E. D. Landreth, then a student at McMurry, heard the talk and recalled that Norris "was smart, clever and persuasive"—but he also saw through Norris's demagoguery. "That night I heard him attack all higher institutions of learning including the Baptist schools and some of the foremost leaders of his own denomination," Landreth recalled. "My regard for the speaker began to wane hurriedly."[117]

In 1925, the Northwest Texas Conference did have to deal directly with a fundamentalist-inspired issue related to evolution. In 1925, Lewis N. Stuckey, the pastor of the Polk Street church in Amarillo (the conference's largest), introduced a proposed standing rule that would require the conference to withhold money from any school whose president would not certify the orthodoxy of its faculty.[118] The resolution was signed by Stuckey and eleven other conference leaders, including future Texas Lt. Gov. John Lee Smith, W. M. Pearce, J. H. Hamblen, McMurry President J. W. Hunt, and Clarendon College President George Slover.[119] With such support, especially from the college presidents, the annual conference expressed no opposition; the resolution became known as Standing Rule Number 9.

In all likelihood, the college presidents supported the resolution because it meant that individual faculty members could be sheltered from being singled out by fundamentalists on a witch hunt. In a sense, the resolution signaled to professors to not be outspoken if they believed in evolution. Stuckey made a pointed reference to the theory in his resolution:

> There is no teacher in our school, within my knowledge, who believes or teaches that man had his origin in a lower form of animal life. All the teachers of our institution, within my knowledge, believe without mental reservation, equivocation, or without interpretation other than that of the accepted standards of our Methodist Church, in the interpretation of both the Old and the New Testaments, and in every statement of the Apostles' Creed.[120]

Similar resolutions passed by other Texas conferences provoked conflict between college faculties and the conferences. SMU President C. C. Selecman did not sign the affidavit, resulting in the loss of Northwest Texas funds for one year.[121] However, the two colleges of the Northwest Texas Conference accepted the stipulation quietly. At McMurry, according to historian Paul Lack, Hunt "simply swore to the doctrinal purity of his faculty without quizzing or badgering them" on the question of orthodoxy.[122]

The orthodoxy rule lasted only a year. In 1927, the conference, after considerable debate, retreated from its hard stand by rescinding Standing Rule Number 9; in its stead, the Board of Education simply recommended that its college trustees "use all care and diligence in seeing that the faculties . . . are both sound in faith and Christian in character."[123] Thus, Northwest Texas Methodists found a way to sidestep a potentially divisive issue. However, their Baptist brethren in Lubbock would not let the issue die and, in 1932, mounted an attack on an ordained Methodist clergyman and son of a Methodist bishop, Texas Tech history professor John C. Granbery, who like John Rice would subsequently lose his job.[124]

By 1928, with their colleges established and the fundamentalist controversy set aside for the time being, Northwest Texas Methodists were ready to move forward. But national economic conditions, especially in agriculture, foretold approaching problems. Those problems were already being reflected in the conference's statistical reports. Membership growth fell from a 6 percent annual rate in the mid-1920s to less than 1 percent for 1928 and 1929. Only seven new churches were founded during the last two years of the'20s.

On October 29, 1929, "Black Tuesday" rocked the New York Stock Exchange as the market lost a third of its value in one day, triggering the beginning of the Great Depression. When the conference met two weeks later in Pampa, the impact of the stock market collapse was still weeks away. Only the "State of the Church" report made any reference to economic conditions, when it noted a downturn in gifts for benevolence and explained that it was "due to the fact that a large territory of our Conference suffered from severe drought conditions."[125] Few, if any, of the assembled could sense what lay ahead. The worst was yet to come.

Chapter 5

“What Troubles We Have Seen”

As the Great Depression settled in on the nation, folks in the Northwest Texas Conference did what they had always done in tough economic times: rely on themselves. They could do that because, in 1930, a great majority of its 700,000 residents still lived on the farm or in rural, almost self-sufficient communities. Typical of the West Texas spirit during hard times was the attitude exhibited by Methodists in Adrian, west of Amarillo. In 1927, drought and economic depression had already hit the little wheat-farming town, but hard times did not deter progress. Even though people were out of work, they built a new church. Their pastor recalled: "Most people would have tried to argue that they were not financially able to build a Church, but these people said, 'Well, it is a good time to build, as we have nothing else to do . . . .' They were fine people."[1]

The drought of the early 1930s was much harder on Northwest Texas than the Depression. Dry weather extended well into the decade and was at its worst in 1934 and '35. People suffered from the lack of rain.

The pastor at Roby in 1930–31, J. Howard Scoggins, recalled how desperate people were:

> We went through one year without rain; no crops were grown. The second year, no rain, not even moisture for grass. The fields were barren as winter, milk cows and work teams were disposed of; chickens died for want of feed. There was no public work; no work on the farms. . . . I knew men who traveled on foot to Sweetwater, even as far as Abilene trying to find work. I saw them come back, not having found work, with their shoes worn off their feet.[2]

The continued dry weather led to the birth of the "Dust Bowl," as thousands of acres of plowed land, especially in the northern Panhandle, literally blew away with strong spring winds. The dust storms began in 1931 and worsened with each dry year. Especially notable was the "Black Sunday" storm of April 14, 1935. Propelled by winds of 80 and 60 miles per hour in Amarillo and Lubbock, a black wall of dirt rolled through the Panhandle and South Plains and destroyed hopes for a wheat crop that year.[3]

Remarkably, many West Texans did not lose heart amid the adversity. "Our people have been sorely tried during the last few months," a pastor reported to the 1931 conference, "but these trials have had a tendency to turn their hearts more toward God."[4] In many communities, people helped one another. As E. D. Landreth noted, "Because of faith in the country and in God, the teachers and bus drivers said, 'We will take script and redeem it later;' the filling stations furnished gas for the busses with very little pay; the doctors cared for the sick; the funeral homes buried the dead, hoping a day would come when they could be paid; and through it all the people stayed close to God and the church carried on its ministry of helpfulness."[5]

As crops dried up and prices continued to sag, church giving fell rapidly. By the 1931 conference, total gifts were off nearly 40 percent from the million-dollar-plus reports of the mid-1920s. Churches tried to reduce their benevolence apportionments by "slashing" their rolls, eliminating inactive members. In the Northwest Texas Conference, at least twelve churches dropped from their rolls 100 or more members each, but at the same time they reported a substantial number of professions of faith. In spite of the hardships, membership continued to increase and totaled more than 66,000 at the end of 1931. However, in 1932 the conference's churches dismissed 10 percent of their membership. Gifts continued to fall from a historic high of nearly $1.4 million in 1928 to one of the conference's lowest totals ever, $580,600, in 1932—a drop of 58 percent.[6] Remarkably, total membership continued to rise.[7]

Without a doubt, throughout the tough times, Methodists in Northwest Texas kept a proper focus and faith. Church leadership also reflected a positive and proactive approach. For example, a long report of the Committee on Temperance and Social Service, presented at the 1931 annual conference, outlined a Christian view of the national economic crisis. It was intelligent and well-written, apparently the work of temperance secretary and Texas Tech history professor John C. Granbery. The report exhorted the membership to practice a dynamic faith in the face of the Depression:

> It has seemed to us, strange that men should starve because they produce too much food, go naked because they have made too many clothes, and sleep on benches in parks because they have built too many houses. The most tragic feature in the world situation is the fact that many who are able to work and want to work can find nothing to do. They do not claim that the country owes them a living and are not asking for charity. All that they demand is a chance to work and live with self-respect. We assert the inherent right of all men to work . . . . Our Christian brotherhood is a mockery when we grind men down and then offer them the dole. . . . We do not discharge our obligations to the poor and needy by offering them charity; we must establish an economic order in which they will have a chance to become self-respecting persons by being self-supporting. We must give them the opportunity to develop whatever capabilities they have.[8]

Rev. Vernon and Viola Henderson. Photo from Viola Henderson, *The Love Story of Vernon N. Henderson and Viola M. Henderson,* courtesy of Gene Henderson.

Unfortunately for Granbery, an ordained Methodist minister and the son of a Methodist bishop, Baptists and other conservatives took issue with Granbery's broader "Social Gospel" and political views. In 1932, he became the target of a Lubbock fundamentalist crusader, school superintendent Marcus Homer Duncan, who was also the brother-in-law of America's best-known fundamentalist Baptist preacher, J. Frank Norris, of Fort Worth. On his radio program, Norris accused Granbery and other Texas Tech professors of waving "the red flag of Sovietism and the black flag of atheism." As a result of such sensational publicity, the Texas Tech board of directors fired Granbery and others in 1932.[9] Fortunately, no other ministers were caught in the 1930s fundamentalist attacks.

Most of the Northwest Texas Conference preachers had no time for politics—they were too busy trying to meet the needs of their families and parishioners. They struggled as best they could with reduced salaries. At Halfway, the church did not have the money to pay the preacher, so the ladies of the church "went to Mr. Lewellen's field and picked cotton to pay the pastor's salary."[10] Most of the preachers in the farming areas accepted commodities such as food, gasoline and car repairs in partial payment of their salaries.[11] Some churches could not afford a pastor at all. The Avoca church went without one for ten years during the Depression.[12] Statewide, Methodist giving was down by 50 percent in 1933 and some bishops received no salary at all.[13]

However, there were a few bright spots. For example, in spite of a total crop failure at Lamesa, its Methodist church gave nearly $16,000 to pay for its new organ.[14] Mrs. Marvin Menefee remembered how church members helped their pastors with periodic "poundings": "The 'surprise' poundings . . . were a great supplement to the meager salaries. What fun and how comforting it was to stock the pantry and cabinet with canned fruit, vegetables (many home canned), flour, sugar, and other staple goods and meat stored in the frozen locker at the store furnished by the owner."[15] Viola Henderson recalled a most welcome pounding that she and her husband, Vernon, received in late 1931—the first of many:

> People began arriving soon after supper bringing in eggs, sacks of sugar, flour, home canned and commercial canned fruits, vegetables, fresh and canned meats, egss and more eggs. When it was over, we counted eleven dozen eggs and one member remarked, "Well preacher, eggs are not worth anything but to give to the preacher. . . ." Many times these "poundings" were life savers and always greatly appreciated.[16]

Churches also cooperated with the conference during the national banking crisis. At the 1932 annual conference, the treasurer expressed his appreciation for "the number of Cashier's Checks and the currency brought in this year, and so few personal checks," and appealed for payment in "Cashier's Checks, Money Orders, Post Office Orders, or Currency"[17] The conference cut expenses as best it could and even considered selling a partial interest in its new camp at Ceta Canyon to another "evangelical type" church.[18]

A double blow for McMurry

As the national economy suffered, so did Methodist institutions around the state and nation. McMurry College, only in its seventh session when the Depression started, struggled financially. In the fall of 1930, the college closed the boys' dormitories, and the following year it made all the remaining dorms "cooperative," meaning that students would do all the work in exchange for reduced fees. This allowed some students to stay in school.[19] In March 1932, the college's trustees met to consider whether to keep the school open and decided that "the best policy was to continue."[20] The college probably survived only because it was the only Methodist school in the Northwest Texas Conference.

McMurry faced an even bigger crisis in 1934 with the loss of its beloved president and founder, J. W. Hunt. Only 59, Hunt suffered from a heart problem, but many believed that the stress and worry brought on by the college's financial struggles during the Depression was the cause of death.[21] His passing also meant that the Northwest Texas Conference had lost one of its greatest leaders. A product of the pioneer community of Estacado on the South Plains, Hunt had been a cowboy and journalist before he entered the ministry; most of the churches he served were in the ranching country in the upper Panhandle, and at Snyder and St. Paul's in Abilene. "He was a preacher of marked ability, who [held] tenaciously to the fundamentals of the Christian religion and preached them with great power," wrote O. P. Clark;—"a Christian statesman recognized everywhere and honored for his unusual strength in this field [of education]."[22]

E. D. Landreth, who would enjoy a long and distinguished career in Northwest Texas after attending his first conference in 1921, remembered Hunt as a "giant" in the conference, "one of the outstanding men I have ever known." He noted that Hunt "never saw a university from the inside . . . but he was a very well educated man" and "a master of words and phrases."

> His great mind was so filled with information, knowledge from history and literature, that he seemed always perfectly prepared for any occasion even though he often spoke on short notice. In eleven short years, from the opening days of McMurry, he had given his life to the college and died at heart failure in the very prime of his useful life.[23]

McMurry students and friends donated money for the construction of a room adjacent to the library in the Administration Building, which was named the Hunt Memorial Library.[24] The Northwest Texas Conference dedicated its 1934 *Journal* to Hunt's memory.[25] But his life and con-

The Northwest Texas Conference's delegation to the 1940 first General Conference of the re-united Methodist Church included the following: standing (L to R), R. B. Bryant, Stamford; D. P. Yoder, Snyder; Rev. W. C. House, Amarillo; Rev. W. M. Pearce, Pampa; Rev. E. E. White, Plainview. Seated (L to R), Jim Willson, Floydada; Rev. J. O. Haymes, Big Spring; R. H. Nicholas, Vernon; Rev. O. P. Clark, Lubbock. Photo from J. M. Willson Papers, Southwest Collection, Texas Tech University, Lubbock, Texas.

tributions to the conference deserved more, and perhaps at that time the school should have been renamed in his honor.

Other "giants" in the land

Obviously, Hunt was not the only great leader in Northwest Texas in the 1930s. Blessed with dedicated and remarkable men, the conference generally functioned smoothly and efficiently, even through the hard times of the 1930s. Bishop Hiram A. Boaz, who had pastored at Abilene in the late 1890s and later served as its bishop from 1930 to 1938, lauded the men of the Northwest Texas Conference: "I knew nearly all the preachers and felt at home among them," he later recalled. "No finer group of men can be found in Methodism. They are friendly, brotherly, loyal and efficient. Breathing the ozone of West Texas they have developed a distinctive type of citizenship."[26]

Landreth also singled out several conference leaders in his autobiography. Among others, both he and Boaz mentioned J. W. Hunt, Sam Hardy, W. M. Pearce, O. P. Clark, L. N. Lipscomb, M. M. Beavers, W. M. Murrell, and J. O. Haymes.[27]

Landreth took special notice of Haymes for his rapid rise in leadership:

> Haymes [came] into the Conference as a college graduate, one of the few in that 1914 class. Now, after a successful pastorate at Spur, at age of 34, he decided to go to seminary for his theological degree. He came out of the seminary recognized as a leader in the Conference and within four short years he was a presiding elder. He has been one of our finest leaders ever since.[28]

Although they never were singled out as conference "giants," H. B. Coggin and many other dedicated preachers worked under difficult circumstances during the tough years. Coggin, as pastor of the Hawley Circuit in 1931, was headed to his church at Center Line but found his road blocked by high water in the Clear Fork of the Brazos, caused by a heavy rain upstream. Not content to return home, Coggin swam the river to keep his appointment. While only three were at church that raining day, the next month, the church was full. Word about his daring swim across the Brazos encouraged his flock.[29]

The wives and families of Methodist preachers also sacrificed in remarkable and unusual ways. Mrs. George Turrentine recalled that shortly after her husband had been assigned to the church at Texline, she found out that the parsonage was inhabited with skunks and thus set up housekeeping in a hotel room Then Presiding Elder W. M. Pearce, asked George to add the Hartley and Channing charges for the rest of the year. Mrs. Turrentine recalled the challenge: "We moved, literally, every two weeks. I do mean move: clothes, dishes, pots, pans, wash tub, books, three children and a dog. . . . If you think that was fun, try it just for once."[30]

The legendary Vernon Henderson, who as of 2008 was very much alive and living in Abilene at age 105, was just beginning his long ministry when the Depression hit. After graduating from McMurry in 1929 and attending SMU for theological graduate work, he and his McMurry sweetheart, Viola Martin, married in September 1931. (She would be his bride for the next 75 seventy-five years, until her death at age 100 in March 2007.) Ready to be appointed to a church, Henderson was admitted on trial at the Northwest Texas annual conference meeting in Vernon in November 1931 and hoped to get a church of his own.[31]

Just before the bishop read the appointments, he learned that there were not enough positions available. However, the outgoing presiding elder of the Plainview District approached Henderson and said: "I have five communities . . . that will make a good circuit when we get the Methodist people in them organized into a circuit. . . . Will you accept this challenge?"

"What could I say?" recalled Henderson in his memoirs. "I was prepared for the ministry, had been accepted on Trial, and beside the gin job would soon be over. My answer had to be affirmative." Thus, with pride, Henderson heard his name called to be the pastor of the Fieldton circuit, even though he knew there were "no organized congregations, no Sunday Schools, no salary, no mission apportionments, as well as no place to live."[32] With the demonstration of such faith as that of Vernon and Viola Henderson, work in the conference carried on in spite of the Depression.

The changing face of the conference and Methodism

Such devotion made a difference in the Northwest Texas Conference as Methodist work continued to grow despite economic hardship. However, some of the growth was due to the region's move from rural to urban. Also, the conference grew with the addition of several Oklahoma churches. Perhaps because of new railroad lines that linked the Oklahoma Panhandle to Texas, the churches of the Panhandle district of the West Oklahoma Conference petitioned the General Conference in 1930 to allow them to merge into the Northwest Texas Conference. The move added churches at Goodwell, Hooker, Optima-Baker, Texhoma, Tyrone, Union and Felt, which included 1,063 members.[33] To accommodate the new churches, the conference created the Perryton District out of the upper portion of the Amarillo District to serve with the Oklahoma churches.[34] This arrangement lasted for eight years.

The conference's boundaries also grew at the south end in 1934 when the General Conference in 1934 added Midland and Glasscock counties to Northwest Texas. However, two churches in Callahan County at the extreme southeastern corner of the region, Cross Plains and Cottonwood, left the Northwest Texas Conference and joined the Central Texas Conference. This move was highly unusual, as there is no record in the *Discipline* or conference journals of a change for that part of the conference's boundary. In all likelihood, those churches found participation in conference activities in far-off Lubbock and Amarillo too difficult and must have some found some form of extralegal dispensation to make the move.[35]

Dramatic changes

Other changes in the 1930s would, in the long run, be much more dramatic. Population shifts and reunification with the Methodist Episcopal Church brought gradual change to Northwest Texas; the change would be difficult for the rural-oriented, conservative Methodist churches of the region.

The Depression and drought accelerated the shift of the population of Northwest Texas from rural to urban. For the first twenty-five years of its history after 1910, the Northwest Texas Conference was decidedly rural in its makeup and expansion. During that time, it had averaged establishing nearly six new churches per year, and most were rural. For example, fifty-four of the fifty-nine new churches established from 1920 to 1933 were in rural or small communities. However, by the middle of the Depression in 1934 and 1935, six of the seven new churches founded were in cities that already had at least one Methodist church, reflecting a shift of population from rural areas to cities.[36] Of the twenty-two new churches established from 1934 to 1945, twelve were located in the larger towns and cities of the conference, all of which already had Methodist churches. Of the ten new rural churches, four were in areas affected by the growth of the oil and gas industry rather than agriculture, such as Sunray (1936), Denver City (1938), Sanford (1939), and Sundown (1943).[37]

Changing lifestyles and a shifting population dramatically impacted Methodist evangelism. As long as people remained engaged in agriculture in isolated rural areas, the two-week summer revival or camp meeting was a major factor in Methodist outreach. Virtually every church, regardless of size or location, held a revival. Rufus Kitchen pastored the seven-church Paducah Circuit, and his daughter Christine Kitchens recalled the full schedule for her family: "In the summer, we had two week revivals at each church—fourteen weeks without stopping! We would live in school houses, homes, empty houses, whatever!"[38]

After automobiles and improved roads made Americans mobile, people had less time for church activities. The change is reflected in the following trend: in the early 1920s, the conference reported more than 4,000 professions of faith each year, averaging one for every ten members. By 1930, the average was one for every twenty members, and by 1936, only one for every twenty-five members.[39] New church growth also declined, primarily due to the saturation of the area with churches. There was no longer a church frontier, an "outside row" to be settled and saved. Only twenty-three new churches were organized from 1931 through 1940.[40] However, during the '30s, the conference gained approximately 10,000 new members during a period when the total population for the region actually declined. By 1940, the conference had nearly 75,000 members and once again could boast that nearly one person out of every ten within its bounds was a Methodist.[41]

Conference leaders were concerned with the drop-off in evangelism and made periodic efforts to renew old-fashioned revivalism. In 1931, a renewed emphasis produced a total of 3,880 professions of faith, but that amount was the highest for the decade.[42] By 1940, the era of a revival in every church was over. One-third of the 417 churches did not have one.[43]

One church that was still holding revivals in the '30s was at Flomot. Dallas Denison, who pastored at Matador at the time, was asked to preach a two-week summer revival at Flomot. On the last night, he extended the service until 2:30 a. m. to allow four friends to go four miles and bring back to the church "a lost friend" who was converted after reaching the church. Denison reported that the revival saw thirty-eight conversions and fourteen rededications: "The next year, they built a new church spiritually and physically."[44]

Edging toward democracy

Change also brought new challenges to Methodism's historic episcopal structure. The South's Methodist Church had long seen dominant control by bishops.[45] However, most Methodists in the Northwest Texas Conference seemed satisfied with the system. Their major dissatisfaction probably was with the appointment process.

Prior to 1940, nearly all appointment decisions were made at conference behind closed doors during the meetings of the bishop and his Cabinet. "No preacher had been consulted as to his wishes, needs or abilities about moving or staying," recalled Mrs. J. E. "Bess" Shewbert many years later. "No congregation was given a choice of who their minister would be."[46] Many preachers had no idea where they were going to be assigned, and thus the most dramatic time at the annual conference was always at the end, when the bishop would read the appointments. As Bess Shewbert described it, "all silently strained to hear the destinies of all, especially to hear their own name."[47]

Mrs. Shewbert was probably not aware of the work that each presiding elder did during the year in order to make appropriate recommendations to the bishop. And she was probably not aware of how some congregations expressed themselves. One preacher learned the hard way how a congregation had a vote in his selection. This pastor had moved to McAdoo in 1928 and soon found himself in a salary dispute with the church. After serving only one year there, he learned something about the politics of preaching:

> I heard later that I could have probably stayed for this second year had it not been for the fact that some Baptist people made the statement to some Methodist that, after all, the members of the Methodist Church have absolutely nothing to do with who is their Pastor. Then, some smart Methodist said, "We will just show you." So, they called the Presiding Elder and told him I would just have to be moved."[48]

The presiding elder followed the church's advice, and the preacher soon found himself in another community, where he remained only one year. "Most of my pastorates were short," he recalled with some chagrin.[49]

National unification and its impact

The Methodists (like many denominations) had split over slavery in 1844, creating two major denominations: the Methodist Episcopal Church, and the Methodist Episcopal Church, South. By 1876, the organizations began discussing reunification, but sectionalism prevented any progress. In the early 1920s, both denominations moved closer to reunification when a "bi-jurisdictional plan" was defeated because three-fourths approval was required. Nationally, 52 percent of Southern Methodists favored unification—but the Northwest Texas Conference voted overwhelmingly against it in 1925 and joined with its neighbor, the Central Texas Conference, as the only two conferences west of the Mississippi River to vote that way.[50] Without a doubt, the Northwest Texas vote was due in large part to the modernism-fundamentalism debate that was raging in Texas at the time, and the conference was not ready to join with the more liberal Northern Methodists.[51]

But reunification was only a matter of time. The Methodist Protestant denomination began negotiations with the Methodist Episcopal Church in 1928 to produce a plan for unity. Throughout the early 1930s, a number of national Methodist events produced additional sympathy toward unification, including the sesquicentennial celebration of the 1784 Christmas Conference held in Baltimore in 1934, and the publication of a new Methodist hymnal by the three major Methodist denominations in 1935.[52]

By 1937, the Northwest Texas Conference had changed its mind about unification. By a vote of 246–11, the conference approved the question on unification at the November 1937 conference.[53] In the annual conferences of the ME Church, South, the total vote was 7,650 for and 1,247 against. Only the North Mississippi Conference voted against the plan.[54]

The next year, the Northwest Texas Conference elected delegates to the Uniting Conference, scheduled for 1939. This process not only indicated who the respected leaders of the conference were at that time but also demonstrated the unity of spirit within. Four of the designated six clergy delegates were elected on the first ballot: J. O. Haymes, presiding elder of the Amarillo District; C. R. Hooton, pastor at First Church,

Plainview; O. P. Clark, presiding elder of the Lubbock District; and W. M. Pearce, pastor at First Church, Pampa. Such unanimity would not be a trademark of the conference in future years.

Voting remained tight for three more ballots, but on the fourth, E. E. White, presiding elder of the Plainview District, was elected. On the fifth ballot, C. A. Bickley, presiding elder of the Abilene District, was named as the sixth and final delegate.[55]

Lay delegates included some of the most prominent leaders of the smaller communities in Northwest Texas: R. H. Nichols of Vernon, D. P. Yoder of Snyder, J. M. Willson of Floydada, and R. B. Bryant of Stamford. Also elected were Mrs. C. M. Randal of Seymour, who was the conference president of the Women's Missionary Society, and S. H. Condron, a college dean from Canyon.[56] All those elected had also served as delegates to the 1938 General Conference.[57]

Sent as alternates were three pastors (L. N. Lipscomb, pastor of Lubbock, S. H. Young of Sweetwater, and C. C. Grimes of Amarillo,) and Presiding Elder Cal C. Wright. Lay reserves were A. M. Braswell of Clarendon, McMurry dean R. G. Boger, Mrs. N. G. Rollins of Abilene, and T. V. Ellney, of Perryton.[58]

The historic Uniting Conference met in Kansas City from April 26 to May 10, 1939.[59] With relative ease, the delegates passed the articles leading to unification, and at the close, the *Daily Christian Advocate* boldly proclaimed in a banner headline, "The Methodists Are Now One People."[60]

As with the formation of America's federal government, Methodist unification was made possible by compromise. As a result, much of the church's power shifted from the Council of Bishops and the General Conference to six jurisdictional conferences—five geographical and one racial—that in turn were given power to elect the bishops for their region or race.[61] Black churches were grouped in their own jurisdictional conference. Unification also brought equal representation of the laity in the annual conferences and a democratic governance structure for the church within the General Conference.[62] At the same time, unification brought a liberalization of the national church, which was not theologically compatible with many of the longtime conservative members of the Northwest Texas Conference.

The impact of unification on the conference was minimal in terms of physical change but profound in other ways. The new denomination became "The Methodist Church" and thus forced thousands of churches to change their signage by dropping the term "Methodist Episcopal Church, South."[63] Also, unification changed the title of presiding elder to district superintendent; the Woman's Missionary Society became the Women's Society of Christian Service,; and the Epworth League became the Methodist Youth Fellowship.[64]

Other changes came about even before unification. During the pre-unification maneuvering, the 1938 General Conference of the ME Church, South, had voted to allow each pastoral charge a lay delegate rather than an at-large number from each district. With the change, lay representation in the Northwest Texas Conference more than doubled, from ninety-one in 1938 to 183 in 1939.[65]

This expansion of conference delegates brought even more subtle changes in the way that Northwest Texas functioned. For the future, it meant that only the larger cities of the conference could provide enough home and hotel space for the delegates. By 1938, for example, the conference had met in sixteen different communities during its twenty-eight-year history, including Houston for the 1936 joint Centennial Conference. Clarendon, which hosted the first 1910 conference, also hosted it in 1915, 1920, and 1933 for a total of four times. Abilene likewise had hosted the conference four times; Plainview, three; and Lubbock, Vernon, Sweetwater, Memphis, and Quanah, two each. By 1938, Pampa, Stamford, Canyon, and Big Spring had hosted the conference one time each. The 1938 session in Memphis marked the last time it would meet in one of the smaller communities of the region.[66] By 1939, the conference's work had become important enough to prompt radio stations in Amarillo, Lubbock, Big Spring, and Abilene to broadcast live the announcement of the ministerial appointments at the closing session.[67]

The growth also meant that at the annual conference, there was less time for oral reports. Prior to the 1940s, every pastor was required to defend his year's work in public before the bishop. E. D. Landreth recalled how important the process was: "Every man reported. The Bishop saw him and heard him and often asked him questions on points of importance, especially as to conversions and admissions to the Church and on the Conference collections or benevolences. Happy was the preacher who could give the good answer, 'Everything is full, Bishop.' "[68] Such accountability undoubtedly produced a stronger effort from preachers.

Other changes were cosmetic. Unification made the conference a part of the South Central Jurisdiction, which encompassed conferences from both the Northern and Southern denominations. The churches of the Oklahoma Panhandle that had been added to the Northwest Texas Conference in 1930 were returned to the West Oklahoma Conference by the Uniting Conference, but this loss was offset by the addition of five former "Northern" Methodist churches in the upper Panhandle: Dalhart Pine Street, Darrouzett, Follett, Sanford, and Ureka.[69]

Pine Street (now Dalhart Lakeview) and Follett, had a long and colorful history with the Methodist Episcopal Church. Shortly after Dalhart was established in 1901 at the confluence of two important rail lines, a small group of Northern Methodists moved from Clarendon to the new town. Among them was Rev. G. W. Graham, who in 1902 founded a new Methodist Episcopal church in the booming new town of Dalhart. For a building, members went back to Clarendon, dismantled the original 1880 ME church, secured its original bell, reclaimed its organ from a nearby home, and shipped all of it by rail to Dalhart! However, according to one account, the church's removal from Clarendon raised the ire of some residents:

> [T]radition says that the citizens of Clarendon, indifferent to the fate of the church before, became disturbed at its loss, and a large crowd gathered at the depot, determined to prevent its removal, and that the three Dalhart men drew six-shooters and held the mob off until the train pulled out.[70]

Once safely in Dalhart, the structure was rebuilt and served as the home for the Pine Street church until the congregation built a new sanctuary in 1962 to become Lakeview.[71] The church honored its historic bell with a tower that allows it to be seen from all directions. According to Lillie Mae Hunter, its peals "still sprinkle the Sunday morning air with blessing."[72]

The Follett church was also begun by Northern Methodists in the Stillwater community in the Oklahoma Panhandle in 1903, but it moved in 1918 across the state line to the new town of Follett, Texas, when the railroad came through. It was a member of the Oklahoma Conference of the Methodist Episcopal Church until reunification in 1939.[73]

Opposition to unification

Not every Northwest Texas Methodist embraced unification. A few withdrew from the new denomination and aligned with a splinter group of Southerners who formed the Southern Methodist Church. This group, as one historian wrote, "set up a polity that eliminated the episcopacy and a theology that elevated racial segregation to an article of doctrine."[74] In Abilene, an independent Methodist church, perhaps established in the 1930s, joined with the Southern Methodists after the new denomination was established, first as the Methodist Missionary Church and later as the Southern Methodist Missionary Church. It closed about 1970.[75]

Still another impact on Northwest Texas from unification emerged a few years after the fact and led directly to the formation of a yet another new Methodist denomination. This story centered on the popular pastor of the First Methodist Church of Abilene, J. H. Hamblen, father of one of America's most famous songwriters, Stuart Hamblen.

J. H. Hamblen was a longtime leader in the Northwest Texas Conference; he joined it by transfer in 1909 and served several churches throughout the conference, including prestigious appointments at Hamlin, Crowell, Clarendon, Stamford, First Church, Sweetwater, and First Church, Abilene. He also served as presiding elder for the Stamford District from 1926 to 1929.[76]

However, long before unification, Hamblen had become concerned about Methodism's embrace of "modernism" in the seminaries and colleges and in Sunday School literature.[77] While serving as pastor at First Church, Abilene, he quit using denominational literature in Sunday School and Vacation Bible School and soon was questioned by the bishop as to why he "would not put on the program," as Hamblen phrased it.[78] Hamblen's reluctance to use Methodist literature created friction within First Church, and in 1944, the church's Official Board rejected a motion to ask for his return.[79] However, Hamblen—who had served ten years at First Abilene in two separate tenures—was convinced that the pressure came from Bishop Charles C. Selecman, and that the Cabinet had begun "to try to move me out":

> They undertook to move me away across the country to an old, rundown church. I knew it was a concocted affair that he [Selecman] was back of it all, so I told them point blank that I would not go to that place. It was not that I was too good to go, but I was not going to do something just to please somebody who was out of the will of God.[80]

True to his word, Hamblen refused the appointment, and in the final session of the November 1944 annual conference, he gained the floor and "spoke to a point of personal privilege, and on his request, the Conference granted him a sabbatical leave."[81]

Hamblen and his wife moved to a small house in Abilene, and sometime during 1945 he began preaching to a small group of First Church's disgruntled members in an Abilene home—a practice he knew to be "against the law of the church."[82] By September 1945, in spite of warnings from the bishop and district superintendent, Hamblen began holding regularly scheduled services on Sundays and Thursdays. Two months later, in November, the annual conference met at St. Paul's in Abilene. Hamblen, after a tearful meeting with the bishop and Cabinet, voluntarily asked for honorable withdrawal from the denomination, even though he knew he would have to forfeit forty years of pension credit:

> I then stood on the Conference floor . . . and stated that I could not conscientiously remain in a church where modernism predominated and where the leaders did not believe in and uphold the Articles of Religion of Methodism; where the Sunday School literature was filled with doubt of the inspiration of the Bible and the fundamental doctrines of evangelical Christianity . . . [and] where the young preachers . . . no longer believed the cardinal doctrines of our church.[83]

Hamblen's withdrawal sent shock waves throughout the conference and, to a certain extent, the national church. Before the annual conference was adjourned, Selecman felt compelled to address the issues raised by Hamblen by instructing his pastors "on preaching the fundamental doctrines of the Christian faith"; he also "voiced his conviction that Methodist literature and Methodist Ministers are true to these doctrines."[84] Several years later, longtime pastor E. D. Landreth wrote in his autobiography, "He [Hamblen] left us, or did we leave him, as he maintained?"[85]

But Hamblen's ministry was not finished, and his withdrawal led directly to the founding of not only a new Methodist congregation but also a new denomination: the Evangelical Methodist Church. He founded and pastored the new Evangelical Methodist Church of Abilene, and then in May 1946 presided over the founding of the Evangelical Methodist Church denomination in Memphis, Tennessee, of which he became the general superintendent.

In 1950, in an effort to find his successor, Hamblen recruited a dynamic 24-year-old East Texas Methodist preacher to take his place at the "mother" church of the new denomination.[86] The young preacher was Ed Robb, a man, who in later years would become strongly influential in the Northwest Texas Conference and Methodism in general.

Robb grew up in the railroad town of Marshall, served in the Navy during World War II, and surrendered to preach in 1946. Licensed by the Longview District in the Texas Conference, Robb by 1950 found himself in conflict with fellow East Texas pastors over eschatological (end-time) doctrine. At the time, Robb was a premillenialist, which did not sit well with more traditional Methodist preachers. Because of his doctrinal differences, Robb was already giving thought to leaving the denomination when Hamblen contacted him. After being "called" to the Evangelical Methodist Church in Abilene in 1950, Robb resigned from the Texas Conference, telling the bishop that "the views of modern day Methodism are so greatly different from my own":

Ed Robb as young preacher. Photo from Edmund W. Robb, *Contending for the Faith: The Ed Robb Story*. Used by permission.

> I believe in the virgin birth, the deity of Christ, His personal return, revivals of religion, and the Wesleyan doctrine of perfect love. The churches and schools no longer believe these things. If I am to follow my convictions I must go to a church I agree with.[87]

It would not be the last time that Robb would challenge the Methodist Church over his convictions.

Robb stayed only three years in the Evangelical Church. Disappointed that Hamblen kept appointing unqualified ministers, Robb resigned after the denomination accepted a man who had withdrawn from a Methodist Church conference because of "questionable financial dealings"; Robb decided that he "would rather be associated with clean liberals than dirty fundamentalists."[88] He resigned in the fall of 1953, joined the Northwest Texas Conference, and subsequently pastored several churches before becoming a full-time evangelist in 1966.

Meanwhile, the Abilene Evangelical Methodist congregation built a church a few blocks from First Methodist Church, remained there for a number of years, and then moved to its present location on the San Angelo Highway in far south Abilene.[89] According to the Evangelical Methodist Church's Web site, the denomination in 2007 had churches in twenty-seven states, including fourteen churches in Texas, four of which are within the bounds of the Northwest Texas Conference (Abilene, Sweetwater, Slaton, and Wilson).

World War II

Meanwhile, adherents of the new and unified Methodist Church rejoiced about their new denomination, but the euphoria was soon tempered by the outbreak of war in Europe in September 1939 and the U.S entry after Japan's attack on Pearl Harbor in December 1941. Longtime conference member and treasurer J. Edmund Kirby remembered well the days after Pearl Harbor. He was 33 years old and had been preaching for fourteen years. As with many of his colleagues, the war forced him to choose between being a conscientious objector or to register for the draft: "After praying most of the night . . . , I came to the conclusion that I would register, but would support and help those in my church and community . . . who chose to be objectors."[90] He also recalled the impact of the war on the region:

> The draft took many from every community and others left jobs and moved to communities and worked at jobs that contributed to the war effort. Ration books were issued . . . for meat, bacon, sugar, coffee, . . . gasoline, tires, etc. The mileage one could drive was determined by the kind of business one was in.[91]

Kirby received a ministerial deferment, and he was never called up. However, many others were. During the war, Texas contributed more than 750,000 troops to the military, including 12,000 women. The Northwest Texas Conference shared in that commitment, and in addition sent twenty-two pastors into the chaplaincy. Also, its churches ministered to thousands of soldiers stationed at bases in Childress, Dalhart, Hereford, Lubbock, Midland, Sweetwater, Pampa, Big Spring, Vernon, Lamesa, Abilene, and Amarillo.[92]

Both the Depression and the outbreak of World War II dramatically slowed the conference's growth. Whereas membership had grown in the ten years after World War I at 6 percent a year and had nearly doubled to more than 60,000 in 1927, the rate of growth fell to just 1.5 percent per year for 1927 through 1940. During the war years of 1941–45, growth edged up only slightly to nearly 2 percent per year.

However, because the war displaced soldiers and civilians alike, the denomination in 1941 began requiring churches to report the number

Group of Methodist ladies at a Lubbock meeting, c. 1940s. Reeves Photography photo from Northwest Texas Conference Archives, McMurry University, courtesy Annette Nall.

of non-resident and/or inactive members. At that time, the Northwest Texas Conference reported 68,453 active and 8,190 inactive or non-resident members for a total of 76,643. By the end of the war in 1945, it reported 64,004 active members, but the inactive count had risen by more than 10,000 to 18,434.[93] Evangelism suffered during the war years. In 1942, the conference staged a School of Evangelism in Abilene because one-fourth of its churches reported no professions of faith in 1941, and 116 more had five or less.[94]

Without a doubt, the Depression and World War II changed the face of America. The population displacement brought on by economic hard times, and the war demands for manpower for the military and industry, introduced "an unprecedented mobility" in America's social structure that would expand further after the war.[95] The Methodist Church, and the Northwest Texas Conference, would face a tremendous challenge in coping with the rapid change from the era of small rural churches and membership to a rapidly growing urban population.

In 1944, Martha A. "Grandma" Rogers of Wheeler died at age 101.[96] Since the 1880s, she had been active in rural Methodist churches in the Panhandle, and her annual visits to conference were legendary. "If we ever had a new Bishop . . . who did not know about Grandma Rogers and he failed to call for her report," recalled E. D. Landreth, "she would rise up and make it without invitation. She was a pioneer woman of great wit and deep spiritual insights and spoke wisely and well."[97] With her death, much of the memory of the old Northwest Texas Conference and of old-time Methodism faded.

As the nation faced a new era in the postwar world, Methodists and the Northwest Texas Conference faced a new era as well. What lay ahead for the conference could never have been imagined by anyone.

CHAPTER 6

"Yet out of all the Lord Hath brought us by His Love"

Although postwar America was far more urbanized than before, Northwest Texas still had a rural look and feel. But the upheavals of the Depression and World War II took their toll. The total number of churches or "preaching places" had dropped from 409 in 1940 to 373 in 1945, with nearly all of the losses coming in rural areas.[1] The number of part-time churches fell from 279 to 217, and the number of full-time churches rose from 130 to 156. Even though the part-time churches accounted for 58 percent of the total number of churches, they represented less than 25 percent of the total membership. For example, in the Abilene District in 1945, only seventeen of fifty-three churches were full-time stations, but these accounted for 80 percent of the district's membership.[2]

Postwar challenges

At the end of the war, Methodists did not think about rural or urban but rather focused on bringing about spiritual restoration. In 1944, the General Conference called for a national revival, which it named the Crusade for Christ. Organized at conference and district levels, the Crusade included fundraising for war relief, educational gains, and evangelism. More than $25 million was raised nationally, and the evangelistic effort recorded 787,207 additions to the Methodist Church in September 1946.[3]

The Northwest Texas Conference enthusiastically participated in the Crusade and exceeded its 1946 goal of 13,876 total additions by 121. Although the number may have been inflated by returning veterans, it also included 5,142 on professions of faith, —the largest number ever for the conference before or since.[4] Not since the summer revivals of 1921 and 1922 had the conference seen such high numbers of professions of faith.

The influx of new members was directly attributed to the success of the Crusade for Christ and its evangelistic emphasis, as statistics for the years immediately following show a significant drop in numbers. The intent of the Crusade, however, was more than numbers. Conference Bishop Charles C. Selecman noted what the Crusade intended to do: "Our churches were to be awakened to want them, and win them, and teach them, and hold them."[5] Because of the Crusade's success, the immediate future looked bright for the Northwest Texas Conference.

Not wanting to lose the momentum of 1946, the Conference Evangelism Committee strongly encouraged its churches to use radio programs and Methodist literature in their evangelistic efforts, but the committee also asked that churches not forget the fundamental foundations of old-time Methodism: "We . . . must go back to tent and camp meetings. The General Board is urging such and we join them. Visitation evangelism must not be forsaken . . . . Let us seek and save the lost."[6] The committee also reported the establishment of eight new churches and the re-opening of three more. Membership for 1946 had reached nearly 86,000, with nearly 70,000 listed as active.[7]

Urban churches

Since the late 1930s, the conference had been making a concerted effort at establishing suburban churches in growing cities. In 1939, Lubbock Methodists worked to establish a new church, but it was not without controversy. Some wanted a new church in rapidly growing southwest Lubbock; others wanted a church to serve the Texas Tech community. Bishop Ivan Holt assigned R. L. Kirk to start a church to serve the college's community; Kirk recalled that all he had to work with was "a vacant lot that the church did not own . . . with no parsonage, membership or church."[8]

The church without a home became St. John's, and the congregation first met in the Tech Theater, a movie house owned and operated by future Texas Gov. Preston Smith, located next to the Texas Tech campus. Under the ministries of Kirk and future Bishop Alsie Carleton, the church grew rapidly and had 1,000 members by 1948.[9] In the ten years after the establishment of St. John's, all of the major cities saw the creation of new churches: Epworth, Aldersgate, and Fair Park in Abilene; Overton, Forrest Heights, and Pioneer Memorial in Lubbock; Trinity and Wyatt Memorial in Amarillo, St. John's in Plainview; St. Mark's and Asbury in Midland; Buena Vista and Wesley in Borger, and North Birdwell Lane in Big Spring.

One of the greatest challenges of the postwar period for Northwest Texas was providing adequate college student ministries. Because of the masses of returning soldiers who could attend college through federal government support, the colleges within the conference's boundaries grew rapidly. In 1945, the five annual conferences of Texas launched a special $440,000 campaign to provide for 13 new campus centers across the state. For its part, the Northwest Texas Conference raised and/or received $85,000 for student facilities at Texas Tech and West Texas State.[10]

Changing from old to new

In May 1949, the Northwest Texas Conference at its fortieth annual session celebrated the 210th anniversary of the very first Methodist conference—and it had good reason to celebrate. Total membership topped 90,000 for the first time, per capita giving was over $44, and total giving was over $3.5 million. Moreover, the conference boasted 324 Church Schools with an enrollment of nearly 62,000. And for the first time, the conference had more full-time churches (184) than part-time (155).[11]

The growth brought changes. One of the last vestiges of old Methodism passed in 1946, when the Northwest Texas Conference changed its annual meeting date from November to late May. From the earliest days of Texas Methodism, annual conferences had always been held in the late fall, probably because of the predominately agrarian society that it served. In 1942, a group in the conference tried to move the meeting time to the spring, but the resolution was defeated by a vote of 88–85.[12] The close vote probably reflected the growing influence of city churches versus rural ones. However, by the end of World War II, it had become clear that the shuffle of pastors at the end of the year worked a great hardship on families, and thus the change was made to allow ministers' children to finish a school year without disruption.[13]

Another focus of old Methodism was also passing away: its opposition to alcohol use and sales. Since the conference's founding in 1910, its Board of Temperance had railed against alcohol use and had promoted state and national efforts such as Prohibition. But by 1951, the board had virtually given up the battle; in its 1951 report to the conference, the board noted that "it is generally admitted that Methodists have been lax in their support of the United Texas Drys and the temperance movement in general."[14] However, the board continued to encourage support for anti-alcohol movements.

Still another characteristic of old Methodism that began to change was the total authority of the bishop and Cabinet to make appointments. The change came gradually, but pastors and churches slowly gained some headway. Weldon Butler recalled an illustrative incident. After serving as director of the Wesley Foundation at West Texas State at Canyon, he was offered a church in the older part of the conference, and its district superintendent "talked in very glowing terms about the church." However, Butler checked with the conference statistician and learned that the superintendent's description did not match the facts.

> I was surprised that the truth was not told to me and I made up my mind to remain at Canyon. The . . . DS caught me in the sanctuary of the church later that day and really gave me a tongue lashing and told me I had better learn the truth about things, that "we run this Conference," and that I had better accept without question what was offered to me. The threat was made that if I did not, that I would never get anywhere in the Conference.[15]

But Butler did not give in, and he accepted an appointment to a church in a newer community in the upper Texas Panhandle.

Bishop William Martin. Photo courtesy Annette Nall.

One of the first previews of new Methodism was introduced in the Northwest Texas Conference in May 1945. Lillie Hester, daughter of Rev. and Mrs. J. N. Hester, was licensed to preach by the Lubbock District Conference. This action was the first for the Northwest Texas Conference, and perhaps was the first in Texas.[16] However, her licensing was not admittance on trial into the Northwest Texas Conference; it only allowed her the liberty to preach if asked. Full ministerial rights for women in Methodism were more than ten years ahead.

Another significant change introduced in 1949 was the naming of William C. Martin as bishop of the Northwest Texas Conference. Martin, who was one of the last bishops elected by the ME Church, South, at its last General Conference in 1938, had been pastor at First Church Dallas when elected but was sent to California for his first assignment. However, after the 1939 Uniting Conference, he was returned to the new South Central Jurisdiction and assigned to the Kansas-Nebraska Area, where he remained until being appointed to administer the Northwest Texas, North Texas, and Central Texas conferences.[17]

Martin arrived at a time when the conference was about to experience even more growth. Unlike World War II, the Korean War in 1950 did little to deter conference growth; in fact, the war, coupled with the

Communist "scare" of the early '50s, probably stimulated church growth and attendance. In the '40s, conference growth had kept steady pace with the region's 20 percent population gain for the decade. During the early 1950s, church membership continued to grow at a steady 3 percent increase per year, primarily because of expansion of the Sunday School. In 1951, average attendance jumped by more than 10 percent to nearly 36,000, fueled by sharp increases in the Plainview and Lubbock districts. The Plainview District noted that its additions in church membership averaged one addition for every 15.8 members. Conference-wide, the average was one for nineteen members.[18]

Church growth was fueled in large part by the rapid expansion of the agricultural industry, especially on the South Plains. With abundant water resources furnished by irrigation, coupled with the availability of inexpensive natural gas, South Plains farmers found they could offset recurring drought conditions. Lubbock and Amarillo became major distribution centers for agriculture-related technology, and both communities grew at rapid paces. By the mid-1950s, both cities were swelling at a rate of more than 6,000 per year.[19]

At the same time, churches also grew in the 1950s as people embraced traditional family values. A steadily growing prosperity allowed young families to buy homes in the new suburbs of Abilene, Midland, Amarillo, Plainview, and Lubbock. And because of the postwar "baby boom," new parents sought churches in order to get religious training for their children. In a sense, the children led the families into organized religion.[20] The 1950s became the decade of the church in America, and especially in the Northwest Texas Conference.[21]

Establishing infrastructure

Throughout the decade, the Methodist Church created and implemented programs after program that attempted to emulate the highly successful Crusade for Christ of the late 1940s. The first program, the Advance for Christ and His Church, was established by the General Conference in 1948; by 1949, the Northwest Texas Conference had already raised thousands of dollars.[22] Less evangelistic than the Crusade for Christ, this program emphasized a broader ministry and gave conferences and churches the opportunity to "personalize" their support; according to Bishop Martin, as outlined in his biography, "these could be building projects, churches, schools, hospitals, missionaries, scholarships, and relief work at home or overseas . . . . Every congregation in The Methodist Church was expected to accept the support of an Advance Special equal to its benevolence budget."[23] Martin played a strong leadership role in the national Advance campaign. In 1952, the Advance became a regular program for the Methodist Church and is still a major force in missions. By 2008, Methodists had given more than $1.2 billion through the Advance program.[24]

In 1952, Texas Methodists joined together to support a program called the All Texas Methodist Revival, but the effort failed to match that of the Crusade for Christ. Yet the Northwest Texas Conference's weekly worship attendance steadily rose and topped 40,000 for the first time in 1953. Evening worship services drew 19,127 weekly.[25]

Also in 1952, the Northwest Texas Conference made its first major changes in district alignment since the late 1930s. The Perryton and Clarendon Districts were divided among the new Pampa and Childress districts as well as the older Amarillo District. The Big Spring District replaced most of the old Sweetwater District, with the western portion placed in the new Brownfield District, which was largely carved out of the western half of the Lubbock District. The older Abilene and Stamford districts remained virtually intact. With the new alignment, each district had approximately 30 charges.[26] The Childress District had the largest number of churches (45); the Amarillo District had the smallest (30).[27] There would be no more changes in district alignment until 1965.

The conference camping saga

The early 1950s also saw the first major change in the conference's camping program since the acquisition of the Ceta Canyon campgrounds in the 1920s. Camping had always been an integral (yet somewhat controversial) part of Texas Methodist life, especially in frontier rural areas when churches gathered for camp meetings that lasted for a week or more.[28] Entire families participated, with each family providing for its own meals. After automobiles came into widespread use, the camp meeting generally gave way to summer revivals, which retained the form of camp meetings without overnight camping.

In the early 1900s, the Methodist youth program, the Epworth League, took the lead in Texas to provide a site for camping. In 1905, its first camp was held on the shores of Corpus Christi Bay on what is now North Beach, north of downtown Corpus Christi. The site had a private pier, a bathhouse, a dormitory/dining hall, and tent sites. Its ten-day summer program attracted thousands from across the state. After a storm damaged the facility in 1915, the camp moved up the coast to Port O'Connor, but a 1917 storm wiped out three new buildings and thus ended coastal camping for the Epworth League.[29]

In 1915, the Northwest Texas Conference began consideration of Palo Duro Canyon southeast of Amarillo as a suitable site for an Epworth League encampment, but apparently no action was taken at that time.[30] The following year, just as Epworth camping was fading, a Sunday School teacher in Memphis, Texas, started a camping program of her own for girls—an initiative that led directly to the establishment of organized camping in the Northwest Texas Conference. For three years, Mrs. T. C. Delaney took a group to a ranch a few miles east of Wellington, but around 1919, she moved her summer camp to Palo Duro Canyon and then to Ceta Canyon, naming the program "The Northwest Texas Girls' Camp of the Methodist Church."

Mrs. Delaney's girls' camp, usually held in August, attracted ten to the first camp and thirty-two years later.[31] Camping was quite primitive. As Bethany Williams recalled in later years, "Most of the time we slept on cots under the trees and cooked our own meals on rocks placed in strategic spots."[32]

Meanwhile, the Central Texas Conference made overtures to Northwest Texas in 1923 about joining it in establishing a camp at Lake Worth near Fort Worth. The conference's three-person committee appointed to review the proposal consisted of M. M. Beavers, J. P. Patterson, and Mrs. Delaney. Needless to say, the committee was less than enthusiastic about the offer, as sentiment was strong that Northwest Texas should have its own facility. The committee recommended that the conference participate and cooperate but have no part in finance or administration. At the same time, it recommended that the conference appoint a permanent encampment committee with representatives from each of the conference's interest groups. The committee further recommended that Mrs. Delaney be appointed to the new committee until the "Women's Missionary Conference" annual meeting.[33] That appointment marked one of the first times, if not the first, that a woman was appointed to a major conference committee.

Mrs. T. C. Delaney. Photo from Gabie Betts Burton, comp., *History of the Northwest Texas Conference Woman's Missionary Society.*

At the 1924 annual conference, the Encampment Committee reported that it was trying to obtain a tract in Palo Duro Canyon, and thus the conference designated it as a temporary board of trustees, empowered to receive and hold property.[34] But no deal could be made until 1927. That year, the camp trustees reported the acquisition of 315 acres for $6,000 that was "free of all encumbrances," thanks to the generosity of "friends of the camp" who had donated money or purchased lots on which private cabins could be built.[35]

However, the report was not well received on the floor of the 1927 conference. Apparently there was significant opposition to the proposal, and some questioned the financial arrangement. A young McMurry student, Marvin L. Boyd, witnessed the debate and recalled the event years later: "[the committee chairman] went on to say that [the report] didn't mean that the property was entirely free of debt. It simply meant that some friends of the Conference, some individuals had put up the necessary money and they were satisfied with the arrangements that had been made about how they would be repaid."[36]

Others, and presumably those from the southern end of the Conference, argued that Northwest Texas should be taking advantage of the

Girls' camp at the Ceta Canyon tabernacle, c. 1940s. Photo from Northwest Texas Conference Archives, McMurry University, courtesy Annette Nall.

Central Texas Conference's offer to share its facility at Lake Worth near Fort Worth. Boyd recalled the strong tenor of the debate:

> [T]hey had quite a hassle and quite an argument. I remember they had to extend the time and the worship service started late that day. Mrs. Delaney, herself [who was secretary of the camp board of trustees], was one of the main ones who spoke in favor of the plan . . . [and] I remember Gaston Foote was one who spoke in favor of it. But a good many members of the conference, some of them conference leaders, were pretty strong in their opposition. Well, anyhow, the vote was finally taken and by a majority that wasn't too large, the conference voted to accept and approve the report of the committee. I've often thought that the Northwest Texas Conference just came within a gnat's eyelash of losing Ceta Canyon that day."[37]

Mrs. Delaney's influence probably carried the day, for by 1927 she had demonstrated the effectiveness of well-organized camps. In time, the Ceta Canyon Camp had a new auditorium provided by the Women's Missionary Society, as well as a dam to create a swimming pool. An old ranch house was enlarged to provide a residence for a camp caretaker.[38]

By the late 1920s, Mrs. Delaney's girls' camp was a highly organized affair and attracted campers and leaders from all over the Panhandle and South Plains. In 1929, at what was billed as "The Tenth Annual Camp," workers included women from Fort Worth, Hereford, Chillicothe, Memphis, Heald, O'Donnell, Canyon, Stratford, Shamrock, Miami, and Amarillo. Conference native Marie Crane, a missionary from Cuba, served on the staff for that year.[39] In June 1928, the new campground also hosted the first laymen's retreat, which proved highly successful. With the camp well established, in 1929 the conference appointed a program committee to assist Ceta Canyon's trustees in camp planning and ministry.[40] By 1939, camp attendance and other events attracted 2,500 people annually.[41]

After World War II, and after extensive remodeling and enlargement of facilities, Ceta Canyon was in high demand. In 1950, the trustees reported 4,484 camp attendees, but it is not clear whether these were all at Ceta Canyon or included the district camps. With a reported fifty-nine conversions and an additional commitment of fifty-nine to full-time Christian service, camping had become an essential part of the conference's ministry.[42]

Beginnings of Butman

However, the distance involved and the onset of the Depression and World War II limited attendance at Ceta Canyon from the southern part of the conference. As early as the 1930s, the Abilene District had established its own summer camps, which were held at the Presbyterian Encampment at Buffalo Gap southwest of Abilene. These camps were for children of intermediate age, thirteen to fifteen. A camp for "young people" began in 1945. These camps continued at Buffalo Gap into the 1950s.[43] The Stamford District, and perhaps others, used the Baptist encampment at Leuders.[44]

In 1953, a long-held dream of a camp for the southern part of the conference became a reality. Sam Butman, who had moved to Mulberry Canyon southwest of Abilene in 1882 as a nineteen-year old, subsequently acquired ranch holdings in the beautiful hills along the Callahan Divide. For years, Mulberry Canyon was a close community of small farms and ranches scattered along Elm and Mulberry creeks. With their own schools, churches, and even a community band, Mulberry Canyon residents often celebrated and worshipped together in the summer at a tabernacle built in 1928. The Butmans hosted an annual July 4 rodeo and picnic at their ranch up until the outbreak of World War II.[45]

After World War II, Sam Butman dreamed of building a new church as well as a summer camp in Mulberry Canyon. In 1950, he acquired the site of the old Butman School near the old tabernacle and gave funds for the construction of Pioneer Memorial Methodist Church in memory of his wife Madge.[46] The new church represented a consolidation of the churches of the old Blair Circuit, Blair, Nubia, Pleasant Valley, and White Church.

Butman's concept for a summer encampment called for giving 40 acres next to the new church and tabernacle in the flatlands of Mulberry Canyon. However, Orion Carter, pastor at Big Spring, Elra Phillips, the new pastor at Pioneer Memorial, and Edgar Irvine, manager at Ceta Canyon, suggested to Butman that he give acreage located in the cedar-covered hills. Marvin Boyd related Butman's response: "My goodness alive," Butman retorted, "this forty acres I am offering to give you down there is good land. I can give you a whole mountain of that cedar brush if you want it."[47]

But the preachers wanted the cedar brush country; and, true to his word, Butman subsequently gave them and the conference a deed for about 232 acres of Mulberry Canyon land that lay near the historic route of the Butterfield Trail near Mountain Pass. At the annual conference in May 1953, Butman—in the presence of four of his children—made the presentation of the deed to Bishop Martin before a grateful assembly.[48]

At long last, the southern half of the conference had its own campground, but much was left to be done. Camping began at Butman in 1956 even before all facilities were in place. Darris Egger recalled an intermediate camp during the very hot summer of 1956: "The girls stayed in cabins and the boys in tents. My, but it was hot. The mosquitoes were very hungry. We got little sleep. We probably prayed that Methodists would become very generous very soon, so we could also be housed in cabins with screens on the windows."[49]

For several years, campers at Butman would struggle with facilities that did not match those at the older Ceta Canyon camp, leaving many to feel that the former was the "stepchild" of conference camping.[50] This feeling did not go away, and in fact camp rivalry and other issues would cause additional divisions in the conference in future years.

A hospital for the conference

With a college and two camps in place, the conference lacked only two entities that would round out its ministries: a hospital and a retirement center. Acquisition of a hospital would be a major task, but not an impossible one, thanks to the leadership of one of Lubbock's longtime Methodist and civic leaders, Dr. M. C. Overton.

Overton, with his partners Drs. J. T. Krueger and J. T. Hutchinson, had developed Lubbock Memorial Hospital as the region's primary care facility. Overton also gave generously to Methodist causes, including land and building fund donations for Overton Methodist Church in Lubbock. Overton apparently encouraged his colleagues to consider giving Lubbock Memorial to the Northwest Texas Conference.[51] The longtime pastor of Lubbock's prestigious First Church, H. I. Robinson, also must have played a large role in encouraging the doctors to give the hospital to the conference. Regardless, in September 1948, the hospital board discussed a "tentative proposal" to give the facility to the Northwest Texas Conference.[52]

With little opposition and no discussion, the Northwest Texas Conference voted in 1949 to work with Lubbock Memorial "regarding the acceptance of the hospital as the property of the Northwest Texas Annual Conference.[53] Robinson invited an officer of the General Conference's Board of Hospitals and Homes to visit Lubbock and review the proposal. Although the outcome of that visit is not known, it apparently set in motion the move toward the conference's acquisition.[54] But events moved slowly.

Methodist Hospital, c. 1960. Photo from Lawrence L. Graves, ed. *A History of Lubbock.*

Meanwhile, the hospital was ready in 1951 to begin construction of a 280-bed facility on the west edge of the city at a cost of $3.5 million. In 1952, it also began a medical office building, the Krueger, Hutchinson and Overton Clinic.[55] Thus, the dream to open the hospital under church auspices was not fulfilled at the time. In August 1953, the new hospital and clinic opened to the public as Lubbock Memorial Hospital. It was a substantial facility, valued at more than $4 million, but with it came substantial debt: $1.75 million.[56]

But perhaps to no one's surprise, in mid-September 1953 the board of trustees voted to "give" the hospital and clinic to the Northwest Texas Conference. Louise Allen and Michael Carmichael, who wrote a history of the hospital, explained the reason:

> [The hospital] presented an awesome number of responsibilities, not the least of which was the financial burden it represented. . . . Officers of the Lubbock Memorial Foundation were practicing physicians also and, as such, had only a limited amount of time to devote to management and decision making. Throughout the period of construction—from the beginning of planning, in fact—they had never lost sight of their earlier, and somewhat unique, proposal to divest themselves of their newly acquired property by "giving" it away.[57]

The conference, apparently aware of the pending vote, responded quickly by bringing in "a special Study Committee" that had already been appointed by the General Conference's Board of Hospitals and Homes. The committee was in Lubbock on September 20, four days after the trustees' vote and included the executive secretary of the Hospital and Homes Board, Dr. Karl P. Meister, along with; current and former administrators of Methodist hospitals in Fort Worth, Houston, and Kalamazoo, Michigan; and J. E. Shewbert, Lubbock District superintendent. After a tour and face-to-face meeting with the hospital board, Meister explained that his committee would make a recommendation but that the decision rested solely with the Northwest Texas Conference.[58]

The Study Committee met four more times in Lubbock in October and November 1953, and on November 30, Meister wrote to Bishop Martin that the committee was "convinced that nothing less than the total property and complete service, under one management, should be considered." The Hospital and Homes Board recommendation concluded the following:

> The possibilities of a great institution to minister to human suffering under the auspices of the Church are present in this situation. These recommendations [to accept the hospital and clinic] . . . provide the basic foundation for what we believe to be one of the foremost opportunities of the church and community in Kingdom building.[59]

The conference was faced with a big decision. It would be taking on not only unprecedented indebtedness but also an obligation to ensure that the hospital remained financially solvent. Some Methodist and Lubbock community leaders believed that the debt obligation was too much; others believed that Lubbock and its trade area was too thinly populated to support such a large hospital.

Martin issued a call for a special session of the conference, scheduled to meet on January 29, 1954. But prior to the session, Shewbert formed a steering committee of prominent Lubbock Methodists to drum up support from among the seven Lubbock churches. While the committee was doing its work in Lubbock, Shewbert lobbied fellow conference members, urging them to come to the session "with an open mind, listen to all discussion and then vote."[60]

The January 29 special session drew one of the largest crowds ever for a conference, with 850 packed into the new sanctuary of Lubbock's First Methodist Church. The debate was long but orderly. The proponents lined up speakers from all levels of churches, as did the opponents. Probably the most prominent opponent was E. D. Landreth, pastor of St. Paul Church in Abilene. After nearly four hours of debate, the conference voted 190–45 to accept the hospital and clinic. The crowd reportedly "cheered" with the announcement of the vote and then immediately elected a 24-member board of trustees.[61]

On April 1, 1954, with incorporation papers all signed and filed, Lubbock Memorial Hospital was officially transferred to the Northwest Texas Conference and was given the name "Methodist Hospital, Lubbock, Texas." Elmer Paul was named as its first administrator. Sadly, H. I. Robinson, who perhaps more than any other pushed for the acquisition, died on April 10, 1954, at age fifty-seven in the very hospital he worked so hard to get.[62] Dr. Overton also lived to see the changeover and died in September 1955. He and his family also gave $120,000 to build the Wesley Methodist Student Center for Texas Tech in 1952.[63]

Trying to keep up

The postwar boom continued to bolster the Northwest Texas Conference. Year by year in the 1950s, the Northwest Texas Conference continued to grow steadily. The year 1954 saw the conference at its brightest. Membership topped 100,000 for the first time. The conference comprised 264 pastoral charges, 328 churches, and 320 Sunday Schools that averaged 39,352 per Sunday—an increase of 10 percent over the previous year. [64] The year also saw the construction of seventeen new church buildings, and First Lubbock's new "Cathedral of the West" was well under way.[65] Four new churches were added in 1955.[66] Yet in spite of increased attendance, church leaders began to note that growth was not keeping pace with general population gains—"we are humbled and ashamed of our shortcomings," noted the chair of the conference's district superintendents in 1955.[67]

Also recognizing that baptisms and professions of faith were slipping, the conference's Board of Evangelism called for churches to stage simultaneous revivals during the last week in March 1957. The effort resulted in a slight increase in professions of faith, briefly halting a downward trend. However, Sunday School growth continued to surge, topping 40,000 in average weekly attendance by the mid-'50s, and this trend continued into the early '60s.[68] In the 1950s, the church owed much of its success to the success of its Sunday Schools.

As a testimony to the growth of the conference churches in suburban settings, the 48th annual conference was held in May 1957 at San Jacinto Methodist Church in Amarillo, a church that centered in Amarillo's first suburb, marking the first time that the conference was held in a suburban church.[69] The setting was appropriate; during the '50s, the conference established at least twenty-eight new churches, twenty-three of which were suburban churches. But new church plantings could not keep pace with the loss of approximately forty-six rural churches. As a result, the total number of churches in the conference continued to edge downward, declining from 331 in 1950 to 313 in 1960.[70]

A half-century celebration

In May 1960, the conference celebrated its 50th anniversary during its 51st annual session, held at Polk Street Amarillo. It was a significant occasion because of the anniversary and the anticipated loss of its beloved bishop, William C. Martin. As previously mentioned, Martin was one of the last bishops to be elected by the Methodist Episcopal Church, South, in 1938. His twelve-year tenure as head of the Northwest Texas Conference would be regarded by many as the conference's golden age.[71] According to J. O. Haymes, Martin's name became synonymous with the term *Bishop* because of his longevity with the conference.[72] He was one of the last of the bishops appointed to the Northwest Texas Conference who had previous experience as a bishop.

Martin liked the Northwest Texas Conference and served it remarkably well, even though he was often thrust into firestorms of national controversy due to his election in 1952 as president of the National Council of Churches.[73] His experience was reflected in his work. "The Conference has enjoyed the leadership of several great bishops,"

Haymes noted, "but none was more greatly appreciated for wise counsel, diligence, and brotherly spirit than W. C. Martin."[74] The Conference's *Journal* for 1960 noted that Martin had been "in the vanguard of our social concerns with his patient, thoughtful and courageous leadership," yet "never [lost] his evangelistic passion."[75] During Martin's administration, he ordained 315 new deacons and elders in the Northwest Texas Conference alone.[76]

The conference showed its unprecedented appreciation for Martin by staging a farewell banquet attended by 1,100 people. It also presented him with a new car.[77] When he died in 1984, a writer from the Northwest Texas Conference recalled that Martin "was ever among the leaders for the expansion of the Christian ministry of the Church in mission outreach, evangelism across all strata of people."[78]

Despite the decline in church numbers, the 1960 conference also celebrated its continued numerical growth during the 1950s. Total membership had grown during the decade by 13 percent, down from the 25 percent growth rate for the '40s. The conference also reported Sunday School enrollment of more than 81,000, with an average attendance of more than 41,000. There were 128 Methodist Men's groups, with nearly 5,000 enrolled, and 259 Women Societies of Christian Service, with more than 12,000 members.[79]

Fifty years had been good to the conference, and the conference was good for Northwest Texas. It had created in 1952 the Administrative Council to improve coordination of conference missions and programs. It had added hundreds of new churches; it had built nearly $36 million worth of buildings and was contributing more than $7 million for all purposes. Clearly, the conference was riding the same wave of prosperity that swept the region in the '50s. Per capita giving had increased from $13 in 1910 to $66 in 1960, and most of that increase occurred in the 1950s.[80]

Moreover, the conference had kept pace with population growth. By 1960, Northwest Texas had just over 1 million residents, an increase of 228 percent over its 1910 population of 333,386. The conference's growth for the same period was just over 205 percent, from 34,650 to nearly 106,000. Methodists could still proudly proclaim, as they did in 1910, that 10 percent of all the men, women, and children in Northwest Texas were members of a Methodist church. That in itself was a most remarkable accomplishment; nationally, most churches of any denomination failed to keep pace with population growth.

By 1960, the Northwest Texas Conference must have been perceived nationally as a shining star. During the decade, four of its former or current members were elected as bishops. In 1952, native son Bascom H. Watts, was elected; in 1960, Eugene Slater, pastor of Polk Street Church, W. Kenneth Pope, pastor at First Church Houston., and Kenneth Copeland, pastor at Travis Park in San Antonio, were elected. Slater had served Polk Street Church for ten years, and his election as bishop marked the first time that an active member of the Northwest Texas Conference had been elected.[81] Pope had grown up in the Northwest Texas while his father, W. M. Pope, served as pastor at Aspermont, Paducah, Shamrock, Tulia and Dalhart. Pope also attended Clarendon College.[82] Copeland had pastored at Haskell in the 1940s.

Also elected by the 1960 Jurisdictional Conference was Paul Galloway, pastor at Boston Avenue in Tulsa. Galloway was assigned to the newly-created San Antonio-Northwest Texas Area. Created in part to relieve Bishop Martin of one of his three conferences, the new area matched Northwest Texas with a South Texas area for the first time. Galloway must have been pleased to have been assigned to one of the most successful conferences in the nation, Northwest Texas. As Haymes noted in the conclusion of his fifty-year history of the Northwest Texas Conference, "The hopes for the future are bright, visibility unlimited.'"[83] But probably no one in 1960 could see the dark cloud of division on the horizon.

Chapter 7

“Fightings without and fears within, Since we assembled last.”

The year 1960 dawned with bright hope for the Methodist Church. Nationally, its membership had grown steadily to nearly ten million members, an increase of 9 percent over the previous decade and well ahead of national population growth of 6 percent.[1] The General Conference's program that year called for a "Decade of Dynamic Discipleship" and for local churches to have "an evangelistic initiative."[2] In the Northwest Texas Conference, all appeared to be holding steady. Because its area's population had grown by 25 percent during the 1950s, its membership growth had pushed its ranking to 10th of the eighteen annual conferences of the South Central Jurisdiction. Northwest Texas reported 2,769 professions of faith in 1959, which ranked 11th of the eighteen conferences.[3]

How Lubbock got the conference office

As the conference continued to grow, so did its bureaucracy, most of which was centered in Lubbock. Over a forty-year period, partly by default and partly by its central location, Lubbock had become the conference's administrative center, even though there was still no centralized conference office. In 1920, the conference had established the office of conference Sunday School secretary with a paid salary, and also for the first time authorized a part-time salary for the conference treasurer.[4] However, all officers of the conference, except for the bishop, conducted business from their homes across the region. In 1926, the Sunday School secretary became the conference Sunday School superintendent, and that office shifted from Plainview (W. H. Terry) to Abilene (B. W. Nance), where it remained until 1929. In 1929, J. W. Watson of Lubbock took over, and the conference apparently purchased a residence in Lubbock for the secretary.[5]

In 1930, the General Conference unified the Board of Education, the Epworth League, and the Sunday School Board into a single body, with the head being designated as the "executive educational secretary." Watson became the new secretary and remained in Lubbock.[6] Nance moved to Lubbock to become "dual extension secretary," along with J. L.Willis, who had moved to Lubbock from Borger. Thus, by the end of 1930, Lubbock had become the headquarters for an important arm of the conference.

Although different men held the position as executive educational secretary, the office remained in Lubbock. Watson served four years until 1933, followed by W. E. Hamilton for fourteen (1933–47), and Uel D. Crosby (1947–53). By 1948, the Educational Office at 1917 23rd (which was also a residence) included not only Crosby but the director of youth work and the director of children's work.[7] In early 1954, Charles Lutrick replaced Crosby, who had returned to a pastorate.

Meanwhile, in 1952, the General Conference laid out guidelines for a new format by which to better guide conference programs. A Conference Planning Commission called for the establishment of a Quadrennial Administrative Council that would be charged with the "responsibility for giving guidance and leadership to the Annual Conference Program."[8] When approved by the conference, the new Administra-

This building in Lubbock became the Northwest Texas Conference office in 1964. Photo by author.

tive Council included the bishop, the district superintendents, representative pastors from each district, the presidents of various conference interest groups, and conference and district lay leaders, for a total of approximately 70 people.[9] Eugene Slater, pastor at Polk Street, was elected as the new Administrative Council's first chairman, a position he held for eight years.

At that time, in addition to the executive secretary of education, the conference treasurer and secretary were located in Lubbock, but in three different office locations. By 1959, eight of the eleven conference officers (not including district superintendents, or the bishop, who officed in Dallas) resided in Lubbock, but most apparently maintained their offices at their residences or churches. Clearly, there was a need for a central office for the rapidly growing conference.

In 1961, the conference realized a dream with the acquisition of a central office. With the help of Floydada businessman and layman J. M. Willson, the conference moved into a building at 8108 Avenue H in south Lubbock.[10] In 1964, the Avenue H property was exchanged for what is now the present Conference Office Building at 1415 Avenue M, and the staff moved into the remodeled structure in September.[11]

For the first time, all of the conference offices were housed in the same place. In 1973, the building was renovated for expanded use; it was dedicated in January 1974.[12]

Urban growth vs. rural losses

During the first half of the decade, the Northwest Texas Conference continued to grow in membership, primarily thanks to the planting of new churches in rapidly growing urban areas. From 1959 through 1963, Amarillo and Lubbock witnessed the establishment of three new churches in each, and additional churches were started in Brownfield, Andrews, Abilene, Big Spring, Hereford, Crosbyton, Dumas, and Lamesa.[13]

St. Stephen's Church in Amarillo had a remarkable beginning. In 1962, recognizing that the city was growing toward the southwest, the Amarillo Board of Missions acquired four acres on Western Avenue. After a lot of door-knocking by a new young pastor, Dan Solomon, a congregation formed in a nearby elementary school and soon had more than two hundred in attendance. In September 1963, the congregation moved into a new building, with 564 attending worship services. By 1968, St. Stephen's membership topped 1,000, even though Amarillo's population was in a slow decline.[14]

Church planting was a little more difficult in Andrews. In 1959, the community had nearly 10,000 residents but only one Methodist church: Means Memorial. That congregation and the Big Spring District took the lead in trying to organize a second church for the community and soon purchased property. In January 1960, the pastor at Means sent a letter to 261 unaffiliated Methodist families, inviting them to either join Means or become charter members of the new church. Sadly, there was only one response to the mailing!

Miffed at the poor results, the pastor decided that the new church was not needed, but at the insistence of the district superintendent, he proceeded with organizational plans. In March 1960, the new church was organized with forty-six charter members, forty-three of whom were from the Means Memorial membership. Soon the new church, which was subsequently named Wesley, had attendance of eighty or more, and by 1962 it had completed a new building. Unfortunately,

Andrews began to experience an economic downturn due to cutbacks in the oil industry. During the '60s, the city lost 30 percent of its population, prompting Wesley church historian Flo Patterson to label it as "The Years of the Great Move-out."[15] Thus, the new church grew slowly and by 1967 had 169 members.[16] Unlike St. Stephen's in Amarillo, the new Andrews church did not have much new housing in its neighborhood to boost its growth substantially.

Nationally, nearly all church growth began to decline after 1960. The dramatic increases that came after World War II were gone. The situation only worsened for Methodists as they continued to lose their historic bastion of strength, rural churches. In Northwest Texas, the change was sobering. For example, Stonewall County once had twenty-one Methodist churches. By 1930, there were only six, and by 1950, only two. In 1960, the Peacock church merged with Aspermont, leaving only one in the entire county. The change caused the Aspermont pastor to reflect on the awesome responsibility that his church faced:

> The rural church in Stonewall County has followed the way of the rural schools and consolidation has had its effect . . . . Still one wonders if we have not, in withdrawing from these communities, left many people without spiritual leadership. The Methodist Church in Aspermont has inherited the background of all these churches and must seek to minister to these people in all these places.[17]

In the first half of the '60s, losses of rural churches were masked by continued urban growth. Thus, when the conference welcomed its new bishop, Paul Galloway, it was seemingly business as usual. Galloway, who had previously served as pastor of the prominent Boston Avenue Church in Tulsa, was anxious to implement his own program, but following the beloved William C. Martin would prove to be a challenge.

Streamlining the conference

Galloway lost no time in making some changes. In September 1960, he called a Special Conference and reorganized the Administrative

Council, renaming it the Conference Council. He directed that the council chairman be the bishop rather than someone elected by the council. He also stipulated that the council should have an executive secretary, and he gave that responsibility to J. Weldon Butler. [18]

Butler, who had been serving as pastor at St. Paul's in Amarillo, was shocked when he learned that the new bishop had appointed him without consultation to replace Charles Lutrick as the new executive secretary of the conference Council and Board of Education. "I knew nothing about that job and cared less," Butler recalled. "When I told this to the Bishop, he informed me that, interested or not, I was being appointed to the Lubbock office."[19] Although upset with the decision, Butler accepted his fate and served in the position for three years. In 1963, Galloway appointed Marvin Boyd as council executive secretary. Boyd would serve in the position for five years.[20]

Galloway's abrupt style also surprised the Cabinet. Vernon Henderson, one of the district superintendents, recalled the Cabinet's first meeting with him:

> When Bishop Galloway arrived, [he was] a very weary man, for he had had a difficult time with the Southwest Texas leadership. Marvin [Boyd] handed him the full list of the appointments we had worked on, frankly, we were very proud of our work. After reading through them, he laid the papers on his table and said, "This is the worst list of appointments I have ever seen." We were shocked.[21]

After getting over the jolt of Galloway's style, the Cabinet settled into its business, and Henderson later recorded that the bishop "was most courteous and friendly to the attendants in the conference session, and also in the meetings with his Cabinet."[22] Butler described his relationship with Galloway as "fine, but at times very hectic." Galloway "reversed himself so many times that I had difficulty determining what his policy or decision was," Butler recalled, but "I soon learned to laugh instead of cry."[23] And, all survived. Galloway made a concerted effort to visit nearly every church in the conference during his first two years, and his diligence paid off as growth continued.[24] In 1962, the churches reported 2,910 professions of faith, including nearly 2,000 by baptism.

In 1963, a special committee appointed by Galloway recommended that the conference reduce the number of districts from nine to eight in the near future.[25] The realignment vote was postponed until the spring of 1965, when the committee recommended that the number of districts be reduced from nine to seven. The 1965 annual conference debated the issue, and, in spite of a motion by prominent businessman J. M. Willson, Jr. to have seven districts, the motion was defeated. A compromise finally emerged, calling for eight districts, with seven "as soon as flexibility in apportionments makes this feasible."[26] The motion carried.

As a result, the Stamford District's territory was divided between the Abilene and Childress districts.[27] In 1968, the Childress District became the Seymour District and was enlarged slightly at the expense of the Abilene District. In 1970, the number of districts was reduced to seven, with the Brownfield District churches being divided among the Plainview, Lubbock and Big Spring districts. This was the last change in district alignments for the next 21 years.[28]

Galloway served the Northwest Texas Conference for only four years, marking the first time since 1930 that any bishop had stayed less than five years. His background may have been too liberal for the Northwest Texas Conference, or he may not have liked the great distances he had to travel. Regardless of the reason, the 1964 Jurisdictional Conference did not return him after his four-year tenure. To replace him, it named former Amarillo Polk Street pastor Eugene Slater, who had served the Kansas Area during his first four years as a bishop.

In September 1964, Northwest Texas welcomed Slater with open arms, pleased to get a bishop "who came from among us."[29] Slater's arrival coincided with the conference's best year in terms of growth, as membership increased to its highest level ever: 108,399. At the time, there were 301 churches organized in 252 pastoral charges, with 202 "effective" pastors and district superintendents assisted by fifty supply pastors. Professions of faith for the year totaled 2,758, and baptisms, 1,767. Church attendance averaged 42,431 and Sunday School attendance, 40,187.[30] The numbers were strong enough to make any bishop proud.

One of Slater's first tasks was to reorganize the Conference Council in order to give it more structure as the program arm of work. In 1965, the conference approved a new council constitution. One distinct change was the restoration of an elected chairperson. Slater had served in that capacity while he was a pastor in the conference and prior to his election as bishop.[31]

Changing times signal trouble

Unfortunately, Slater's assignment as bishop to the Northwest Texas Conference coincided with an abrupt stop in membership growth on the local and national levels. There had been signs of coming change. The number of churches in Northwest Texas had been declining for some time because of the consistent loss of rural congregations. Additions by baptism had sharply declined in 1963, dropping off by more than 10 percent.[32] Church School enrollment had also been gradually declining since 1960 and was down by nearly 4 percent by 1965.

Overall church membership in 1965 dropped by 465, less than 0.5 percent, prompting the district superintendents to report at the annual conference that "we are disturbed over this record."[33] But it got worse. In 1966, the losses became dramatic: baptisms dropped by 10 percent, professions of faith, 14 percent, and Church School attendance, 5 percent, in just one year.[34]

However, no alarm bells went off. At the time, Methodist attention was focused on other business. All five Texas annual conferences met together for the first time since 1936 in a great convocation at SMU.[35]The occasion was the celebration of "five great anniversaries' of Methodism, which included the 100th anniversary of the founding of the North Texas Conference and the original Northwest Texas Conference, which comprised the present Northwest Texas and Central Texas conferences. It also marked the 200th anniversary of Methodism in America and the 50th anniversary of SMU.[36] At its close, attendees had to suffer through the reading of 2,000 appointments in the final session.[37] The session also marked the first ever missed by the venerable O. P. Clark, who had been involved in a car accident; he had attended 60 consecutive annual conferences.

The great anniversary celebrations did nothing to stem the declining tide of membership loss, especially in Sunday School enrollment and attendance. Denominational leaders tried introducing new teaching materials for children to change the downward trend, but to no avail. After 1966, Sunday School losses became dramatic and averaged nearly 5 percent per year, and by the end of 1970 stood at 58,308—25 percent below what it had been in 1960. Vernon Henderson, who was serving as the conference's associate executive secretary, wrote a series of thoughtful articles on the problem for the *Texas Methodist* to encourage renewal of Sunday School efforts. Henderson concluded that the Sunday School was the key to the church's future; that "the chief cause of dropouts in the Adult Division . . . is the lack of motivation to search for the fulfillment of basic human needs in this relationship"; and that poor teaching methods, poor or no preparation, and indifference were major contributors.[38]

Otherwise, church leaders were at a loss to explain the declines, except to ask for greater evangelistic efforts. Thus, it was easy for Slater to agree to Ed Robb's appeal to be appointed as a full-time evangelist. In July 1966, the dynamic preacher left St. Paul's at Midland and moved to Abilene to establish his base. As previously mentioned, Robb had begun his ministry in the Texas Conference at Marshall, but in 1950 he left the Methodist Church and moved to Abilene to pastor the Evangelical Methodist Church that had been founded by J. H. Hamblen. After three years, he left that denomination and joined the Northwest Texas Conference, where he was appointed to Quitaque and later to Amarillo, Hamlin, and Midland.[39] At Midland, he had led St. Paul's to nearly double in size during his four years there.[40] When he became a full-time evangelist, Robb was soon holding tent and stadium revivals throughout the conference and nationwide.[41]

However, Robb's approach—a return to old-style revivalism—was not generally followed in the conference. For example, the Evangelism Committee's report for 1967 called on the churches "to explore methods for evangelistic action in the churches of the district" and listed fifteen recommendations; however, none of these included holding a revival meeting.[42]

The renewed evangelistic efforts perhaps stemmed the losses, as overall church membership remained flat for two years and then began to decline slowly. By the end of 1970, membership had dropped

5 percent for the decade to 103,530.[43] Church attendance and Sunday School average attendance had fallen 10 percent. Ten churches closed or merged. And for the first time in many years, the conference failed to raise its assigned apportionment for World Services and Conference Benevolences.[44]

By 1968, it had become apparent that the numerical decline of the Northwest Texas Conference and the national church was not going to be easily reversed. But answers about the cause of the decrease were elusive. Slater, in his last address as bishop of Northwest Texas, outlined the problem before the 1968 South Central Jurisdictional Conference:

> One is tempted to rationalize and say that much of the [San Antonio-Northwest Texas] Area is rural and that population in the rural area is declining, which is true. Then, too, the fact that many churches have engaged in cleaning the membership roll in keeping with the requirement of the Discipline accounts for further statistical losses. Even so, we must confront the fact that our evangelistic efforts, and more importantly, our quality of Christian life have not been such as have moved large numbers of persons to unite with our churches and become actively involved in the life of the congregations.[45]

As overall membership continued to decline, pressure mounted on district superintendents to change the trend. "Although we live in an area where the population is gradually decreasing," they noted in 1968, "we must not give in to despair or discouragement. The fields are still 'white unto harvest.' "[46] They put some of the blame for the decline on the church's boldness in taking a stand on such volatile issues as the Vietnam War and civil rights. Their report quoted a "good Methodist layman" who had stated: "I am proud to be a Methodist for the Methodist Church is seeking to meet the relevant issues of the day. Of course, it is dangerous to stick your neck out in such times, but a church that does not try to deal with relevant problems is stagnant. Thank God for the Methodist Church, for it is trying to deal with the real and relevant issues of the day."[47]

"Real and relevant issues"

West Texans have never been prone to get deeply involved in "real and relevant" national issues, but events such as the Cuban missile crisis in 1962, followed by the tragic 1963 assassination of President John F. Kennedy and growing opposition to the Vietnam War set the tone for years to follow. And as attempts at integration in the South turned violent, church leaders found themselves thrust into the heart of a growing national moral crisis.

On April 4, 1968, on the eve of one of the most important meetings of the General Conference, civil rights leader Martin Luther King Jr. was assassinated in Memphis, Tennessee. Riots broke out in more than 125 cities nationwide.[48] The ugly scenes in the streets and on television tempered the tone of the General Conference three weeks later in Dallas as it moved to create a new denomination. But out of it came the new United Methodist Church when Methodists and the Evangelical United Brethren (EUB) merged to create the new denomination. The Northwest Texas Conference had voted 350–0 to merge with the EUB.[49]

The merger effected Northwest Texas in two significant ways. First, it hastened full integration of black churches into the Methodist Church—the EUB had insisted on the dissolution of the minority Central Jurisdiction, one of the last vestiges of the old Southern church that had effectively kept black churches segregated within the denomination.[50] Full integration, which began in 1965, was finalized by 1970. The African-American West Texas Conference had at dissolution 134 churches, more than 16,000 members, and ninety-one ministers in full connection. These churches were assimilated into the North Texas, Southwest Texas, New Mexico, and Northwest Texas conferences on an equal footing.[51] Only five were within the bounds of Northwest Texas: these included Abilene Plum Street, Amarillo Wyatt Chapel, Lubbock Mount Vernon, Midland Hollowell Chapel, and Levelland St. Luke's. These churches had a combined total membership of 549; Mount Vernon was the largest, with 215 members.[52]

Abilene Plum Street Church is one of the oldest in the Northwest Texas Conference. Established in 1905 as St. Paul Methodist, the little church met in homes until it could build its own structure.[53] Lubbock

Mount Vernon was established in 1925 as Caprock Methodist Episcopal Church. It underwent two more name changes (Mosley Chapel and John Wesley) before adopting its current name in 1940, shortly after it was placed in the segregated Central Jurisdiction after merger of the Northern and Southern Methodist churches.[54] Amarillo's Wyatt Memorial was organized in a home around 1946, with seventeen members, and continued to meet in homes until it acquired a building in 1951.[55] It became Community of Grace after its merger with Forest Hills Church in 1997.[56]

The national merger of the Methodist Church and the EUB also brought about a new administrative alignment. To have a balance among jurisdictional districts, the South Central Jurisdiction was given an additional bishop. At the same time, the Jurisdictional Conference's College of Bishops realigned the conferences, moving the Spanish-speaking Rio Grande Conference administration from the Houston Area to the San Antonio Area. Perhaps because of this change, Northwest Texas was paired with the New Mexico Conference to create a new area, the Northwest Texas-New Mexico Area."[57]

The change in areas was significant for both Northwest Texas and New Mexico. Prior to 1960, Northwest Texas had been a part of the Dallas-Fort Worth Area for many years. In that role, the conference often did not receive the attention of the more urban Central and North Texas conferences with which it shared a bishop. Similarly, New Mexico shared its area with the Oklahoma Conference, which had three times as many members.[58] Thus, with the joining of Northwest Texas and New Mexico in a new area, the two "stepchildren" found themselves thrown together. Northwest Texas was the "big brother," with a 15 percent advantage in membership over New Mexico.

In the episcopal election, a product of Northwest Texas, Alsie H. Carleton, and Don Holter, the president of the St. Paul School of Theology, emerged as the leading candidates. The contest pitted Midwest against Southwest. Thirteen ballots were required before Carleton was chosen.[59] And much to the delight of the Northwest Texas delegation, he was immediately assigned to the new Northwest Texas-New Mexico Area.

The creation of the new area prompted a brief competition between New Mexico and Northwest Texas for the bishop's headquarters.

Northwest Texas had never had a bishop live within its bounds. Lubbock and Albuquerque mounted campaigns to attract the bishop's seat, but Albuquerque was chosen, primarily because of its better air and rail connections, and because jurisdictional leaders wanted to provide a "strong Protestant presence" there to work with the Catholic Archdiocese that was also located there.[60] It perhaps was an appropriate solution; New Mexico furnished a home for the homegrown bishop from Northwest Texas, Alsie Carleton.

Bishop Alsie Carleton. Photo from *Northwest Texas Conference Journal*, 1971.

Carleton had spent much of his life in Northwest Texas. He graduated from McMurry, and pastored in the region for most of his career, serving churches at Trent, Clyde, Baird, Lubbock St. John's, and Big Spring First before transferring to the North Texas Conference where he pastored University Park in Dallas.[61] Widely loved in the conference, Carleton assumed its leadership just in time for some of its most difficult days.

Other changes by the historic 1968 General Conference were not particularly welcomed in Northwest Texas. One approved resolution called for "limited support of nonviolent civil disobedience," a decision that was not popular, especially among Southern Methodists.[62] Also, many Texas Methodists felt that the new UMC had embraced a "theological liberalism which made Christianity little more than ethical humanism."[63] As a result, individuals and churches began to seek ways to express concern and to make an impact through selective giving, supporting alternative mission efforts, and turning to lay witness missions and other renewal groups.[64]

It was a difficult time for the church at large. Nationally, church attendance continued to decline; young adults stayed away from church in droves, with a 34 percent decline in two years among thoses of age twenty-one to twenty-nine.[65] In the Northwest Texas Conference in

1968, professions of faith dropped 29 percent under the previous year, and baptisms dropped 22 percent. Worship and Sunday School attendance were also down by similar amounts.[66] Perhaps in an effort to soften the sharp impact of the decline, church statisticians no longer distinguished between adult and infant baptisms.

One other significant change in the Northwest Texas Conference came in 1968. Dr. Cecil R. Matthews relinquished his positions as secretary of the annual conference and editor of the annual *Journal*, jobs that he had handled for twenty and twenty-one years, respectively. In addition, S. Duane Bruce became the new executive secretary of the Conference Council, replacing Marvin Boyd, and the position's title was changed to program director.[67] Bruce recalled the changeover:

> This was a real challenge, but I gave it my best. The [new] Council on Ministries concept as adopted by the General Conference called for all ministries . . . [to] be coordinated in the one Council . . . . This made sense to me, but some of the brethren accustomed to all the boards and agencies didn't like giving up their "little thrones." Some of them who had been leaders in the Conference never did accept the Council on Ministries concept.[68]

Two attendees of the 1910 Northwest Texas Conference, Cal Wright, and E. L. Yeats, were on hand for the 1969 annual conference—the 60th such session.[69] The old-timers witnessed the discussion of several national political issues—debates on topics that they probably had never witnessed before. From the conference floor, a lay delegate from Friona introduced a resolution to be presented to the 1972 General Conference that expressed concern about the denomination's support of civil disobedience: "We affirm the necessity of a society rooted in law and of a citizenry who respect law," the resolution noted, and went on to say that civil disobedience was acceptable as long as it was done within the context of the law and dissidents were prepared to live with the consequences of their actions.[70]

While not directly opposing the resolution, the conference's more liberal members quickly responded. Ted Dotts, pastor at Idalou, called for an amendment that would provide for a year's study of the issue; Ed Robb, the conference's conservative evangelist, spoke against the amendment, as did two prominent laymen: Judge Neil Daniel of Abilene and Judge Rod Shaw of Lubbock.[71] Another amendment was offered that somewhat softened the tone of the resolution by commending the General Conference for its "forthright defense of Christian conscience."[72] That amendment passed, as did the amended resolution. Clearly, the Northwest Texas Conference was on the side of "law and order," a term that became quite popular in future U.S. presidential elections.

During the same session, the conference questioned the report of the Board of Christian Social Concern about a statement about whether members of the Official Board should be selected from abstainers from alcohol. The report stated that the General Conference had moved away from "legalism" in this area, which some interpreted to mean that it no longer took a hard stand on alcohol. It also noted that Methodists had "seen a decreasing response among adults to total abstinence as a way of life . . . both within and without the membership of the United Methodist Church."[73] One delegate offered an amendment to the report, calling for a return to the historical Methodist position of "total abstinence."[74] After an extensive debate—which was punctuated by "an unidentified lady [who] came before the conference and forcefully claimed that Methodists should quit watering down their beliefs"—the conference finally dismissed the attempted amendment and accepted the principle of "witness by Christian example."[75]

The emerging political division within the conference's ranks became even more apparent in 1970. In April, the conference met in a special called session to consider the recommendations of a special study committee on the conference's ministry. The call for such a panel came at the 1968 conference.[76] The most controversial of the recommendations dealt with the way that delegates were to be elected to the general and jurisdictional conferences. The study committee called for a nomination process that would limit the election ballot to 25 clergy and 25 lay delegates, selected through an initial secret ballot. In previous elections, all clerical and lay members of the conference were listed on their respective ballots. Why the proposed change was controversial is unclear. Perhaps some members felt that the new process would lead to party-style politics; others probably held to the old adage "If it ain't broke, don't fix it." The vote was close: 186 for and 179 against.[77] Although the new procedure did not last, it did initiate a new level of lobbying within the conference as delegates began to vote along conservative vs. liberal lines.

Other issues dealt with salaries, the appointment process, moving expenses for pastors, and the preferred number of conference districts. The latter provoked considerable discussion, probably reflecting a growing division over the role of district superintendents and the administrative cost related to that office. In the end, 243 delegates voted to retain seven districts, while 137 called for a five-district arrangement.[78]

By 1970, division within the conference was obvious enough that one pastor was able to define it. Bob Ford, then pastor at Rotan, published an article in *The Northwest Texas Log*, a little journal edited by Ted Dotts and designed to allow free expression among the conference's ministers. In March 1970, Ford wrote that the division could be defined as "the polarization of evangelism versus social concern or activism or involvement:

> There has already been some confrontation in this regard. I am not sure of the outcome of these encounters, but I feel sure that there will be more, and I rejoice in the possibilities for dialogue this can bring about. What I am fearful of is that there will be a tendency toward polarization in which no one can really win and everyone can lose.[79]

Ford added some wise and prophetic advice for his colleagues:

> We must learn to listen to each other, no matter where we stand theologically. To listen means we must not be afraid of honest, hands-on confrontation of views. This is the risk of reconciliation which must be constantly taken if we are to be able to live on the boundary line of our time. But this will require work. . . . Most of all it will require love—a love which realizes that each one of us is loved by God as he is and not because of a certain theological position.[80]

But Ford's advice to "listen" and to "love" generally went unheeded for a number of years, and the conference drifted toward fracture. However, division was not exclusive to Northwest Texas—it was even more pronounced at the national level. A special 1970 General Conference met in St. Louis to complete the details of the 1968 merger of Methodists with the United Brethren. A flurry of petitions nearly overwhelmed the session; volatile issues such as race relations, campus unrest, firearms control, and the Vietnam War were never addressed as a large number of delegates withdrew, forcing the conference to sputter to a halt before the work was completed. Some blamed the failure on Southern delegates supposedly opposed to social concerns.[81]

A few weeks later in its regular annual session, the Northwest Texas Conference approved a resolution calling for "Reconciliation in a year of turmoil." The document took a somewhat "middle-of-the road" approach to the nation's problems: it reminded youth that they "need to be heard, but there are other voices too"; it recognized that minorities had vital needs, yet it noted that "we must recognize that no one has ever been redeemed by threats." With such ambiguity, it is no wonder that the resolution passed unanimously.[82]

But ambiguity could not spare Northwest Texas from additional controversy. By 1971, the national debate on abortion rights spilled into the conference floor. Groups such as the National Organization for Women had risen to national prominence and led the fight to overturn laws that made abortion a crime. Within the conference, pro-abortion activists persuaded the Board of Christian Social Concerns to introduce a resolution that called for legislative revision of Texas' abortion laws. "The option of terminating an unwanted pregnancy is an individual right," stated the resolution, "and should be the privileged decision of the person directly involved."[83] The motion prompted a lengthy debate that spilled into the afternoon. One controversial paragraph (unfortunately, it is not recorded in the *Journal*) was deleted, but the revised resolution passed by a vote of 205–112.[84] Such action contributed to the groundwork that led up to the U.S. Supreme Court's famous *Roe v. Wade* decision in 1973, which declared the abortion laws of most states to be unconstitutional. (The winning attorney who represented "Roe" in the famous decision was Sarah Ragle Weddington, the daughter of longtime Northwest Texas Conference minister H. Doyle Ragle.[85]) The Vietnam War also divided Methodists nationally, especially after the Council of Bishops publicly condemned President Lyndon Johnson for his escalation of bombing in 1965.[86]

As the church was drawn more and more into national issues, some Northwest Texas Conference lay members became more vocal about a perceived liberal drift in the denomination. The district superintendents reported in 1971 that there "has been the questioning, searching desire of the laity for responsible information . . . . Some have misinterpreted this very justifiable desire as only criticism and opposition. However, generally our people have been most supportive and responsible to program and fiscal challenges."[87]

Some Northwest Texas laypeople and pastors were probably not happy with the "theological pluralism" doctrinal statement that was unveiled at the 1972 General Conference. This statement, strongly influenced by prominent SMU theologian Albert Outler, outlined four guidelines for Methodist belief: Scripture, Christian tradition, experience, and reason. It also endorsed "Christian social action," reported *The Texas Methodist,* "including some of the activities that have raised controversy in church circles in recent years," and "a sensitivity to the semantic concerns of some women's liberationists."[88]

One Methodist layman expressed his frustration with the new doctrine in the *Texas Methodist* in an August 1972 commentary:

> I am afraid that we Methodists have drifted into an emphasis of social needs and the values of Christian fellowship until it has become difficult for our youngsters to see the differences between the Christian Church and many fine civic organizations which offer the same challenges and satisfactions.[89]

It was only a matter of time before the dissension took on a "party" distinction. By the early 1970s, conference preachers found themselves being labeled as either "evangelical" or "liberal," a process that created the perception of two distinct camps. In an informal group discussion, six Lubbock-area preachers noted that there was also a third "camp:" One participant noted that "one of the men said he actually felt that theologically he stood somewhere in between the two 'camps.' Another member of the group, who many would definitely place in one camp, said he, too, felt that his theological position was in the middle."[90]

The observer of the discussion thoughtfully offered a solution to the perception of division. "The need . . . is not that we should all end up with the same theology," he wrote. "What we need to do is to have men sit down together and try to see each other as persons. . . . It is time we quit talking about each other and began talking to each other."[91] His words also went unheeded—for the next thirty years.

Ecumenicalism and the Lay Witness movement

Still another movement in the 1960s that was probably not well received by some in the Northwest Texas Conference was ecumenicalism. Prompted in part by the coming-together of the Evangelical United Brethren with the Methodist Church, there was considerable discussion in church literature about the merger of several denominations into a single church. In 1966, seven Protestant denominations worked to draft a plan of union, but little progress was made except for the unification of the Methodist and the EUB denominations in 1968.[92] But on the local level, an ecumenical spirit came from an unexpected direction: the Lay Witness Mission movement. This phenomenon quickly crossed denominational lines and became very popular within the Northwest Texas Conference.

Founded by an Alabama Methodist pastor in 1962, the Lay Witness movement quickly spread, especially among the more evangelical churches in the South and Southwest. It offered training and a simple formula that encouraged average Christians to share their personal testimony about what God had done their lives. By 1972, more than 1,200 Lay Witness Missions had been scheduled for Methodist churches nationally, and that many or more in other denominations.[93]

The conference leadership was not certain what to do about the new movements. "The spirit of ecumenism moves like West Texas winds, with high and low centers across the area, not always consistent in strength or direction," reported the district superintendents in 1969. "Numerous churches in every district have experienced true spiritual renewal and direction in these [Lay Witness Mission] experiences."

Not certain whether to embrace the movement, the district superintendent report took a middle ground: "This movement, 'led' and 'fed' by laymen, in addition to all the other effective programs and avenues of evangelistic effort in our churches can be the spiritual tonic for an anemic membership."[94]

It should be noted that long before many in the conference could even spell the word, ecumenicalism had been a part of the Northwest Texas fabric. From the beginning, conference preachers encouraged participation in joint Sunday Schools and revivals, especially in rural areas. However, two churches in the Northwest Texas Conference were far ahead in ecumenical action. Beginning in the early 1900s, the Methodist and Baptist congregations in the Canyon community east of Lubbock shared a school building, and then in 1927 jointly built a church. In 1971, the two congregations built a new modern sanctuary.[95] Each supported their own pastor, but the congregations held joint revivals and Sunday Schools.[96] The churches continued to worship together until 1986, when Canyon Baptist Church apparently disbanded.[97] Canyon United Methodist Church is still in existence.

In 1971, retired pastor E. D. Landreth took note of the conference's historic embracement of ecumenism. "In 1921, the word 'ecumenical' was not in common usage," he wrote in the *Texas Methodist*. "It probably could not have been pronounced by many of the preachers, yet among the visitors introduced to the [1921] Conference were two Baptist ministers, a Christian minister, a Presbyterian minister, an Episcopal rector, and a Catholic priest, and this was fifty years ago."[98]

During the height of the ecumenical movement in 1968, Bishop Carleton told a reporter that he thought the trend had some limitations: "I don't think we are going to cease to be Methodists or Baptists or Catholics," he said, but "we are going to stand together and work together, while recognizing our differences." And he thoughtfully added: "I don't want to see us get wrapped up in ecumenism and let that take all our steam while we let up on evangelism. We forget to win people to Christ."

Carleton also noted that there was a link between evangelism and the new church renewal movements, such as the lay witness mission: "We need to evangelize in the ways that are effective today," he told the

Texas Methodist, "and I think part of the work of the renewal groups . . . is evangelism."[99]

What caused the decline of the 1960s?

Carleton's call for a renewed evangelistic effort echoed the words of virtually every bishop who has presided over the Northwest Texas Conference before or since his tenure. In times of church decline, it seemed apparent that the church needed to be more evangelistic, but the causes for the downturn that struck the conference and the denomination in the mid-1960s go far beyond a lack of evangelical emphasis, and are numerous and complex.

One obvious reason for the conference's losses in the 1960s was population loss. For more than eighty years, the region had grown steadily, except for the Depression years of the 1930s. In the mid-1960s, the region was hit with drought and other factors that contributed to an economic slowdown on the high plains.

The closure of Amarillo Air Force Base in 1964 had a marked impact on the local economy; the city's population slipped into decline, losing 8 percent in only six years.[100] On the South Plains, the irrigation boom that followed the extensive drought of the early 1950s peaked in the 1960s.[101] By the mid-'60s, the spread of irrigation to area farms had run its course. In addition, below-normal rainfall from 1963 through 1966, coupled with a downturn in commodity prices, hastened an exodus from many farms.[102] For example, cotton production fell dramatically after 1965, dropping more than 40 percent by 1967.[103] Population of communities that depended primarily on farming peaked and then turned downward after 1965. Thus, it is no wonder that the growth of the always rural-oriented Northwest Texas Conference peaked in the mid-1960s.

The rural-to-urban shift in population was another major factor. By 1960, the population of the sixty-seven counties in the Northwest Texas Conference had climbed to just over 1 million, a 25 percent increase over the 1950 total. However, only five urban counties—Potter, Randall, Lubbock, Taylor, and Midland—grew rapidly. These had gains of 72 percent; Midland County almost tripled in population because of an expanding demand for petroleum products. But of the other, more rural counties, thirty-two actually saw decreases in population during the '50s, and in the 1960s, the decrease became even more dramatic: fifty-five of the sixty-seven counties lost population. The '60s saw the entire region drop in population by more than 50,000, and the sixty-two rural counties lost nearly 11 percent of their population.

The 1960s were a watershed period for the rural counties of Northwest Texas. After World War II, irrigation and farm mechanization brought new prosperity to the region, but by the mid-1960s, these changes also meant continuing population decline in rural areas. For example, the number of family farms in Lubbock County that produced chickens for home or market consumption declined from nearly 2,000 in 1950 to just 129 in 1969.[104] This dramatic drop indicates that the number of farm families dropped rapidly, and thus it is no wonder that the conference's rural churches were disappearing.

National trends and changing social values also contributed heavily to church losses. After World War II, membership in nearly all mainline Protestant denominations grew steadily, but, according to one account, "church sociologists have judged that period as a time of numerical growth without corresponding spiritual revival."[105] "We went to people's homes and had them sign membership cards," recalled one Arkansas bishop. "Then they never showed up in church, and we never called back. But we had more members on our rolls."

Northwest Texas leaders agreed with this assessment. "We appear to be near the close of a long siege of negativism designed to destroy the Church," the district superintendents reported to the 1972 conference. "Such negativism came on the wave of massive membership additions in the 1950s and the Death of God theology of the 1960s. [But] In the 1970s, the church still stands."[106]

Other leaders assailed "the numbers games" of churches trying to build membership without discipleship as being a factor in church losses of the 1960s. One authority on church growth, Lyle Schaller, said that church growth in the '50s reflected "the priority of the church at that time. We placed a pretty high priority on evangelism and church development then. Later, our priorities changed."[107]

However, priorities of society also changed dramatically. Dr. Terry Matthews, a church history professor at Wake Forest and a graduate of Duke University, noted how the change occurred:

> As William Willimon and Stanley Hauerwas have observed in a recent book, *Resident Aliens: Life in the Christian Colony,* there was a time when the Church was quite literally "the only show in town." It had little or no competition for people's attention. If you wanted to go anywhere, if you wanted to get out of the house, you went to church or Sunday School. There were few other options.
>
> The Sabbath was sacrosanct. You didn't see people mowing their yards in those days, or even raking their leaves on Sunday. It was a day of rest, and few dared challenge the conventions of the day. Church, home and state worked together in a three way partnership to instill "Christian values" in people. And when most people looked around them, they saw a society that was "good, wholesome, and reasonable." It was as if God was on his throne, and all was right with the world.
>
> But then things began to change . . . . Slowly, but surely, people began to discover that they had options other than going to Church on Sunday. Restaurants, Movie Theaters, Malls, a whole host of alternatives to the church began to offer themselves to folks. And in surprisingly short order, what had been a day of rest, had became little different from any other day of the week.[108]

By the 1960s, America had become a highly mobile society. No longer bound to rural community centers such as the church, the baby-boomer generation born after World War II often chose lifestyles different from those of their parents' generation. By the 1960s, television, recreation, sporting events, and other diversions competed with the church for attention. And in West Texas, a superb rural-to-urban highway system ensured that country folk could participate in the diversion.

Other forms of religious expression also began to draw members away from mainline Protestant churches. By the late 1960s, the charismatic movement, with its emphasis on the "gifts of the Spirit" and emotional experience, began to affect Episcopal, Lutheran, Anglican,

Catholic, and Methodist churches nationwide. Pentecostal churches began to experience growth, often at the expense of the older mainline denominations. One example is the rise of Trinity Church in Lubbock. Founded in 1960 as Highland Assembly of God, Trinity became an "independent" nondenominational church in 1967, and by 1969 had moved twice to larger facilities.[109] A three-week revival in the early 1970s tripled membership, and weekly attendance was 1,000 or more. Without a doubt, much of its new membership included former Baptists, Lutherans, and Methodists.

By 1972, the new United Methodist Church was beginning to recognize that its membership losses were not temporary and that rather dramatic changes were in store. Its membership was rapidly becoming urban, but it could not abandon its rural heritage. Moreover, minorities within the church were finally getting a voice, and the church as a whole found itself embracing a broad diversity. Although the changes may have been welcome in the Northeast, the more conservative members of the Northwest Texas Conference became somewhat uncomfortable with the more liberal church as a whole. Moreover, the General Conference also made sweeping changes in organizational structure. It established a new Council of Ministries that provided broader representation of church interest groups, including minorities. It also created a new structure for boards for Global Ministry, Discipleship, and Church and Society.[110]

The new structure also affected the Northwest Texas Conference. In a special conference in September 1972, delegates approved an organization plan that made the new Conference Council on Ministries a stronger, more centralized group than the previous Administrative Council had been. Among other things, the new Council on Ministries was charged to "coordinate district programming, evaluate the work of the district council and conference staff, implement general conference level programs and other specialized help to sub-district, district and local councils on ministries."[111]

The year of 1972 became a watershed year for the Northwest Texas Conference. Even though the General Conference and the Northwest Texas Conference faced difficult challenges with declining membership, some church leaders hoped that the worst had passed. On the one hand, the new administrative structure with its centralized Council on Ministries gave mobility to the deployment of new programs and causes; on the other hand, others began to question the church's need to be caught up in causes at the expense of evangelism and other basic functions of the local congregation. As a result, Methodist soil became fertile for even more discontent.

Chapter 8

"Fightings without and fears within"

Continued

By the early 1970s, church leaders had begun to recognize the significance of the denomination's losses and, to a certain extent, the root cause of the loss. Sunday School attendance nationally had dropped nearly 23 percent from 1959 to 1974.[1] In the Northwest Texas Conference, it dropped 40 percent in 10 years following 1963.[2] During the same time, the number of Sunday School members joining the church dropped 89 percent.[3] Conference leaders were quick to recommend a solution: "Surely our number one task in the future should be evangelism," the district superintendents reported in 1974. "Our number two task should be the church school. They go together." A Duke professor, John W. Westerhoff III, told a Sunday School conference in 1975: "If it were not for the Sunday school, the church would have died long ago. Nevertheless, Sunday schools in small mainline churches are sick, sick in part because they have tried to become modern church schools and failed."

But many believed that the problems went deeper than just Sunday School. Nationally, some challenged seminary training, mission efforts, and involvement in social concerns. These issues had already started to divide Northwest Texas ministers, but during the 1970s, the local conflicts did not necessarily mirror national issues. The charismatic movement, a surprising student protest at McMurry, evangelical issues, and summer camp conflicts demanded much of the stage. However, all issues were interrelated, and it is difficult to determine whether the national church issues had a greater impact on Northwest Texas or whether Northwest Texas had the greater impact on national issues. Regardless, the 1970s can be characterized as a war of words, but it played out with some grace and civility.

The spiritual wars

The first major issue within churches in the conference was the growing charismatic movement. By the early 1970s, this phenomenon had hit Northwest Texas, fueled in part by the lay witness mission movement, new Pentecostalism, and a new wave of independent churches. The movement reached across all denominations. In Lubbock, a Baptist pastor led his congregation into the movement by abolishing all but one Sunday School class for adults, dropping traditional literature, changing the music program to a praise format, and preaching messages that emphasized the gifts of the Spirit. Traditional Baptists soon began to leave the congregation, but they were replaced by new charismatic adherents.[4]

In some Methodist churches, the movement caused division; within others, it provided an opportunity to learn.[5] Max Browning, pastor at Shallowater, organized a "Holy Spirit Conference" for his church in 1974 "in order to help our people better understand the issue and make a more intelligent and less emotional response." He told the *Texas Methodist* on the eve of the event, "There is probably no single issue in Christian theology that has generated the interest, confusion and controversy within the local church like the doctrine of the Holy Spirit and the spirit-filled life."[6]

For the program, Browning invited Ted Dotts and Ed Robb, leaders from both the liberal and conservative sides of the conference, as well as leading Pentecostal theologian David du Plessis, considered one of the founders of the modern charismatic movement.[7] Dotts recorded his own observations of the conference and commended the Shallowater church for its "good service for all of us." He provided a summary of du Plessis's message for the *Texas Methodist*, which he described as a "constant affirmation of the forgiveness of God in Christ":

> All extraordinary gifts of the Spirit are to be normed by the fruits of the Christian through whom these gifts may be questioned by folks as ordinary as "thee and me," because any Christian can ask about the fruits of the Spirit: love, joy, peace, patience, kindness, goodness, fidelity, gentleness, and self control (Galatians 5:22). Those who claim extraordinary gifts and do not reveal the fruits are making a false claim.[8]

The Shallowater conference certainly did not quench the charismatic movement on its own, but it demonstrated a willingness to hear diverse issues through the traditional Methodist approach of reason and intellect.

Many churches in the Northwest Texas Conference experienced another form of spiritual renewal in the Lay Witness Missions that began in the mid-1960s. The program involved laypeople who usually traveled to another church for a weekend program of testimony and sharing. These were official programs of the church, sponsored by the General Board of Evangelism. The first one in Texas was in 1964 at Corpus Christi.[9] By 1968, the Northwest Texas Conference's Board of Evangelism had issued a call for a Lay Witness Mission in every church in the conference.[10]

These missions proved to be very popular in Northwest Texas. "The lay witness, in my opinion, was a powerful movement in the church," recalled Eddie Allsup. "It was lay centered and got people excited about Christ and the Church and enthusiastic about sharing their witness."[11] Because some pastors were shying away from revivals and personal evangelism efforts, a Lay Witness weekend often became a substitute for holding revivals.

"Good News" and the theological war

Nationally, the Lay Witness movement helped to give rise to still another renewal effort in Methodism: a forum that came to be known as the "Good News" movement. In 1966, pastor Charles Keysor, of Elgin, Illinois, wrote a stimulating and controversial article for *The Christian Advocate* in which he contended that "the silent minority" within the Methodist Church had no voice: "It is not represented in the higher councils of the church," Keysor wrote:

> Its members seem to have little influence in Nashville, Evanston, or on Riverside Drive. Its concepts are often abhorrent to Methodist officialdom at annual conference and national levels. I speak of those Methodists who are variously called "evangelicals" or "conservatives" or "fundamentalists." A more accurate description is "orthodox," for these brethren hold a traditional understanding of the Christian faith.[12]

Keysor's appeal for unity among "orthodox" Methodists struck a chord, and he founded the magazine *Good News* to continue his dialogue. In 1970, nearly 1,600 Methodists from across the nation joined Keysor in Dallas at the first "Convocation of United Methodists for Evangelical Christianity," sponsored by *Good News*. The program included Keysor, Bishop Gerald Kennedy from Los Angeles, the famous missionary and evangelist E. Stanley Jones, and the president of Asbury Theological Seminary, Dr. Frank Stanger.[13]

The convocation set the tone for an agenda that called for a "reform of Methodism from within" and focused on such diverse issues as the "domination of liberalism within the denomination," "a general state of apathy within the church," and "the past tendency of evangelicals to concern themselves only with spiritual concerns." Speakers also emphasized "the need for a revival emphasis on repentance, conversion, and personal faith in Christ among existing church members," and the need to restructure "programs, literature and seminaries to reflect the Lordship of Christ in our secular culture."[14]

Although the convocation took no steps to create a formal caucus, it determined to have future annual conventions. *Texas Methodist* editor

Spurgeon M. Dunnam III covered the convocation for his paper and asserted prophetically that the meeting would have a profound impact on Methodism. "Despite the lack of official pronouncements, two things are perfectly clear," Dunnam noted. "The evangelicals are a significant presence with no intentions of giving up their membership in the United Methodist Church. And they intend for this presence to be felt at all levels by the church in the future."[15]

R. L. Kirk, pastor at Aldersgate United Methodist Church at Abilene, became the contact point by 1970 for Good News interests in the Northwest Texas Conference.[16] The message and pronouncements of the Good News convocation were well received by many in the conference's laity and ministry. Convocation participants apparently went home and made calls to their district superintendents. At the 1971 Northwest Texas annual conference, the chairman of the bishop's Cabinet, Marvin Boyd, noted in the district superintendents' report that "emerging in the conference has been the questioning, searching desire of the laity for responsible information regarding our programs and general boards and from our national church leaders. Some have misinterpreted this very justifiable desire as only criticism and opposition."[17]

Conflict on campus

Without a doubt, a new wave of religious conservatism was rolling through Northwest Texas in the early 1970s, stimulated in part by the Lay Witness movement and reaction to the violence of the late '60s. This new conservatism subsequently came into conflict with the more liberal establishment within the United Methodist Church. The first major sign of theological and/or political division within the conference appeared at McMurry College in clear form in the spring of 1972.

By the early 1970s, many McMurry students were more conservative and evangelically oriented than those of the '50s. However, as the college replaced retiring faculty members with new professors who were inclined to be broader and more diverse in their teaching, conflict was inevitable. One of those new hires was Dr. Robert Monk, and he recalled the issues: "Innovations in teaching style and content, open support of the Civil Rights movement, questioning of Vietnam," he noted, "and, of all things, sponsoring dancing on the campus was welcomed by many students, but also brought resentment and resistance from several quarters."[18]

The "resistance" formed ranks in the spring of 1972 and polarized into two groups, "liberal" and "evangelical." According to McMurry historian Gary Shanafelt, the evangelical group "became increasingly critical of McMurry's religious courses and professors," and a group of thirty students "presented a petition to the Board of Trustees requesting a complete overhaul of the teaching philosophy of the religion faculty."[19]

The petition, in the form of a letter to the board, was very specific:

> We feel that strong Biblical Theology . . . is not being presented on our campus. Instead a bankrupt liberal theology is being taught. The result has been disastrous. Our campus, we feel, is too much like any other secular campus. The permissive attitude taken has resulted in an immoral atmosphere. . . . It is debatable whether our Religion Department and campus ministry are meeting the basic needs of a student community thirsting for the "Good News."[20]

According to Shanafelt, the trustees did meet with the students, but the religion professors were not invited.

However, Johnny Robertson, one of the self-proclaimed "Dirty Thirty" signers of the petition, remembered differently: "We were sent to the general student body grievance meeting in the Fine Arts Building to meet with one member of the Board of Trustees who would bring a final report of all student grievances presented that day to the Trustees," recalled Robertson. "The auditorium was filled with student groups."[21] Robertson, who presented on behalf of the thirty petition signers, said that he focused the group's grievance on the unfair interpretation of pluralism: "My argument was that pluralism was used to question the historic teachings of the church and of our NWT [Northwest Texas] local churches specifically, but pluralism in the hands of McMurry wouldn't allow the positions or views of the textbooks and teachers to be questioned in a like manner."[22] It was a point that would be repeated many times over by Methodist evangelicals in future years.

According to Shanafelt, McMurry President Thomas Kim "felt constrained to reaffirm the right of the faculty to teach its courses as it saw fit, without outside interference." Indeed, Kim strongly defended the faculty in a memorandum to the trustees:

> The function of the Department of Religion is different than the function of a local church. I believe so strongly in my own Christian faith to know that Christianity will emerge as a strong and viable faith for me and for others, even after close scrutiny and careful comparison with other religions. The academic freedom of the Department of Religion to examine all possible religious experiences and, at the same time, affirm our fundamental Christian commitment, is vital to the intellectual integrity of the Department of Religion and of the College.[23]

Although the issue did not go away easily, Kim allowed normal attrition of faculty to provide the opportunity to hire a professor who would please the evangelical side, and he led in forming the Christian Outreach program that sent teams of students, both liberal and evangelical, to minister in area churches.[24]

Although the issue may have calmed down on campus, it continued nationally and in Northwest Texas. At the 1972 General Conference, evangelicals failed to get any of their resolutions approved, prompting Good News founder Charles Keysor to charge that the process was not open to minority viewpoints and determined that evangelicals needed to be more politically aggressive.[25] The same idea arose in Northwest Texas: "That [issue] spread throughout our Conference," Darris Egger recalled, "and that's when it became both a doctrinal question and a power struggle—who is going to be in power."[26] Influenced in part by national movements, individual pastors—and to a certain extent individual churches—began to identify with both local and national identities in the new power struggle.

Perhaps because of the new conservatism and as a concession to the conference's evangelicals, Bishop Carleton appointed the dynamic evangelist Ed Robb to the pulpit at St. Luke's in Lubbock in 1974. Robb,

Bishop Alsie Carleton and the 1974 Cabinet: standing (L to R), Carlton Thomson, Darris Egger, Ted Dotts, J. Weldon Butler; seated (L to R), O. A. McBrayer, Clifford Trotter, Bishop Carleton, Marshall Rhew. Photo from *Northwest Texas Conference Journal*, 1974.

after more than seven years in full-time evangelism, said he was exhausted and asked Carleton for a church appointment, and preferably to Trinity First in El Paso. But the bishop had other ideas and moved Lubbock St. Luke's pastor, Carlton Thomson, to the Plainview District and appointed Robb as St. Luke's pastor. As Robb recalled, "The conference was stunned that the Bishop had put me in one of its strongest churches."[27]

Robb saw the opportunity to demonstrate the power of effective evangelism in church growth. He soon made an immediate impact at St. Luke's, a church where membership had fallen by nearly 30 percent by charge conference removal in the year prior to his arrival. During his tenure of two and a half years, worship average attendance nearly doubled, increasing from 485 to 794, and total membership rose from 1,602 to 2,188 by the end of 1976. Clearly, Robb appealed to evangelical-oriented Methodists, as most of the church's growth was by transfer from other United Methodist congregations.[28] However, the church also reported fifty-four professions of faith for 1974—more than twice the number from the previous year—and seventy-four for 1975. Due in part to the church's inability to expand in its location, Robb returned to full-time evangelism in September 1976.[29]

The seminary war

While at St. Luke's, Robb's impact went far beyond growing a church and the conference. His role as a conservative evangelist thrust him into a national spotlight, especially through the Good News organization, which gave him a public forum for his campaign to return Methodism to its historical evangelistic roots and orthodoxy. While he was still pastor at St. Luke's, Robb spoke in 1975 at the sixth annual Good News Convocation at Lake Junaluska, North Carolina, delivering a landmark speech to 2,000 attendees. Primarily, he challenged the United Methodist Church to reform its seminaries: "We have a sick church which is suffering from weak, ineffective ministerial leadership," he declared. "The seminaries bear a major portion of the responsibility."[30]

Like those in the McMurry "Dirty Thirty," Robb also questioned whether the new Methodist doctrine of "pluralism" worked only for the liberal side:

> By pluralism, do we mean that the evangelicals can pay the bills, receive members and follow the program determined and directed by liberals? By pluralism do we imply that it is disloyal to question the program, literature or schools of our denomination? Is the episcopacy and bureaucracy of our church demonstrating the same attitude toward evangelicals that the Church of England's leadership showed toward the Methodists of the 18th Century?[31]

To give evangelicals a voice in theological training, Robb proposed three recommendations: 1) "that two of these seminaries be entrusted to evangelical boards of trustees and continued as official United Methodist seminaries"; 2) that "every official theological school" be required "to invite competent evangelical scholars to join their faculties, especially in the fields of Biblical and systematic theology"; and 3) "that greater support be given to the established independent theological seminaries, especially those of the Wesleyan-Arminian tradition.[32]

Robb emphasized his third point with this illustration:

> I know of one annual conference in United Methodism that provides $1,000 scholarships annually to every student from its area who attends a well known, independent evangelical seminary. This money is contributed by concerned laymen and churches. That conference now has between 25 and 30 students enrolled in evangelical schools. Every cent of this money is sent through the conference treasurer. This is bringing about significant evangelical renewal in that conference.[33]

(To fill in the blanks, Robb was referring to the Northwest Texas Conference; the seminary in question was Asbury, which is located in Kentucky, far from Texas.[34])

Robb concluded his stirring address with this declaration:

> Let us serve notice, here and now, that we will no longer turn over our converts to the theological liberals who neither understand nor teach the Biblical faith. Let us serve notice that evangelicals will no longer be silent concerning the great issues of the church, and follow blindly their impotent policies. We are dedicated to evangelical renewal within the United Methodist Church. *We are not going elsewhere.* Rather, we propose to radically alter the direction of our great denomination.[35]

The speech must have rattled windows in Nashville, and it certainly did so in Dallas. Albert Outler, the primary framer of the doctrinal statements of the new United Methodist Church, took offense with at least one of Robb's statements—that no seminary was teaching the historic Wesleyan biblical perspective. Outler, who was editing a voluminous work on John Wesley's sermons, wrote what Robb later termed "a scorching letter" to the *Texas Methodist* and charged that Robb's "salvo" was "a sin against both truth and charity":

> It is sad that a well-meaning man should lodge a blanket indictment against the entire lot of United Methodist theological schools in terms so unjust that they are bound to wreak incalculable damage to the cause of theological education in the UMC—which is, as we all know, in grave enough peril already.[36]

Texas Methodist editor Spurgeon Dunnam promptly called Robb and read the letter to him over the phone. Robb recalled that he "prayed about it for about fifteen minutes" and then called Outler and made an appointment. Outler related the outcome of the meeting in the summer of 1975:

> [T]here were not many of us in an other-cheek-turning mood [after Robb's blast]. My own indignation was especially "righteous" since I was deeply involved, with others, in a protracted, earnest crusade to recover and re-present John Wesley (not only to Methodists but to other Christians as well) as a significant theologian and as a fruitful resource for contemporary ecumenical theology. My response was less than conciliatory; after all, what was there to expect but another salvo in reply?
>
> It was, therefore, downright disconcerting to have Dr. Robb and some of his friends show up in my study one day with an openhearted challenge to help them do something more constructive than cry havoc. Needless to say, I've always believed in the surprises of the Spirit; it's just that they continue to surprise me whenever they occur!
>
> Here, obviously, was a heaven-sent opportunity not only for a reconciliation but also for a productive alliance in place of what had been an unproductive joust. Moreover, as we explored our problems, some unexpected items of agreement began to emerge. For example, there was the recognition, first off, that too many evangelicals (especially in the Methodist

> tradition) had made it all too easy for the liberal establishment to freeze them out on the grounds that they had not paid the going price for full academic respectability. All too often, John Wesley's warmed heart is celebrated by those who ignore the import of that richly stored head of his and that superb set of scholarly tools that he kept burnished throughout his long career.[37]

The "productive alliance" was Outler's and Robb's formation of "A Foundation for Theological Education," designed primarily to give support to evangelical graduate students for terminal degrees to allow them to teach at the seminary level. Robb was its first board chairman. The alliance indeed has been productive—during the thirty-two years since its inception, the foundation has given approximately $2.5 million to theological graduate students and as of this writing was supporting nineteen John Wesley Fellows with $150,000 in scholarships.[38]

The student wars

As previously noted, Robb's landmark speech to the Good News Convocation cited "one annual conference" that was providing scholarships to "a well-known independent theological seminary." This policy began in the Northwest Texas Conference in the early 1970s, when Abilene pastor R. L. Kirk Jr. and others began raising funds to provide scholarships to Asbury Theological Seminary. In his position as pastor of Aldersgate United Methodist Church, located across the street from McMurry, Kirk played a large role in employing and mentoring young preachers and securing scholarships.[39]

Kirk had been one of the first in the conference to attend Asbury, where he received his master of divinity degree in 1955.[40] However, according to Rex Mauldin, "the Board of Ordained Ministry had trouble trying to be convinced that [R. L.] was educated" and made him obtain a second master's degree at Iliff, a Methodist seminary in Denver, before he could be admitted as a full elder.[41] Jim Smith, R. L.'s longtime friend, said: "Even though his dad [R. L. Kirk Sr.] was district superintendent, they didn't let R. L. come straight back into the Conference .... There was some pretty strong feelings among some leaders . . . that

Asbury was not really accepted as a place to get a theological degree."[42] Smith indicated that this may have been due in part to the school's placement on academic probation in the 1950s.

Other than Kirk, most Northwest Texas ministerial students went to SMU to attend Perkins School of Theology, the official school for the South Central Jurisdiction. For example, in 1962, of the twenty-eight Northwest Texas students appointed to attend school, sixteen were enrolled at Perkins, three at Drew (New Jersey), and two each at Yale and Iliff. One each went to five other seminaries, but none was enrolled at Asbury.[43] However, by 1968, Perkins students had dropped to twelve, while St. Paul in Kansas City attracted six, and two were attending Asbury.[44]

Jim Smith from Northwest Texas, who would later become pastor of St. Stephen in Amarillo, was one of those enrolled in Asbury in 1966.[45] While he was still in high school, Smith met the outstanding young evangelist and Asbury professor Robert Coleman. "We had a tremendous revival [in Tulia] . . . and it was a major turning point for many of us and for that whole church," Smith recalled. ". . . Out of that revival, I felt that God was calling me to preach and that was kind of a new experience because I had never considered that before. I never really thought that I would in any way go into any kind of church related vocation. "[46] Smith also became friends with Kirk, who was serving as pastor at Gruver, where Jim led a summer youth meeting and dated his future wife, Lu Ann Cator. "[Kirk] was about 12 years older than I was . . . . We became very good friends. "[47]

Smith recalled being told by a conference leader that if he went to Asbury, he "might as well not come back to Northwest Texas, that there probably would not be a place" for him. But Smith noted: "That was never true . . . . Before I graduated [in 1969], the district superintendent [Jordan Grooms in Brownfield District] called me and said 'I want to appoint you to a church.' "[48]

As Smith, Jim Terry, and other Asbury graduates began to prove themselves in the conference, a spontaneous revival brought new distinction to Asbury College and its seminary. In 1970, a routine fifty-minute chapel service turned into a spiritual awakening; according to one report, it continued "185 hours non-stop 24 hours a day" and "continued for weeks" and spread to other schools and seminaries across the country.[49] News of the event gave the school broad publicity.

By 1972, five Northwest Texas students were enrolled at Asbury and nine at Perkins.[50] But only two years later, Asbury pulled into the lead as thirteen conference students chose Asbury; twelve went to Perkins, three to Iliff, and one to Duke.[51] By 1974, Northwest Texas students comprised 5 percent, or fourteen of the 269 full-time United Methodist students enrolled at the Kentucky school, and included seven of the "Dirty Thirty."[52] Clearly, Kirk's efforts on Asbury's behalf were paying off, and to show its appreciation, the school honored him with an honorary doctor of divinity degree in 1975.[53] At the time of Kirk's death in 2002, his son Robert estimated that his father had "helped upwards of 150 men and women interested in evangelical seminary education."[54]

By the late 1970s, Asbury became the school of choice for a majority of Northwest Texas students. Smith credited the lay renewal movement with being a major reason for the change: "A lot of youth were touched by the Lay Witness Mission movement," he recalled. "[They] came out of that experience with a desire to serve in some way . . . and wanted to go somewhere to have more of an orthodox theological training, and Asbury offered that."[55] The trend continued well into the 1980s and '90s. In 1978, Asbury attracted twenty Northwest Texas students; fifteen went to Perkins, and ten others were attending six other seminaries.[56] In 1980, Asbury had twenty-five, its highest number ever, and Perkins had seventeen.[57]

The student wars were over, and Asbury had won, at least for the time being. It would take years, though, before the Asbury influence would become dominant on the high plains.

In the foxhole

Meanwhile, back in the Northwest Texas Conference, Bishop Carleton's response to the theological and seminary wars was to surround himself with strong Methodist leaders. At the same time that he appointed Robb to Lubbock St. Luke's, in early 1974 he returned Marvin Boyd to the Conference Council on Ministries for a second term as program director. As previously mentioned, he also added Carlton Thomson from pastor at St. Luke's to his Cabinet as superintendent of the Plainview District. Other superintendents were experienced and included Darris Egger, Clifford Trotter, former conference program director J. Weldon Butler, O. A. McBrayer, and Marshall Rhew.[58]

The Cabinet also included Ted Dotts, whom Carleton had appointed in 1970 to the Pampa District, —a move that surprised many at the time because Dotts represented the conference's "liberal" wing. Apparently some other members of the Cabinet did not agree with Carleton when he announced this appointment; according to one legend, when the bishop left the room for a few minutes, he returned to find an egg had been placed in his chair! Such irreverence apparently did not faze Carleton; Dotts served a full term as district superintendent and, according to Rex Mauldin, "did an excellent job."[59]

Carleton's district superintendents must have struggled with the McMurry issue as well as how to deal with declining numbers. Based on the tone of their report to the 1974 annual conference, Rhew, the senior member of the Cabinet, had the unpleasant task of telling the conference the bad news about the decline; he introduced his remarks by saying: "No district superintendent in his right mind would ask for this job. If you don't like this report, please blame my brothers in the Cabinet."[60]

Rhew pointed out that in 1973 the conference had "again broke the 100,000 barrier," but this time, the numbers were on the way down. He noted that the conference could "take some comfort" in knowing about the downward spiral of the general population for the region for the past ten years, pointing out that all of the districts, except for Lubbock and Amarillo, had lost population.

The district superintendents also noted programs that were working and encouraged the conference to consider "visitation evangelism" concepts such as the Evangelism Explosion touted by Presbyterian minister D. James Kennedy in Florida. Kennedy used this to help grow his church to a membership of 2,700 in eleven years. "At least one of the members of this Conference [Rex Mauldin] has gone to Florida to study it," noted Rhew. "The Dalhart Central Methodist Church now has 22 members trained for this kind of visitation and they have had 77 persons to confess faith in Christ in 7 ½ months."[61]

Rhew also pointed out that the conference planned a strong evangelism emphasis through a pastor's school and in the 1975 annual conference. He noted that "great improvements have been made in the literature for the Methodist Church School," but "more will need to be done than simply to improve the literature . . . in order to get our enrollment and attendance back to where it belongs." On the positive side, Rhew also noted that in 1973 the conference had reached its highest record in giving—more than $9 million—and had overpaid World Service and Conference Benevolences for the second year in a row.

The conference increased annual giving to more than $10 million in 1974. Northwest Texas was one of the leaders in per capita giving, averaging $128, which topped the national average by 18 percent and the other South Central conferences by 25 percent.[62] And thanks to renewed evangelism efforts, Northwest Texas saw its membership decline drop to less than 1 percent over the previous year. The 1975 district superintendent report also noted that, after evaluation and removal of more than 8,000 "ghost members" from church rolls, actual membership had increased by 1,150 over the previous four-year period. Yet it also pointed out that "the church school is in crisis," as evidenced by a 25 percent drop in average attendance over a four-year period.[63] The district superintendents renewed their call for effective evangelism and more emphasis on missions.

Northwest Texas was not by itself in reporting losses. In 1975, fourteen of the seventeen conferences in the South Central Jurisdiction reported losses, with the most dramatic drops in Kansas and Nebraska.[64] Nationally, Methodist membership had dropped back to 1960 levels.[65] But Methodists were not the only ones dealing with membership losses in the mid-1970s. The American Baptist, Lutheran, Episcopal, and Presbyterian groups all reported losses. Only the Southern Baptist, Assembly of God, Latter-day Saints, and Nazarene denominations reported gains, and most were modest at that. The Mormons were the nation's fastest-growing denomination.[66]

Delegate wars: Round 1

By 1975, the theological and student wars had driven a wedge into the conference. That year, the conference had the task of electing delegates to both the General and Jurisdictional conferences. The process required fourteen clergy and fifteen laity ballots to elect four to General Conference, five to Jurisdictional, and three reserves. The *Texas Methodist* reported that the lay delegates were all new and that many of the clergy delegates were new. The prolonged balloting seemed to indicate that many were looking for change. But the conservatives were far from winning the battle, as the conference elected Clifford Trotter, Charles Lutrick, and Darris Egger—all traditional "mainline" Methodists. In addition, it also elected Dotts, who had long been the liberal spokesman for Northwest Texas.

At the same 1975 session, twelve ministers retired who had a combined service record of 406 years, including longtime influential leaders Marvin Boyd and J. Edmund Kirby. Thus, it is no wonder that the *Texas Methodist* noted that the 1975 Northwest Texas annual conference session "marked the end of one age and the beginning of a new era."[67]

By 1976, conference leaders seemed to feel that some issues had been put to rest, and all worked to be positive. In the spirit of the nation's bicentennial celebration, the annual session was held jointly with New Mexico at the Baptist retreat center at Glorieta, New Mexico, near Santa Fe. Perhaps trying to impress their New Mexico brethren that "all is well" in Northwest Texas, the district superintendents presented a carefully worded report to the assembly:

> The feeling is alive throughout the Conference, that we have passed the depression and are now on our way again with new life and vigor. The optimism following World War II, the uncertainty and the pessimism of the intervening years, are now past, and again we have taken some of the lessons of history that life does not consist in the abundance of things, but in the inner presence of the living God. "[68]

Indeed, the conference reports showed that baptisms and professions of faith increased for the year—but total membership continued to slide downward, largely because, according to the superintendents, "many churches dropped members by Charge Conference action, and because several small churches closed their doors. "[69] Indeed, the practice of purging membership rolls of inactive or absent members was a historic practice of Methodism. Unlike the Baptists, whose doctrine of "once saved, always saved" ensured that any adherent would be on a church roll for life, Methodists had faithfully maintained the practice of removal, in part because churches could reduce their apportionments by keeping their membership up to date. Thus, the conference membership report, although reflecting a continued downward trend, at least portrayed a more realistic view of real membership numbers.

The 1976 district superintendent report also alluded to the continuing undercurrent of dissent within the conference as it concluded with an appeal for "unity within His Spirit" and for "team work and a spirit of appreciation, unity and continuity."[70]

Shortly after the annual conference, Carleton was selected to give the prestigious Bishop's Address to the 1976 South Central Jurisdictional Conference. Apparently he took careful note of his superintendents' report at conference and perhaps used it to chide those who were just counting numbers: "Now is the time . . . for United Methodists to cease counting our losses and being pleased that so many inactive persons are being removed from our church rolls . . . . ," he eloquently declared. "A pastor is not a good shepherd unless he feeds his sheep and goes out to find the forgotten and the lost. A church is not a Christian church unless it goes out as members of Christ's body to seek and save the hurt, the hungry, and the lost." Carleton called on his brethren to formulate effective preaching, to develop stronger Church schools, and to "give priority to the local church."[71]

Carleton also spoke to the positive and negative sides of the new Methodist doctrine of "theological pluralism." On the one hand, he said that pluralism had always been a part of Methodist tradition: Citing Albert Outler, Carleton told the assembly that "Wesley's understanding of pluralism is that the basic commitment of faith is salvation by faith in Jesus Christ, and . . . [Wesley] calls upon Methodists to build on that base by using Scripture, tradition, experience and reason as tools of 'free inquiry' and 'serious reflection.' " But he also noted that pluralism could cause divisiveness and "deviate into self-centered individualism": "It can easily become 'Parallelism,' and be not only divisive, but outright heretical. If our pluralism negates, wipes out, neutralizes, and immobilizes our Wesleyan heritage of 'connectionalism' and sound Biblical theology as taught by Mr. Wesley, then we are of all people most foolish."[72]

Sadly, the immediate future for Northwest Texas seemed to be "parallelism" rather than pluralism. Although dissent within the conference was not yet fully organized by the mid-'70s, on the national level, a fracture was developing within the General Conference. In 1974, a group organized itself as the "Evangelical Missions Council" and in 1975 constituted itself as a "supplemental" world missions agency for evangelical missionaries. This group contended that the World Division of the Board of Global Ministries favored "liberation and sociopolitical action" and slighted "efforts toward personal conversion."[73] Such a division within the church's work in effect gave individual churches a choice of support and helped to begin an erosion of traditional giving through the apportionments process. It also hastened the process of individual pastors being labeled as "evangelical," "mainline," "traditional," "middle-of-the road," or (heaven forbid) "liberal." The practice was unfortunate, and the characterizations for the most part inaccurate. For example, by national standards, a Northwest Texas "liberal" would be called a moderate at best or even conservative in other parts of the nation.

In 1977, dissent and division within the conference became more apparent, partly due to the denomination's and the conference's call for greater evangelistic efforts. "Evangelism is probably more important today in the life of the United Methodist Church," wrote conference program director Darris Egger in the *Texas Methodist*. "Losses in membership. Church school attendance, attendance at worship service point to the need of effective evangelism."[74] Later that year, thirty-four from the Northwest Texas Conference attended the Dallas Focal Point Evangelism Conference and accounted for ten percent of the attendance.[75]

However, traditional revival evangelists felt that they were being left out of the renewed evangelistic mix; the National Association of United Methodist Evangelists complained that they "were not where the efforts of the larger church should be." Most of the sixty members were from the South, where traditional evangelism was practiced in smaller churches.[76] The new evangelical preachers coming out of

Asbury also felt discriminated against; according to Johnny Robertson, Asbury evangelicals found themselves facing a Conference Board of Ministry that was not sympathetic to their beliefs:

> The biggest objection we got was to [our] belief that the Bible was the Word of God and the final authority for faith and practice. Sometimes the debates got very intimidating to young men seeking entrance to the United Methodist ministry. To deal with this threat to conservative and Asbury grads, we asked our district superintendents to place us on the Conference Board of Ministry. After lots of confrontations we started getting an evangelical on that board here and there. This same pattern was reproduced all over the annual conference infrastructure. Tensions grew higher with each annual conference.[77]

As tensions increased and conference membership numbers continued to decline, pressure continued to mount on the bishop and Cabinet to find a solution, and none was forthcoming. By 1977, the "liberal vs. evangelical" issue continued to seethe, forcing the Cabinet to make one of its strongest statements ever at the annual conference: "Our connectionalism is still rent by 'party spirit,' " reported O. A. McBrayer in the 1977 district superintendents' report. "In spite of our General Church's admonition to 'pluralism,' we have difficulty in practicing the principle in day-to-day issues. So long as any of us put down another by attitude or deed, the 'whole body' suffers.[78]

And "the whole body" continued to suffer. In 1978, conference membership had dropped to 92,904, and church attendance declined by 3.5 percent.[79] Yet giving was up more than 11 percent, a factor that implied that Methodists were prospering and those who were dropping out were not faithful supporters of the church.

The camping war

One other major issue that percolated to the surface in the 1970s was probably unique to Northwest Texas. This issue, more than any of the others, became a dividing point that forced churches and individuals to make a distinct choice between "evangelical" and "liberal." That issue was the conference's summer camping program.

With the addition of Camp Butman in the southern part of the conference in the 1950s, as well as improvements to Ceta Canyon in the northern part in the 1960s, the Northwest Texas Conference was poised to have one of the nation's finest Methodist camping programs. In 1964, more than 7,000 took advantage of Ceta Canyon's facilities in thirteen weeks of camping and thirty-three other events during the year.[80] Camp Butman reported 2,513 attendees in 1963 and was having difficulty in attracting campers due to its lack of quality facilities, summer heat, and lack of support from churches in the southern part of the conference.[81] In 1964, the conference approved a plan that created separate administrative committees for each of the campgrounds, with separate managers provided for each.[82] By 1968, the conference director's office was serving as a clearinghouse for camp dates and schedules.[83]

Prior to 1971, the camping program was driven primarily by districts, with each holding their own camps primarily for elementary and junior high children. Jim Smith, who had just returned to the conference in 1969, recalled preaching at a junior high camp that summer and witnessed the effectiveness of evangelism in a camp setting. "I came out of that [experience] and said to the directors that we need this kind of opportunity for our high school kids as well as junior high," he said. "Both of the directors [of the junior high camp] said, 'Well, we used to have a camp like this for high school, but . . . the Conference won't let us have it any more.' "[84] Determined to get something going, Smith and Max Browning, as members of the conference Board of Evangelism, asked the board to ask the Conference Youth Council to set up a new camp that would have an evangelistic emphasis. The request was approved, and in the spring of 1970 the Youth Council concurred.[85] The result was the "Youth Inner-Life Camp" for high school-age youth.[86] This camp, the first of what would later become known as the "One Way Camp," started at Butman in 1970 and attracted about sixty-five. The following year, the Inner-Life Camp attendance topped 100 and had already outgrown the Butman facility.

As early as 1968, the conference had conducted "experiments" in "cooperative camps" that would reach across district lines.[87] With

Camp New Dawn participants enjoy a lively squirt gun game at the Butman Methodist Camp. Camp New Dawn was established in 1972 and continues at both Butman and Ceta Canyon camps. Photo from Butman Methodist Camp, courtesy Carolyn Street.

the development and growth of the Inner-Life Camp, which was designed to be conference-wide, camping leaders decided that perhaps it was time to review the overall camping program. In 1971, the council revamped the entire camping program by offering five junior high and five elementary camps conference-wide, with three at Ceta Canyon, and two at Butman. In addition, the council planned to offer camps for "youth, adult, family, and other camp enterprises."[88]

One of the special camps planned for 1972 was for mentally disabled adults. Spearheaded by Kathryn Peddy (later Goddard) of Lubbock, Camp New Dawn began a long record of service to the conference. The five-day camp provided a wonderful experience for disabled adults long before such programs as the Special Olympics. The camp grew rapidly, with forty-nine attending in 1974, and by 1980 had eighty-two campers and twenty-five counselors.[89]

Camp New Dawn became one of the brightest stars of conference camping: "Responses from the workers in Camp New Dawn indicate they feel privileged to have such opportunities," wrote Vernon Henderson. 'One such counselor put it this way: 'I thank you for the wonderful privilege of serving at New Dawn. I cannot remember ever having a more gratifying experience.' "[90] By the early 1990s, New Dawn had expanded to two camps.

Jim Smith recalled that, for the regular camps, the camping committee felt that "two different styles of camping were creating too much tension and differences, and so they began to try to figure out a way to reconcile the two and put them together:"[91] But the issue could not easily be resolved. Smith and other supporters of the Inner-Life Camp wanted an evangelical emphasis. The others were reluctant to allow it. "We never did put the two camps together," Smith said.

Instead, in 1974, the Camping Committee, in an effort promote the separate camps on an equal basis, insisted that the camps be named "Youth Camp Number One" and "Youth Camp Number Two." That year, Camp Number One was the more traditional camp, and Number Two was the one with evangelical emphasis.[92] The following year, the numbers were reversed, with the evangelical camp being Number One.[93] The change was inspirational: Smith recalled that it was an easy move from "Camp Number One" to a new name: " [Hugh Daniel] came along and said, 'Well, we are Youth Camp One, so let's just call it Youth Camp One Way.' " Smith concluded, "It wasn't a well thought-out intention; it was just something that happened."[94]

But the name stuck. The *Texas Methodist* described the camp slated for June 1975 as the "One Way conference-wide event." Youth Camp Number Two was named "Learning to Love" and was also promoted as being conference-wide.[95] In 1976, the One Way camp drew 360 campers, one of the largest in conference history.[96] Due to its success, at least one other conference imitated the One Way camp idea; the North Texas Conference began a camp with a similar theme but named it "Impact."[97]

Because of the success of the high school One Way camp, Smith said, in 1976 he asked that the conference start a One Way camp for elementary children. "The Conference Camping Committee (CCC) turned down our request," he recalled. ". . . They just said, 'you can't do it.' "[98] But Smith said that he noticed that there was no camp scheduled for the week of July 4 at Ceta Canyon, and he determined to take advantage of it. His church at Floydada joined with Lockney and Plainview in planning a Good News Camp for elementary children for the summer of 1977 and involved R. L. Kirk, Hugh Daniel, and Jim Terry.[99] "Word got out and others began to call . . . ," Smith recalled. "It was the largest elementary camp of the whole schedule, unannounced and unpublicized, but they had 160 elementary-aged children at that camp."[100]

In 1976, the One Way Camp at Ceta Canyon reported an attendance of more than 400. Its popularity caused its leaders in October 1977 to seek to establish a second One Way camp at Ceta Canyon as well as one for Butman. They also asked that they be given the opportunity to participate in planning and directing junior high and elementary camps.[101] As a result, the Conference Camping Committee reorganized all the camps and included the One Way elementary camp in its schedule. Of the fifteen camps scheduled for 1978, seven were One Way camps of all age levels.[102]The One Way Camp at Butman in 1978 attracted only 135, but the *Texas Methodist* reported that "several experienced campers called [it] the best 'One Way' ever."[103] The Ceta Canyon One Way camps for 1978 were well attended.

After the summer camping season of 1978, a new tension descended on the conference. Apparently the success of the One Way camps created some concern among the traditional camp leaders. In addition, the Camping Committee was getting requests for a number of diverse camps, including music and nature. And as the number of camps expanded, programming was becoming more difficult. At the same time, the committee recognized that coordination and control of the camping program was slipping out of its hands. Even though it was charged with being responsible for conference camps, the committee realized that nearly half were primarily virtually independent, and thus it appealed to the bishop for some resolution. Specifically, the committee wanted clarification of its supposed "umbrella" authority over all the camps and a way "to bring about a healing and reconciling attitude in the camping program of our conference."[104]

Bishop Carleton then called a joint meeting with his Cabinet, the Executive Committee of the Conference Council on Ministries, the CCC, and "invited representatives of the 'One Way Camp.' " Thirty-five participated in the discussion on November 10, 1978, and all issues and concerns were laid on the table. The dispute clearly focused on the expansion and success of the One Way camps. As discussion progressed, the initial proposals offered all called for camps that included the different "styles," with co-deans, one from each "side."[105] But no consensus was reached that day.

The discussion continued the following day during the regular meeting of the CCC. Apparently, during the intervening hours, some on the committee must have hammered out the Great Camping Compromise of 1978. Rita Crowell, who was the associate director of the Council on Ministries, presented a two-fold plan: traditional and One Way camps would be offered at both sites, provided that scheduling and directors for each be cleared through the CCC, and all camps would become conference-wide. The old adage "If you can't lick 'em, join 'em," seemed to be an appropriate way to settle the dispute. The CCC concurred. The motion passed, and the program committee began immediate work on scheduling under the new plan. For the summer of 1979, the committee planned eighteen camps, eight of which were designated as One Way.[106]

For the first time, the Camping Committee's 1979 annual report to the conference mentioned the term "One Way." It noted that camp to be attended "by anyone in that age group, regardless of where the camp is located" and attempted to define the difference between it and "traditional" camping:

> [One Way] reflects a particular style of camping which emphasizes first-time commitments to Christ, Bible study, and personal witness, as well as Christian growth. Camps not so designated are our more traditional camps, which emphasize Christian growth, nurture and discipleship, as well as opportunity for first-time commitment. All of our camps are uniquely Christian, centering on the understanding of, love for, and commitment to God our Father, as revealed in the Son, Jesus Christ.[107]

"What's in a name?" The Butman dilemma

Although probably disturbing and stressful to some, the camping controversy had a two-fold impact on Northwest Texas: it sharply increased the number of campers, and it probably contributed to the saving and renewed development of Camp Butman. Although its setting among the cedar trees in Mulberry Canyon offered a respite from the surrounding plains, Camp Butman had no running streams, as did Ceta Canyon. As previously mentioned, from its founding in 1953, the Butman site struggled to attract funding and campers. For several years, the conference ran the camp at a deficit. In 1964, Butman got its own Conference Camp Committee, but the administrative change was not enough to recruit additional support.

Throughout the '60s and well into the '70s, Camp Butman ran a deficit, but according to Darris Egger, "The Council on Finance and Administration was long-suffering and patient."[108] Also, after 1964, when each camp had its own administrative committee, competition for conference funding increased; because Butman served a smaller area, it generally only received one-third of the funds, while Ceta Canyon got two-thirds.[109]

The situation had become serious, but some unusual circumstances over a two-year period helped rescue the camp. In 1977, as the Butman Advisory Committee discussed ways to make the camp more appealing, a member suggested changing its name to the "Mulberry Canyon Retreat Center." The motion passed and was sent on to the Conference Camping Committee and then on to the conference, where the change was passed without opposition in 1978.[110]

But there was one problem: no one had thought to consult with members of the Butman family, descendants of land donor Sam Butman. "Naturally, the Butman families were hurt and angered by the proposal," Egger noted, "and especially by the fact that they were never consulted."

> This [issue] united these Methodists of Mulberry Canyon as well as many others throughout the southern part of the Conference. Letters were written, telephone calls made. Resolutions were forthcoming, attorneys were consulted.[111]

Bishop Carleton tried to defuse the situation when he wrote a family member, explaining that the only intent was a "desire to strengthen, enlarge, and make more effective this camp site" and that he would inform the appropriate boards of the family's desire to put the name back on the camp. When an attorney representing members of the Butman family questioned whether the change "may have been a reflection on the nature of the family," conference officials quickly took note and began to look for a resolution in earnest.

In September 1978, Pioneer Memorial Church in Mulberry Canyon provided them with one by passing a resolution calling on the Conference to make the name "Butman Methodist Camp," as it had always been intended to be. A few weeks later, the Conference Camping Committee approved a similar resolution unanimously; in May 1979, the Conference concurred and the name was restored.[112]

However, the Butman crisis was not over. In February 1979, in the midst of the name change discussion, the Cabinet and Conference Council staff voted 10–2 to recommend the sale of Butman because the camp had historically run a deficit. A month later, the Camping Committee met to consider the recommendation and found a room full of Butman supporters. Egger was a member of the Camping Committee and an eyewitness to the meeting: "Carloads of people arrived to attend," he wrote. "One plane was chartered in Sweetwater to carry interested and concerned people to the Lubbock meeting. Tension was not only in the air, you could feel it in every conversation."[113]

Butman's supporters carried the day with the committee, which declined to approve the Cabinet and staff recommendation to sell the camp. Instead, the committee proposed a major new study of the conference's camping program and, as previously mentioned, restructured the schedule to allow for both traditional and One Way camps.[114]

At its 1979 session, the conference accepted the Camping Committee's report and appointed a review study committee. Meanwhile, another wrinkle in the Butman saga popped up in the summer of 1979 before the study committee could meet. Egger, the Abilene District superintendent, learned in August that conference program director Marvin James had held "informal discussions" with the executive committee of McMurry College's board of trustees. James had proposed giving

Butman Camp to McMurry. Egger, who had served as the conference program director from 1975 to 1978 and who had helped orchestrate opposition to the name change, fired off a rather sharp letter to James, noting that the new study committee had not met and that "no one is in a position to begin informal discussion about Butman Camp."[115] Apparently James took Egger's letter to heart and must have decided to let the study committee deal with the Butman issue.

Armistice

The "One Way" camp and name change issues brought attention to the need for improved camping facilities, especially at Butman. Moreover, the issues forced the conference to take a hard look at camping's successes and failures. After the 1979 annual conference, study committees were appointed to review every aspect of both camps. The review began in the fall of 1979, and the resulting report clearly indicates that extensive discussion and planning were involved. In February 1980, the special Conference Camping Study Committee presented its report to the Conference Camping Commission and the Council on Ministries. Interestingly, the report avoided the evangelical-vs.-traditional controversy of the '70s. Also, it made no mention of a possible sale of Butman. Instead, it focused on organizational structure and needed improvements at the two camps.[116]

The report vested programming and policy control of both camps in the Conference Camping Commission, but it also created separate boards of trustees for each camp that had maintenance and budgetary responsibility. The report also set the apportionment division at two-thirds for Ceta Canyon and one-third for Butman[117] In May 1980, the goals and recommendations of the special study committee were presented in a slide presentation at the annual conference. After questions were asked from the floor, the report was adopted.[118] Thus, after ten years of contention, a new era for conference camping was ready to begin, and the period of what one pastor termed "dysfunctional tension" seemed to be drawing to a close.[119]

Although there was still some contention over scheduling, the camping issues did begin to settle. The *Texas Methodist* reported that camps attracted 2,000 for the summer of 1981. The One Way elementary camp alone attracted 400.[120] The paper reported that the season was "a huge success" and gave much credit to the hard work of the Camping Commission.[121] Its chair, Albert Lindley, had served for eight difficult years and was probably very glad to pass the gavel to his successor, Eddie Allsup. Among other things, Rev. Allsup began encouraging churches to have "Camp Promotion Sunday."[122]

In his 1982 report to the conference, Allsup noted that the new administrative structure for camping was going through "some growing pains" but that everything pointed to the development of a "healthy and mature" program. And he noted that the dual camping system that provided for evangelical (One Way) and traditional camps "seek to express the theological diversity in our annual conference, while at the same time affirm the United Methodist principle of theological pluralism."[123]

By 1984, both the evangelical and traditional camps had evolved to what in essence became a permanent program. That year, the Camping Commission offered a total of thirteen One Way and traditional camps for elementary, junior high, and senior high at Butman and Ceta Canyon. Of those camps, seven were classified as One Way, five as traditional, and one as creative arts for elementary.[124] Promoters of the evangelical and traditional camps each had an opportunity to define their programs in a June 1984 issue of the *United Methodist Reporter.* The director of the One Way Senior High Camp, Michael O'Connor, said that "we seek to challenge the camper to come and discover the meaning of discipleship, calling the camper to be a student, a follower with Jesus as teacher and leader." Lynn Moore, director of the traditional camp, said the experience there would be "to discover life as God intended it; to embrace our Lord as He desires; to care for people around [us] as Jesus did; to love, laugh, and really live."[125]

In a larger sense, the controversy and its ultimate solution of camps for dual and diverse theology served as a microcosm of what would take place in the conference as a whole during the remainder of the twentieth century. The traditional camps would become more evangelical as the conference would become more evangelical. The controversy produced many benefits, and in the end (in Eddie Allsup's words), the Northwest Texas Conference would ultimately have "one of the best camping programs in the general church."[126]

Northwest Texas Conference evangelist and noted artist Kenneth Wyatt presented the Conference in 1984 a copy of his painting, "Offer Them Christ," which depicts John Wesley giving those instructions to Thomas Coke as he and others departed for America in 1784. Photo courtesy of the Foundation for Evangelism. Used by permission.

A bright future?

Meanwhile, positive things were happening in other aspects of the conference's work. Giving was at an all-time high. In 1977, perhaps recognizing the financial opportunity that a prosperous church offered, Bishop Carleton challenged both the Northwest Texas and New Mexico conferences to raise $2 million to build a new campus center at McMurry, and they responded positively[127] Carleton was "untiring" in his efforts to raise funds for the building, and his work was rewarded when the college dedicated the new facility in December 1979 and named a chapel in the building for him and his wife, Artha. The new structure also provided "a snack bar, meeting rooms, bookstore, game room, faculty lounge, and offices for religious life and campus center staff."[128]

In 1980, Louis Schowengerdt was elected as a bishop and was appointed to the Northwest Texas-New Mexico Area, a post he would hold for twelve years. He was a rare commodity in that he became a bishop while serving as a conference council director rather than as a pastor of a large church. A product of Missouri, Schowengerdt personified the "Show Me State": he told a reporter after his election that his idea of supervision was to "identify the restraining and enabling forces, and go with the enabling forces."[129]

By the early 1980s, with the spiritual, student, theological, and camping wars having run their course, the conference seemed to be settling into a new era of cooperation. Also by 1982, the tide of fifteen years of continual membership loss seemingly had turned. In that year, membership decline had lessened to only 352, and professions of faith, baptisms, and Sunday School and church attendance all increased over the previous year.[130] One of the largest gains was posted by the new Korean church in Lubbock, an encouraging sign for a conference that had few minority members. In addition, Lubbock's new LakeRidge church grew by nearly 33 percent.[131]

The year 1984 was special: for the first time, Lubbock hosted the quadrennial meeting of the South Central Jurisdiction—the regional association of what was then seventeen annual conferences in eight states—whose primary purpose is to elect new bishops. Attending the three-day meeting that July were 364 delegates.[132] Also, the Northwest Texas Conference joined with others in celebrating the bicentennial of Methodism that year.[133]

The celebration was also a time of reflection, and studies revealed the continuing shift from rural to urban and from small to large. By 1984, 40 percent of the national denomination's membership belonged to 1,411 churches that had 1,000 or more members. Twenty-two churches had 4,000 or more members, with eighteen of these located in Oklahoma, Louisiana, and Texas. Yet Methodism was still the domain of the small church. 60 percent of the membership belonged to 36,670 churches, most of which had less than 300 members.[134]

In the Northwest Texas Conference, membership was slightly more balanced—approximately 35 percent of its 88,000 members belonged to the seventeen churches of 1,000-plus membership. However, more than 6 percent of the entire conference belonged to one church: First, Lubbock, with its 5,722 members.[135]

In 1984, the conference also held its 75th annual conference. In spite of membership losses, it was still a strong conference, with 199 pastoral charges and 243 churches.[136] Bishop Schowengerdt, who was in his fourth year as the presiding officer, gave his assessment of the recently held General Conference, declaring that its delegates "were independent in their thinking and refused to be swayed by oratory from ultraliberal or other pressure groups": "The winds of change are blowing in the United Methodist Church, and the denomination is moving toward a middle of the road position."[137] Impressed by the audience's enthusiastic response to the bishop's remarks, a reporter for the *United Methodist Reporter* observed that "leaders . . . in the Northwest Texas Conference are ready for the challenge to move toward a strong and unified church and to unite in a strong and dedicated return to the Wesleyan tradition to 'Offer them Christ.'"[138] But unbeknown to Schowengerdt, the "winds of change" would become a gale within the denomination before the century's end.

Chapter 9

"And still He doth His help afford"

The last fifteen years of the 20th twentieth century were the most difficult for the Northwest Texas Conference since the Depression. However, the problem was not economic hardship but internal dissent. Theological and political differences, coupled with a continuing decline in membership, created an uncomfortable environment that permeated local congregations and annual sessions. The "good old days"—those robust years of growth during the first half of the conference's history—had become a faint memory.

During its first fifty years, from 1910 to 1960, the Northwest Texas Conference founded nearly 200 new churches and tripled in membership as it rode the wave of the region's agrarian settlement. From 1960 to 1985, it founded only thirteen churches, closed seventy, and lost nearly 19,000 members—18 percent—at a time when the region was rapidly shifting from a rural to an urban environment. The conference obviously needed to change its approach, but what was it to be? One solution was to renew efforts in two areas: evangelism, and Sunday School.

A call for evangelism

In the early 1980s, in an effort to stem its steady membership loss, the conference buzz words had become once again "evangelism," "Sunday School," and "establish new churches." In November 1982, the Texas bishops hosted a statewide convocation on evangelism in an effort to rekindle a Methodist zeal for the lost. In March 1983, the conference held its own "Congress on Evangelism," with Charles Allen as the featured preacher. The event attracted "a full house" to Lubbock's First Church.[1] According to the district superintendents' report to Annual Conference later that year, the effort "sparked a renewed interest in our primary priority, evangelism .... We feel we are on our way to reversing our membership losses .... We are beginning to be in earnest about evangelism."[2]

Because conference Sunday School attendance had dropped 36 percent in the 1970s, the Council on Ministries made its growth one of its priorities in 1982, and some churches began using literature that was more "biblically based" than previous lessons. There was an immediate response, as average Sunday School attendance for 1982 rose by 222.[3] But the gain was short-lived, as attendance dropped in 1984.

Douglas Wofford, who in 1982 had replaced Marvin James as conference council director, was exasperated with the situation when he reported in his column in the *United Methodist Reporter* in October 1983 that, in spite of a two-year emphasis on evangelism, the conference lost an additional 428 members. "Our actual gain or loss seems to be affected by Charge Conference action ...." he noted. "We spend as much time removing people from our rolls as we do bringing people into the fellowship of the church."[4] However, the traditional practice of charge conference removal at least provided a more realistic reflection of church membership and discipleship. Some denominations never remove a name from their church rolls.

By the mid-1980s, church leaders had to face a hard reality: the United Methodist Church was literally dying, and membership decline was accelerating. Between 1968 and 1983, national membership fell by 1.6 million as 1.9 million Methodists died.[5] Undoubtedly, the trend was the same in Northwest Texas; rural churches were closing primarily because members had died or moved away. On average, the conference was losing more than 1,000 members each year to death alone.[6]

The General Conference's response was a call for 1,000 new churches to be established from 1985 to 1988 in a program called "Church Alive." One writer, Thom Gallen, noted an appropriate formula for new church growth, calling for more emphasis on churches in minority communities: "If we are serious," he wrote, "we need to look for rental space, store fronts, homes, abandoned churches or buildings. Much of the growth of the fundamentalist churches . . . has come about in the abandoned churches of mainline denominations." He also noted that "elitism," the continued movement away from the poor and working class, "threatens the denomination's historic pluralism. We need to develop and renew churches in all community settings."[7]

The Northwest Texas response to this call was to continue its emphasis on evangelism and Sunday School growth and to make an effort to start new churches. The latter was a practice almost forgotten: from 1964 until 1979, when LakeRidge in Lubbock was established, the conference had founded no new churches except for Christ Church in Levelland, a merger of two older churches. In an effort to rekindle new church starts, the conference resurrected an old idea: the "Builder's Club," which had been formed in 1961 to raise money to assist start-up churches. The new effort was named "The Society of Phillip," and in 1983 it set a goal to start four new churches in four years and raise $400,000.[8]

A few new churches

LakeRidge's rapid growth gave some hope for a turnaround. When it moved into its new 375-seat sanctuary in 1981, 460 attended the first service, and the church grew rapidly.[9] Other new churches included Lubbock Korean (1981), Plainview San Juan (1981), Borger St. Andrew (a 1982 merger of Phillips and Bunavista), Lubbock Aldersgate (1985, formerly East Broadway) and Amarillo Christ (1985)—the first new church in Amarillo in twenty-three years.[10]

Two new churches in the Midland area rounded out growth for the 1980s. In the little community of Greenwood, near Midland, laypeople, with the assistance of St. Mark's pastor Jack Riley and Big Spring District Superintendent Rex Mauldin, started first a Sunday School and then a church—a sequence reminiscent of pioneer days. The new Greenwood church was established in November 1986.[11] Three years later, Bethel Church in Midland was opened as well.

However, the new churches did little to stem the tide of loss. Membership and Sunday School enrollment and attendance all declined by 1 to 2 percent per year in the late 1980s. In 1986, Bishop Schowengerdt noted that perhaps Methodists had learned a lesson too late to stop the loss. "Statistics show that, prior to 1940, nearly every Methodist Sunday School had more in attendance at class sessions than were staying for morning worship," he wrote. "Since then, we have concentrated on morning worship with the subsequent neglect of the Sunday School, particularly for adults."[12] A statewide Sunday School rally in 1987 in Houston, attended by forty-nine from Northwest Texas, could not stem the loss.[13]

"Heal the wound that will not heal"

Northwest Texas was not alone in dealing with losses. Only fifteen of seventy-three Methodist annual conferences reported gains in 1986; losses were greatest in the Northeast and Midwest. Texas growth was at a standstill.[14] In 1987, the denomination also experienced a number of negative state and national reports, including an athletic scandal at Southern Methodist University that resulted in the NCAA imposing its "death penalty" on SMU's the football program. A prominent Dallas pastor was forced to surrender his credentials after admitting to an affair with the daughter of a deceased bishop; a retired bishop died from AIDS; and a female pastor in Maine was forced to resign after admitting a lesbian relationship.[15]

Fortunately, the Northwest Texas Conference escaped sensational public scandals and was pronounced "in good health" in 1989 by an outside consultant: Dr. Robert Schaller, author of the book *Creative Leadership.* He told conference leaders: "Comparatively, you're in better health than the whole church is. We have some conferences . . . in crisis situations—you're not." But he also pointed out that "you are clearly aging and shrinking . . . . Persons born in 1910–1930 are the most loyal to a denomination than any generation in American history. When this generation dies off, we'll have problems." That situation, he said, combined with the lack of recruiting younger members, accounted in part for the numerical decline.[16]

Bishop Lewis Schowengerdt. Photo from *Northwest Texas Conference Journal,* 1981.

Schaller made some interesting predictions, many of which would become true in the near future. He said that retirement benefits for clergy would dominate the church's agenda, and he also noted the possibility that United Methodism would become primarily a Southern denomination by 2020 if rapid declines in other parts of the nation continued. He also said that, to grow, the church needed to reach young adults, and the way to do that is through larger churches that can offer more programming, noting the emergence of the megachurch movement in America.[17]

Bishop Schowengerdt, who in 1988 had been appointed to a third term to the Northwest Texas-New Mexico Area, apparently did not agree with Schaller's assessment of the conference's health. At the 1990 annual conference, Schowengerdt noted the losses of 1964–89, which included 33 and 53 percent losses in worship and Sunday School attendance respectively, and gave one of the most passionate appeals ever made from the conference pulpit, "to heal the wound that will not heal":

> We are living in a time when many persons are lost through drugs, self-centered materialism, sexual abuses, racism, poverty, and despair. Some call this the "cut flower generation," out to have a blooming good time and they don't care what happens next. . . . [The present society] wants to go to church to feel good . . . . I would like to charge . . . this conference to change the image from Christians who want chocolate-covered communion wafers and Jacuzzi Christianity to Christians who know what it means to be at the cross of Jesus.[18]

He also chided Methodism's propensity for over-organization. "We spend all our energy and all our time talking to ourselves," he said. "Pastors tell me that 95 percent of their time is spent on church organization." Indeed, as membership levels declined, the conference consistently tried about every nine or ten years to re-invent its organizational programs, and Schowengerdt's tenure was no exception. In 1981, the Administrative Council structure was abolished and replaced with a reorganized Conference Council on Ministries, along with numerous other changes.[19]

But somewhere in the changes, the mission of the local church got lost, and by the end of the decade, the bishop called for another restructuring to focus "on making local congregations more vital."[20] In 1990, the conference adopted a new organizational plan that created a "Conference Ministry Team" at both the conference and district levels.[21] According to a report in the *United Methodist Reporter,* the new structure would provide "impetus for district and conference programming [to] come from grassroots United Methodists."[22]

At the same time, the conference voted to reduce its districts from seven to six; this time, the historic Seymour District was the casualty. Its churches were divided among the Abilene, Plainview, and Pampa districts.[23] Before it dissolved, the district's pastors and laity compiled a thorough history of the district and its current and closed churches and placed it in the archives of the Northwest Texas Conference at McMurry.

Another significant change took place in the council office. Rex Mauldin, who had succeeded Douglas Wofford in 1987 as conference council director, served until June 1991, when the bishop appointed Mauldin to the Lubbock District superintendent's position. The bishop and Cabinet made a bold move in replacing him: they selected Louise Schock, who had been the associate council director for three years.[24] A diaconal minister and certified Christian educator, Louise became the first woman, as well as the first layperson, to serve as council director for Northwest Texas, even though she had only been in the conference for three years. She recalled how surprised she was when she was asked to meet with the bishop and Cabinet:

> I thought they were going to tell me who was going to be the new council director . . . . When I got there, [Bishop Schowengerdt] said, "We want you to do it." I said, "Bishop, I can't do it. I am a lay [person]." We had something in our conference bylaws that said [the council director] had to be an ordained person. But the Bishop said, "*The Discipline* says it can be clergy or lay, and *The Discipline* supersedes the conference bylaws.[25]

A new role for women

Schock was the first female conference director in the regular conferences of the South Central Jurisdiction, and one of the first in the nation. Her dramatic 1991 promotion gave women a much larger presence in conference administration—a change that had been long in coming. Nearly fifty years before, the Lubbock District Conference in 1945 had licensed Lillie Hester as a local minister, the first in Northwest Texas and perhaps in the state.[26] In spite of this exceptional action, even though the General Conference had approved the full ordination of female clergy in 1956, conservative Northwest Texas was very slow to embrace the concept. Instead, it reluctantly embraced "deaconesses," a long-accepted title that allowed a woman to serve in the church but without full clergy rights. In 1960, three deaconesses were serving in Northwest Texas: Rachel Divers, Helen Reeves, and Barbara Sommerville.[27]

In 1962, the conference, without any fanfare, ordained its first woman as a local elder: Viola Nethery Apple.[28] Appointed as an associate to her husband on the Spur Circuit, Rev. Apple apparently served the conference only one year as an associate but was listed as a non-appointed supply pastor for two years. Her name does not appear in any records after 1964.[29]

In 1978, twenty-two years after the General Conference's decision to allow the ordination of women, Northwest Texas, also without fanfare, ordained its first women as elders in full connection who became full-time pastors: Hazel House and Sammie Ellis Teeter. Perhaps the conference thought that no one would take notice that two of the candidates had longer hair than the other eight—all men. But Tom Nagle

Rev. Sammie Ellis. Photo from Northwest Texas Conference Office, courtesy Rosemary Prumer and Rev. Ava Berry.

did, and he reported the historic event in the *Texas Methodist*. "It almost went unnoticed . . ." he wrote. "Few people realized that there was, within this peaceful and seemingly routine annual conference, a history-making moment. The fact that two women were among the group waiting to be ordained . . . did not seem to cause any stir."[30]

But female preachers had caused a stir in the conference. Jordan Grooms, when he was the Brownfield District superintendent, told of his first appointment of Hazel House as a local pastor in the late 1960s to the church at Bula. Soon afterward, he said, five men in the church drove to Brownfield to meet with him and told him that having a female preacher would "finish off the church" and would undo their hard work to keep the church open. Grooms, perhaps one of the most genteel district superintendents to have served the conference, told the men that their pastor "loved the Lord and would do a good job," and he refused to make a change. He encouraged them to give her a chance.

Six weeks later, Grooms made a call on the little church on Sunday morning, and word of his arrival must have preceded him. "These same five men met me outside," he said. "They told me, 'Don't you dare move her!' I said to them, 'Well, you sure have changed your tune.' One said to me, 'Well, even old men can change!'"[31] When the next district superintendent, Weldon Butler, moved House to a new appointment five years later, he said he "got some rather angry calls" from the men at Bula and that "one man had said that he was going to whip me for moving her."[32]

In addition to Bula, House pastored at Estelline, Enochs, Amherst, Colorado City, Andrews, and Sundown/Whiteface. After her death in 1991, a member of the Bula Church wrote about her pastorate there: "We were mostly unhappy at first with the appointment of a woman pastor, but we all cried when she left . . . because she was just what we needed."[33]

Rev. Hazel House. Photo from Northwest Texas Conference Office, courtesy Rosemary Prumer and Rev. Ava Berry.

Even before the first full ordination of women in Northwest Texas in 1978, a few women had already been serving as local lay pastors, mostly in rural churches. Ruth Cooper may have been the first; in 1959, she began a three-year pastorate at White Flat-Flomot and also served at Three Way (1962–65), Lubbock Forrest Heights (associate, 1965–69), and Nolan (1975–80).[34] Others who began pastoral ministries before 1978 include House (1967), Fay Brown (1972), Alvareta Griffin (1977), Sammie Ellis (1977), and Jo Carr (1977).

Carr also became the first woman to be appointed as a district superintendent, serving the Pampa District from 1989 until 1993.[35] She was Northwest Texas' first female clergy delegate to the General Conference, elected in 1991.[36] She brought a wealth of missionary and intellectual experience to the ministry but experienced some difficulty in being accepted as a pastor. However, she was quick to note: "There was so much more welcome than difficulty. . . . In the first church I served [as pastor], the chairman of the board resigned; in the second church, the finance secretary resigned! But the people were so welcoming. After the first two or three Sundays, when they realized we were eating out of the same lunchbox, reading the same gospels, [they were] just very welcoming."[37]

Rev. Ava Burdine Berry had a similar experience of reluctant acceptance. At her first appointment at Throckmorton-Elbert in 1996, one family left the church, but thanks in part to a show of support from a fellow pastor, the community quickly accepted her:

> Moving day, I received the most wonderful show of support that the whole community could see. The Baptist pastor was the first person at the truck to help us unload. Brother Cliff became a good friend. From the beginning his actions said to the community, this clergyperson is my equal and peer and friend in ministry in this town. I shall never forget his act of grace.[38]

Unfortunately, other Northwest Texas churches refused to accept women as pastors. In 1999, the bishop wanted to appoint Berry to a Panhandle church, but the congregation absolutely refused to accept a woman. At the same time, another female pastor in the Abilene District was denied an appointment. However, some churches were accepting. Berry was appointed in 2000 to Clyde, where the departing pastor was Rev. Dixie Robertson. It marked the first time in Northwest Texas that one clergywoman followed another at a single church.[39]

Open Hearts, Open Doors, Open Minds?

By far the most divisive issue in the United Methodist Church in recent years has been the church's relationship to homosexuals. On the national level, the question of gays in the church surfaced in 1972 when the Social Principles Study Commission, after a four-year study, recommended language for the *Book of Discipline* that affirmed homosexuals "as persons of sacred worth" and that said Methodists should "welcome them into the fellowship of the church."[40] The final statement said that "all persons are entitled to have their human and civil rights ensured, although we do not condone the practice of homosexuality and consider this practice incompatible with Christian teaching."[41]

A large majority of Northwest Texas Methodists agreed with the stand. A 1971 survey by the *Texas Methodist* indicated that 85 percent of the respondents believed homosexuality to be abnormal and not acceptable, and 45 percent said that one could not be both a Christian and homosexual.[42] In 1982, the Amherst church, upset because a Methodist bishop had ordained a known homosexual, introduced a resolution at the annual conference expressing opposition to the ordination and asked the conference to go on record as viewing "homosexuality as a sin and contrary to the will of God.[43] Although the motion's language and content were debated, the resolution passed. The vote was not recorded in the *Journal*.[44] However, liberal conference leaders introduced another resolution affirming that "all persons are sacred in the sight of God and should be ministered to by the Church so that reconciliation and redemption may occur regardless of race, color, creed or sexual identity." This resolution also passed.[45]

The 1984 General Conference had heated debates about new language for the *Discipline*, but it passed legislation that denied ordination or appointment to "self-avowed practicing homosexuals" and also prohibited the giving of church funds for gay causes.[46] The issue rose again at the 1988 General Conference. This time, it created a committee to study homosexuality, which recommended to the 1992 conference a more moderate stand, including "their rightful claims to same-sex relationships."[47] The report was highly controversial and virtually polarized the denomination, setting the stage for a stormy General Conference in 1992. The conference delegates voted to "receive" the report but did not make any significant changes in the church's stand on homosexuality.[48]

The debate served to further divide the Northwest Texas Conference along liberal and evangelical lines. The issue had become a major cause for evangelicals, helping them to gain more prominence in the 1970s.[49] The board of the Good News movement called for "a positive, Biblical ministry under the spirit of Christ to liberate the homosexual from his enslaving sin."[50] Within the Northwest Texas Conference, in at least one instance, the bishop had to move a minister from one church to another due to the pastor's support of the gay issue, and it became more and more difficult to match pastors with churches.

A few other issues also demanded Northwest Texas Conference attention in the '80s and early '90s, and it went on record as opposing abortion on demand, the construction of nuclear waste deposit sites in the Panhandle, a statewide lottery, and pari-mutuel gambling.[51] One of the closest votes came in 1989, when the conference narrowly defeated a resolution that called for the General Conference to modify the *Discipline* in order "to more explicitly secure the rights of the unborn."[52] The vote reflected the conference's continued movement toward a more conservative makeup.

One bright spot in the 1980s was Bishop Schowengerdt's appointment of Faye and W. L. Armstrong Jr. to the mission field to serve in Indonesia. Their service was supported entirely by the Northwest Texas Conference.[53] Faye taught at a Methodist seminary, and her husband taught people how to make bricks with which to build their own churches.[54] This was a second time of service for the Armstrongs in the Far East.

The Asbury triumph

The Methodist doctrine of pluralism provides for theological diversity within the church. But within Northwest Texas, that provision further divided its clergy, especially as the region—and the nation—continued to move to the right in the 1980s and '90s. By the mid-1980s, the majority of ministerial students sponsored by Northwest Texas (where for many years the pastors had been trained in Methodist seminaries) were attending the conservative evangelical independent Asbury Seminary—perhaps encouraged in part by "supplemental" scholarship money being provided over and above the conference allotment by individuals interested in strengthening the conference's evangelical wing.[55] For example, in 1983, Asbury had seventeen conference students, nine were at Perkins, and four were at St. Paul's. As the conference continued to decline in membership, its student enrollment also declined. Yet the Asbury margin held—of the six students enrolled in 1992, four were at Asbury and two at Perkins.[56]

The effort of conference evangelicals to train students began to pay dividends in the 1980s and afterward as the students returned to Northwest Texas. Unfortunately, because of the polarization of conference preachers along evangelical and traditional lines, returning students found themselves being labeled even before they had a chance to prove their worth or theology. One returning student said he left the conference after being denied a position because he was not "evangelical." Still another chose not to return to the conference after receiving his education because he knew he would have to be an evangelical to advance, and he knew he could not align with that side.[57]

Yet by the mid-1990s, a student's seminary choice was no longer an issue in the conference, partly because there were so few students. Only two were appointed to attend school in 1995, both to Perkins. In 1996, the conference had seven attending seminary: two each at Perkins and Asbury, and three at three other seminaries.[58]

Delegate wars: Round 2

The political labeling within the conference became most apparent in the '80s as both sides in effect formed caucuses to advance their cause, especially for the elections of delegates to general and jurisdictional conferences every four years. In 1979, considerable pre-conference posturing occurred as some pastors tried to block certain individuals from being elected. As a result, seventeen ballots were required to elect delegates to general and jurisdictional conferences. The vote made the division in the conference apparent but also indicated that the traditional and more liberal side was strong. The moderate Charles Lutrick, known as "Mr. Methodist" for his long service to the national church and his encyclopedic knowledge of the *Discipline,* was chosen on the first ballot, and liberal leader Ted Dotts on the second. Moderate Clifford Trotter was picked on the fourth. R. L. Kirk, from the evangelical side, was chosen on the sixth ballot as the fourth delegate for the General Conference. Most of the other delegates and alternates for jurisdictional conference were moderates.[59]

The 1983 elections for the 1984 conferences followed a similar pattern, with Charles Lutrick being elected first, followed this time by evangelical Charles Whittle. Dotts, along with moderate Ira Williams, rounded out the selections for the General Conference. For the jurisdictional event, evangelicals Kirk and Rex Mauldin, were chosen along with a slate of moderate leaders: Bruce Parks, Clifford Trotter, and David Hamblin. The two alternates were moderate Sam Nader and evangelical Jim Smith.[60]

By 1987, the evangelicals showed an even greater strength. On the first ballot cast for General Conference delegates, the top three vote-getters were Whittle (eighty-five votes), Lutrick (eighty-one), and Kirk (seventy-eight), followed by Trotter (sixty) and Smith (fifty-eight). Dotts, the conference's longtime liberal leader, received fifty votes.[61] The top four vote-getters were subsequently elected in succeeding ballots for the General Conference, and Smith, along with fellow evangelicals Tom Fuller and Thomas Thompson, were chosen as jurisdictional delegates. Parks and Dotts also were elected, along with Keith Wiseman and Mauldin as alternates.[62]

About the time that the evangelicals thought that they had won the delegate wars, the liberal side trumped them in 1991's election with the choice of a woman. Jo Carr, who was serving as the Pampa District superintendent, was elected on the first ballot. Others elected that year were evangelicals Jim Jackson and Kirk, along with liberal Bobby McMillan. All those elected to the Jurisdictional Conference were evangelicals.[63] Carr and McMillan's elections were quite a surprise, especially to Carr. "We had no plan, no nothing," she remembered, and indicated that she might have made a difference in the delegate wars "if I had stayed with it. [But] I [was not] politically oriented and I didn't give it what I should have afterwards, but then, I didn't know what that was."[64]

The twenty-year war ended in 1995. That year, with Smith elected first on the second ballot, almost the entire slate of General and Jurisdictional delegates represented the conference's conservative side.[65] However, in the elections of 1999 and 2003, a more balanced slate was elected. Pastors of several larger churches were chosen: the moderate Lane Boyd and evangelicals Bill Couch and Smith were elected as delegates or alternates to the General Conference in those years, and moderate Richard Edwards was elected an alternate in 1999. After 2003, because of the conference's loss of membership, Northwest Texas was allotted only two clergy delegates. By 2007, the arduous and divisive struggle had moderated (see Chapter 10); Lubbock District Superintendent Jimmy Nunn, a moderate evangelical, was chosen on the second ballot, with Amarillo Polk Street pastor Lane Boyd, a moderate, on the seventh. The alternates were an evangelical and a moderate.[66]

A new bishop in the midst of the storm

In 1992, in the midst of the delegate wars and political posturing, the Northwest Texas Conference got a new bishop. Louis Schowengerdt retired after twelve (probably long) years of his exclusive service to the Northwest Texas-New Mexico Area. Weldon Butler, who served on the

Cabinet under the previous bishop, Alsie Carleton, found working with Schowengerdt more challenging and described his appointment process as "divisive":

> Bishop Carleton was the very picture of punctuality and business, but Bishop Schowengerdt was fairly slow and deliberate and walked at a more leisurely pace. In appointment making, Bishop Carleton started at the very top and worked down to the smallest church. Bishop Schowengerdt skipped around and I was uneasy with this procedure for fear that the Cabinet would leave somebody out . . . and some people would be hurt because of this process. Also, Bishop Carleton insisted that the Cabinet work as a team and be responsible for all the appointments . . . [and] sought to eliminate competition between superintendents, while Bishop Schowengerdt thought that competition was good.[67]

Another member of the Bishop's Cabinet, Rex Mauldin, recalled that Schowengerdt "took the appointive process very seriously": the bishop "considered himself to be the CEO of a large Church and his task was to make sure the right pastor went to the right church," Mauldin remembered. "In order to accomplish this task he took us to Albuquerque and had the Cabinet meet with the human resource officials . . . of New Mexico Power and Light. He [also] tried to give corporate leadership in every area and insisted on being the chair of every important committee."[68] If there was any doubt about Schowengerdt's institutional Methodism, it was put to rest when he addressed the Northwest Texas Conference for the first time in 1981 and told the delegates that "there was a great deal of energy . . . being used to try to save the local churches, but not enough energy . . . given to save the world," and he affirmed his belief in "connectional churches."[69]

To replace Schowengerdt, the church named another "freshman" bishop, Alfred L. Norris, to serve the Northwest Texas-New Mexico Area. Already distinguished because he was only the second bishop in the history of the South Central Jurisdiction to be elected on the first ballot, Norris brought a whole new set of credentials to the Conference.

The Bishop's Cabinet in 1998 probably had to withstand the "the slings and arrows of outrageous fortune" as a result of the stormy 1998 Annual Conference: (L to R) Kenneth T. Metzger, Louise K. Schock, Earl N. Blair, Bishop Alfred L. Norris, Henry Salley, W. Vernon O'Kelly, C. Edward Allsup, and Lynn D. Moore. Photo from 1998 *Northwest Texas Conference Journal,* courtesy Pat Williamson.

A native of Louisiana, he had served as pastor of two of the largest African-American churches in the Louisiana Conference; he had served as a General Conference delegate four times; he had served as district superintendent; and prior to his election as a bishop, he had served as president of Atlanta's Gammon Theological Seminary from 1985 to 1992.[70] Rev. Jo Carr, leader of the Northwest Texas delegation to the Jurisdictional Conference, told the press what she saw in the new bishop: "I have already seen in him sincere warmth and openness," she said, "and know that he is also a man of deep faith and personal commitment, a proven administrator, and a great preacher.[71]

Norris's first word to the conference was "evangelism," and it must have pleased the evangelicals. His second word was "education," and that must have pleased the liberals. "Evangelism, Education, Equipment of the saints," he wrote in September 1992, "these three, but the greatest of these is—all three!"[72] Norris, with his broad experience in pastoring and administration, was probably the best choice to try to deal with the fractured Northwest Texas Conference.

Norris described the division as a "line of demarcation—on one side was the Perkins graduates, and on the other, the Asbury graduates," he recalled. "Sometimes it seemed that 'Never the twain shall meet.' They seldom agreed on much."[73] In an effort to bridge the chasm, Norris appointed Asbury graduate Lynn Moore, as the Big Spring District superintendent. "That was my attempt to say to the entire Conference, and particularly to the Asbury contingent that I don't have any problem where you went to school," he said. "I did it . . . to try to bring varying viewpoints to the Conference, and especially to the leadership table."[74]

Strong feelings

National events did little to help Norris find common ground. As a prelude to the 1992 General Conference, an extracurricular movement within Methodism was gaining support. A program known as Reconciling Ministries began in the early 1980s in an effort to develop "a program in which local churches will declare their support for the concerns of lesbians and gay men."[75] Before the 1992 General Conference, fifty churches in seventeen states and the District of Columbia had declared themselves to be Reconciling, along with four annual conferences.[76] In addition, the General Conference's Commission on Christian Unity and Inter-religious Concerns voted to be a Reconciling commission. This action prompted the Northwest Texas Conference in 1990 and 1991 to ask the General Conference to cut off funds to the commission, because, according to an Abilene pastor, the panel had "placed itself in the position of promoting homosexuality . . . and has lined itself up with a gay caucus."[77] In October 1991, the General Conference's Judicial Council ruled that it could find "no evidence" that Methodist funds were being used to promote homosexuality, and thus took no action to cut the commission's funding.[78] In 1992, the Judicial Council subsequently upheld the commission's right to allow gay and lesbian members.[79]

As previously mentioned, a study committee presented a report on homosexuality to the 1992 General Conference that presented a positive acceptance of homosexuality, but the conference voted only to "receive" the report and not to accept it. However, the General Conference modified the *Discipline* slightly, affirming that "all persons, regardless of age, gender, marital status or sexual orientation, are entitled to have their human and civil rights ensured."[80]

In 1996, a breach developed among the bishops when fifteen released an independent statement prior to the General Conference affirming their support of gay and lesbian inclusion, including the right to be ordained.[81] The stand polarized the General Conference; the motion to keep the *Discipline*'s language intact passed, but 40 percent of the delegates voted against it.[82] The conference also rejected a proposal to allow noncelibate homosexuals to be ministers and passed a ban prohibiting same-sex marriages by preachers.[83]

Norris soon found out how strongly Northwest Texas, especially the laity, felt about homosexuality. At the Breakfast with the Bishop event at the annual conference, laypeople were given the opportunity to ask the bishop questions. Norris remembered that the most frequently asked question had to do with homosexuality. He said that his "pat" answer was to support the *Discipline* and state that he stood "by the position of the Church."[84] He reiterated that position in an address to the 1996 annual conference. According to the 1996 *Journal*, "he made clear that the worship services celebrating sexual diversity, which are being held during Conference week, are not organized or sanctioned by the Conference or Agenda Committee."[85]

The church label wars

The national debate about homosexuality in the 1980s and '90s led to a new era in Methodism: the "labeling" of churches. As previously mentioned, the Reconciling Ministries movement of the 1980s called for churches to become "Reconciling," and it continued to gain momentum in the 1990s. Meanwhile, the "Transforming" movement emerged from the West in 1988, when a group in the California-Nevada Conference became concerned with both the "homophobic" attitudes and the new "accommodationist" group within Methodism; the group "sought instead a compassionate approach that would offer the hope of transformational healing to those struggling with unwanted same-sex attraction and behavior."[86] Soon churches were being asked to become "Transforming Congregations."[87]

Partly in response to the Reconciling and Transforming movements, as well as others in 1994, a group of evangelicals headed by the president of Asbury Theological Seminary called a meeting to "consult about the future of the United Methodist Church" and to "confront the crisis of faith within."[88] As a result, more than 800 Methodists met in Atlanta, Georgia, in 1995 and produced "A Confessional Statement" that called for (among other things) "all laity and all clergy to confess the person, work and reign of Jesus Christ."[89] The statement also included a list of specific concerns, such as "experimenting with pagan ritual and practice; consuming the world's goods without regard for the poor; accommodating the prevailing patterns of sexual promiscuity, serial marriage and divorce; resigning ourselves to the injustices of racial and gender prejudice; condoning homosexual practice; and ignoring the Church's long-standing protection of the unborn and the mother."[90] Thus, the Confessing movement was born, and its supporters called on churches to accept still another label.

Before the Northwest Texas Conference could take action on joining the Confessing movement, Nebraska minister Jimmy Creech sent shock waves through the denomination and nation in 1997 when he performed a "covenant ceremony" for two women—a seemingly clear violation of the General Conference's 1996 ban on gay marriages.[91] Creech's action immediately reignited the homosexuality debate in Methodism, especially after an initial trial failed to convict him of violating the *Discipline*.

In response, the national leader of the evangelical Good News organization, James Heidinger II, sent nearly 250,000 letters to Methodist laity and leaders asking the faithful to sign a petition calling on the bishops "to do whatever is necessary, including a call for a special session of General Conference, to stop the occurance [sic] of homosexual marriages within the UM Church." His organization also warned: "If this issue is not dealt with decisively, local churches may be forced to withhold certain apportionments in protest."[92] In his cover letter, Heidinger wrote, "From the non-stop telephone calls, faxes, and e-mails we have received, I can only conclude that our church is angry, demoralized, frustrated, and in a state of turmoil."[93]

Without a doubt, Heidinger's letter prompted churches to flood annual conferences nationwide with resolutions opposing gay marriages, and Northwest Texas was no exception. On the eve of the 1998 Northwest Texas annual conference, an ad hoc committee of four pastors circulated a letter to delegates promoting five resolutions on the gay marriage crisis. The language of two of the resolutions came directly from the national Confessing and Transforming movements. The "Confessing" resolution, "A Call for Doctrinal Integrity," represented the word-for-word the text of the Confessional Statement that came out of the

1995 Atlanta meeting, which called for a return to the fundamentals of the faith, a repudiation of homosexual practices, and a requirement that all new preachers agree to the resolution's affirmations.[94]

The "Transforming Conference" resolution was more moderate, calling on the conference to follow the rule of the *Discipline* to oppose the practice of homosexuality, while at the same time "to be in ministry to those persons who struggle with the reality" of it.[95] However, a third resolution—"A Response to the Theological Crisis in the United Methodist Church"—called on the church to make "preaching, teaching, or advocating the practice of homosexuality as a valid sexual expression and alternate life style . . . a chargeable offense" for conference clergy members.[96]

The committee also proposed two other resolutions. One was "A Call for Prayer in the Midst of Crisis"; the other, "A Resolution Toward Charity and Freedom in Ministries," was much more dramatic and potentially explosive. It called on the conference to implement a study to produce a plan "whereby those local congregations or ordained persons who no longer wish to remain in the United Methodist Church may be given a just and equitable way to withdraw."[97] The resolution specifically called for the "possible diversification of ministries including the 'birthing' of new entities for ministry with a just and equitable distribution of church properties, pensions, and any other shared church resources."[98] In other words, if enacted, a church, whether pro-gay or not, could possibly withdraw from the conference and the denomination.

By the time of the printing of the 1998 pre-conference *Journal*, five additional resolutions relating to gay marriage had been added to the agenda. One was especially disconcerting: it called on the conference "to design a plan for the withdrawal of the Northwest Texas Conference from The United Methodist Church, and to design a plan for the joining of an existing Methodist General Conference or the creation of a new Methodist General Conference with their foundations rooted in the authority of the Scriptures."[99]

Already on edge because of having to deal with the potential loss of Lubbock's Methodist Hospital, the 1998 annual conference promised to be the stormiest ever. Prior to debate on the many resolutions, Bishop

Norris and the Cabinet tried to defuse the gay issue by issuing a strong statement vowing to "hold all clergy accountable to the United Methodist *Discipline*," whose language strictly forbade same-sex marriage ceremonies.[100] Then Rev. Richard Edwards introduced a "Call to Harmony" resolution, which asked the conference not to vote on three of the more controversial resolutions. A heated debate ensued, and the delegates voted against the "Harmony" resolution, 283–162.[101]

The vote cleared the way for consideration of all the resolutions. First up was "A Call for Doctrinal Integrity." Norris ruled that a portion of the resolution was out of order. One pastor proposed deletion of another controversial statement, but his amendment was defeated. Just prior to the vote, Rev. Elizabeth Sisco rose to a point of order questioning whether the resolution was constitutional. Norris later ruled that it was because he interpreted it as "a mere expression of the opinion of the Annual Conference and not as a rule binding upon local churches."[102] The resolution passed, 287–158.[103] The resolution to make Northwest Texas a "Transforming conference" passed with apparently little opposition.

Late in the afternoon, the resolutions debate resumed. The one that called for a special General Conference session to deal with the gay marriage issue was withdrawn by its author, Rev. Steve Holston. However, Robert Hawkins, a layman from Hart, then moved the acceptance of his interesting and potentially explosive resolution that called on the bishop to appoint a committee to design a plan of withdrawal from the United Methodist Church. Fortunately, it never came to a vote, as Norris immediately ruled that the resolution was out of order under the provisions of the church's constitution.[104]

That action set the tone for the remainder of the day. Rev. Tom Mills moved the adoption of the "Charity and Freedom" resolution, which implied a provision of church withdrawal. Without hesitation, the bishop also ruled it to be in conflict with the church constitution. During the debate on the "Theological Crisis" resolution, the bishop ruled several parts out of order, after which its author, Steve Holston, withdrew it from consideration.

With the most controversial resolutions overruled or withdrawn, the session considered what was left. One of these, which proved to be most important to the conference's future, was titled "A Call for Conversation." Presented by Christ Church, in Levelland, this resolution noted that the conference was "experiencing division as a result of the theological diversity" and called on the bishop to appoint a task force of diverse individuals and empower them to engage an outside facilitator in order to "seek ways of restoring the Christian love for one another."[105] With some discussion and an amendment to shorten it, the "Call to Conversation" was approved.[106]

The actions of the 1998 Northwest Texas annual conference had local and national impact. Norris's decision to allow the conference to assume the "Confessing" and "Transforming" labels was taken before the General Conference's Judicial Council, the church's "supreme court." In late October 1998, the council ruled:

> An Annual Conference may not identify or label itself as an unofficial body or movement (such as, but not limited to, a "Confessing Conference", "Reconciling Conference", or "Transforming Conference"). Such identification or labeling is divisive and makes the official bodies of the Church subject to the possibility of being in conflict with the *Discipline* and doctrines of The United Methodist Church.[107]

Within the same decision, the Judicial Council also reversed its 1991 ruling against Northwest Texas that had allowed the General Commission on Christian Unity and Interreligious Concerns to identify itself as a "Reconciling commission."[108] With these decisions, the practice of conference labeling theoretically had come to an end.

But in the fall of 1998, prompted by the conference's debate about Transforming and Confessing labels, St. John's Church in Lubbock took action toward naming itself as a "Reconciling" congregation.

Long known as a liberal church, St. John's was among the first, if not the first, in the nation to adopt the slogan "Open hearts, open minds, open doors"—a phrase now widely used by the General Conference. Over many years, St. John's had started open ministries for the poor, giving legal aid, food, and food vouchers. It led in giving training for female pastors. It was the first to employ an African-American student intern.[109] It was the conference's leading church in interfaith studies, inter-ethnic activities, and addressing social issues.[110]

As the national debate on homosexuality ratcheted up in the mid-1990s, St. John's Sunday School classes began studying the subject and invited speakers with gay and lesbian ties, a move that drew sharp criticism from other Lubbock pastors.[111] In spite of the opposition, St. John's continued to study the issue—for four years. Finally, after the firestorm label debate at the 1998 annual conference, St. John's voted 155–38 in October 1998 to identify as a Reconciling congregation.[112]

The decision prompted another round of resolutions for the 1999 annual conference. During its session, six resolutions dealing with human sexuality and labels were passed. One took direct aim at the St. John's decision. The resolution stated that "any congregation within the Northwest Texas Conference that has taken on any such label be required to reverse that action."[113] The vote was close: 137–117 in favor of the resolution. After the vote, Bishop Norris stepped out of the chair and, at the request of Rev. Ted Dotts, spoke to the constitutionality of the resolution.[114] Although his decision was not recorded in the daily journal, Norris overruled the resolution, saying that the conference had no authority to adopt the measure because it was "an attempt . . . to legislate authority which has not been granted by *The Discipline*."[115]

However, once again Norris' decision was appealed to the Judicial Council. At its October 1999 session, the council ruled that a local church could not "label itself as an unofficial body or movement" because the process "is divisive and make the local church subject to the possibility of being in conflict with *The Discipline* and doctrine of The United Methodist Church."[116] Ironically, the ruling created strange bedfellows: it was opposed by the opposite-poled national Reconciling and Confessing movements. Moreover, many churches that had embraced the labels simply ignored the ruling, and apparently still do.

Thus, through two difficult years, the Northwest Texas Conference vented its frustration over the gay movement, and the process had a twofold effect. First, the conference's actions affected national events by forcing judicial decisions that barred conferences and churches from adopting labels. Second, the continued division within the conference finally convinced some leaders that they needed to look for a way to reconcile.

Meanwhile, Norris was somewhat appalled by the whole process and language, saying that all churches should be "transforming, confessing, and reconciling." "My theology says that all congregations are reconciling," he said. "When you single out a congregation, and say 'This one is and the rest of you aren't,' [it's wrong]. I think all congregations are theologically supposed to be reconciling as all of us are being 'reconciled to God.' "[117]

For some, the process was painful. One of the conference's new female pastors recalled the damage that the labeling practice did to individuals: "these labels when spread about actually brought pain, exclusion, and judgment," she said, "and yes, even as in my case, being blacklisted as unacceptable to be considered as lay delegate to General/ Jurisdictional Conference, [even though] I considered myself to be a moderate evangelical still passionately believing that salvation is through Christ alone."[118]

The moderate middle

Without a doubt, the controversies of the '80s and '90s took a heavy toll on the Northwest Texas Conference. It became more and more difficult for the bishop and Cabinet to match churches with pastors. As longtime elders retired, the conference had to rely more on local pastors and retirees to pastor its smaller churches. It would be easy to cite intra-conference dissension as a major cause for the decline of full-time elders in relation to local pastors. It is true that the number of full-time elder pastors decreased from 144 in 1984 to eighty-three by 2006—45 percent of the total number of pastors. The number of full-time local pastors increased during the same period from fourteen to thirty-three. The number of churches being pastored by part-time locals and retirees also increased dramatically.[119] However, the conference's trend only reflected the national trend; in 2006, 45 percent of all American United Methodist churches were pastored by elders in full connection; 28 percent were pastored by local pastors, compared to 29 percent in Northwest Texas.[120] Rising insurance costs, coupled with the lower pay scale for local pastors, may have contributed to the increase in the use of local pastors.

Also, the conference was spared from major withdrawals by church members. With the exception of a start-up Lubbock congregation, The

Springs Church, no established church did what one in Kingsbury, California did. Members there withdrew totally from the denomination and created Kingsbury Community Church, a move that represented "the highest percentage of loss ever for a United Methodist congregation."[121] Moreover, although Northwest Texas membership continued to decline in the '90s, its remaining members kept giving; in 1999, the year following the most controversial annual conference, total gifts set a record of nearly $45 million.[122]

In spite of the division, an active "moderate middle" was always at work in the conference. Darris Egger and Robert Monk wrote in 1997 that in spite of the strong differences, "members of the conference . . . remain convinced that our future is bright, for, as it has been throughout our history, God's gracious Holy Spirit will lead us to new unity and allow us to continue our proclamation of Christ-like love among our neighbors."[123]

Similarly, Rev. Ava Berry recalled that "the faithful folks who did not resort to rhetoric and debate" stabilized the ship and brought the conference through its most difficult times. "They continued to faithfully preach the gospel, teach the gospel and live the gospel . . . . The moderate middle held the reins to keep this conference from being torn asunder. The years of conflict and rancor were also years of faithful, 'steady in the saddle' passionate ministry for those not caught up in the swirling conflict."[124]

Methodist Hospital

Bishop Norris had to face one other issue during his tenure, and this one made him lose considerable sleep. For more than fifty years after its acquisition in 1954, Methodist Hospital in Lubbock had been one of the Northwest Texas Conference's shining stars. Its early years were challenging. In the late 1950s, the hospital found itself with a growing debt. "Some doctors and other hospitals in the area thought that, since it was now a church hospital, it would take care of all the charity cases," recalled longtime hospital chaplain William Wayne Cook. "This threw the Conference into so much debt that it had to borrow money to continue to operate. At one time, we were keeping the hospital open practically on a day to day basis, and seriously considered closing."[125]

The School of Nursing also came under conference control with the acquisition of the hospital. The school was one of the oldest institutions in West Texas. Dating from 1918, when students transferred from the Post Training School in Post to Lubbock, the School of Nursing operated under the auspices of the Lubbock Sanitarium (1918–41), its successor Lubbock General (1941–45), Lubbock Memorial (1945–54), and finally Methodist Lubbock.[126] In 1959, the school moved into a new building adjacent to the hospital, and in 1960 it added a residence for student nurses.[127]

In spite of its difficult start, Methodist Hospital soon began major expansion. In 1961, five stories were added to the north wing, funded in part by more than $250,000 contributed by churches of the Northwest Texas Conference.[128] In 1966, it added a million-dollar wing for operating rooms.[129] In 1970, the hospital began a campaign to build a 200-bed addition at a cost of more than $8 million. One quarter of that was to come from a $2 million dollar donation drive, which according to the administrator's report to the conference was "the largest single hospital campaign ever conducted in this area."[130] About the same time, a deadly tornado struck Lubbock on May 11, 1970, demonstrating the hospital's need for additional space as it treated 400 patients in the hours immediately following the storm, without the benefit of a water supply.[131]

The new wing opened in the late summer of 1974, but renovations on the older wings continued for two more years. When the remodeling was completed in 1976, Methodist was a 500-bed facility.[132] But expansion was not finished. In 1982, the facility announced plans to build a new south wing to add 166 beds—a $42.6 million facility. By the time that ground was broken in 1984, the cost had risen to more than $44 million, and the building permit was the second largest in Lubbock history.[133]

Twenty-four years of expansion after 1961 was all under the direction of Methodist Hospital's capable administrator, George Brewer. When Brewer took over the institution in 1961, it was deeply in debt; twenty years later, it was financially sound and, as reported by then-Mayor Pro Tem Alan Henry, had "grown into one of the finest hospitals anywhere."[134] William Poteet became the hospital's new CEO in 1986.[135]

Expansion continued unabated. In 1987, the hospital opened a new birthing center at a cost of $3.6 million.[136] In 1991, it launched its biggest project ever: a $67 million expansion to add two stories to its south tower and two five-story parking garages. Also in 1991, the hospital gained widespread recognition when it hosted the region's first heart transplant.[137] When the newest facilities opened in 1992, the hospital announced that it had provided more than $18 million in charitable and non-reimbursable care during the previous year. In addition, it was supplementing the conference's $100,000 contribution to its chaplaincy program by an additional $407,000.[138]

But by the early 1990s, the national hospital industry was in trouble. Mounting debt and changes in federal programs helped to create problems as Medicare reimbursement changed from expense-based to case-based formulas. As a result, hospitals were no longer able to get full reimbursements at their own rates. With decreased revenue, the industry witnessed a wave of mergers after 1988.[139]

In spite of the industry's difficulties, Methodist continued to expand rapidly. By 1995, it was managing hospitals in Plainview and Levelland; on its Lubbock campus, it opened an endoscopy center, a new six-story heart center, and a women's and children's clinic. The additional space brought the hospital's bed capacity to 920.[140] However, it also increased its debt to more than $200 million.[141]

If Methodist Hospital was in financial trouble, it was not apparent to the conference in 1995. Its reports consistently indicated expansion into various aspects of health service. Perhaps its officials no longer thought it necessary to keep the conference informed. After all, the church no longer "owned" the hospital. In 1979, the conference had in effect relinquished its title by transferring land and ownership to the institution's board of trustees. This move was made in order to protect the conference from liability and litigation.[142] However, the conference continued to appoint the trustees, and many people apparently assumed that the conference was still the sole owner.

In 1995, in the midst of expansion and acquisitions by national hospital corporations like HCA and Humana, rumors began in Lubbock that the hospital was for sale. In January 1996, startling news from Methodist Hospital produced even more speculation. On January 4, hospital CEO William Poteet, abruptly announced his resignation, catching the community—including the trustees and Bishop Norris—by surprise.[143] When asked to comment about the sale rumor, board Chairman Alan White, told the press that the "hospital isn't for sale." "It is financially sound," White said. "We are not selling out to anyone."[144]

However, White flew from Lubbock to Albuquerque to meet with the bishop and had to tell him that the hospital was in fiscal trouble and that something needed to be done. Norris remembered the conversation:

> Basically, he asked me how would I feel about the hospital being bought by one of these big hospital corporations . . . . I didn't have to hesitate on that one. I said absolutely not. It's Methodist Hospital and it's going to stay Methodist Hospital as long as it can stay Methodist Hospital. I don't want it to be swallowed up by some big corporation.[145]

White returned to Lubbock and, according to Norris, "did all he could to save a dying situation." With the tremendous debt, White and the board had little choice but to make a deal with longtime rival St. Mary's of the Plains Hospital, a Catholic institution owned by the Sisters of St. Joseph of Orange, California. On January 28, 1996, the *Lubbock Avalanche-Journal* reported that Methodist and St. Mary's were planning to merge. According to the paper, the two facilities "had been discussing a merger for several months" because "it would allow both hospitals to eliminate duplicate services and because the two hospitals' service areas overlap."[146]

The next day, White and St. Mary's President Charlie Trimble confirmed that the two institutions were going to merge and that each would own 50 percent of the new corporation. Neither made any mention of the Methodist debt problem, but it became obvious that it was a major factor in the merger as St. Mary's, with half the assets of Methodist, subsequently gained 50 percent ownership as well as control of the new governing board. But as one St. Mary's official said, it was "much more of a merger than a buyout."[147]

A few months later, Methodist Hospital, perhaps in an effort to justify its devastating losses, published a full-page flier in the August 2, 1996, issue of the *United Methodist Reporter.* It noted that the hospital had incurred $290 million in losses through unrefunded health care as well as declining patient and surgery counts.[148] "It was a painful time," remembered Norris.

Although some may have questioned whether Methodists and Catholics could share a hospital ministry, it became apparent that such arrangements were not unique. Within a few days of the merger, High Plains Baptist Hospital and Catholic-owned St. Anthony's Hospital in Amarillo announced plans to consolidate.[149] If the Baptists and Catholics could work together, surely there was hope for a Methodist-Catholic relationship!

It took more than two years to work out the details of the Lubbock merger. During that time, the new institution was known as the "Methodist-St. Mary Health System," and there was no indication that this would not be its permanent name. In their reports to the conference in 1996 and 1997, hospital officials made no mention of a potential name change or the huge debt absorbed by the St. Mary's system. In fact, a resolution presented by the hospital and approved by the conference in 1997 indicated that the name would be the "Methodist-St. Mary System.[150]

Perhaps St. Mary's officials thought it was unfair to retain the name "Methodist" and not include "Catholic," especially since the latter bore the brunt of the financial outlay in the merger. For whatever reason, both names were dropped in favor of a neutral name: Covenant Health System.[151] For two years, White served as the initial chairman of the new system. However, the final agreement, approved at the stormy Midland annual conference in June 1998, stated that the Methodists would appoint eight board members and the Catholics eight as well as the chair, thus giving controlling interest to the Sisters of St. Joseph.[152]

Also, the agreement regulated the conference's relationship to the new Covenant System to only being able to approve the members of the board of the Methodist Hospital System, the entity that owned 50 percent of Covenant. The Methodist board in turn would appoint eight members to the Covenant System. The final agreement included these stipulations:

> The Covenant Organizations will . . . not be "owned or controlled" by the Conference or any annual, jurisdictional or central conference or any agency of the United Methodist Church . . . . In that respect, the Conference will not have any reversionary right in the property or assets of any of the Covenant Organizations, except to the extent [Methodist Hospital] System will have certain reversionary rights . . . . [Methodist Hospital] System is not required to obtain the approval of the Conference for any action, other than the approval of members of its board of trustees.[153]

The agreement did provide that a Methodist would be involved in hospital administration at a vice presidential level. Rev. Ted Dotts, who had served the hospital during the merger as theologian in residence and ethicist, was hired by Covenant in 1999 as senior vice president for Methodist community relations.[154] In his first report to the conference, Dotts said that "United Methodists will find the values and goals of Covenant Health System representative of our Lord Christ Jesus."[155]

Since the merger, the conference has continued to support chaplain work at Covenant facilities, budgeting annually $110,000 for that purpose. In a sense, this ministry was returned many-fold, as Covenant reported that in 2006 alone it provided $110 million in hospital services for "indigent, uninsured, and low income patients."[156] Today, Covenant has 1,352 licensed beds and employs more than 4,000 people.[157]

Even though the Methodist Hospital story had a somewhat happy ending, Norris recalled that living through the revelations and negotiations was a "very painful" time. "It was the only thing in those days that kept me awake at night," he remembered. "[It was] a 'no win' situation."[158]

Attempts to stem the tide of loss

During the 1990s, the Northwest Texas Conference's membership continued to slide downward in spite of renewed efforts in evangelism, reorganization, and education. Death continued to be a leading villain, taking 1,000 or more a year. In 1992, in spite of nearly 1,254 by professions of faith, the Conference , conference membership fell to 74,399.[159]

However, for the first time in eight years, the conference recorded an increase in average attendance at morning worship.[160] In 1993, a loss of only 342 members was the lowest that it had been in years.[161] Unfortunately, the historic downward trends returned in 1994 as the conference lost in all categories except for giving. That year, its members gave nearly $31 million for all church causes, an increase of 1.4 percent.[162]

In the 1990s, the conference renewed its effort to plant new churches. In 1990, Lubbock planted Crossroads, in west Lubbock; in 1992, Amarillo started a new congregation on the far west side, Wesley Drive. The conference's combined City Board of Missions in 1995 proposed three new churches in the Abilene area, three for Amarillo, and one each in Lubbock and Wolfforth.[163] However, most of the plans never materialized. Only a Lubbock church—The Springs, which was started in 1996 and organized in late 1997—began with modest success and by 1999 boasted a weekly attendance of 300. However, its history as a Methodist church was short-lived, as the congregation withdrew from the denomination two years later and refunded the conference more than $44,000 in start-up costs.[164] The loss of what could have been a major new church left a vacancy in far southwest Lubbock.

Also in the 1990s, the conference began to take a closer look at its efforts to reach minorities. Historically, Methodists were open to minority inclusion within the denomination, but at the same time they supported a form of segregation when the church created a separate conference for African-American churches in 1939. Hispanic churches also were segregated in a separate conference.

After the creation of the United Methodist Church in 1968, African-American churches were integrated in 1970 into the majority conferences. In one 1971 case in Northwest Texas, an African-American church in Levelland, St. Luke's, merged with the white congregation at Wesley; the two formed a new church, Christ United Methodist.[165] (This process was repeated in Amarillo in 1997 with the merger of Wyatt Memorial and Forest Hills churches, which formed the Community of Grace church.[166]) However, most Hispanic congregations remained separate; the Rio Grande Conference served twelve Spanish-speaking churches in Northwest Texas in 1975; these included churches in Abilene, Amarillo, Big Spring, Brownfield, Hereford, Lamesa, Lubbock,

Muleshoe, Plainview, Sweetwater, and Tulia. The largest of these was La Trinidad Church in Lubbock, with 139 members.[167]

National inclusion of minorities did very little toward integrating individual churches. By the mid-1970s, 88 percent of all churches in the South Central Jurisdiction had no non-white members, and less than 5 percent of church membership was minority.[168] The small minority churches struggled, especially in Northwest Texas.

In 1976, the Northwest Texas Conference created the Lubbock Cooperative Parish for five smaller churches in an effort to help "each church make the most of its talents."[169] In time, the organization became known as the Lubbock Inter-Ethnic Parish and included six churches: two Anglo (Agape and Asbury;), two Hispanic, (Emmanuel and La Trinidad), a Korean Church, and an African-American church (Mount Vernon).[170] The conference, along with St. John's in Lubbock, had assisted a group of Korean families in starting the Korean United Methodist Church in Lubbock in 1981.[171] A similar program—the Amarillo Cooperative Cooperative Parish—had linked the San Jacinto, Tenth Avenue, Buchanan Street, and Wyatt Memorial churches in Amarillo.[172]

In 1986, the church at Memphis began a program to help local Hispanic families at Christmas and then expanded its outreach to teach classes in Spanish and English. It even hired a Catholic to teach the Methodist Sunday School in Spanish.[173] However, such efforts made little difference in total outreach. By the mid-1980s, the face of Methodism had not changed. The denomination was far behind all other denominations in ethnic growth. Nationally, United Methodists gained only 5 percent in minority membership from 1975 to 1985, while the Assembly of God saw a 48 percent increase and Southern Baptists, 70 percent.[174] Northwest Texas fared no better and in 1988 called for aggressive recruiting of minority members.[175]

About the same time, First Church Hereford stepped in to assist the struggling San Pablo Church with its community in bringing it into the conference.[176] In 1988, the Plainview District employed Sergio Gonzalez, a native Ecuadorian, to be a circuit rider for the Plainview District in an effort to strengthen Hispanic work in the area. Within a year, the young pastor was working with Hispanic groups in Plainview, Abernathy, and Dimmitt.[177] Rev. Gonzalez found the work "challenging," but he made progress. However, his work came to an end in late 1989 after the Immigration and Naturalization Service refused to grant him a work permit.[178] His departure dealt "a strong blow to the unique program."[179]

After Gonzalez's departure, there was little progress in minority work until 1996, when the conference started the Shalom Worship and Outreach Center in Brownfield. In 1997, the conference also helped bring about the Community of Grace. church merger in Amarillo. "I really wasn't for it at first," recalled Bernice Mitchell, who had been a member at Wyatt Memorial for 48 years. "When they said, 'Let's merge with Forest Hills,' it seemed like I was lost, out in the desert with nowhere to turn. I felt uncomfortable at first, but now I am not."[180]

Modest success

By the end of the 1990s, the conference showed a modest gain in minority growth, especially among Hispanics. In 1990, conference minority membership totaled 698 of 77,549, less than 1 percent; by the end of the decade, minority membership was 1,185 of 70,439, or 1.6 percent.[181] The conference had only four Hispanic churches, and one of those, the new Shalom church in Brownfield, would be closed by 2003.[182] Moreover, the Conference had only nine minority clergy out of 368 full and retired members—2.4 percent of the total.[183] However, it should be noted that eight Hispanic churches within the bounds of the Northwest Texas Conference are a part of the Rio Grande Conference, and their membership is not included in Northwest's statistics.[184]

As the twentieth century drew to a close, the conference continued to sustain gradual losses in membership, but in 1999 it showed modest gains in worship attendance, baptisms, and professions of faith. Moreover, giving increased over the previous year by 22 percent to a record $44 million.[185] Obviously, growth was no longer the priority that it had been in the first fifty years of the conference's history. In 1999, the conference conducted a survey among clergy and laity asking what its greatest emphasis should be. A majority of respondents indicated that strengthening spiritual growth and commitment was most important, followed by increases in youth ministries and efforts to increase worship attendance. Only 29 percent of the respondents indicated that attraction and enlistment of new members should be the most important, and only 28 percent believed that an increase in biblical preaching and teaching should be the top priority for emphasis.[186]

During his tenure from 1992 to 2000, Bishop Norris led the conference through some of its most difficult and challenging times, especially during the stormy 1998 debate about homosexuality and labeling. An excellent preacher, Norris was loved and widely respected. In 2000, the Conference Episcopacy Committee asked that he be returned, but the South Central Jurisdiction transferred him to the prestigious Texas Conference in Southeast Texas. Norris, as the only minority bishop to serve Northwest Texas, said that the experience was "positive":

> I could not have been received any better than I was out there. The Northwest Texas Conference . . . affirmed me at every turn. There were some instances where, theologically we might have butted heads, but I never had any relational problems, none whatsoever. . . . Some of my African-American colleagues were very concerned when I was assigned out there. One . . . was livid because he felt I was being sent to a situation where I wouldn't be welcomed and supported. But what people don't understand is . . . that, in most instances, the area to which you are assigned has given some indication that they would welcome you and that they do want you to come. I really believe that was the case with Northwest Texas and New Mexico. They basically said, "We'll take you." The door was open, and you walk through it with a positive attitude.[187]

At some point during his tenure, some of the conference's political leaders began to adopt Norris' positive attitude. Tired of the theological and political fighting, the conference, as previously mentioned, endorsed "A Call to Conversation" in 1998, calling on the bishop to "appoint a task force . . . whose theological ideas represent the diversity present in this Conference . . . [in order to] seek ways of restoring the Christian love for one another."[188] Recognizing that the infighting needed to come to an end, some conference leaders began to define ways to heal the breach. It would not come quickly or easily, but for the first time in nearly thirty years, some pastors and laity began to look for common ground. The approaching new millennium brought a promise of better days ahead.

Chapter 10

"And are we yet alive?"

At the special 2008 joint session of the Northwest Texas and New Mexico conferences at Glorieta, New Mexico, Charles Wesley's stirring question, "And are we yet alive?," rang out once again, this time in a bold and dynamic new arrangement. For a hundred years, delegates have sung the hymn, but never has the question been more important than it is today as the church and the conference continue to decline slowly in numbers. However, unlike the controversial 1998 annual conference, the 2008 session was joyous, reflective, and inspiring. Clearly, something had changed in ten years.

Part of the change may be attributed to the conference's desire to renew itself in the twenty-first century and to finally set aside its differences. Like many groups in America, Methodists began planning years in advance for the new millennium. In the early 1990s, through the General Conference's Vision 2000 program, Northwest Texas launched its own planning. a 1992 workshop drew more than 900 people from across the conference for training in programs designed to enhance the local church ministry.[1] In 1997, the program's name was changed to

TEAM Work, with a theme of teaching, equipping, assisting, and motivating local churches to make disciples; and it also evolved into a strategic planning device.[2] As an outgrowth, Bishop Norris appointed a "Dream Team" of clergy to work in strategic planning.

Although the work of the TEAM program and the Dream Team produced a thoughtful report on conference organization, much of the effort was lost in the fallout from the homosexuality debate that gripped the 1998 annual conference. However, the Dream Team's 1999 report accurately identified and listed the historical issues dividing the "evangelical right" from the "theological left," including "Asbury versus Perkins theology, Rio Grande versus Northwest Texas Hispanic ministry, [and] confessing movement versus reconciling movement." The report also listed other issues as well, including the conflict between "boomer/buster generation values versus builder/silent generation values, affirmation of global ministries support versus withholding global ministries support . . . , [and] on-the-caprock frontier world versus off-the caprock settler world view."[3]

The Dream Team's recognition of such subtle differences as "on-the caprock" versus "off-the caprock" attitudes reflected well its understanding of the regional distinctions of Northwest Texas. The report offered a nine-point solution that emphasized strengthening the conference's weaknesses rather than trying to "discuss" theological differences, and it called on leaders to "deliver with excellence" their efforts to strengthen local congregations.

With the Dream Team's foundation document in place, a step was made toward reversing the conference's dramatic division. At the 2000 annual conference, members of St. John's Church in Lubbock renewed the effort to bridge the "diversity" gap and sponsored a renewed "Call for Dialogue and Conversation" resolution. The conference concurred and charged the bishop with appointing a committee that would "hold conversation on issues that arise from the diversity present and to work ways of restoring a covenant relationship within the Annual Conference."[4]

Like the Dream Team report, the "Dialogue" resolution did not solve the problem, but it was another step. In 2001, the diversity committee reported that it had met and acknowledged that "relationship is crucial" and committed to trying to create "small groups where covenant is emphasized and dialogue, possible."[5] The idea of covenant took root, although it was not obvious at the time. "Even though it was a good experience for those who were on it," recalled Eddie Allsup, who served as the facilitator for the group, "it did not have much [immediate] impact on the Annual Conference."[6]

A bishop for the task

The task of continuing to restore relationships fell to a new bishop. In 2000, after the South Central Jurisdiction appointed Norris to the Houston Area, it assigned to Northwest Texas still another "freshman" bishop: Max Whitfield, who was elected that same year.[7] A native of Arkansas, Whitfield brought a wealth of experience as a district superintendent and as a former director on the General Board of Global Ministries. He also brought a passion for unity. Shortly after his election, and before he knew of his appointment to the divided Northwest Texas Conference, Whitfield told a reporter in 2000 that divisions in the church can be overcome if "we keep people talking to one another. Our unity is in Jesus Christ. When we work on a personal level, we find common ground."[8] He soon had opportunity to put his philosophy to work.

One of Whitfield's first tasks was to get to know the conference and to see if it matched outsiders' perceptions. That image "was not good," he recalled. "It was a reputation of being an annual conference that was anti-United Methodist church, that individuals from the conference just weren't the best folks to be around, [and] that they were extremely conservative, and always in a fight." Although some of that reputation may have been deserved, Whitfield noted that his investigations proved otherwise: "I did not find the conference as rancorous as it had been portrayed in the rumor mill . . . . [Instead, I found] individuals that were very willing to work, [and that] there was greater diversity within the Conference than what I had anticipated."[9] In addition, Whitfield said he found some active leaders who realized that change needed to occur, recognizing that the discord was "not benefiting the kingdom of God."[10]

He also recognized that retirements were helping to change the tone of division. From 1997 to 2004, forty-eight—nearly one-half—of the ac-

Bishop Max Whitfield and 2008 Cabinet: (Left to Right) Randy Hollums, C. Edward Allsup, Namiqa Shipman, Bishop Whitfield, T. Todd Dess, Ava Burdine Berry, and James G. Nunn. Photo from *Northwest Texas Conference Journal*, 2008.

tive elders retired. The turnover began to be of benefit as old personal feuds faded. Whitfield also credited predecessor Alfred Norris for starting the process of restoration. "Although [his tenure] was pretty stormy," Whitfield said, "[Bishop Norris] laid some foundations for individuals to work together, and I reaped the benefits of what he did."[11]

Whitfield took a three-fold approach as he applied his "common ground" philosophy. First, he wanted to get to know the pastors and congregations; second, he wanted to "let them know that I was going to focus time and energy on how to make disciples of Jesus Christ;" and third, he wanted to approach people "without assumptions" as to what their theological position was in the past.[12]

Sobering events

In the midst of the bishop's early efforts to restore unity, dramatic international events intervened on September 11, 2001, with the terrorist attacks on the United States and the tragic loss of thousands of innocents. Without a doubt, 9-11 changed America, and it may have helped to change attitudes within the Northwest Texas Conference. In 2002, the annual conference's theme was "Building Bridges to Wholeness"; its sessions took on a more somber tone than before, and without conflict. The 2003 conference, except for the election of delegates for General and Jurisdictional conferences, was also calm and uneventful; even the elections went smoothly, with a more balanced result. Bill Couch and Lane Boyd were elected for the General Conference on the second and fourth ballots—a far cry from the late '70s and '80s, when ten or more ballots were required.[13] The 2004 conference also reflected an absence of controversy; gone were the calls for dialogue and new resolutions on homosexuality. The only excitement was the hilarious way that longtime resolutions chair Bobbye Shaw announced her own retirement: "If there is anyone I have NOT insulted, I apologize," she told the conference, "and if I have, likewise."[14] Her humorous resolutions, which closed every session of the conference through its stormiest years, may have served as a glue to help keep things together.

New covenants

In 2004, the Council of Bishops determined to focus its energies in a way "to lead the church in making disciples of Jesus Christ for the transformation of the world."[15] Whitfield took the message to heart and began a careful effort to bring the leadership of the Northwest Texas Conference into a sharper and clearer focus on that purpose. For assistance, he contacted Craig Robertson of Kentucky, one of the principal developers of the Leadership Incubator program, which was first used in the Kentucky annual conference in 2001.[16]

Initially, twenty-four pastors and laypeople were invited to participate in two groups, which met for eight hours once a month for a year. According to Whitfield, the selected individuals were not chosen because they represented a particular theological or political view. "I did pick people that had voice and ear to the entire Annual Conference," he said, "and from that perspective, it was more of identifying the individuals who are being listened to—the natural leaders . . . . It turned out that we had people from all kinds of theological perspectives."[17]

The initiative worked. Not only did the program teach leadership, but it brought different sides to the table for the first time in many years. Inspired to follow the bishop's call to take "Bold, New Directions," twenty-three participants in the first year's incubator sessions hammered out a resolution for the 2005 conference that called for the development of a "Ministry Action Plan for the Conference through an environment of loving God (each member of the team in covenant for spiritual growth); learning (constant review and comparison of best practices); and leading (developing Ministry Action Plan for the Conference)."[18] Whitfield emphasized the need for change when he told the 2005 conference: "The church has tried to be a business instead of a church, and we are dying. We must stop giving lip service to Jesus Christ and start following Him."[19]

Over the next two years, dozens of conference leaders participated in incubator groups. And out of the initial sessions came the idea for the Bold New Directions Task Force, which soon began to define totally new concepts of organization, based on a "growing trust." Dot Harris, one of the task force members, told delegates in a pre-conference video message: "The winds of change have already begun to blow through the Northwest Texas Conference, not only to our churches, but to us personally as well, and we are excited about that. But, sometimes, change is hard, is difficult and can be a little bit scary."[20] At the 2006 conference, Francie Pittman reported a "growing trust among the task force" and challenged conference delegates "to 'really see' what is being done in ministry throughout the Conference."[21]

The process was difficult; individuals who once had despised one another found themselves working together. Mike Shafter, one of the participants, related that the experience was life-changing: "God began to change my life in radical and unbelievable ways," he said. "He changed who I was as a person; He changed my leadership skills and my style; He began to do amazing things to me that moved my life to another level."[22] Participants learned the importance of relationships and soon began to apply it to a proposed new model for the conference.

"When we were real clear about vision, mission and values, and some of the strategic directions we wanted to go, then we started looking at present structure," Whitfield recalled. "I realized that the way we were operating was like a wheel with the spokes running out [from the annual conference] and there was no coordination of ministries. Annual Conference is not a good planning session."[23]

Taking a bold new direction

After months of hard work and testing, the Bold New Directions team hammered out a draft of major reorganization. At the 2007 conference, it presented its first draft of a comprehensive "re-inventing" plan that envisioned "a bold, new way" of organizing the conference, moving away from a tiered centrist structure to that of a cohesive relational structure. It called for a structure that promoted "inviting, nurturing, equipping, and deploying" individuals as a part of the process "for making disciples."[24] At the same time, the plan called for capital investment in church extension and revitalization; as a result, the Council on Finance and Administration recommended that the conference enter a capital campaign to raise $3.2 million to support the concept and to build a new service center.[25]

The task force confessed that its work represented "the combined efforts of team members who allowed themselves to be transformed by love, informed by study, and equipped for leadership." It also told the conference that it stood "at an important crossroad where we can continue on our present course of slow death or choose deep change."[26] The conference took the message to heart; in a strong show of unity, especially after two team members told how the experience had drawn them together, both resolutions passed without opposition. The bishop called a special conference to meet in Lubbock in January 2008 to consider the new organizational plan.[27]

By the beginning of 2008, the reorganization plan had a new name: DINE, an acronym for "deploy, invite, nurture, and equip." In January, the special session gave it "overwhelming support." Whitfield was especially pleased: "We have established the framework for us to better serve the local churches in our mission of making disciples of Jesus Christ."[28] The parallel capital campaign also had a name, "Build, Renew, Rejoice," and it proved to be one of the most successful in conference history. At the 2008 annual conference, campaign leaders joyfully announced that pledges totaled to date $3,773,347.12, exceeding the goal by more than $500,000. Nearly 75 percent of the conference's churches had made pledges, along with 70 percent of the pastors and fifty-five individuals.[29]

Without a doubt, the many incubator sessions had a profound, and perhaps a saving, impact on the Northwest Texas Conference. The process directly led to a major change in the way that the conference approached its purpose and, for the first time in many years, helped to revive its historic goal of making disciples of Jesus Christ. Whitfield told students in Oxford, England, in 2007 that the process went beyond its original purpose to develop "spiritual leaders"—it also led to "the formation of persons in their daily walk with Jesus Christ," he said. The "participants learned a new style of leadership and the necessity of living in covenantal relationships with those seeking to fulfill the Church's mission of making disciples for the transformation of the world."[30]

Challenges of decline

The need and urgency for change became more apparent with each passing year. In 2000, conference membership fell by 1 percent, down to 70,000. Deaths accounted for most of the decrease, with more than 1,000 conference-wide—a 3 percent increase over the year before. Professions of faith declined by nearly 12 percent, but average attendance rose by 15 percent to more than 30,000 weekly.[31] In 2001, professions of faith increased by 6 percent over the previous year, and then increased slightly in 2002.[32] In 2003, total gifts topped $43 million, a 10 percent increase over the previous year, but short of 1999's record high of nearly $45 million.[33]

Moreover, the conference showed a membership increase in 2003 for the first time in many years. Baptisms also increased slightly.[34] However, 2003 was only a blip in an otherwise downward slide; membership loss from 2000 to 2006 averaged 704 per year; worship attendance declined from an average of 25,515 in 2000 to 22,749 in 2006. Church School membership also fell by 25 percent during the same period, but average attendance loss was not as dramatic. A very important bright spot in numbers was in professions of faith. From 2000 to 2006, churches averaged 935 per year, and in 2006, there were 963.[35]

After 2000, as the conference continued to decrease in membership and churches, it sought ways to improve efficiency, which led to the painful task of once again reducing the number of districts. In 2004, the conference voted to go from six districts to four, a move that eliminated two historic districts: Plainview and Pampa.[36] For its first sixty years, the conference had functioned with eight or nine districts, then dropped to seven in 1970 and then six in 1991. The new reduction eliminated the Conference's second-oldest district, Plainview, which had been created in 1906. (The Abilene District was formed in 1883.)[37] It shifted the far eastern portion of the Plainview District to Abilene and the west part to Lubbock. Some churches west of Lubbock were moved to the Big Spring District, and most of the Pampa District was folded into the Amarillo District.[38]

The reduction brought new challenges. Rev. Jimmy Nunn, superintendent for the Lubbock District, saw his church load increase from forty to fifty-nine, but he told a reporter that in spite of the travel and increased responsibility, "Whatever we've got to do, I'll do."[39] To assist the district superintendents, the conference implemented a plan for sub-districts and church groupings. Annual district conferences also were scheduled to become a part of annual conference sessions.

Starting new churches

A hard-learned lesson for the Northwest Texas Conference has been that growth usually comes from the establishment of new congregations rather than from trying to increase the size of existing congregations. The hallmark of the conference's first fifty years was the establishment of more than 200 new congregations from 1910 to 1960. During the next forty years, only twenty were founded. As previously noted, the conference took steps in the 1990s to plant new churches, but it soon found that the process was much more difficult than it once was. For example, the failure of The Springs Church to develop as a Methodist congregation in southwest Lubbock in the late '90s prompted Lubbock leaders to seek an alternative method of church planting, and this time they looked to landlocked St. Luke's Church for assistance.

In 2001, St. Luke's, which had long before outgrown its parking space, accepted the task of starting a new church and carefully considered several options. In 2004, its membership approved a plan whereby the southwest Lubbock location was to become a second campus rather than a new church, to be named St. Luke's Southwest.[40] The work started slowly. For four years, the congregation met at a school, then a movie theater and storefront, before breaking ground for its own sanctuary in January 2008.[41] By that time, the new campus was reporting weekly attendance of 160, and the new church was well under way.[42]

In Amarillo, the historic San Jacinto Church took at different course. Begun in 1924 as one of the conference's first suburban churches, San Jacinto had grown by 1960 to more than 2,000 members. But as with many rural churches, its members began to die or move away from the neighborhood, and by 2005 its average worship attendance was less than 100—in a facility designed for 2,000. Rather than wait for a slow death, the congregation voted in February 2005 to sell its facility and move to a storefront location in a newer neighborhood.[43] It also changed its name to the Covenant Fellowship.

Preparations for the first new Methodist church in Abilene in forty-four years began in June 2006. Named The Journey, the new congregation held its first service in January 2008, with 170 in attendance.[44]

Work beyond the church

The work of the Northwest Texas Conference cannot be measured only in numbers of churches, or total members, baptisms, and donations. From its founding, the conference has stretched far beyond its boundaries through the Methodist connectional system, and it continues to do so today. The conference and its churches have created a rich legacy of service through the establishment or support of several institutions, and these continue to serve a broad constituency.

In 2007, Northwest Texas Conference churches gave more than $75,000 to the Methodist Mission Home in San Antonio, led by a $51,000 gift from First Church, Canadian.[45] Similarly, the conference has been a major supporter of the Methodist Children's Home in Waco. Founded as an orphanage in 1890 by the original Northwest Texas Conference, the home gained widespread attention when the famous evangelist Abe Mulkey began to support it through offerings taken at his revivals.[46] The Northwest Texas Conference churches and individuals continue to support the home through special offerings and gifts, and the conference appoints two of its trustees. In 2006, Northwest Texas churches gave more than $200,000 to the Children's Home.[47]

The Wesley Community Center in Amarillo has grown into a major facility since its establishment in 1953. Photo by Annette Nall.

Another longtime benevolence of the Northwest Texas Conference has been the Lydia Patterson Institute in El Paso, a historic mission school that offers grades 8 through 12.[48] In 2007, the school enrolled 467 students and was the only United Methodist institution in the United States that served a predominately Hispanic population.[49] In addition to individual and church contributions, the Northwest Texas Conference budgeted $28,282 for Lydia Patterson in its 2008 budget.[50]

Closer to home: Wesley Community Center, Amarillo

Another of the conference's long-time benevolences is the Wesley Center in Amarillo. Founded in 1951 by members of the Women's Society of Christian Service (WSCS) at Polk Street Church in Amarillo, the center initially offered instructions in sewing and cooking and a baby clinic for the predominately Hispanic neighborhood of east Amarillo. In 1953, the conference's WSCS accepted the center as one of its projects.[51] In 1967, Rev. Jacinto Alderete became the center's first executive director and served for thirty-one years until his retirement in 1998.[52] He led in completing a major building expansion in 1982. The center continues to provide guidance in diverse programs for families at all levels, including recreational classes.[53] In 2008, the conference budgeted $50,000 for its programs.[54]

Youth and camping programs

Youth work has taken various names and directions over ten decades. In 1916, the conference sponsored its first Epworth League Conference at Vernon, which drew about forty. Interest grew rapidly, and the 1922 youth assembly attracted more than 400 to a meeting in Clarendon.[55] Two years later, more than 500 attended the four-day conference at Amarillo. The meetings were patterned after the format of the annual conference at which the youth elected councils and officers.[56]

In 1931, the league changed its name to the Methodist Youth Organization; in 1940, it changed again to the Methodist Youth Fellowship (MYF). Prior to 1931, the annual assemblies were held in the conference's larger cities, but the McMurry campus became the permanent home in 1931 because of the availability of boarding space.[57]

Annual assemblies continued throughout the 1940s and '50s and were popular with Methodist youth. Many of those who were elected to office later became prominent leaders in the Northwest Texas Conference.[58] One of the last large rallies was held in 1969 in conjunction with the annual conference and met on a Sunday afternoon as a joint session with the conference. That same year, youth work was removed from the Board of Education and placed under a Department of Youth Ministry and renamed United Methodist Youth.[59] After 1969, conference youth work took a different direction as more emphasis was placed on the summer camping programs for youth.

Among all the bright spots in its history, the Northwest Texas Conference has produced three crown jewels: its Butman and Ceta Canyon camps and McMurry University. Over the years, the two camps have become first-class facilities, thanks to the conference's recognition of their importance in ministry, and perhaps in part to competition between the northern and southern parts of the conference. Both Ceta Canyon and Butman have been upgraded in recent years with new facilities and minister to more than 3,500 campers annually.[60]

In 2007, more than 2,000 took advantage of the camping program.[61] For the summer of 2008, Butman hosted six camps, including a New Dawn Camp for mentally challenged adults, and GRACE Camp for children with an incarcerated parent. Begun in 2002, GRACE Camp for a time was offered at both sites, but only at Butman in 2008.[62] Butman's schedule for other camps were for traditional elementary, junior high, and high school. Ceta Canyon's program in 2008 called for eight camps, including New Dawn, four One-Way, and three traditional camps. In addition, it hosted a Family Camp for all ages for the July 4 weekend in 2008.[63]

The importance of the camping program is best summed up in a testimony by David Thomas, a football star from Wolfforth and a player for the New England Patriots:

> Ceta Canyon will always have a special place in my heart. While growing up, I attended several One Way camps. It was at one of these camps that I accepted Jesus Christ into my life as my Lord and Savior. The camps I attended helped build my relationship with the Lord and enhance my spiritual growth. The memories of the prayer chapel, tabernacle, worship services and the counselors will always be with me.[64]

McMurry University

McMurry is a testimony to the strong love of Christian education that permeated the Northwest Texas Conference from its beginning. The sole survivor of the early efforts to build colleges, McMurry emerged from the difficult days of the Depression and World War II to become one of the premier private church-related schools in the Southwest. In 1940, enrollment was 436, but it fell nearly 50 percent after Pearl Harbor as most of its male students went into the military. However, at war's end in 1945, enrollment skyrocketed to more than 600; it continued to climb steadily in the '50s and then skyrocketed again in the early '60s to more than 1,700 in 1964.[65] Ironically, the school's enrollment began to decline at the same time that Northwest Texas Conference membership had peaked.

The 1970s were difficult years for the college as declining enrollment, increased growth of state schools, and declining federal support created financial crises on campus. But thanks to strong support from the Northwest Texas and New Mexico conferences and their churches, giving increased to offset the loss of other funds.[66] The decade's crowning achievement was the construction of the United Methodist Campus

Center, a $2.5 million facility paid for in large part by fund drives spearheaded by Bishop Alsie Carleton through the New Mexico and Northwest Texas conferences. (See Chapter 8.) By 1986, the school had rebuilt its enrollment to more than 1,700.[67]

In the mid-1980s, about the time that the college's future was looking its brightest, the federal government began a new round of cuts. McMurry President Thomas Kim told the Northwest Texas Conference in 1985 that the administration of U.S. President Ronald Reagan was "propounding a series of serious cuts in federal aid to higher education" and that additional cuts by the state of Texas were adding to the crisis.[68] About the same time, McMurry's "big-sister" institution, Southern Methodist University, received the NCAA's "death penalty," which led to the suspension of its football program.[69] In spite of the crises, McMurry continued to survive and expand, and in 1990 it changed its name to McMurry University to reflect its broad liberal arts program.[70]

In 1992, Kim retired after serving as president of McMurry for twenty-two years. During his tenure, the college had eighteen straight years of balanced budgets, saw its endowment increase from $3 million to $25 million, and witnessed $21 million in new building construction or renovations.[71] Kim left some big shoes to fill, and his successors struggled through difficult financial crises. Although total enrollment sagged to less than 1,400 in the fall of 1998, full-time students increased to 1,097—the highest number in twenty-five years.[72] That same year, the school was recognized by *U.S. News and World Report* for its overall quality and value.[73]

The Northwest Texas Conference has supported McMurry financially from its beginning. Although the conference's current (2009) budgeted amount of $125,000 is divided among all Texas Methodist schools, the conference also provides funds for ministerial scholarships and campus ministry to students.[74] In addition, McMurry receives a large portion of its funding directly from churches and individuals from throughout Northwest Texas and New Mexico.

Since 2000, McMurry's enrollment has held steady and even increased to 1,466 in 2008, its largest since 1993.[75] In 2007, McMurry received its largest gift ever: a bequest in the will of Betty Jo Mowry of Lubbock estimated to be worth $9.3 million.[76] That gift helped the university launch a major capital campaign as a forerunner for its approaching centennial in

In 2008, the McMurry track and field team captured the school's first ever national championship at the NCAA Division III Outdoor Championship Meet in Oshkosh, Wisconsin. Photo from University of Wisconsin-Oshkosh Sports Information Department, courtesy Kennan Timm. Used by permission.

2023. In March 2008, the school announced a $53 million "Shaping the Future" campaign, which according to the *Abilene Reporter-News* "will focus on four areas: science and math, $20 million; enhancing academic achievement, $6 million; developing a faculty for the 21st century, $10 million; creating an ideal environment for living and learning, $17 million." Included would be a new science and math facility and a center for "leadership, excellence, and virtue."[77]

McMurry students helped make the spring of 2008 one of the school's best. In May, its track team capped off the 2007–08 school year by winning the NCAA Division III Outdoor Track and Field championship, the university's first-ever national championship in any sport.[78]

Student work

As exemplified by its investment in McMurry and other Methodist schools, the Northwest Texas Conference has had a long-standing commitment to Christian education and to providing ministries to students beyond the church-affiliated campus. In 1917, even as it struggled to aid its own schools at Clarendon and Stamford, the conference appropriated funds for Southern Methodist, Texas Woman's College (aka Fort Worth Polytechnic), Southwestern University, and the Wesley Bible Chair at the University of Texas.[79] When Texas Tech opened in the fall of 1925, the conference began to shift its resources for student work there and at the West Texas Teachers' College in Canyon.[80]

In the 1930s, during the brief period when the Oklahoma Panhandle was included in its territory, the conference also provided funds for student work at Panhandle A&M College in Goodwell. In 1931, the workers at Goodwell, Canyon, and Lubbock reported that they had approximately 1,200 Methodist students under their care at the three institutions. Thus, at the time, approximately one out of every five students in the three Panhandle schools was Methodist![81]

The conference continued to support college ministries even as the Depression deepened. In 1932 and again in 1933, it designated $1,485 for the three state-supported campuses, and $1,520 in 1934.[82] Prior to the mid-'30s, local churches also carried much of the load in campus ministries. In Lubbock, First Church began to employ directors of education in 1932 who were charged to work with Tech students. In September 1935, director B. F. Jackson Jr. rented a duplex apartment to serve as both a residence and the home of the Wesley Foundation. Jackson left in November 1935 and was replaced by Cecil Matthews, who was to serve as associate pastor of First Methodist and as part-time director of the Wesley Student Center.[83]

During its first fifteen years, as the Tech Wesley Foundation grew, it moved from an apartment to a larger house, and then to a still larger house. In 1941, Matthews became its full-time campus minister, a position he would hold until 1968.[84] In the late 1940s, after years of planning, long-time Lubbock physician M. C. Overton and his family gave the conference $120,000 to provide for a new building for the Wesley Foundation, Lubbock.[85]

Matthews had a profound impact on Methodist student work. According to J. O. Haymes, "[Cecil] and his wife Faye have wielded an influence on several generations of students . . . . Some of our most effective preachers and missionaries are ex-Tech students who, under the aegis of

Cecil and Faye, have gone out to serve and bless multitudes of people."[86] Matthews retired from the Wesley Center at Tech in 1968, but he promptly moved to Canyon and served there for five years until 1973.

Former Tech student Gene Sorley, replaced Matthews as director in Lubbock, followed by Roger Loyd in 1974. According to historian Robert Monk, the two brought new perspectives to Methodist student work: "Both Gene and Roger were trained in the newer theologies and were certainly better attuned to the changes in student perspective," Monk wrote. "But, their programs tended to represent the 'liberal' positions in the conference theology."[87]

Loyd also had strong ties to Perkins Seminary. As a result, when Ed Robb became pastor at Lubbock St. Luke's, the Tech Wesley Foundation found itself competing with Robb's church for students. Loyd recalled the conflict: "[Robb] was very clear that he was pulling in a whole other direction than I was pulling," he said, "and neither of us would quit what we were doing."[88] With a strong emphasis on youth, Robb appealed to students and soon had the entire Tech football team attending services at the beginning of the season.[89]

After Loyd left the foundation in 1980 to move to an administrative position at Perkins, Steve Moore became the new director at Tech. His appointment marked a decided change in the Wesley Foundation program. A graduate of Asbury, Moore began a ministry that more represented the conference's conservative theology, according to Monk:

> Moore was very effective in drawing into the Wesley Foundation at Tech students of this [evangelical] persuasion and doing a good job of evangelizing those who had little or no church background. His innovations in the campus ministry, among other programs, included the use of mission programs unrelated to Methodism; interns, usually recent graduates, who served a year or two as assistant campus ministers; and a successful program of recruitment of ministers, missionaries, and other campus ministers. The interns and folks who went into missions raised their own salaries through support from conservative churches and as recent graduates were effective evangelists on campus.[90]

The success of Moore's ministry contributed greatly to the development of the Northwest Texas-Asbury Seminary connection; at the same time, it may have contributed to a reduction in the number of ministerial students attending McMurry.[91]

Methodist student work at West Texas A&M in Canyon may have begun with the opening of the school in 1910 through support of the First Methodist Church in Canyon. In 1923, its pastor, M. M. Beavers, appealed to the Conference's Women's Missionary Society for a worker, and the ladies responded by assigning Jessie Green and later Mrs. Tom Delaney, the founder of Ceta Canyon Encampment, to the task. Volunteers continued the work for two years.[92] Mrs. Delaney also taught Bible at West Texas.[93]

But it was not until late 1940s, under the leadership of First Church Canyon's pastor Hubert Thomson, and layperson Isabelle Burrus, that a facility and full-time director were obtained. A successful capital campaign raised money for a building, which opened in September 1949.[94] For the first full-time director, the bishop appointed a brand new minister, J. Weldon Butler.[95] Butler later recalled the surprises he found when he arrived in Canyon:

> We had been told in Dallas that the new Student Center contained a 3-room apartment . . ., but when we arrived the concrete floor had not even been completed! . . . We finally . . . bought some cots which we pitched in the unfinished Student Center at night . . . even though there were no windows yet installed . . . and no bathroom facilities. We went to bed late and arose early in order to avoid being a public spectacle while we dressed and undressed. . . . The other surprise was that no plans had been made to furnish the building! I was told that furnishing the building would be MY responsibility.[96]

Such was the life of a campus minister. Butler said that churches of the community responded by donating money for furnishings and that, on the night before freshmen registration in September 1949, "we all stayed up until well past midnight helping to complete the laying of the tile floor so that we could open the building to the students on the first day of registration!"[97] In 1968, the Canyon center moved to still another new and larger building, where it resides today.[98]

The conference's next student outreach was at South Plains College in Levelland. In 1995, the conference began supporting Bible studies for students in January, and in the following summer it chartered a Wesley Foundation. In 1996, the new foundation acquired a building near the campus.[99] By 1999, the South Plains Foundation was sponsoring mission trips and also serving more than 1,000 lunches a semester.[100]

Today, the Northwest Texas Conference focuses primarily on student ministry work at Texas Tech, West Texas A&M, South Plains College, and McMurry, and; it also provides limited support to SMU. In 2008, it budgeted nearly $500,000 for campus ministries in 2009, with nearly half of that amount designated for the Wesley Foundation at Texas Tech.[101] The Tech student program in 2007 included weekly luncheons, Bible study, and small group sessions that ministered to more than 150 each week.[102] Similarly, the West Texas A&M Wesley Foundation ministered to approximately eighty students each week through weekly worship gatherings and small cell groups.[103]

The conference investment in student work continues to return interest. According to the Texas Tech Wesley Foundation Web site, more than 200 students served by its facility have gone into full-time ministry.[104] In 2008, the conference began planning to extend campus ministries to additional junior college campuses.

Africa University and the Black College Fund

But that's not the end of the story for student work. The Northwest Texas Conference joined with all other conferences in supporting through apportionments the new Africa University. Established in 1992 in Zimbabwe with forty students, Africa University awarded more than 350 degrees and certificates in 2008, in the midst of the political turmoil that grips the country.[105] The conference also supports the Black College Fund , which provides funds for eleven historically black United Methodist schools, including Wiley College in Marshall,, and Huston-Tillotson University in Austin.[106] For Africa University and the Black College Fund, the Northwest Texas Conference budgeted more than $100,000 in 2009.

In addition, the conference has provided for ministerial student support at all levels. Although hampered by the Asbury-Perkins rivalry of the late twentieth century, Northwest Texas has tried to maintain strong support for students studying for the ministry. But even with a substantial increase in conference budgeting for ministerial support from nearly $36,000 in 1969 to more than $210,000 in 2009, the funds could not keep up with inflation.[107] Also, 75 percent of the 2009 budget was designated for support of the thirteen Methodist seminaries.[108]

Retirement centers

In addition to its youth and student work, the Northwest Texas Conference has for nearly fifty years given support to senior ministries, primarily through retirement centers. In 1960, Hereford residents asked the conference if it would be interested in owning a retirement home. That year, the annual conference approved a resolution calling for the establishment of "the Northwest Texas Home for Older Adults", established a governance system and board of trustees, and appointed Rev. Donovan R. Davidson as its executive director.[109] Davidson worked tirelessly to raise support, traveling over more than 60,000 miles and made 106 appearances on behalf of the project during his first year of service.

The conference accepted an offer of $100,000 in 1961 from an unnamed "incorporated foundation" to provide funds for the construction of the new home, to be named King's Manor.[110] The new facility opened in September 1962[111] By 1963, thirty-three residents were living in King's Manor. It also opened Westgate, a nursing unit, in October 1964.[112]

Meanwhile, in 1963 the conference's Board of Hospitals and Homes purchased a fifteen-acre tract in Abilene for a retirement facility there, to be modeled on King's Manor.[113] Thanks to a substantial gift from two West Texas ranching families, Mr. and Mrs. Frank Sears and Mr. and Mrs. John Sears, the new entity was named Sears Memorial Methodist Center. It broke ground for a $200,000 facility in March 1966 and opened it in December of that year. Within three months, the facility was full, with thirty-three residents, and had a waiting list.[114]

In the 1980s, the two retirement homes distinguished themselves. In 1981, the Sears Center received a fourth straight Certificate of Superiority from the Texas State Health Department, marking the first time that a retirement home had ever achieved this honor.[115] In the mid-1980s, both homes underwent major expansion. Sears, prompted by a 600-name waiting list, increased its capacity to 115 in its nursing center and ninety-three in its retirement center in a $3.8 million expansion project.[116] King's Manor expanded to include seventy-four nursing beds, thirty-three retirement apartments, nineteen cottages, and five residential homes. It also added a licensed day-care facility for children.[117]

In 1993, Sears expanded its operation to Amarillo when it acquired from the Evangelical Lutheran Good Samaritan Society a retirement home and nursing center and renamed it the Canyons Retirement Community.[118] Sears' new presence in the Panhandle seemed to be an answer to prayer; by the early 1990s, King's Manor, according to an internal report, was suffering from "a lack of leadership, management and accountability" and needed major overhaul in administration and governance.[119] At the request of conference officials, Sears assumed ownership and management of King's Manor for two years. With the aid of Hereford volunteers, who raised $170,000, as well with additional money provided by Sears, King's Manor was brought up to standards within two years. In 1996, Sears released the property at no cost to a new Hereford-based board of trustees, but the facility remained part of the Northwest Texas Conference ministries.[120]

Since 1996, King's Manor's growth has been slow but steady. In 2002, it added home health and hospice care to its services, and in 2004 adult day care.[121] According to the King's Manor Web site, the facility continues to offer "a wide range of services for all levels of care including: Adult Day Care, Child Day Care, Independent Living, Assisted Living, 24 hour-Nursing Care, Home Health and Hospice. . . . With over forty years of service, [King's Manor] has earned a reputation of commitment to the social, mental, physical and spiritual well being of our residents at all levels of care."[122]

Meanwhile, after the mid-1990s, Sears Methodist Center expanded rapidly into many areas of health care and outside the bounds of the Northwest Texas Conference. In 1995, Sears opened its first Alzheimer's care facility: Windcrest, located in Abilene. In 1997, it opened the J. Paul and Polly Craig Methodist Retirement Community in Amarillo, a $30 million project that was reportedly "the largest most complex retirement community under construction in Texas and the single biggest building project in Amarillo."[123] In 1997, Sears acquired the Parks Good Samaritan Village in Odessa (renamed Parks Methodist Retirement Village) and added home health care services.[124]

In 2002, Sears opened one of its most ambitious projects ever: a joint venture with the Texas Tech University Health Science Center in Lubbock. U.S. Sen. Kay Bailey Hutchison dedicated the Mildred and Shirley Garrison Geriatric Education and Care Center. This 72,000-square-foot, state-of-the-art care facility on the campus of the Texas Tech University Health Sciences Center included 120 beds, sixty beds for skilled care and sixty for Alzheimer's and other age-related dementia care.[125]

Also in 2002, Sears began plans for a facility in Waco and initiated a cooperative arrangement with the Central Texas Conference, and; two years later, it opened the Wesley Woods Alzheimer's Care Center in Waco. In 2004, it opened its new Wesley Court Retirement Center in Abilene, a facility for independent retirees that included homes, apartments, assisted living, and a nursing center, and assumed management of the Lamun-Lusk-Sanchez Texas State Veterans Home in Big Spring.[126]

In 2006, Sears celebrated the 40th anniversary of the opening of the original Sears Methodist Center in Abilene, a facility that had increased its capacity from its original thirty-three residents to 170 during its four-decade history. At the same time, it added a new retirement center in Tyler and took over management of two more veterans homes in El Paso and McAllen. With a ministry throughout the state, the Sears Methodist Center provided $3.6 million in unreimbursed charitable care in 2006.[127] That amount increased to $4.3 million in 2007. Sears Methodist Retirement System Inc. employed more than 2,000 people with an operating budget of more than $90 million in 2007. It currently serves approximately 2,000 residents throughout Texas on thirteen campuses in eight cities.[128] In 2007, the Northwest Texas Conference and 164 of its churches contributed more than $73,000 to the Sears and King's Manor programs through apportionments.[129]

Lay organizations

Lay groups for both men and women have been important parts of the growth and ministries of the Northwest Texas Conference. In the conference's early days, all of the ministers, officers, and committee members were men. Thus, women's activities were conducted as auxiliaries, primarily through two organizations: the Women's Foreign Mission Society, established in the old Northwest Texas Conference in 1880, and the Women's Parsonage and Home Mission Society, which first appeared in the conference in 1895.[130] In 1911, a year after the old Northwest Texas Conference divided, the two (and sometimes rival) women's societies merged into a single organization, primarily at the insistence of the General Conference. By 1917, the Northwest Texas's Women's Missionary Society had 121 societies and 3,127 dues-paying members.[131]

Much of the early success of the Missionary Society was due to the work and longevity of Lena Elva Hyder Rollins, daughter of one of the conference's early Abilene ministers, J. A. Hyder. Mrs. Rollins served as president of the society from 1918 to 1936. She also served as a leader in the Women's Laity League, a group that in 1918 successfully campaigned for women's laity rights. She was one of the first female General Conference delegates (1922), and was the first woman to deliver a commencement address at McMurry (1928).[132]

In 1940, after the re-unification of the national Methodist Church, the society, whose name changed once again to the Women's Society of Christian Service, had nearly 10,000 members in 248 Northwest Texas Conference churches. By 1941, a parallel organization for working women was organized as the Wesleyan Service Guild (WSG). By 1952, the WSG included 82 units with nearly 2,000 members.[133] The total conference membership for both organizations in 1952 was nearly 13,000.[134]

Even though many women began working outside the home in the 1950s, the two organizations maintained combined memberships of approximately 10,000 for several years and then rose to a new peak in 1968, when there were 11,000 members in 221 WSCS and WSG groups.[135] In 1972, after the 1968 creation of the United Methodist Church, the two groups were merged under the new name of United Methodist Women.

By that time, membership had fallen to 9,000.[136] But even as conference membership began to decrease and as more women went to work, the United Methodist Women held their own for a while; in 1979, the organization had nearly 10,000 members and gave $257,011 to mission work and other causes during the year.[137]

However, during the 1980s and '90s, as still more women went to work outside the home, UMW membership fell sharply, and by 1998 it had less than 5,000 members. By 2006, membership had fallen to 3,443. Yet, UMW continued to give to its mission causes; in 2006, it gave more than $175,000 to support its programs.[138] In spite of its losses, UMW remains deeply committed to its long heritage of mission support and work. In 2007, its activities included its annual Conference School of Missions, participating in leadership training, lobbying the legislature, sponsoring retreats, holding missions studies for churches, and staging its annual meeting.[139]

In 1944, the wives of conference pastors organized for their first meeting, with sixty in attendance. They established a tradition of having a luncheon on the last day of the conference.[140]

Men

Laymen's work in Methodism and the Northwest Texas Conference was slow to develop, due in part to the nature of the episcopacy system and its vestment of power in the all-male clergy. By 1940, laypeople had a much greater voice, and shortly after World War II they began to play a larger role in conference affairs. Encouraged by a strong conference Board of Lay Activity, the first annual Laymen's Retreat was held at Ceta Canyon on a weekend in August 1946, with seventy-five in attendance. Although it was a modest start, the event would within fifteen years attract more than 600 laymen and pastors.[141]

In 1947, the General Board of Lay Activity began chartering local Methodist men's groups; by 1950, Northwest Texas had fifty-two men's organizations.[142] By 1954, there were 105 "Men's Clubs" with 4,000 members.[143] Four years later, the movement peaked at 139 clubs with more than 5,000 members in conference churches.[144]. At the conference level, the emphasis of men's work was stewardship, as well as helping to raise funds for the Builder's Club (later the Society of Phillip), which was dedicated to raising funds for new churches.[145] At the local level, emphasis was on fellowship and service. At Wellington, for example, the men's club built a house for a retired minister.[146]

As church membership declined, so did the United Methodist Men's clubs. By 1979, membership had declined to less than 1,200. By 1997, however, some of the loss had been made up as membership climbed to nearly 2,200, but it then fell back to 1,702 by 2006.[147] At the conference level, the United Methodist Men have been relatively inactive since 2001.

Roundup

One of the conference's most successful programs in recent years has been Roundup, the yearly August gathering that hosts dozens of workshops on church and outreach activities. One of the earliest was held at Oakwood Church in Lubbock in 1983 and was promoted as a conference-wide "Church Growth Seminar."[148] Over the years, the conference continued to hold leadership workshops at least every other year in August, usually in Lubbock.[149] In 1991, it offered a four-day leadership training program at McMurry, "Transformation 2000," that featured ten workshops.[150] By 1996, the conference was annually promoting its "Fall Roundup," to be held on a Saturday in Lubbock in late August. The 1996 program featured a variety of workshops offered cafeteria-style, and more than 200 responded.[151]

The following year, the program was expanded to include thirty-eight workshops, and it attracted 228 from fifty-six churches. In 1998, the conference promoted the program more than ever, and people responded as more than 600 from sixty churches participated.[152] Over the next ten years, conference leaders enhanced the program and invited the New Mexico and Rio Grande conferences to participate. In 2005, eighty workshops were offered. First United Methodist Church Lubbock's new activities center and educational complex became the ideal place for the event, and in 2006, 800 attended one or more of the eighty-five workshops offered.[153]

In 2008, Roundup offered its largest program to date, with ninety workshops; there were sessions for adult and children ministries, Bible study, communications, evangelism, lay leadership, missions, pastoral leader-

Participants of all ages help to make the annual Roundup a big success. Jody Holland's session in 2006 attracted a full house. Photo from Northwest Texas Conference Office, courtesy Karla Abernethy-Thetford.

ship, small member churches, spiritual growth, stewardship, United Methodism, world religions, worship and music ministries, and youth.[154]

Archives and history

Another longtime and successful program of the conference has been its devotion to preserving its history, thanks to the zeal and energy of a handful of pastors and laymen. In 1940, the conference created its Historical Society, probably as a result of the 1939 creation of the unified Methodist Church. Of the first five Historical Society directors, four were longtime members of the conference: Cal C. Wright, O. P. Clark, J. T. Griswold, and Lloyd H. Jones.[155] Initially, the Historical Society had little to do, but in time it encouraged the writing of memoirs by pastors that would provide a valuable record of Conference history. The year 1949 marked the appearance of Griswold's wonderful book, *From Dugout to Steeple*, which covered conference history from the 1890s through World War II.

A few years later, two different biographies examined another original member of the Historical Society, Cal C. Wright. In 1978, McMurry published Joseph Stamey's book, *With God in the Light—Cal C. Wright: A Theological Biography.* Four years later, Wright's daughter, Fern Schmidt, wrote *The Devil Stalker*, an account of her father's early days as an itinerant preacher.

In 1958, the Historical Society asked Dr. J. O. Haymes, the retired pastor of Lubbock's First Church, to write the 50-year history of the conference, and he began work immediately. In preparation for that publication, the society in 1959 published its first report in the conference *Journal,* a two-page "History of the Northwest Texas Conference," written by another charter member of the Historical Society, the venerable O. P. Clark..[156] This brief summary served as a prelude for Haymes' book, which was published in 1961 as *History of the Northwest Texas Conference, The Methodist Church: The First Fifty Years, 1910-1960.* Highly detailed, the book was written primarily from the annual conference journals but also includes thumbnail sketches of nearly every church in the conference as well as biographical information on all pastors who had died from 1910 to 1960.

In 1968, another chairman of the Conference Historical Society, E. D. Landreth, published his memoirs, *The Missing Book,* in order to "practice what he preached":

> During these years [as chairman of the Historical Society] I constantly exhorted my brethren to shake off their lethargy, lay aside their modesty, and write down interesting memories in order that precious historical materials might be preserved for posterity. Many unrecorded and irrecoverable facts are tragically lost with the passing of each churchman because too few will go to the trouble to write.[157]

Landreth was quite right. Fortunately, the national church gave some assistance to history when in 1968 it created the General Commission on Archives and History and required each conference to create such a commission.[158] Northwest Texas promptly responded, and its new commission immediately began to encourage pastors to prepare memoirs and for each church to write its history. Moreover, commission Chairman Dallas Denison called on each church to "share historical materials such as old pictures, clippings, documents, [and] rare books" for deposit in the conference office.[159] One of the first to respond to the new appeal for memoirs was longtime pastor E. L. Yeats, whose book, *Lights and Shadows in the Itinerant Ministry,* appeared in 1972.

Although several ministers responded to Dennison's appeal by developing their personal stories, his call for materials to be deposited at the conference office failed to produce significant results. When Robert Monk was appointed chairman of the Archives and History Commission in 1972, he journeyed to the conference office inquiring about archival materials. The staff showed him a cardboard box on a lower bookcase shelf that contained several volumes of Women's Society histories and an elementary school hymnal! In the understanding of the conference staff, that box constituted the archival material. The task of a newly formed commission was obvious as members began to work toward establishing a conference archives at the McMurry University Library.[160]

By 1975, the new Northwest Texas Conference archives had grown in importance. In 1977, Jewell Posey, who had retired from a long career as a student and teacher at McMurry, became the conference archivist, a position she held until 1999. Her assistant Pat Williamson, became the new archivist and continues to serve in that capacity.[161] In recent years, the archives have served as a research center and catalyst for additional books. One member of the Archives and History Commission, Darris Egger, wrote several books utilizing the archives' resources: *Prairie Parsons* (1990), *Butman Methodist Camp in Mulberry Canyon* (1994), *A Church Named St. Paul* (1995), and his own autobiography, *It Was Just Yesterday: Remembering 80 Years of Memories and Experiences* (1999). In 1985, he also wrote a succinct history of the Abilene District that was never published.

Two other book-length autobiographies deserve mention. In the early 1990s, J. Weldon Butler self-published a well-written memoir, *Called by Grace,* which recalled his years as campus minister, pastor, and district superintendent. And at age ninety-seven, the venerable Vernon Henderson wrote a delightful memoir, *Fifty-Three Rungs Up Jacob's Ladder And Still Climbing* (1999) covering his sixty years of service to the conference as pastor, district superintendent, editor, and conference officer. (As of this writing in August 2008, Henderson was planning his 106th birthday in September 2008!) Over the years, many former pastors have written short sketches of their careers, but none reaching the depth of these two writings.

Churches responded positively to appeals by the Archives and History Commission for church histories. By 1991, 169 of the 238 churches in the conference had written histories for deposit in the archives. Since that time, several more have been added as a large number of churches celebrated centennials or other anniversary dates. In addition, two districts, Seymour and Pampa, compiled excellent histories of their churches prior to their merger into other districts.

Where did all the people go?

Since 1965, the Northwest Texas Conference has lost 40 percent of its membership. Some of the reasons are obvious: a) rural population in the area declined in the non-urban counties of Northwest Texas by 14 percent since 1960, resulting in the loss of rural churches and membership in areas where Methodism had historically been strong;[162] b) the loss of an aging membership through death; c) a changing society that no longer was loyal to a particular denomination or doctrine; d) a changing church that no longer emphasized personal evangelism; e) the failure to maintain a strong, biblically-based Sunday School program;[163] f) a reluctance to plant new churches; and g) a failure to attract a growing Hispanic population.[164]

Loss of population does not explain why the church has failed to grow in growing urban areas. For example, from 1970 to the present, the population of Amarillo and Lubbock has grown by 43 percent. Much of this growth was among Hispanics, who accounted for nearly 25 percent of Amarillo and Lubbock's population by 2000.[165] Yet during the same time, the Methodist churches in those communities have experienced a combined loss of more than 6,500 members, or nearly 23 percent of their 1970s totals.[166] Moreover, Hispanics accounted for only 221 of the 19,283 members of the Northwest Texas Conference churches in Lubbock and Amarillo in 2006.[167]

Methodist church historian and elder Robert Sledge, who taught history at McMurry for many years, notes additional reasons for the church's decline, including a centralization of control away from the local church, a proliferation of committee and paper work, a shift of the ministry from a "calling" to a "profession," a loss of denominational distinctiveness through succeeding mergers, and a shift in evangelical emphasis from community to family:

> [I]n our time, the churches with the best record for making new Christians are the suburban churches who have younger families raising their children in church, and having them join via membership classes. The principal source of converts has become our own children. But, we are having fewer children.[168]

Sledge's noting of a shift from community to family is telling. It has long been a characteristic of mainline Protestant churches to focus their local ministry on their own kind, either by economic status and/or ethnic origins. Thus, the church's passion was for those who were "just like us." But as communities became more diversified with the infusion of larger numbers of minorities, the pool of folk "just like us" began to shrink. In January 2008, Bishop Whitfield, without apology, told the conference what its problem was:

> First, we must cease being a social club for like-minded, economically homogenous, white middle and upper middle class people who have forgotten Jesus came to save this world. Until we focus on the young, people of color, and the poor, we cannot save those Jesus died to redeem. White, middle class, well educated people are only a small part of our communities and most of them have little interest in looking and behaving like Jesus. We must become the community that truly reflects Jesus to the world. Second, we must seek to discern how God is going about this business. The business of redeeming the slaves is not something we invented. I can also assure you that God is not waiting around until we tell God how to respond. We need to be on our knees with open hearts and minds to listen for a word from the Lord.[169]

You are not alone

Northwest Texas Methodists are not alone in suffering losses. The Nebraska Conference had by 2004 lost 65,000 members since 1968.[170] By 2008, the national United Methodist Church had lost 2.6 million members, or 24 percent since 1968. The Evangelical Lutheran Church saw its national membership drop by nearly 8 percent in the fifteen years after 1990.[171] In fact, nearly every mainline denomination has lost substantial membership since the 1960s. By 2007, even Southern Baptist churches, which rarely purge membership rolls, reported decline in members and baptisms.[172]

A recent survey of 35,000 adult Americans revealed that 44 percent had left the faith in which they were raised, usually shifting from mainline Protestant denominations or Catholicism to conservative evangelical churches. According to Alan Wolfe, a professor of political science at Boston College, evangelical churches draw members by appealing to day-by-day concerns rather than to doctrinal position. "It's not hellfire and damnation," he told *The Wall Street Journal* in 2008, but concerns about money and social problems—"a therapeutic side to faith."[173] Wolfe's contention matches that of author Tex Sample, who wrote in 1990 that America's values changed after World War II from believing in "self-denial" to a practice of "self-fulfillment."[174]

This change in America's value system explains in part the development of the charismatic movement, the growth of a new pentecostalism, and the emergence of "praise and worship" style of music. People who are seeking a personal manifestation of spirituality often find it in a body that literally believes in all the "gifts of the Spirit." As a result, all over the country, new and independent evangelical churches have appeared, many of which follow a pattern of establishment, marketing, and worship as taught by a number of prominent independent pastors. This approach followed in large part a model established by Bill Hybels, who in 1975 founded the now-famous Willow Creek Church in suburban Chicago, Illinois. Utilizing a market-driven philosophy, Hybels utilized contemporary music and language, dramatic skits, and multimedia presentations, all choreographed to coincide with a sermon that focused on current issues.[175]

Hybels's church grew rapidly, and its success contributed to the rise of the megachurch—churches that are defined as having a "weekly sustained attendance" of 2,000 or more. According to the Hartford Institute of Religion Research,, the number of such churches nationally increased from 350 in 1990 to more than 1,200 by 2008.[176] Of these, 34 percent were nondenominational, 26 percent were Baptist, and only 5 percent were United Methodist. More than two-thirds of the megachurches embraced an evangelical or charismatic philosophy.

In 2007, according to the magazine *Christian Report*, the most influential of the new megachurches in Texas were Fellowship Church in Grapevine, The Potter's House in Dallas, and Lakewood Church in Houston.[177] The creators of these churches avoided denominational labels, utilized modern marketing strategies that target men, and made wide-spread use of television advertising as well as telecasting services. Their pastors—Ed Young, T. D. Jakes, and Joel Osteen—have become widely known as speakers and authors.

Lubbock's first independent megachurch is a good example of the origins of the movement and its impact on the Northwest Texas Conference. Started even before the modern megachurch movement, Trinity Church was originally founded in 1960 as Highland Assembly of God, a Pentecostal church, and then became independent in 1964. According to the church's Web site, Trinity Church now averages 2,000 in weekly worship and had more than 5,000 for Easter services in a special 2005 convocation.[178]

Interestingly, of the 190 Texas churches that the Hartford Institute for Religion Research has identified as megachurches, only twelve are within the bounds of the Northwest Texas Conference: four in Amarillo, four in Lubbock, three in Abilene, and three in Midland. Of these, five are Baptist, two are Church of Christ, and four are nondenominational. The only United Methodist megachurch on the Hartford list is LakeRidge in Lubbock, which shows to have an average attendance of 4,000.[179] (However, in 2006, LakeRidge reported that its average worship attendance was 1,191.)[180]

Regardless of whether the Hartford Institute's list is accurate, one can be assured that many of these churches have attracted thousands of former mainline Protestants, including Methodists. According to a 2005 article in *Newsweek,* megachurch growth has done little to change America's worship attendance percent. In 1966, a Gallup Poll reported that 44 percent of Americans said they attend worship services weekly; the 2005 *Newsweek* poll reported 45 percent, reflecting only a 1 percentage point change.[181]

But how well do the big megachurches minister, especially those that utilize national and worldwide television? An interesting study is to compare the record of Houston's Lakewood Church to the Northwest Texas Conference as a whole. Lakewood's weekly attendance averaged approximately 25,000 in 2003, making it the largest church in America.[182] In 2003, the Northwest Texas Conference averaged 23,898 in weekly worship attendance.[183] Lakewood's contributions in 2003 were $47.5 million. Northwest Texas' total giving was $43.6 million.[184]

In a 2005 *Houston Chronicle* article on Lakewood, the newspaper cited church expenses of $45 million that included $14.1 million for general and administrative expense, $2.4 million for fundraising, and $5.7 million for television production. According to the paper, the church also spent nearly $20 million on "program services," which included "missions, television ministry, worship services and other church activities."[185] According to *Forbes.com,* Lakewood spent $12 million for television airtime alone in 2003.[186]

At the same time, the 218 churches of the Northwest Texas Conference spent approximately $44 million, of which $39 million went for local church support and maintenance, including the salaries of 173 pastors and dozens of other church support personnel. In addition, they gave $4.4 million to causes beyond the local church at the conference, national, and world levels. They also supported hospitals, nursing homes, colleges, student centers, children's homes, missionaries, seminaries, ministerial students, and community centers, as well as retirement pensions for 339 retired clergy or surviving spouses. They also preach a doctrine that has much more substance and depth than that of Osteen's therapeutic, simplistic, feel-good, self-help, "be happy" teachings.[187]

You will never be alone

In their century of connectional service, the United Methodist churches of Northwest Texas have recorded nearly 200,000 professions of faith and almost that number of baptisms.[188] Since its founding, the conference and its churches have given well over a billion dollars to all of its causes. Over and over across the years, their pastors have proclaimed faithfully the gospel; members have reached out to help others; and hundreds of men and women have dedicated their lives to full-time Christian work. The conference's history reflects the dedication of the itinerant preachers and their families, often at great personal sacrifice and sometimes in the midst of danger. Their service built a great conference.

One of those long-time pastors, Cal Wright, recalled the evangelical zeal of those early days:

> When time for the evening service arrived, we were filled with the Holy Ghost, and were ready to receive the Word. We expected conversions, and God gave us our expectations. The spiritual inspirations give us heavenly experiences. These were the days of purification and dedication. We were in tune with God. The witness of the Spirit continued with us. Methodism grew mightily. Our circuit riders knew the love of God, and in sincerity and love they preached of conviction, repentance and faith, of Christian love, of spiritual witnessing, redemption through the blood of Christ, restitution, purity of the Christian life and the judgment to come. We were made proud of our Methodist teachings and traditions and on through the fall and winter months we continued "doing good" by having experience meetings, by personal evangelism, and in our public worship.[189]

Somewhere along the way, in the 1950s and '60s, some may have lost their zeal amidst theological and ecumenical issues; some got caught up in charismatic and other movements; still others found themselves at odds with their brothers and sisters in Christ. But in His own time, God provided leaders to give "Bold, New Directions," and one can hope that many have rediscovered what it means to "make disciples of Jesus Christ for the transformation of the world."[190]

In 1881, when Peter Gravis and young J. T. Hosmer set out from Seymour on their long mission trip to Mobeetie and Clarendon, they struck out in a "Bold, New Direction," doing so with expectation and great faith. Gravis commented on the eve of the trip that "Methodism can and will do much for this country, and it is firmly planted. We now have a membership of 24 in Seymour."[191] By 1964, Seymour's twenty-four had become 108,000! It is a lesson about what faith and work can accomplish when God's people strike out in bold, new directions.

Appendix A

Methodist Churches within the Bounds of the Northwest Texas Conference, 1873-2008

Compiled by David Murrah and Pat Williamson from annual conference journals and county, district and church histories

Author's note: This list includes approximately 630 churches and preaching points but is not complete. The conference journals did not list consistently churches in every circuit. Churches without known founding dates are listed at the end of the table.

Churches	County	Date Founded	Date Closed	Notes
Albany	Shackelford	1873		
Belle Plain	Callahan	1877	1931?	merged with Eskota and Rowden
Buffalo Gap	Taylor	1878	1985	
White Church	Taylor	1878	1951	merged with Blair and Nubia to become Pioneer Memorial
Potosi	Taylor	1879		originally Lytle Gap until 1904
Abilene Potosi	Taylor	1880		
Pease City	Foard	1880	?	
Seymour	Baylor	1880		
Abilene First	Taylor	1881		
Epworth	Hale	1881	1893	founded by ME minister, merged into Hale Center
Margaret	Hardeman	1881		
Shep	Taylor	1881	1985	
Sweetwater First	Nolan	1881		
Vernon First	Wilbarger	1881		
Anson	Jones	1882		
Colorado City First	Mitchell	1882		
Merkel	Taylor	1882		
Big Spring First	Howard	1883		
Snyder First	Scurry	1883		
Throckmorton	Throckmorton	1883		
Baird	Callahan	1884		ME church started in 1882
Quanah First	Hardeman	1884		
Bradshaw	Taylor	1885	1984	
Eula	Callahan	1885		
Haskell	Haskell	1885		

Midland First	Midland	1885		
Moran	Shackelford	1885		
Tuscola	Taylor	1885		
Benjamin	Knox	1886		
Chillicothe	Hardeman	1886	?	originated at Jackson Springs, moved to railroad town in 1887
Roby	Fisher	1886		
Rochester	Haskell	1886	2006	
Thalia	Foard	1886	1978	pews and pulpit given to Lubbock Korean Church; communion table and piano to Vernon Faith
Avoca	Jones	1887		moved to railroad town 1906
Cataline (see Allison)	Hemphill	1887		see Allison
Childress First	Childress	1887		
Claude	Armstrong	1887		met in home of pioneer rancher Charles Goodnight
Crowell	Foard	1887		
Lake View	Hall	1887	1998	
Lipscomb	Lipscomb	1887	?	first church organized north of Canadian River
Lockett Wesley Chapel	Wilbarger	1887	1960	
Timms City	Lipscomb	1887	?	
Vernon Wesley Chapel	Wilbarger	1887	1965	merged with Vernon First, 1965
Allison	Wheeler	1888		started as Cataline and Zybach
Amarillo Polk Street	Potter	1888		
Arlie	Childress	1888	1977?	
Banister	Foard	1888	1891?	merged with Crowell
Clarendon	Donley	1888		J. T. Hosmer preached in 1887
Colemelle		1888	?	
Della Plain	Floyd	1888	?	
Estacado	Lubbock	1888	1960	
Fairview	Jones	1888	?	
Plainview First	Hale	1888		
Aspermont	Stonewall	1889		
Big Valley	Hardeman	1889	1921	merged with Medicine Mound 1921
Canyon	Randall	1889		
Cone	Crosby	1889	1969	
Dora	Nolan	1889	?	became Slater Chapel
Fargo	Wilbarger	1889		
Fresno	Collingsworth	1889	1957	merged with Wellington Trinity

Hale Center	Hale	1889		
Harold	Wilbarger	1889	?	
Medicine Mound	Hardeman	1889	1967	merged with Chillicothe, 1967
Nolan	Nolan	1889		
Rayner	Stonewall	1889	1904	
Wellington First	Collingsworth	1889		
Bethel	Jones	1890	1948?	
Boyd Chapel (near Anson)	Jones	1890	1940s	Members transferred here from Neinda, 1908; building may have been moved to Anson to serve Bethel Memorial.
Camp Springs	Scurry	1890	1979	
Carey	Childress	1890	?	
Coldwater	Sherman	1890	?	
Double Mountain	Stonewall	1890	1919	
Emma	Crosby	1890	1914	
Fairview	Haskell	1890	?	
Farmer's Valley	Wilbarger	1890	?	
Floydada	Floyd	1890		
Goodlett	Hardeman	1890	1985	
Goree	Knox	1890	2003	first organized at Old Goree; reorganized 1906 by J. B.Curry
Lockney	Floyd	1890		
Mack	Wilbarger	1890	?	
Memphis	Hall	1890		
Mount Pleasant	Stonewall	1890	1920	
Nugent	Jones	1890	1969	
Panhandle	Carson	1890		
Pinkerton	Knox	1890	1922	
Vera	Knox	1890		
Elizabeth	Hall	1891	1905	Turkey church formed in 1905
Hitson	Stonewall	1891	1911	
Hulver	Hall	1891	?	
Loco Bethel	Childress	1891	1958	
Tulia First	Swisher	1891		
Afton	Dickens	1892	1978	first called Cottonwood
Epworth	Wilbarger	1892	?	
Gail Doward Chapel	Borden	1892	1991	became Dorward Chapel, 1959
Lake View	Hale	1892	1995	

Lubbock First	Lubbock	1892		12 charter members, met in schoolhouse and courthouse, suffered fire in 1917
Matador	Motley	1892		
Newlin	Hall	1892	1950	church organized 1909
Paducah	Cottle	1892		
Roscoe	Nolan	1892		
Truscott	Knox	1892	1997	
Turkey	Hall	1892		first located at Elizabeth in 1891
Tye	Taylor	1892		
White Flat	Motley	1892	1966	
Flomot	Motley	1893	1991	began as a Presbyterian church, joined Northwest Texas Conference in 1903 to become Quitaque
Gilliland	Knox	1893	?	
Canadian	Hemphill	1894		
Dunn	Scurry	1894	1988	
Miami	Roberts	1894		preaching began in 1893, organized 1897
Dumont	King	1895	1982	
Estelline	Hall	1895	1984	
Oplin	Callahan	1895	1966	
Abilene Caps	Taylor	1896		formerly Borden Chapel
Channing	Hartley	1896		oldest existing Methodist church north of Canadian River
Kirkland	Childress	1896	1960	merged with Sparenburg; grocer W. C. Furr and wife were charter members
Perryton	Ochiltree	1896		originally at Ochiltree, moved to Perryton 1919
Bush Knob	Throckmorton	1897	1950	
Putnam	Callahan	1897	?	
Round Timber	Baylor	1897	?	
Ruby	Nolan?	1897	?	
Westover	Baylor	1897	1959	
Bedford	Callahan	1898	1901?	
Cedar Grove (near Putnam)	Callahan?	1898	1901	
Clairemont	Kent	1898	?	
Dodson	Collingsworth	1898	1965	merged with Wellington First, 1965
Dozier Glen Davis	Collingsworth	1898	1984	originally Dozier; named 1947 for Glen Davis who was killed in military, merged with Wellington First
Gillespie	Knox?	1898	1909	merged with Thorp
Mount Olive	Stonewall	1898	1940	

Red Springs	Baylor	1898	1922	
Thorp (formerly Gillispie)	Knox	1898	1950	merged with Munday
Farmer	Lubbock	1899	?	
Hereford First	Deaf Smith	1899		
Northfield	Motley	1899	1946	
Shinnery Grove	Stonewall	1899	1927	
Altus (Abilene District)		1900	?	
Bala (Grow)	King	1900	?	
Clyde	Callahan	1900		
Hooleyan (Hardeman County)	Hardeman	1900	?	
Koger	Throckmorton	1900	1938	
Leavitt	Haskell	1900	?	
Loraine	Mitchell	1900		
Maybelle	Baylor	1900	?	
Munday	Knox	1900		
Ogden	Baylor	1900	?	
Plainview	Haskell	1900	?	
Red Hill	Collingsworth?	1900	1947	
Stamford, St. Johns	Jones	1900		100-ft. church tower, highest between Dallas and El Paso
Trent	Taylor	1900		church organized 1901
Aberdeen	Cottle	1901	1957	merged with Qual and Fresno to become Wellington Trinity
Dalhart Central	Dallam	1901		first called Southside
Dumas First	Moore	1901		
Newman	Fisher	1901	?	
Shamrock	Wheeler	1901		preaching began in 1892 in area
Spearman	Hansford	1901		originally at Hansford, relocated to Spearman 1919
Stratford	Sherman	1901		
Tell	Cottle	1901	1999	
Alanreed	Gray	1902	1957	
Fairview	Fisher	1902	1943	
Higgins	Lipscomb	1902		preaching began in the 1880s
High Point	Childress	1902	?	
Hobbs	Fisher	1902	1927	
Lynn	Lynn	1902	?	
McLean	Gray	1902		

Olton	Lamb	1902		
Rule	Haskell	1902		
Salt Fork	Collingsworth	1902	1955	merged into Wellington Trinity
Summerfield	Castro	1902	?	
Dalhart Lakeview	Dallam	1903		was Pine Street ME Church until 1939, became Lakeview in 1962.
Dickens	Dickens	1903	2000	
Dumas Middlewell	Hartley	1903		
Follett	Lipscomb	1903		originated in merger of Stilwater and Ivanhoe, Oklahoma, as ME church, relocated to Follett in 1918.
Hamby	Taylor	1903		
Heald	Wheeler	1903		began as Rowe Mission, 1904
Quail	Collingsworth	1903	1955	merged into Wellington Trinity
Quitaque	Briscoe	1903		originally Presbyterian, see Flomot
Snyder Union	Scurry	1903		
Spring Creek	Wilbarger	1903	1910	
Spurlock Chapel	Sherman	1903	1983	
Tahoka	Lynn	1903		
Wheeler	Wheeler	1903		
Abilene Wylie	Taylor	1904		
Brownfield First	Terry	1904		
Delvin	Cottle	1904	?	
Groom	Carson	1904		
Guion	Taylor	1904	1973	
Knox City	Knox	1904	1968	merged with O'Brien
Lamesa First	Dawson	1904		
Stanton	Martin	1904		
T Bar	Lynn	1904	?	
Vega	Oldham	1904		
Abilene Fairmont	Taylor	1905	2006	see Abilene Southwest Drive
Abilene Plum Street	Taylor	1905		originated as St. Paul, an African-American congregation
Abilene Southwest Drive	Taylor	1905		originally Fairmont, after fire, renamed Southwest Drive, 2006
Blackwell	Nolan	1905		originated as a Methodist Protestant church, but joined Northwest Texas Conference before 1939 unification
Bovina	Parmer	1905		
Brazos Valley	Baylor	1905	1925	
Cross Roads	Collingsworth	1905	?	

Dimmitt	Castro	1905		
Eskota		1905	1974	
Glazier	Hemphill	1905	?	
Guthrie	King	1905	1968	
Happy	Swisher	1905		
Johnson Chapel	Stonewall	1905	1920	
Kelly	Collingsworth	1905	1964	
Lawn	Taylor	1905	1974	merged with Tuscola
Leila Lake	Donley	1905	1965	first named McCullough Memorial, renamed 1953, merged with Clarendon, 1965
Ochiltree	Ochiltree	1905	1919	church relocated to Perryton, 1919
Ovalo	Taylor	1905	1979	
Seagraves	Gaines	1905		
Seminole	Gaines	1905		
Shady	Baylor	1905	1938	
Shinnery Lake	Stonewall	1905	1925	
Sylvester	Fisher	1905	2005	
Umbarger	Randall	1905	?	
Carney	Knox	1906		see O'Brien
Chalk	Cottle	1906	?	
Coahoma	Howard	1906		
Dunlap	Cottle	1906	1950s	
Eli	Hall	1906	1940s	Sunday School established in 1896; also known as Twin Buttes
Forty-Two	Throckmorton	1906	1918?	
Garden City	Glasscock	1906		
Hamlin First	Jones	1906		
Hefner	Knox	1906	1940s?	
Hermleigh	Scurry	1906	?	
Kress	Swisher	1906		originated at Wright, relocated in 1907 to Kress
Lee's Chapel	Collingsworth	1906	1912	
Liberty	Hale	1906	1975	
Lone Star	Throckmorton	1906	?	
Lone Star	Throckmorton	1906	1919	
McCaulley	Fisher	1906		
Morse	Hansford	1906	1970	
Nubia	Taylor	1906	1951	merged with Blair and White to become

				Pioneer Memorial
O'Brien	Knox	1906	1968	formerly Carney; merged with Knox City, 1968
Pampa First	Gray	1906		
Tolbert	Wilbarger	1906	?	
Tuxedo	Jones	1906	1959	originally known as Little Elm
Verbena	Garza	1906	?	
Weinert	Haskell	1906	1999	
Westbrook	Mitchell	1906		
Andrews Means Memorial	Andrews	1907		first church in Gaines County, became Means after fire in 1946?
Brice	Hall	1907	1947	merged with Clarendon
Cross Plains	Callahan	1907		transferred to Central Texas by boundary change, 1934
Draw	Lynn	1907		schoolhouse services started 1905
Elliott	Wilbarger	1907	?	
Hartley	Hartley	1907	1995	
Hash Knife	Baylor	1907	?	
Hawley	Jones	1907		
Hedley	Donley	1907		
Jayton	Kent	1907		
Jud	Knox	1907	1928	
Lueders	Jones	1907		
Roaring Springs	Motley	1907		
Rotan	Fisher	1907		
Texline	Dallam	1907		
Vigo Park	Swisher	1907		
Black	Bailey?	1908	?	
Bomarton	Baylor	1908	1951	
Chalk	Howard?	1908	?	moved to Forsan, c. 1950
Cook's Chapel	Throckmorton	1908	1911	merged with Woodson
Dudley	Callahan	1908	1975	
Fluvanna	Scurry	1908	2001	
Maryneal	Nolan	1908	1965	
Muleshoe	Bailey	1908		relocated from Hurley
Odell	Wilbarger	1908	1965	merged with Fargo, 1965
Peacock	Stonewall	1908	1960	
Peacock	Stonewall	1908	1960	
Post	Garza	1908		
Rocky Point	Throckmorton	1908	?	

Swenson	Stonewall	1908	1941	
Abilene St. Paul	Taylor	1909		
Adrian	Oldham	1909	?	
Amarillo Buchanan	Potter	1909		
Amarillo Tenth Ave.	Potter	1909		
Denton Valley	Callahan	1909	1972	
Gem City	Hemphill	1909	?	
Hockley?		1909	?	
Iatan	Mitchell	1909	?	
Ira	Scurry	1909		
Lazare	Hardeman	1909	1952	
Ogden	Cottle	1909	?	
Pride	Dawson	1909		renamed Welch
Rayland	Foard	1909	1933	merged into Lockett Wesley Chapel
Sagerton	Haskell	1909		
Soash	Howard	1909	1917?	
Spur	Dickens	1909		
Wildorado	Oldham	1909	1990	
Abernathy	Hale	1910		
Barton	Lubbock	1910	1910	merged with Abernathy
Blackland	Nolan	1910	1914?	
Coleyville	Cottle	1910	1937?	
Crosbyton First	Crosby	1910		
Foard City	Foard	1910	1965	shared building with Baptists; merged with Crowell, 1965
Gageby	Wheeler	1910	1982	
Green Valley	Cottle	1910	?	
Lakeview	Lynn	1910	1970	
Lorenzo	Crosby	1910		
Plains	Yoakum	1910		
Plaska	Hall	1910	?	also known as Lodge
Royston	Fisher	1910	?	
Stamford, Ward Memorial	Haskell	1910	1930	
Elbert	Throckmorton	1911		
O'Donnell	Lynn	1911		
Petersburg	Hale	1911		
Rendham	Baylor	1911	?	
Slaton	Lubbock	1911		

White Deer	Carson	1911		
Woodson	Throckmorton	1911	1993	
Wright's Chapel	Stonewall	1911	1935	
Cache Creek	Baylor	1912	?	
Halfway	Hale	1912	1979	
Hood	Knox	1912	1941	merged with Munday
Plymouth	Collingsworth	1912	?	
Stamford Ward Memorial	Jones	1912	?	
Sunnyside	Jones	1912	?	
Ballard	Dawson	1913		see note on Liberty church
Ballard (see Liberty)		1913	1937	merged with Liberty to become Nolan Chapel
Childress King Memorial	Childress	1913	1985	
Littlefield	Lamb	1913		
Valley View	Stonewall	1913	1918	
Carr's Chapel	Hale	1914		merger of Harmony (1904) and Allmon (1912)
Edsall Chapel	Throckmorton	1914	?	
Friona	Parmer	1914		
Genevieve	Stonewall	1914	?	
Grandview	Stonewall	1914	1928	
Hooker	Stonewall	1914	1928	
Longworth	Fisher	1914	1978	
YL	Bailey	1914	1975	merged with Muleshoe
Graham Chapel	Garza	1915		pastor rode 15 miles on bicycle from Tahoka
Lubbock Canyon	Lubbock	1915		
New Lynn	Lynn	1915	?	
Old Glory	Stonewall	1915	1938	
Ralls	Crosby	1915		
Robertson	Lubbock	1915	1957	merged with Lubbock Canyon
Vernon Wildcat	Wilbarger	1915	1971	
Wildcat	Wilbarger	1915	?	
Wilson	Lynn	1915	1999	
Zybach	wheeler	1915	1950	merged iwith Allison
Cook Spring	Haskell	1916	?	
Garlynn	Garza	1916	1943	building sold and moved to Smyer
Grassland	Lynn	1916	1973	church organized 1925; became Grassland-Draw

Idalou	Lubbock	1916		
McAdoo	Dickens	1916		
Rio Vista	Stonewall	1916	1922	
Rio Vista	Stonewall	1916	1922	
Sparenberg	Dawson	1916	1968	merged with Lamesa Northridge
Trinity Chapel	Swisher	1916	1956	became Tulia Trinity
Victoria	Stonewall	1916	1922	
Webster	Hall	1916	?	
Dixie	Lynn	1917	1948	
Lubbock Cooper	Lubbock	1917		originally Woodrow
Plainview	Stonewall	1917	1920	
Acme	Hardeman	1918	1955	became St. Luke's Quanah, merged with Quanah 1962
Sweetwater Bethel AME	Nolan	1918	?	
Whitfield	Swisher	1918	?	
Hackberry	Cottle	1919	1955	
Marilla	Swisher	1919	1944	merged with Quail
McConnell	Knox	1919	?	
Plainview	Wheeler?	1919	1944	
Farmer's Valley	Hardeman	1920	?	
Golden Pond	Stonewall	1920	1942	
Meadow	Terry	1920		J. A. Sweeney preached as early as 1904
Southland	Garza	1920	1978	
Bledsoe	Yoakum	1921	1930s	
Bog Creek	Throckmorton	1921	?	
Carson	Throckmorton	1921	?	
Fairview	Gaines	1921	?	
Hog Creek	Throckmorton	1921	?	
Lubbock Bethel AME	Lubbock	1921		in 1954, became Greater Bethel. Not UMC.
Ropesville	Hockley	1921		
Valley View	Hale	1921	1974	
Booker	Lipscomb	1922		merged with LaKemp from Oklahoma Conference
Hardy	Lubbock	1922	?d	
Hart	Lamb	1922		
Ketron	Haskell	1922	1939	merged with Paint Creek
Morris Chapel	Haskell?	1922	?	merges with Ketron and later Paint Creek
New Deal	Lubbock	1922		

Sudan	Lamb	1922		
Ackerly	Dawson	1923		
Amarillo San Jacinto	Potter	1923	2005	renamed Covenant Fellowship and relocated in Amarillo
Hyman W. T. Scott Memorial	Mitchell	1923	1945	
Shallowater	Lubbock	1923		
Acuff	Lubbock	1924	?	
Amherst	Lamb	1924		
Blair	Nolan	1924	1951	merged with Nubia and White Church 1951 to be Pioneer Memorial
Kelton	Wheeler	1924	1991	
Levelland First	Hockley	1924		
Morton	Cochran	1924		
Anton	Hockley	1925		
Bledsoe	Cochran	1925	1975	
Higginbotham	Dawson	1925	1944	merged with Nolan Chapel to become L amesa Union
Lubbock Asbury	Lubbock	1925		formerly Nineteenth St, merged with Pioneer, 1977.
Lubbock Mt. Vernon	Lubbock	1925		originally Caprock CME, merged with UMC, 1969
Smyer	Hockley	1925	1976	
Borger First	Hutchinson	1926		
Bula	Bailey	1926	1987	
Enochs	Bailey	1926	1984	merged wth Morton
Oklahoma Lane	Parmer	1926		
Phillips	Hutchinson	1926	1982	merged into St. Andrew, 1982
Sweetwater Highland Heights	Nolan	1926		merged with Sixth Street, 1966
Union Chapel	Haskell	1926	?	
Whitharral	Hockley	1926	1968	
Becton	Lubbock	1927	1974	merged with Idalou
Earth	Lamb	1927		
Fairview	Bailey?	1927	?	
Gruver	Hansford	1927		
Hurlwood	Lubbock	1927		
Maple	Bailey	1927	1957	
Progress	Bailey	1927	1965	merged with Muleshoe, 1965
Stinnett	Hutchinson	1927		ME church
CeeVee	Cottle	1928	1984	

Lazbuddie	Parmer	1928		
Owens	Lubbock	1928	?	
Union Chapel	Knox	1928	?	
Janes	Bailey	1929	?	
LeFors	Gray	1929		
Sterley	Floyd	1929	1966	
Wolfforth	Lubbock	1929		
Big Spring Wesley	Howard	1930	2001	
Dermott	Scurry	1930	?	
Stith	Jones	1930	1951	
Briscoe	Wheeler	1931	1977	used Baptist church and attended Baptist Sunday School
Champion	Nolan	1931	1937	merged with Maryneal to become Sweetwater Highland
Darrouzett	Lipscomb	1931		ME church until 1939
Hodges	Jones	1931	1954	
Salt Creek	Cottle	1931	?	
Spade	Lamb	1932		
Spring Creek	Throckmorton	1932	?	
Whiteface	Cochran	1932	1992	
Parnell	Hall	1933	?	
Welch (formerly Pride)	Dawson	1933		
Brownfield Parkview	Terry	1934	1986	
Pampa Harrah Chapel	Gray	1934	1988	merged with St. Paul, 1988
Pampa St. Paul	Gray	1934		
Abilene Grace	Taylor	1935		
Amarillo Westway	Potter	1935	?	
Cotton Center	Hale	1935	1997	first located at Center Plains
Patricia	Dawson	1936	1965	
Samnorwood	Collingsworth	1936	1950	
Sunray	Moore	1936		
Vernon Faith	Wilbarger	1936		originally Texas Street, renamed Faith in 1982
Highland (south of Roscoe)	Nolan	1937	1977	
Nolan Chapel	Dawson	1937	1944	merged with Higginbotham to become Lamesa Union, then Northridge
Denver City	Gaines	1938		
Paint Creek	Haskell	1938	1995	
Lubbock St. John's	Lubbock	1939		

Sanford	Hutchinson	1939	1962	
New Home	Lynn	1940		originally Monroe
Abilene Epworth	Taylor	1943		formerly Willow street, Trinity, Crescent Heights
Sundown	Hockley	1943	2005	
Lubbock Overton	Lubbock	1944	1967	merged with Oakwood
Abilene Fair Park	Taylor	1945	1986	
Amarillo Wyatt Memorial	Potter	1945	1997	originally in West Texas Conference; merged into Northwest Texas, 1970; merged into Community of Grace
Plainview St. John's	Hale	1945	1975	facility became San Juan in 1981
Amarillo Trinity	Potter	1946		
Borger Buena Vista	Hutchinson	1946	1982	merged with Phillips to become St. Andrew
Johnson	Terry	1946	?	
Midland Asbury	Midland	1947	2000	membership transferred to Bethel
Wellman	Terry	1947	2001	succeeded Forrester School House
Big Spring North Birdwell Lane	Howard	1948		originated as Park Place, renamed North Birdwell Lane, 1966
Lubbock Aldersgate (No. 1)	Lubbock	1948	1964	formerly East Broadway, renamed c. 1955
Lubbock Pioneer Memorial	Lubbock	1948	1977	merged with Asbury
Borger Wesley	Hutchinson	1949		
Cactus	Moore	1949	1983	merged with Hunt Memorial
Lubbock Forrest Heights	Lubbock	1949		
Abilene Aldersgate	Taylor	1950		
Forsan	Howard	1950	1973	merged with Big Spring First
Lamesa Clark	Dawson	1950	1962	See Liberty, became Northridge 1962
Midland St. Mark's	Midland	1950		
Pioneer Memorial	Taylor	1951		merger of Blair, Nubia, and White Church
Fatith	Jones	1952	1970	merger of Celtoex and Dovey churches, merged with Hamlin First, 1970
Fritch	Hutchinson	1952		
Hamlin Faith	Jones	1952	1970	merged with Hamlin First
Hereford Wesley	Deaf Smith	1952		
Midland St. Luke's	Midland	1952		
Plainview Grace	Hale	1953		originally Trinity, renamed Grace, 2003
Plainview Trinity	Hale	1953		see Plainview Grace
Snyder Trinity	Scurry	1953		
Amarillo St. Paul	Potter	1954		
Colorado City St. Luke	Mitchell	1954	2003	

Levelland Wesley	Hockley	1954	1971	merged into Christ church
Anson Bethel Memorial	Jones	1955	1960?	
Lubbock St. Luke's	Lubbock	1955		
Midland St. Paul	Midland	1955		
Pioneer Memorial	Midland	1955	1963	
Quanah St. Luke	Hardeman	1955	1969	originated as Acme, merged with Quanah First
Wellington Trinity	Collingsworth	1955	1977	merged with Welington First
Amarillo Wesley	Potter	1956	1988	merged with Tenth Ave.
Tulia Trinity	Swisher	1956	1979	merged with Tulia First
Abilene Elmwood West	Taylor	1957		
Washita		1957	1959	
Three Way	Bailey	1958	1966	
Amarillo Kingswood	Potter	1959		
Amarillo Pleasant Valley	Potter	1959		
Lubbock Oakwood	Lubbock	1959		originally 58th Street
Andrews Welsey	Andrews	1960		
Big Spring Kentwood	Howard	1960	1974	merged with North Birdwell Lane, 1974
Foreman's Chapel (Spur Circuit)	Dickens?	1960	1969	
Hereford San Pablo	Deaf Smith	1960		
Lubbock Agape	Lubbock	1960		originated as Pleasant Ridge
Abilene St. James	Taylor	1962		first called Edgemont
Amarillo St. Stephen	Potter	1962		
Crosbyton Buen Pastor	Crosby	1962	1971	in Rio Grande Conference, merged with El Crosbyton First
Lamesa Northridge	Dawson	1962		see note on Liberty Church
Dumas Hunt Memorial	Moore	1963		
Lubbock St. Matthew	Lubbock	1963		
Levelland Christ	Hockley	1971		merger of Wesley and St. Luke's
Lubbock LakeRidge	Lubbock	1979		
Lubbock Korean	Lubbock	1981		
Plainview San Juan	Hale	1981		
Borger St. Andrew	Hutchinson	1982		merger of Phillips and Buena Vista
Amarillo Christ	Potter	1985	1992	property became Wesley Drive UMC
Lubbock Aldersgate (No. 2)	Lubbock	1985		
Midland Greenwood	Midland	1986	2003	
Midland Bethel	Midland	1989	2006	merged with Midland First
Lubbock Crossroads	Lubbock	1990		

Amarillo Wesley Drive	Potter	1992	2002	merged with St. Stephens
Brownfield Shalom Centro	Terry	1996	2003	
Lubbock The Springs	Lubbock	1996	2000	discontinued as an UMC
Amarillo Community of Grace	Potter		1997	merger of Forrest Hill and Wyatt Memorial
Amarillo Covenant Fellowship	Potter		2005	formerly San Jacinto, relocated and renamed in 2005
Abilene The Journey	Taylor		2006	
Glen Davis (see Dozier)	Collingsworth		1984	merged with Wellington
Ada (Sweetwater Mission)	Nolan		?	Sweetwater Mission, 1911-1914
Amarillo Forrest Hill	Potter		1997	merged into Community of Grace
Amarillo Westover Fellowship	Potter			
Anderson Chapel			1997	
Ashtola	Donley		1947	merged with Clarendon, 1947
Bailey Chapel			1978	
Bethel	Hall		?	
Bethel	Collingsworth		1955	merged with Wellington Trinity 1957?
Big Square	Bailey		1940s	
Black	Foard		?	
Brushy	Knox		?	see Union Chapel
Buck Creek (see Loco)	Childress		?	
Buford	King?		1969	
Busby	Fisher		?	Sweetwater Mission, 1911-1914
Callemelle	Foard		?	
Claytonville	Foard		?	
Cliff (or Clift?)	Haskell?		?	
Cook Springs	Knox		?	
Cotton Wood	Dickens			see Afton
Cottonwood	Callahan			transferred to Central Texas by boundary change, 1934
Cottonwood	Foard		?	
Croton	Cottle		?	
Deep Lake (see Lakeview, Hall)	Hall		?	
Dorn Chapel	?		?	
Dowell	Fisher		?	
Duck Creek	Dickens		1960	
Durham	Borden?		?	

El Paso	Fissher		
Elba	Hardeman	?	
Elm Top	Throckmorton	?	
Fairview	Lubbock?		
Fancher	Baylor	?	
Finney	Kent	?	
Forrester School House	Terry	1947	became Wellman
Gannon	Nolan?	?	
Garden Valley	Childress	1946	
Gatesville	Haskell	?	
Gilliam Pinkerton (see Pinkerton)	Knox	?	
Gilpin	Foard	?	
Girard	Kent	?	
Golan	Fisher	?	
Gomez	Terry	?	
Hancock	Dawson	1957	
Harrisville	Haskell	?	
Hereford Westway	Deaf Smith	1962	
Jameson	Foard	?	
Klondike	Dawson	?	
Lake Creek	Knox	?	
Lakeview	Throckmorton	?	
Lamesa La Trinidad	Dawson		
Lawlis Chapel	Roby	?	
Lenorah	Martin?	1958	
Levelland St. Luke's	Hockley	1971	merged with Wesley to become Christ
Levelview	Baylor	?	
Liberty	Dawson		merged with Ballard, 1937 to become Nolan Chapel, moved to Union 1944, to Lamesa in 1949 to become Union, then Clark in 1950, then Northridge 1962
Lillie	Collingsworth	?	
Lively	Baylor	?	
Lodge (see Plaska)		?	
Lubbock Epworth	Lubbock	1969	
Lubbock Wesley	Lubbock	1978	
Lytle Gap	Taylor		see Potosi
Marcy	Haskell	?	
Marshall	Hardeman	?	

Marshall (Hardeman County)	Hardeman	1949	
Midland Hollowell	Midland		formerly AMC, renamed Visionary Hollowell Community, 2007
Midway	Knox	?	
Midway	Childress	1938	
Mitchell	Callahan		
Moody (near Sweetwater)	Nolan?	?	
Moss Chapel	Callahan?		
Mount Olive	Dawson?	1951	
Needmore	Haskell?		
New Hope	Collingsworth	?	
New Mid	Haskell?		
Oklaunion	Wilbarger	?	
Pleasant Hill	Cottle	?	
Pleasant View	Knox	?	
Polar	Kent	?	
Pool		?	
Pringle	Hutchinson	?	
Pyron	Nolan?		
Ramsdell	Wheeler	?	
Rock Crossing	Wilbarger	1955?	
Rockwell	Taylor?		
Rhoda	Haskell?		
Rogers	Taylor?		part of Tuscola church history
Scranton	Taylor	?	
Shores Creek	Foard	?	
Sibley	Throckmorton	?	
Silverton	Briscoe		
Snyder East Side	Scurry	1966	
South Vernon	Wilbarger	?	
Spring Creek	Hardeman	?	
Spring Creek	Jones	?	merged with Avoca
Sunshine	Wilbarger	?	
Swearingen	Collingsworth	?	
Sweetwater Sixth Street	Nolan	1966	merged with Highland Heights
Tokio	Terry	1959	merged with Brownfield Parkview
Twiner	Knox	?	

Union Grove	Callahan?		
Vivian	Haskell	?	
Vontress	Knox	?	
Wallace	Callahan?		
Ward	Haskell	?	
Wayside	Armstrong		
Wichita	Cottle	?	
Woodrow Cooper	Lubbock		see Lubbock Cooper
Wright	Fisher	1937	

Appendix B

Northwest Texas Conference Composite Statistical Table, 1910-2008

Compiled by David Murrah and Pat Williamson from annual conference journals and county, district and church histories

Journal Year	Total Members	Profession of Faith	Baptisms, all Ages	Worship Attdnce Mbrship.	Church School	Church School Ave. Att.	Grand Total Paid
1910	34,650	3,371	3,092		27,907		$417,781
1915	36,711		2,470		31,594		
1920	41,680	1,993	2,539		32,739		
1925	52,411	3,850	3,504		44,512	24,612	$1,157,974
1930	64,553	3,727	3,024		48,709		$1,022,611
1935	69,614	3,312	2,894		48,913		$719,470
1940	74,844	2,648	2,575		51,448	28,201	$899,769
1945	82,528	3,122	3,016		49,130	25,815	$2,022,829
1950	92,932	3,240	3,486		63,760	32,248	$4,019,602
1955	101,002	3,109	3,765		77,083	40,714	$5,609,049
1960	105,893	2,769	3,311		81,555	41,022	$7,028,808
1961	105,995	2,785	3,181	42,016	80,590	41,318	$7,599,962
1962	106,429	2,910	3,171	46,756	79,900	41,593	$7,870,408
1963	107,203	2,689	2,902		79,522	40,482	$7,946,435
1964	108,399	2,943	3,061		78,597	40,187	$7,860,092
1965	107,938	2,758	2,828	42,431	79,660	39,306	$8,311,568
1966	107,940	2,412	2,433	44,054	77,254	37,386	$8,134,150
1967	106,987	2,363	2,209	40,062	73,784	35,918	$8,373,808
1968	106,511	1,933	1,884	38,738	70,610	33,174	$8,247,201
1969	105,469	1,934	1,804	38,262	64,400	32,179	$7,989,725
1970	103,896	1,676	1,635	36,391	60,363	32,281	$7,993,685
1971	103,530	611	746	35,041	58,308	31,401	$4,889,827
1972	101,154	1,452	1,438	35,063	55,805	30,558	$8,087,007
1973	99,635	1,316	1,323	32,913	54,362	29,078	$8,610,793
1974	98,258	1,454	1,397	31,563	50,385	24,760	$9,315,150

1975	97,082	1,318	1,311	31,300	48,605	22,849	$10,121,421
1976	95,575	1,394	1,344	29,837	45,798	21,587	$12,238,899
1977	94,225	1,342	1,267	29,789	44,992	21,728	$12,770,500
1978	92,904	1,378	1,298	29,081	44,108	20,974	$14,186,462
1979	91,352	1,125	1,146	28,374	43,419	20,515	$14,881,614
1980	89,933	1,410	1,427	28,670	44,158	20,492	$16,202,926
1981	89,479	1,392	1,382	28,437	43,412	20,230	$18,124,670
1982	88,713	1,326	1,404	28,306	43,265	20,008	$20,138,142
1983	88,305	1,230	1,378	28,206	42,304	19,900	$21,959,264
1984	87,953	1,275	1,486	28,230	42,553	20,084	$23,986,868
1985	86,918	1,293	1,557	28,304	42,478	19,887	$25,210,671
1986	86,118	1,463	1,424	28,459	42,804	19,867	$26,113,777
1987	84,806	1,286	1,289	28,341	43,036	20,166	$25,846,410
1988	83,603	1,243	1,237	27,914	42,366	19,673	$26,347,630
1989	81,759	1,185	1,150	26,901	42,049	19,324	$26,679,573
1990	79,758	1,057	1,100	26,900	41,409	18,868	$29,882,618
1991	77,549	1,316	1,274	26,766	40,263	18,648	$29,551,235
1992	75,946	1,155	1,138	26,685	40,040	18,440	$29,749,863
1993	74,399	1,254	1,587	26,749	39,391	18,374	$31,272,172
1994	74,057	1,202	998	26,567	39,585	17,944	$30,428,296
1995	72,920	1,211	1,018	26,455	39,041	17,577	$30,865,846
1996	72,746	1,303	1,069	26,609	38,141	17,143	$32,737,698
1997	72674	1306	1119	26532	38286	16,988	$33,426,980
1998	71616	1044	1239	26351	38,120	16,490	$35,470,415
1999	71,150	916	982	26,038	37,284	16,211	$36,410,345
2000	70,070	1,035	1,022	25,774	36,024	15,538	$44,729,337
2001	69,458	911	991	25,515	35,030	15,371	$37,648,355
2002	68,733	971	963	25,524	34,873	15,222	$39,860,246
2003	67,474	983	890	24,497	34,115	14,532	$39,777,918
2004	68,016	849	919	23,898	32,769	14,192	$43,685,867
2005	66,975	975	895	23,411	32,107	14,115	$46,936,948
2006	65,772	897	784	22,906	25,970	13,407	$49,520,809
2007	65,229	963	800	22,649	26,161	12,880	$48,976,258
2008	64,535	913	824	21,758	25,364	12,382	$49,716,326

Appendix C

Membership Comparison, 1909-1911, compiled from 1909-1911 *Journals*

Original Six Districts of the new Northwest Texas Conference and Three Additional Districts Created in 1910

District Name	Number of societies in circuit, 1909	Members 1909	Number of societies in circuit, 1910	Members 1910	Number of societies in circuit, 1911	Members 1911	Notes
ABILENE DISTRICT							
Abilene First	1	707	1	420	1	476	
Abilene St Paul			1	320	1	357	
Abilene Tenth St.					2	54	
Abilene Mission			3	162			
Albany and Leuders	3	242	3	219			to Stamford Dist 1911
Anson	1	248	1	301	1	308	
Baird	2	249	2	217	2	283	stats for 1911 incomplete
Buffalo Gap			6	306			
Clyde	4	413	3	425	3	437	
Caps	4	220	2	198	4	329	
Cross Plains	6	269	6	283	6	292	
Dudley	5	184					
Denton			4	210	3	183	
Escota	4	208	6	227			
Hawley			3	159	4	272	
Lawn	5	417			4	150	
Merkel	3	573	2	493	1	446	
Moran	3	177					
Nubia	4	253					
Nugent	4	298	4	352	4	356	
Ovalo			6	375	5	387	

Putnam	4	300	4	200	4	201	
Sabanno	3	61					
Scranton			3	240			
Tye	4	371	5	389	5	363	
Trent	2	215	3	263	5	313	
Truby	4	170					
ABILENE DIST. TOTALS	**66**	**5575**	**68**	**5,759**	**55**	**5,207**	
CLARENDON DISTRICT							
Amarillo Polk St.	1	885	1	907			to Amarillo Dist. 1911
Amarillo Buchanan St.							to Amarillo Dist. 1911
Amarillo Houston St.							to Amarillo Dist. 1911
Amarillo Mission			4	202			
Clarendon Station	1	713	1	743	1	625	
Clarendon Mission			2	30			
Claude Station	1	280	1	314	1	273	
Canyon City Station	1	264	1	333			to Amarillo Dist. 1911
Channing Station	1	68	2	76			to Amarillo Dist. 1911
Canadian Station	1	176	1	199	1	127	
Cataline					6	101	
Dumas	2	78	2	89			to Amarillo Dist. 1911
Dalhart Station	1	259	1	290			to Amarillo Dist. 1911
Gem City			4	69			
Glazier Mission		38	5	45	5	72	
Goodnight					4	98	
Groom Mission	6	184	6	179	3	89	
Hedley Mission	5	125	5	210	5	243	
Hansford Mission	3	36	3	44			to Amarillo Dist. 1911
Hereford							to Amarillo Dist. 1911
Higgins Station	1	151	2	151	2	145	
Lakeview	6	349	3	310	4	304	
Memphis Station	1	430	1	443	1	464	
Miami	3	244	3	253	4	290	

McLean	3	209	3	160	2	212	
Newlin Mission			3	161	3	171	
Ochiltree Mission	3	60	3	92			to Amarillo Dist. 1911
Pampa							to Amarillo Dist. 1911
Panhandle Mission	2	107	2	152			Pampa listed in 1910 with Panhandle, moved to Amarillo Dist., 1911
Quail					6	338	
Stratford Station	1	182	1	189			to Amarillo Dist. 1911
Shamrock	2	163	2	249	1	199	
Texline Mission	3	104	2	123			to Amarillo Dist. 1911
Wildorado							to Amarillo Dist. 1911
Wheeler Mission	7	223	5	195	5	229	
Wellington Station					1	383	
Wellington Ct.					7	286	
CLARENDON DIST. TOTALS	**55**	**5,328**	**69**	**6,208**	**62**	**4,649**	Journal reports 5816 for 1909
COLORADO DIST.							
Big Springs Station	1	482	1	543			to Big Spring Dist. 1911
Big Springs Mission	6	142		100			
Blackwell			6	391	2	98	
Colorado Station	1	335	1	320	1	322	
Colorado Mission	3	87			3	15J	ournal reported 18 societies
Camp Springs	7	246	6	225	7	301	
Coahoma	4	251	3	121			to Big Spring Dist 1911
Clairemont	4	138					
Dermott					5	128	
Dunn	8	317	5	379	5	459	Ira added to Dunn, 1910
Fluvanna	2	97	6	195	3	162	
Gail	3	125	2	113			Durham added to Gail, 1910, moved to Big Spring Dist 1911
Hermleigh	3	250	2	200	3	171	

Hylton					4	208	
Iotan			5	194			
Lorraine Mission	4	114	5	166	3	128	
Lamesa	7	201	1	146			to Big Spring Dist 1911
Pride			3	95			to Big Spring Dist 1911
Roscoe and Lorraine	2	465	3	346	2	432	
Roby	4	232	4	246	5	270	
Sweetwater Station	1	341	1	347	1	395	
Sweetwater Mission					5	67	
Stanton Station	1	143	1	96			to Big Spring Dist 1911
Stanton Mission	6	48	8	62			to Big Spring Dist 1911
Seminole	3	137	3	150			to Big Spring Dist 1911
Snyder Station	1	396	1	451	1	471	
Snyder Mission	4	147	4	120			
Soash				30			
Wesbrook	6	304	4	280	6	300	
COLORADO DIST. TOTALS	**81**	**4,998**	**75**	**5,316**	**56**	**3,927**	

PLAINVIEW DISTRICT

Afton			1	143	5	150	
Barton	3	53	1	133	4	162	
Bovina	5	72	1	44			to Amarillo Dist 1911
Brownfield	2	128	2	125			to Big Spring Dist 1911
Crosbyton					3	143	
Dickens	5	146					probably moved to Vernon Dist.
Dimmitt	3	111		151	4	151	
Emma	3	160	2	204	4	79	
Floydada	1	190	1	206	2	222	
Floydada Mission				100			
Gomez	4	98	1	100			to Big Spring Dist 1911
Hale Center	3	178		147	3	163	
Happy			2	167	5	198	

Hereford	1	336	1	366			to Amarillo Dist. 1911
Hereford Mission		15		91			
Jayton			1	94			
Kress	4	179	1	150	2	146	
Lockney	6	200	1	209	2	158	
Lubbock	1	230	1	305	1	295	
Lubbock Mission					3	32	
Matador	3	298	1	215	1	195	
Plainview	1	510	1	563	1	661	
Plainview Mission					4	62	
Post	4	97		84			to Big Spring Dist 1911
Silverton	4	206	2	106	3	195	
Slaton					1	31	
Spur			2	159			
Tahoka	1	131	1	162	1	193	
Tulia	1	250	1	255			
Turkey	4	250	3	320	4	315	
Wildorado	5	67	2	76			to Amarillo Dist. 1911
PLAINVIEW DIST. TOTALS	**64**	**3,905**	**29**	**4,675**	**53**	**3,551**	

STAMFORD DISTRICT

Albany and Lueders					3	144	
Aspermont	2	192	1	173			to Hamlin Dist. 1911
Aspermont Mission	4	84	7	132			
Avoca	2	298	2	293	3	262	Lueders added 1910
Bomerton	4	220	3	202	4	165	
Goree	4	310	3	317	3	265	
Hamlin	2	286	1	346			to Hamlin Dist. 1911
Hamlin Ct.			4	247			
Haskell Mission	5	289	4	137	5	335	
Haskell Station	1	534	1	550	1	508	
Hitson	3	64					
Knox City	4	458	1	192			to Hamlin Dist. 1911

Lone Star					4	67	
McCauley and Sylvester	4	340	2	235			to Hamlin Dist. 1911
McConnell			4	156			
Munday	1	312	1	329	1	300	
Pinkerton	4	304	3	189			to Hamlin Dist. 1911
Rochester			2	249			to Hamlin Dist. 1911
Rotan	3	271	1	275			to Hamlin Dist. 1911
Rotan Mission			6	88			to Hamlin Dist. 1911
Royston	3	111	4	121			to Hamlin Dist. 1911
Rule	2	373	1	158			to Hamlin Dist. 1911
Sagerton			2	112			to Hamlin Dist. 1911
Seymour					1	310	
Spring Creek					8	293	
Stamford Mission	4	104	4	63			
Stamford Station	1	778	1	290	1	652	
Stamford Ward Mem			2	157	2	202	
Thorp			2	212			
Throckmorton					1	116	
Tuxedo	3	312	4	320	5	392	
W. Stamford and Liberty	2	87					
Welnert	6	170	4	179	5	358	
STAMFORD DIST. TOTALS	**64**	**5,897**	**70**	**5,722**	**47**	**4,369**	

VERNON DISTRICT						
Childress Mission	9	222	8	392	9	456
Childress Station	1	514	1	580	1	687
Chillicothe Mission	2	161	4	241	1	247
Chillicothe Station	1	263	1	262	4	259
Crowell Mission	5	275				
Crowell Station	1	331	1	357	1	342
Estelline	2	238	2	261	2	265
Guthrie Mission	8	102	4	132		
Kirkland	6	397	7	508	8	642

Margaret			3	228	3	226	
Olney Mission	2	279					
Paducah Station					3	212	
Paducah Mission	4	206	1	183	6	140	
Quail	5	358	6	300			
Quanah Station	1	485	1	575	1	576	
Seymour Mission	8	60	4	120			
Seymour Station	1	887	1	260			to Stamford Dist 1911
Spring Creek	6	343	7	344			
Tolbert	6	460	3	349	2	403	
Vera	4	260	4	323			
Vernon Mission	4	250	4	269	2	292	
Vernon Station	1	562	1	576	1	610	
Wellington Mission	7	196	6	360			to Clarendon Dist 1911
Wellington Station	1	369	1	350			to Clarendon Dist 1911
VERNON DIST. TOTALS	**85**	**7,218**	**70**	**6,970**	**44**	**5,357**	

AMARILLO DIST. (CREATED 1910)

Amarillo Polk St.					1	906	
Amarillo Buchanan St.					1	93	
Amarillo Houston St.					1	108	
Bovina					4	56	
Canyon City Station					1	284	
Channing Station					2	107	
Dumas					3	95	
Dalhart Circuit					3	32	
Dalhart Station					1	164	
Hansford Mission					5	108	
Hereford					1	300	
Ochiltree					3	133	
Panhandle					1	91	
Pampa					1	98	
Stratford					1	171	

Texline	2	136
Wildorado	4	68
AMARILLO DIST. TOTALS	**35**	**2,950**

BIS SPRING DISTRICT (CREATED 1910)

Big Spring Station	1	462
Blythe		7
Brownfield	2	125
Coahoma	5	216
Gail	2	119
Gomez	3	116
Lamesa	1	102
Lamesa Mission		
Post	1	62
Pride	4	119
Stanton Station	1	127
Stanton Mission	6	25
Seminole	3	158
Soash	5	123
Tahoka	1	157
BIG SPRING DIST. TOTALS	**35**	**1,918**

HAMILIN DISTRICT (CREATED 1910)

Aspermont	1	198
Hamlin	1	348
Jayton	4	96
Knox City	1	211
McCauley	3	341
Peacock	7	162
Pinkerton	3	182
Rotan Station	1	212
Rotan Mission	1	105
Royston	4	167
Rule	1	180

Rochester					3	260
Sylvester					5	228
Sagerton					5	210
Spur					1	163
Vera						no report
HAMILIN DIST. TOTALS					**41**	**3,063**
CONFERENCE TOTALS	**415**	**32,921**	**381**	**34,650**	**428**	**34,991**

Notes

Preface

[1] *The Methodist Hymnal* (Nashville: Publishing House Methodist Episcopal Church, South, 1919), p. 560.

Chapter 1

[1] *Journal of the Northwest Texas Conference, First Annual Session, Methodist Episcopal Church, South* (1910), 62 (hereafter referred to as *Journal*).

[2] Frederick A. Norwood, *The Story of American Methodism* (Nashville: Abingdon Press, 1983), pp. 124-125.

[3] Walter N. Vernon, *Methodism Moves Across North Texas* (Dallas: Historical Society, North Texas Conference, The Methodist Church, 1967), p. 16.

[4] *Ibid.*

[5] Walter N. Vernon, Robert W. Sledge, Robert C. Monk, Norman W. Spellman, *The Methodist Excitement in Texas* (Dallas, Texas: The Texas United Methodist Historical Society, 1984), p.26. Stevenson later pastored in Arkansas. He died in Louisiana at age eighty-nine. The *New Orleans Advocate* noted in his passing, "The history of Methodism west of the Mississippi is more bound up in his life and labors than perhaps that of any other man." C. A. West, ed., *Texas Conference Methodism on the March, 1814–1960* (Nashville: Parthenon Press, n.d.), p. 112

[6] Vernon, *Methodism*, p. 32.

[7] *Handbook of Texas Online*, s.v. "Methodist Church," (http://www.tsha.utexas.edu/handbook/online/articles/MM/imm1.html (accessed February 8, 2006).

[8] Vernon, *Methodism*, p. 33.

[9] Vernon, *et.al., Methodist Excitement*, p. 39.

[10] *Ibid.*, p. 59.

[11] *Ibid.*, p. 65.

[12] According to the official history of the Texas Conference, when Texas was divided into two conferences by the General Conference of 1844, the territory of the area east of the Trinity River took the name "East Texas Conference," and the area west of the river retained the original name. See *Texas Conference Methodism on the March*, p. 133.

[13] *Handbook of Texas Online*, s.v. "Methodist Church."

[14] Vernon, *et.al., Methodist Excitement*, p. 76.

[15] *Handbook of Texas Online*, s.v. "Methodist Church."

[16] Vernon, *Methodism*, p. 92.

[17] Vernon, *et.al., Methodist Excitement*, p. 123.

[18] Macum Phelan, *A History of Early Methodism in Texas, 1817–1866* (Nashville: Cokesbury Press, 1924), p. 485.

[19] *Ibid.*, p. 486

[20] Vernon, et. al., *Methodist Excitement*, p. 124.

[21] Phelan, *History*, p. 487.

[22] *Ibid.*

[23] *The Doctrines and Discipline of the Methodist Episcopal Church, South* (Nashville: Publishing House of the Methodist Episcopal Church, South, 1866), p. 228; Vernon, *et.al., Methodist Excitement*, p. 163.

[24] *Minutes of the First Session of the Northwest Texas Annual Conference of the Methodist Episcopal Church, South, September 26, 1866* (photocopy, Archives of the Northwest Texas Conference, McMurry University, Abilene, Texas, hereinafter cited as NWT Archives).

[25] Ernest Wallace, *Texas in Turmoil* (Austin: Steck-Vaughn, 1965), p. 242.

[26] *Ibid.*, p. 245.

[27] *Ibid.*

[28] Phelan, *History*, p. 491.

[29] *Minutes, 1866.*

[30] *Ibid.*

[31] Peter W. Gravis, *Twenty-five Years on the Outside Row of the Northwest Texas Annual Conference* (Brownwood, Texas: Cross Timbers Press, 1966), p. 40.

[32] Gravis, *Twenty-five Years*, pp.42-43.

[33] *Ibid.*, 43. George Webb Slaughter himself founded dozens of Baptist churches in North Texas and produced a clan of cattlemen, including his most famous son, Christopher Columbus Slaughter. See David J. Murrah, *C. C. Slaughter: Rancher, Banker, Baptist* (Austin: University of Texas Press, 1981).

[34] J. O. Haymes, *History of the Northwest Texas Conference, The Methodist Church: The First 50 Years, 1910–1960* (Nashville: Methodist Publishing House,1962), p.16.

[35] *Journal of the Northwest Texas Conference of the Methodist Episcopal Church, South, 1871.* Hereafter, all references to the Northwest Texas Conference journals will be cited as *Journal* preceded by the year.

[36] Vernon, *et.al., Methodist Excitement*, p. 151.

[37] Elsa McFarland Turner, *A Charge to Keep; First United Methodist Church, Albany, Texas, 1873–1991* (Austin, Texas: Nortex Press, 1991), p. 21. According to J. O. Haymes, J. E. Ferguson, father of future Texas Gov. James E. Ferguson, may have preached the first sermon in Shackelford County on Hubbard Creek "about 1870." He adds, "But it is probable that Milton Jones went to Fort Griffin prior to 1870 while he was pastor of the Stephenville Mission." Haymes, *Northwest Texas Conference*, p. 16.

[38] *Handbook of Texas Online*, s.v. "Fort Griffin, Texas," http://www.tsha.utexas.edu/handbook/online/articles/FF/hnf35.html (accessed February 9, 2006).

[39] Turner, *Charge*, p. 3.

[40] 1975 *Journal*, p. 276.

[41] Carl Coke Rister, *Fort Griffin on the Texas Frontier* (Norman: University of Oklahoma Press, 1956),
p. 204.

[42] Wallace, *Texas in Turmoil*, p. 232.

[43] Robert W. Sledge, "Lytle Gap: A West Texas Frontier Mission, 1879–1889," *Year Book of the West Texas Historical Association* (Vol. 56, 1980), 118.

[44] Vernon, *Methodism*, p. 16.

Chapter 2

[1] Haymes, *Northwest Texas Conference*, p. 16.

[2] *Ibid.* p. 16. See also Robert W. Sledge, "Ghost Churches of South Taylor and Callahan Counties," unpublished typescript (2 pp), 2004, NWT Archives. See also *Texas Methodist*, April 4, 1978, p. 1. Files (1965-present) of the Northwest Texas Conference Edition of the *Texas Methodist* and its successor, *The United Methodist Reporter*, are located in the Northwest Texas Conference Archives at McMurry University.

[3] Sledge, "Lytle Gap," 119.

[4] *Northwest Texas Conference Journal, 1879.*

[5] *Northwest Texas Conference Journal, 1879, 1880.*

[6] *Northwest Texas Conference Journal, 1880*; Vernon, *et.al., Methodist Excitement*, p. 163.

[7] *Northwest Texas Conference Journal, 1880.*

[8] *Ibid.* p. 160.

[9] *Northwest Texas Conference Journal, 1902,* 23-24.

[10] John M. Barcus, "A Trip through the Panhandle," in *Pictorial Directory, First Methodist Church, Seymour, Texas* (n.p., 1948), p. 29.

[11] Gravis, *Twenty-five Years,* p. 52.

[12] *Northwest Texas Conference Journal, 1880,* 161.

[13] Barbara Ledbetter, "Gun Totin' Bible Quotin' Indian Fighter was Graham's First Methodist Parson," *Graham News,* January 26, 1975. Xeroxed copy in Barbara Ledbetter Reference File, Southwest Collection, Texas Tech University. See also Walter N. Vernon, *Methodism*, p. 77.

[14] Tackitt moved from Young County back to Parker County in 1882, apparently to pastor the church at Goshen (five miles west of Springtown), one of the many churches he founded. He died in 1891 at the age of 88.

[15] "The History of the First United Methodist Church, Seymour, Texas," in *Histories, Seymour District of the United Methodist Church* (n.p., 1984), p. 1 of Seymour section.

[16] "Pease City," *Histories, Seymour District*, in "Discontinued Churches in Foard County."

[17] Gravis, *Twenty-five Years,* p. 52.

[18] *Ibid.*

[19] *Ibid.* p. 54.

[20] *Ibid.* p. 54. Gravis recorded this trip apparently in letters that he wrote, and for his book, he simply copied the letters into the text. However, in so doing, he may have gotten some pages out of order. For example, he recounts the beginning of the trip on page 54, but the story line become confused on page 55.

[21] *Ibid.*, p. 56.

[22] *Ibid.*, p. 57; Henry Chenoweth, "Doan's Crossing," Ghosttowns.com Website at www.ghosttowns.com/states/tx/doanscrossing.html. See also J. Marvin Hunter, ed., *The Trail Drivers of Texas* (Austin: University of Texas Press, 1985), pp. 772-775.

[23] Keith R. Owen, "Doan's: Birth and Death of a Frontier Town," *Year Book of the West Texas Historical Association* LXXI), 85-86.

[24] Gravis, *Twenty-five Years,* p. 58.

[25] *Handbook of Texas Online,* s.v. "Greer County," http://www.tsha.utexas.edu/handbook/online/articles/GG/hcg81.html (accessed February 11, 2006).

[26] *Northwest Texas Conference Journal*, 1893, p. 181.

[27] Gravis, *Twenty-five Years,* p. 58.

[28] *Ibid.*, p. 59.

[29] *Ibid.*, p. 61; *Handbook of Texas Online*, s.v. "Mobeetie, Texas," http://www.tsha.utexas.edu/handbook/online/articles/MM/hlm77.html (accessed February 11, 2006).

[30] Gravis, *Twenty-five Years,* p. 60

[31] *Ibid.*.

[32] Fred. W. Rathjen, *The Texas Panhandle Frontier* (Austin: University of Texas Press, 1973), p. 232. See also Pauline Durrett Robertson and R. L. Robertson, *Panhandle Pilgrimage* (Canyon, Texas: Staked Plains Press, 1976), pp.244-246; and *Handbook of Texas Online*, s.v. "Carhart, Lewis Henry," http://www.tsha.utexas.edu/handbook/online/articles/CC/fca53.html (accessed February 12, 2006).

[33] After the Clarendon Methodist Church fell into disuse after 1900, Methodists from Dalhart dismantled the church and moved it and its bell to Dalhart where they established the Pine Street Methodist Episcopal Church, which later became the Lakeview United Methodist Church. The historic bell is still in use. See Chapter 5.

[34] Gravis, *Twenty-five Years*, p. 61.

[35] *Ibid.*, p. 62

[36] *Ibid.*, p. 65.

[37] *Ibid.*, p. 66;

[38] *Northwest Texas Conference Journal, 1881*, 230.

[39] *Northwest Texas Conference Journal, 1902*, 23.

[40] Virginia Browder, *Donley County: Land of Promise* (_______: Nortex Press, 1975), p. 303.

[41] Ruth Magee, ed. *A Century of Methodism in the Eastern Texas Panhandle* (Pampa, Texas: Pampa District of the Northwest Texas Conference, 1993), p. 45; *Handbook of Texas Online*, s.v. "Mobeetie, Texas." In 1887, John M. Barcus, Robert Sheldon, R. M. Morris, and Jerome Harralson made a trip to Mobeetie along the same route that Gravis and Hosmer had followed. There they held a Sunday-Thursday meeting with two services a day. "We had a splendid meeting . . . and they showed us much hospitality," Barcus recalled in 1910. Barcus, "A Trip Through the Panhandle," p. 31.

[42] "James Taylor Hosmer," *Northwest Texas Conference Journal, 1893*, 181; "James Taylor Hosmer," unpublished typescript (4 pp., n.p., n.d) Northwest Texas Conference Archives.

[43] Richard W. Etulain, *Beyond the Missouri: The Story of the American West* (Albuquerque: U of New Mexico Press, 2006), p. 289.

[44] R. F. Dunn, as cited in Haymes, *Northwest Texas Conference*, p. 19.

[45] *Handbook of Texas Online*, s.v. "Baird, Texas;" Putnam, Texas," http://www.tsha.utexas.edu/handbook/online/articles/PP/hlp60.html (accessed February 21, 2006).

[46] Fane Downs, ed., *The Future Great City of West Texas: Abilene, 1881-1981* (Abilene, Texas; Rupert Richardson Press, 1981), p. 6.

[47] *Ibid.*, "Abilene, Texas."

[48] *Northwest Texas Conference Journal, 1881*, p. 231.

[49] Tanner Laine, "Circuit Rider—Gospel on Horseback," *Lubbock Avalanche-Journal*, August 5, 1963. One of Dunn's children was Dr. Sam Dunn, a noted Lubbock physician.

[50] *Texas Methodist*, March 17, 1978.

[51] "History of the First United Methodist Church," *Centennial Celebration, First United Methodist Church, Sweetwater, Texas* (n.p.,1981); Hooper Shelton and E. L. Yeats, *A History of Nolan County, Texas* (Sweetwater, Texas: Shelton Press, 1975), p. 128.

[52] *Lore and Legend: A Compilation of Documents Depicting the History of Colorado City and Mitchell County*, Volume I (Colorado City, Texas: Colorado City *Record*, 1976), p. 50.

[53] *Ibid.*, p. 234.

[54] *Ibid.*, p. 206. Unlike the present, the first and second Northwest Texas Conferences included all of Callahan County, including the Pecan Circuit. The Cross Plains church moved from the Northwest Texas to the Central Texas Conference in 1934 for an unexplained reason.

[55] Robert W. Sledge, "'Ghost Churches' of South Taylor and Callahan Counties" (unpublished typescript, 2004, in possession of author, 2 pp.). Of the missions and preaching points that made up the south Taylor and Callahan counties circuits in 1881, only North Pecan and Lytle Gap, now Eula and Potosi churches, still survive. See also Robert W. Sledge, "Lytle Gap: A West Texas Frontier Mission, 1879-1889," *West Texas Historical Association Year Book* (Vol. 56), 117-132.

[56] One source, "A Brief History of the First Methodist Church in Big Spring, Texas," (undated typescript), notes that the Big Spring church began in November 1882. Another cites July 1883 as the starting date. Probably, the earlier date was the initial effort and official organization came in July 1883. See Joe Pickle, *Getting' Started: Howard County's First 25 Years* (Big Spring, Texas: Howard County Heritage Museum, 1980, p. 226.

[57] 1885 *Journal*, 1885, p. 56.

[58] "History of the Haskell United Methodist Church," (typescript, 1980), NWT Archives.

[59] 1886 *Journal*, p. 41.

[60] Report of the Committee on the Sate of the Church, 1887 *Journal*, 1887, p. 101 (typescript).

[61] "History of the Claude United Methodist Church," (typescript, 1984), NWT Archives.

[62] *Handbook of Texas Online*, s.v. "Southern Kansas Railway," http://www.tsha.utexas.edu/handbook/online/articles/SS/eqs22.html (accessed May 29, 2006).

[63] Logically, Panhandle should have developed as the major city of the region; however, geography determined the difference. The Fort Worth and Denver, which originally planned to turn north near Clarendon to connect with the Santa Fe near Panhandle, changed its route because construction of the line across the Red River was going to be too expensive. As a result, the line continued to the northwest along the relatively level divide between the Prairie Dog Fork of the Red to the south, and the Salt Fork on the north toward present-day Amarillo. The Santa Fe then contracted with the builder of the FW & D, Greenville Dodge, to build a spur connecting its line from Panhandle to the FW & D at Washburn, just east of Amarillo. Washburn was a townsite owned by Dodge's father-in-law, R. E. Montgomery. See David Alan Loving, "H. B. Sanborn and the Early Development of the Texas Panhandle (MA Thesis, Texas Tech University, 1998), pp. 18-22.

[64] 1888 *Journal*, p. 8.

[65] *Our Church History, Allison United Methodist Church* (n.p., 1993). The Cataline church moved to Zybach in 1915 and to Allison in 1930.

[66] *A Century of Methodism in the Eastern Texas Panhandle*, p. 13; Glyndon M. Riley, "The History of Hemphill County (MA Thesis, West Texas State Teachers College, 1939), p. 120.

[67] Ernest Charles Shearer, "A Survey History of Potter County, Texas (MA Thesis, West Texas State Teachers College, 1933), p. 95; Garry Nall, ed., *The Centennial History of Polk Street United Methodist Church* (Amarillo: Polk Street United Methodist Church, 1989), p. 9.

[68] Nall, ed., *Centennial History*, p. 10.

[69] Lynn and Duane Guy, eds., *A Joyful Journey* (Canyon, Texas: First United Methodist Church, 1989), p. 2.

[70] This information is drawn from Appendix A: Northwest Texas Conference Churches: Dates Established. This table and others were compiled from church and county histories and from the Church History files in the Northwest Texas Conference Archives.

[71] *Our Story, Kindred Spirits, We and They, Yesterday and Today* (n.p., n.d.), p. 235.

[72] "A History of the Benjamin Methodist Church" (typescript, undated), p. 1; J. T. Griswold, *From Dugout to Steeple* (find publication info)

[73] "History of First United Methodist Church, Wellington, Texas," (unpublished typescript), p. 3.

[74] Ralph Cooper, *First Methodist Church, Aspermont, Texas: A History of Methodism in Stonewall County, 1890-1967* (n.p., n.d.), p. 9.

[75] "A History of the Crosbyton Methodist Church" (unpublished typescript, c. 1960), n.p.; *A History of Crosby County, 1876-1977* (Dallas: Taylor Publishing Co., 1978), p. 32.

[76] "Epworth, Texas," *Handbook of Texas Online*, http://www.tsha.utexas.edu/handbook/online/articles/EE/hve32.html (accessed June 15, 2006). There is some disagreement among sources as to Graves' settlement in Hale County; the *Handbook of Texas* gives two different dates, 1883 and 1884, and the Hale County history book gives it as 1881. See Vera Dean Wofford, ed. *Hale County Facts and Folklore, Vol. II* (Dallas: Taylor Publishing Company, 1986), p. 389.

[77] Wofford, ed., *Hale County Facts*, p. 402.

[78] *Ibid.*, pp. 389, 402; J. O. Haymes, *History of the First United Methodist Church, Lubbock, Texas, 1892-1976* (n.p.,n.d.), p. 7; Charles E. Lutrick, "The Lakeview United Methodist Church (Hale County, Texas), unpublished typescript, 1995.

[79] L. L. Graves, ed., *A History of Lubbock* (Lubbock: West Texas Museum Association, 1962), p. 452; Alwyn Barr, Paul Carlson and Betty Carr: *First United Methodist Church of Lubbock: A Centennial Celebration, 1892-1992* (Lubbock: First United Methodist Church, c. 1992), p. 5.

[80] Wofford, ed., *Hale County Facts*, p. 389.

[81] Barr, Carlson, and Carr, First United Methodist of Lubbock, p.5; Fane Downs and Robert Sledge, eds., *Pride of Our Western Prairies: McMurry College, 1923-1988* (Abilene, Texas: McMurry College, 1988), p. 6.

[82] 1880, 1892 *Journal.*

[83] 1879 *Journal*, p. 109.

[84] 1881 *Journal*, pp. 122-123.

[85] 1881 *Journal*, p. 247.

[86] 1892 *Journal*, pp. 88-89.

[87] *Ibid.*

[88] "Mack's Tracks: Panhandle rainfall totals all wet," *Amarillo Daily News* (Amrillo.com), September 1, 1999.

[89] Paul Lack, et.al., *The History of Abilene: Facts and Sources* (Abilene, Texas: McMurry College, 1981), p. 17.

[90] Murrah, *C. C. Slaughter*, p. 70.

[91] 1893 *Journal*, pp. 171-173.

[92] Turner, *Charge*, p. 3.

[93] Elva Mae Pittard, *History of First United Methodist Church, Anson, Texas* (n.p., 1982), p.4.

[94] Abe Mulkey, *Abe Mulkey's Budget* ((Waco, Texas: Y. G. Freeman, 1897), p. 12. This rare copy is in the Bridwell Library at SMU. Little information is available on Mulkey. According to the *Handbook of Texas*, Mulkey entered the Methodist ministry in 1885; however, another source implies that he was not licensed until 1891. See Spruill Cook, "Abe Mulkey, 'Exorter' for God and the Orphans" (unpublished typescript, 1964, Bridwell Library, Southern Methodist University), p. 8.

[95] Abe Mulkey, *Abe Mulkey's Budget*, p. 41.

[96] *Ibid.* p. 108. In one of his sermons, Mulkey took note of his critics: "The jackass of today is the doctor of divinity, sitting high up in his pulpit, but getting down and throwing his pen and ink javelin at a little revivalist who is only trying to win souls to Christ." See Mulkey, *Abe Mulkey's Budget*, p. 114.

[97] *Ibid.*, p. 109.

[98] *Ibid.*, p. 110. Mulkey continued to hold revivals in Norhwest Texas in the years ahead. In 1904, he preached for a camp meeting in Callahan County near Cross Plains in a "planked-roof tabernacle." "It was one of the greatest revivals in the history of our church," recalled Cal C. Wright, who was 17 at the time and a student at Fort Worth Polytechnic College. Wright joined the Northwest Texas Conference in 1909 and pastored within it for nearly 50 years. He died in 1971, the second to last surviving member of the pre-1910 Northwest Texas Conference. See Nail, ed. *The History of Texas Methodism, 1900-1960*, pp. 497-499. See also 1971 *Journal*, pp.174-175.

[99] 1893 *Journal*, p. 163.

[100] Griswold, *From Dugout to Steeple*, p. 26; Vernon, *et.al.*, *Methodist Excitement*, p. 156.

Chapter 3

[1] "Desdemona, Texas," *Handbook of Texas Online*, s.v. "," http://www.tsha.utexas.edu/handbook/online/articles/DD/hld18.html (accessed June 19, 2006).

[2] Ed R. Wallace, *Parson Hanks: Fourteen Years in the West* (Arlington, Texas: Journal Print, 1906), pp.44-45; Haymes, *History*, p. 27.

[3] *Ibid.*, p. 72.

[4] *Ibid.*, p. 56.

[5] "Flomot Methodist Church (typescript, undated), NWTC Archives.

[6] 1894 *Journal.*

[7] 1897 *Journal,* p. 14.

[8] Murrah, *C. C. Slaughter*, p. 84.

[9] "Pecos and Northern Texas Railway," *Handbook of Texas Online,*" http://www.tsha.utexas.edu/handbook/online/articles/PP/eqp9.html (accessed June 17, 2006).

[10] Bessie Patterson, *A History of Deaf Smith County* (Hereford, Texas: Pioneer Publishers), 1964),

[11] "Texas Central Railroad," *Handbook of Texas Online.*

[12] W. B. McKeown to Mrs. Julus Weildling, Dumas Texas, Feb. 15, 1941 (photocopy), NWT Archives.

[13] With his strong ties to Dallas through his more famous brother C. C. Slaughter, W. B. Slaughter had brought to Coldwater "big" Baptist preachers to hold summer camp revivals on Coldwater Creek, such as L. R.Scarborough and George W. Truett, pastor of the First Baptist Church of Dallas. (Marylou McDaniel, *God, Grass, and Grit* (Hereford, Texas: Pioneer Book Publishers, 1971), p. 12, 43).

[14] W. B. McKeown, "Making the Survey," *Southwestern Advocate*, March 14, 1935, p. 3. Clipping in W. B. McKeown file, NWT Archives.

[15] McKeown, "Making the Survey," pp. 3, 12.

[16] Lillie Mae Hunter, *The Book of Years: A History of Dallam and Hartley Counties* (Hereford, Texas: Pioneer Book Publishers, 1969), p. 47.

[17] Laura V. Hamner, *Light 'n Hitch* (Dallas: American Guild Press, 1958), p. 250.

[18] McKeown, "The Work Begins to Take Form," *Southwestern Advocate,* May 30, 1935, p. 2.

[19] *Texas Methodist*, September 17, 1976.

[20] Hamner, *Light 'n Hitch,* p. 252.

[21] "History of Methodism in Dumas, Texas," (n.p.,n.d.), p. 5.

[22] W. B. McKeown to Mrs. Julus Weildling, Dumas Texas, Feb. 15, 1941.

[23] McKeown, *Southwestern Advocate,* June 27, 1935, pp.3, 10; Boyd M. McKeown to David Murrah, August 1, 2008, telephone conversation., notes in possession of author.

[24] Elmer D. Landreth, *They Were Called* (Englewood Colorado: Columbine Copy, n.d.), p. 12.

[25] *Gray County Heritage* (n.p. Gray County History Book Committee, 1985), p. 64.

[26] *A Century of Methodism in the Eastern Texas Panhandle* (Pampa District: Northwest Texas Conference, 1993), p. 38. Rancher Alfred Rowe donated a city block to the church for a new building that was begun in 1904. ("McLean Methodist Church" (typescript, n.p., n.d.).)

[27] Griswold, *From Dugout to Steeple*, p. 105.

[28] Kathryn Cotton, *Saga of Scurry* (San Antonio: Naylor Company, 1957), pp. 24-25.

[29] Lack, *et. al*, *History of Abilene*, p. 17.

[30] Abbe, *et.al.*, *Lubbock and the South Plains*, p. 35; Murrah, *C. C.Slaughter*, pp. 104-109.

[31] Jan Blodgett, *Land of Bright Promise: Advertising the Texas Panhandle and South Plains, 1870-1917* (Austin: University of Texas Press, 1988, p. 87.

[32] *Hereford Brand*, November 22, 1907, as cited in Jan Blodgett, "Home, Health, and Happiness in the Panhandle: Land Promotion and Advertisement on the Panhandle and South Plains of Texas, 1890-1917" (MA Thesis, West Texas State University, 1985), p. 211.

[33] "A Brief History of the Methodist Church at Draw" (typescript, 1951), NWT Archives.

[34] Robert H. Kirk, *The Story of A Church that Pioneered and Grew: A Word and Picture History of First Methodist Church, Lamesa, Dawson County, Texas* (n.p: 1947), p. 1.

[35] Griswold, *From Dugout to Steeple*, p. 77.

[36] *Ibid.*, p.77,91-92.

[37] 1907 *Journal.*

[38] Haymes, *History of the Northwest Texas Conference*, pp. 35-37.
[39] Vernon, *et.al.*, *Methodist Excitement*, p. 163.
[40] 1900 *Journal*, p. 26.
[41] *Ibid.*, p. 37.
[42] Vernon, *et.al.*, *Methodist Excitement*, pp. 166-167.
[43] *Ibid.*, p. 165.
[44] 1950 *Journal*, p. 49.
[45] 1909 *Journal*, p. 22.
[46] 1909 *Journal*, p. 22.
[47] Vernon, *et.al.*, *Methodist Excitement*, p. 167.
[48] 1909 *Journal*, p.23.
[49] Compiled from the 1909 *Journal* of the Northwest Texas Conference. The initial 1910 journal for the new Northwest Texas Conference reported a total membership of 31,287 for the previous year. The 1909 Journal reported a total of 32. The statistician did not account for the discrepancy. A terse note on the Recapitulation Table says, "There are many apparent discrepancies in the Statistical Tables, but having nothing to check them against, same appear just as in copy."
[50] *Texas Christian Advocate*, May 5, 1910, p. 1. At that 1910 General Conference, the bishops reported that southern Methodism had grown by more than 200,000 since the last General Conference and total membership was 1.8 million. They reported that ministers were transferring from other Protestant churches to be in the Methodist Episcopal Church South, so that they could be in a "witnessing church, where people told their religious experience and had one to tell." Thus the bishops exhorted, "We pray that our Church may ever remain witnesses of the living Christ and the power of his resurrection."
[51] *Ibid.*
[52] *Texas Christian Advocate,* November 17, 1910, p. 1.
[53] Frederick DeLand Leete, *Methodist Bishops* (Nashville: Parthenon Press, 1948), p. 21.)
[54] Haymes, *History,* p.42
[55] 1910 *Journal.*
[56] *Ibid.*,p. 21.
[57] *Ibid.*,p. 28.
[58] *Ibid.*,p. 33.
[59] *Texas Methodist*, August 10, 1979.

Chapter 4

[1] O. P. Kiker, "A Word from the New Northwest Texas Conference," *Twenty-ninth Annual Report of the Board of Church Extension of the Methodist Episcopal Church, South, 1910-1911*, p. 260.
[2] *Ibid.*, p. 262.
[3] Compiled from U.S. population estimates for 2010.
[4] *Northwest Texas Conference Journal*, 1910, pp. 40-41.
[5] See Appendix C, Membership Comparison, 1901-1911, compiled from 1909-1911 *Journals.*
[6] 1910 *Journal*, p. 73.
[7] This figure is based on a 1910 Conference membership of 34,650, rather than 35,009 as reported by the 1910 *Journal.* J. O. Haymes reported the figure as being 30,009, but he either made a mistake in transcribing the figure or tried to correct what he thought to be an obvious error in the Journal. The 34,650-figure is the author's own calculation based on a recalculation of the statistics reported in the 1910 *Journal*. See Haymes, *History*, p, 54. This information is compiled from the statistics reported in the 1910 *Journal* and the 2006 *Journal.*
[8] "Hamlin, Texas,"*Handbook of Texas Online.*

[9] Haymes, *History*, p. 196.

[10] 1910 *Journal*, p. 7.

[11] Haymes,, *History*, pp. 54-63.

[12] See Vernon, *et. al.*, *Methodist Excitement*, pp. 249-252.

[13] 1909 *Journal*.

[14] 1910 *Journal*, p. 40.

[15] Compiled from the 1912, 1915, and 1916 *Journals*.

[16] *Texas Christian Advocate*, August 24, 1911 (microfilm, Southwest Collection, Texas Tech University).

[17] "History of the First United Methodist Church, Wellington, Texas," (n.p, n.d, typescript), p. 4, NWT Conference Archives.

[18] 1910 *Journal*, p. 62.

[19] *Texas Methodist*, March 11, 1977, p. 1.

[20] See Appendix C: Membership Comparison Table, 1909-1911; 1912 *Journal*, p. 68.

[21] 1912 *Journal*, p. 68.

[22] Paul Carlson, *Amarillo: The Story of a Western Town* (Lubbock: Texas Tech University Press, 2006), p. 81.

[23] In 1914, rainfall for the year totaled over 41 inches in Abilene, nearly twice the average. Lack, *et. al*, *History of Abilene*, p. 17.

[24] Abbe, *et.al.*, *Lubbock and the South Plains*, p. 37.

[25] 1915 *Journal*.

[26] Lack, *et. al*, *History of Abilene*, p. 16.

[27] "South Plains Rainfall, 1915-1992, data disk, in possession of author; *Lubbock Avalanche-Journal*, July 4, 1975, clipping located in Reference File, "Lubbock, Texas: Weather," Southwest Collection, Texas Tech University. The clipping includes rainfall for Lubbock from 1911 through 1974.

[28] David J. Murrah, *The Pitchfork Land and Cattle Company: The First Century* (Lubbock: Texas Tech University Press, 1983), p. 18.

[29] "Facts and Background."

[30] Leota Nash Pirtle, *Look Back with Pride, Look Forward with Hope: A History of the Throckmorton United Methodist Church* (Quanah, TX: Nortex Press, 1976), p. 24.

[31] *History of the Crowell Methodist Church First Seventy-five Years* (n.p.,n.d.), p. 22. One Methodist preacher, Cal Wright, was "sacrificial" in his visitation of ill people throughout his county. See Elmer Landreth, *The Missing Book*, (Englewood, Colorado: by the author), p. 91. While there was wide-spread deaths in Northwest Texas, the region's isolation may have spared many as the flu claimed 675,000 lives throughout the United States. See Molly Billings, "The Influenza Pandemic of 1918," accessed February 27, 2007, online at http://virus.stanford.edu/uda/.

[32] *Lubbock Avalanche-Journal*, March 5, 1971.

[33] "Facts and Background on Influenza Epidemic," from Texas Tech University Health Science Center Pandemic Influenza Initiative website, http://www.ttuhsc.edu/flu/facts.aspx, accessed December 17, 2007.

[34] O. F.Sensabaugh, "Recollections," (Typescript), Hunt Collection, Jay-Rollins Library, McMurry University, as cited in Robert Sledge, "A People, A Place: The Story of Abilene," (draft typescript), n.p., courtesy Robert Sledge. This manuscript is scheduled to be published by State House Press in 2008.

[35] 1918 *Journal*, pp. 5-7.

[36] *Ibid.*, p. 55.

[37] Compiled from Appendix A: Churches of the Northwest Texas Conference, Listed by Founding Date. Rain, or the lack thereof, played a major role in church expansion. During the wet years of 1905-1906, the area saw the establishment of 46 new churches; during the extremely dry years of 1917-1918, only six were founded.

[38] Compiled from 1918, 1919, 1920 *Journals.*

[39] Robert Sledge, *Hands on the Ark: The Struggle for Change in the Methodist Episcopal Church, South, 1914-1939* (Lake Junaluska, North Carolina: Commission on Archives and History, The United Methodist Church), p. 70.

[40] "Mrs. Nat G. Rollins (Lena Elva Hyder: A Woman of Firsts," (unpublished typescript, nd), p. 1, Northwest Texas Archives, McMurry University; Vernon, *et.al., Methodist Excitement*, pp. 229-230.

[41] 1918 *Journal*, p. 18.

[42] 1919 *Journal*, pp. 6-7.

[43] "Mrs. Nat G. Rollins," p. 1; 1921 *Journal*, p. 19.

[44] Haymes, *History*, p. 67. See also Appendix A.

[45] 1919 *Journal*, p. 18

[46] Presiding Elder Report, 1921 *Journal*, p 60. Two districts did not report the number of revivals, but all reported conversions. The report implied that nearly every charge held at least one revival during the year.

[47] 1921 *Journal.*, p.73.

[48] *From the Heart of Hockley County:* Recollections (Dallas: Taylor Publishing Company, 1986), pp. 230-231; Elvis E. Fleming and David J. Murrah, *Texas' Last Frontier: A New History of Cochran County* (Morton, Texas: Cochran County Historical Commission, 2001), pp. 50-52.

[49] *History of the First United Methodist Church, Morton, Texas, 1924-1974* (n.p., 1974), pp. 6-7.

[50] "I. Ernest Walker: Some Reflections on my Life," (Typescript, 1971), NWT Archives. Ernest Walker served in the Northwest Texas Conference from his admission in 1923 to 1942 when he transferred to the Southwest Texas Conference. He retired in 1957 and died in 1983 at the age of 91. He was married to Jennie West, who was the daughter of pioneer Northwest Texas pastor C. D. West. Their son Charles Walker became a pastor in the Southwest Texas Conference. Newspaper clipping, undated, in I. Ernest Walker file, NWT Archives.

[51] *Ibid.*, p. 76.

[52] Compiled from 1920-1927 *Journals.*

[53] T. R. Havins, *Belle Plain, Texas: Ghost Town in Callahan* (Brownwood, Texas: Brown Press, 1972), pp.43-44.

[54] "Belle Plain College," *Handbook of Texas Online*, http://www.tsha.utexas.edu/handbook/online/articles/BB/kbb26.html (accessed February 18, 2007; T. R. Havins, *Belle Plain Texas: Ghost Town in Callahan (Brownwood, Texas:* Brown Press, 1972), pp.42-58. See also District History Committee, "A History of the Abilene District of the Northwest Texas Conference of the United Methodist Church, 1910-1984, (Typescript, 1984, NWT Archives, pp. 17-20).

[55] Vernon, *et.al., Methodist Excitement,*, p. 261. Polytechnic listed three seniors in the Class of 1909, two of which were from northwest Texas—Anson and Amarillo. (*Panther City Parrot, 1910: Year Book of Polytechnic College, Fort Worth* (Fort Worth, Polytechnic College, 1909), located in the R. F. Dunn Papers, Southwest Collection, Texas Tech University.

[56] Vernon, *et.al., Methodist Excitement*, p. 258.

[57] Michael Q. Hooks, "The Struggle for Dominance: Urban Rivalry in North Texas, 1870-1910" (Ph.D. Dissertation, Texas Tech University, 1979), p. 219. A full account of Dr. Boaz's role in this story is found in Hiram A. Boaz, *Eighty-Four Golden Years: An Autobiography of Bishop Hiram Abiff Boaz* (Nashville: Parthenon Press, 1951), pp. 77-89)

[58] Vernon, *et.al., Methodist Excitement*, p. 258.

[59] Hooks, "Struggle for Dominance, "pp. 220-222.

[60] *Ibid.*

[61] 1910 *Journal*, p. 49.

[62] Vernon, et.al., *Methodist Excitement*, p. 258; Olin W. Nail, *History of Texas Methodism* (Austin: Capital Printing Company, 1961), p. 168.

[63] Nail, *History of Texas Methodism*, pp. 162-163.

[64] Vernon, *et.al., Methodist Excitement*, p. 261).

[65] "Clarendon College," *Handbook of Texas Online*, http://www.tsha.utexas.edu/handbook/online/articles/CC/kbc22.html (accessed February 18, 2007). The College's enrollment reached 350 in 1919.

[66] W. M. Stoker, "History of Seth Ward College" (unpublished typescript, West Texas State University, 1977), p. 1, Southwest Collection, Texas Tech University.

[67] "Seth Ward College," and "Central Plains College," *Handbook of Texas Online*, http://www.tsha.utexas.edu/handbook/online/articles/CC/kbc13.html (accessed February 18, 2007); (Herman Ford, "The History and Economic Development of Hale County, Texas (MA Thesis, West Texas State Teachers College, 1932), p. 89.

[68] Vernon, *et.al., Methodist Excitement*, p. 168; Olin W. Nail, *History of Texas Methodism, 1900-1960* , p. 4.

[69] "Seth Ward College," *Handbook of Texas Online.*

[70] 1916 *Journal*, 1916, p. 41.

[71] Vernie Newman, "A History of McMurry College, 1920-1936" (MA Thesis, Texas Technological College, 1937), p. 6.

[72] *Twenty-Eighth Annual Report of the Board of Church Extension of the Methodist Episcopal Church, South* (n.p., 1910), p.266.

[73] *Ibid.*,p. 268.

[74] "Stamford College," *Handbook of Texas Online*, http://www.tsha.utexas.edu/handbook/online/articles/SS/kbs52.html (accessed February 19, 2007).

[75] Newman, ""A History of McMurry College," p. 11.

[76] 1916 *Journal*, p. 41; Darris Egger, "J. W. Hunt," excerpt from an unpublished manuscript in possession of Rob Sledge, sent to author via email February 20, 2007. Egger notes that two preachers filled Hunt's unexpired term at St. Paul until new appointments were made at the 1916 Annual Conference. McMurry University may publish the Egger manuscript in 2009.

[77] 1917 *Journal*, p. 47.

[78] Newman, "A History of McMurry College, p. 11. According to Anthony Hunt, J. W. Hunt's son, the fire was started in a fuse box where a worker had used a penny instead of a new fuse. Darris Egger, *A Church Named St. Paul* (Abilene, Texas: St. Paul United Methodist Church, 1995), p. 109.

[79] 1919 *Journal*, p. 46.

[80] Sledge, *Hands on the Ark*, pp. 66, 79.

[81] Newman, "History of McMurry College," p. 11-12

[82] Fane Downs and Robert Sledge, editors, *Pride of Our Western Prairies: McMurry College, 1923-1988* (Abilene: McMurry College, 1989), p. 6.

[83] Downs and Sledge, ed.,, *Pride of Our Western Prairies*, p. 7.

[84] Report of the Board of Education, 1920 *Journal*, p. 45)

[85] *Ibid.*

[86] Downs and Sledge, ed., *Pride of Our Western Prairies*, p. 8.

[87] Griswold, *From Dugout to Steeple*, p. 163.

[88] 1921 *Journal*, pp. 51-52; Downs and Sledge, ed., *Pride of Our Western Prairies*, p. 8; 1920 *Journal*, p. 45.

[89] 1921 *Journal*, p. 20.

[90] Downs and Sledge, ed., *Pride of Our Western Prairies*, p. 11; Newman, "History of McMurry College," p. 21.

[91] *1923 Journal*, p. 38.

[92] Downs and Sledge, ed., *Pride of Our Western Prairies*,, p.17.

[93] Ethel Harvey, *The Athens of the Panhandle: A History of Clarendon College* (Clarendon, Texas: Clarendon Press, 1958), p. 243.

[94] "Clarendon College," *Handbook of Texas Online;* 1925 Journal, p. 28.

[95] Paul Carlson, *Amarillo: The Story of a Western Town* (Lubbock: Texas Tech University Press, 2006), p. 111.

[96] *Ibid.*, p. 112.

[97] 1926 Journal, pp. 44-45.

[98] Harvey, *Clarendon College*, pp. 245-246.

[99] *Ibid.*, p. 247.

[100] *Ibid.*, p. 249.

[101] *Ibid.*, p. 248.

[102] *Ibid.*, p. 252.

[103] *Amarillo Sunday News and Globe*, June 19, 1927. Reference courtesy Paul Carlson.

[104] 1927 *Journal*, p. 27-28.

[105] *Ibid.*, p. 28

[106] Harvey, *Clarendon College*, pp. 254.

[107] 1928 Journal, p. 45; Harvey, *Clarendon College*, p. 255. Apparently, the changeover was transparent to the community; in her book on the history of Donley County, local historian Virginia Browder described the change this way: "When Clarendon College was transferred from the supervision of the Methodist Conference to the city of Clarendon, the value of the buildings and premise were estimated to be $64,749.00 Thus, thereafter did Clarendon College become a Municipal Junior College." Virginia Browder, *Donley County: Land of Promise* (Wichita Falls: Nortex Press, 1975), p. 310.

[108] Donald E. Green, *Land of the Underground Rain* (Austin: University of Texas Press, 1973), pp. 120-121.

[109] 1928 *Journal*, p. 46.

[110] Carlson, *Amarillo*, p.112; "Amarillo," *Handbook of Texas Online.*

[111] 1929 *Journal*, p. 41.

[112] Sledge, *Hands on the* Ark, p. 138.

[113] *Ibid.*, p. 15.

[114] *Ibid.*, p. 145.

[115] 1921 *Journal*, p. 49.

[116] 1921 *Journal*, p. 16.

[117] Elmer D. Landreth, *The Missing Book*, p. 85.

[118] Sledge, *Hands on the Ark*, p. 148-149.

[119] *Ibid.*, p. 36. Smith at the time was county judge of Throckmorton County. He later served as lieutenant governor of Texas from 1942 to 1946. "John Lee Smith," *Handbook of Texas Online.*

[120] 1925 *Journal*, pp. 35-36.

[121] Sledge, *Hands on the Ark*, p. 149.

[122] Downs and Sledge, ed., *Pride of Our Western Prairies*, p. 20.

[123] 1927 *Journal*, p. 39.

[124] For an excellent discussion of the fundamentalist controversy in Lubbock in the 1920s and 1930s, see Merton L. Dillon's chapter in L. L. Graves, ed., *A History of Lubbock* (Lubbock: West Texas Museum Association, 1963), pp.449-516.

[125] 1929 *Journal*, p. 47.

Chapter 5

[1] J. Neland Hester, "Thirty-Five Years on the Outside Row," (unpublished typescript, 1954) NWT Archives, p. 79.

[2] Scoggins, *From Saddle to Pulpit*, p. 207.

[3] Paul H. Carlson, "Black Sunday—the South Plains Dust Blizzard of April 14, 1935," *The West Texas Historical Association Year Book* (Vol. 67), 6-16.

[4] State of the Church Report, 1931 *Journal*, p. 37.

[5] Scoggins, *From Saddle to Pulpit*, p. 207-208.

[6] See reports in 1928 and 1932 *Journals.*

[7] Haymes, *History of the Northwest Texas Conference*, pp. 84-85.

[8] 1931 *Journal*, Report on Temperance and Social Service, p. 27

[9] Graves, ed., *A History of Lubbock*, pp. 478-479.

[10] *Our Story*, p. 195

[11] Henderson, *Fifty-three Rungs up Jacob's Ladder and . . . Still Climbing, 1931-1999*, (n.p.: by the author, 1999), p. 10.

[12] "History of Avoca United Methodist Church," (np, 1982, pamphlet).

[13] Vernon, *et.al., Methodist Excitement*, p. 268.

[14] Kirk, *The Story of a Church*, p. 3.

[15] *Texas Methodist*, May 13, 1977, p. 1.

[16] Viola Henderson, *The Love Story of Vernon N. Henderson and Viola M. Henderson* ((n.p.:n.d.), p. 11. This wonderful little book was printed for his parents by Gene Henderson about 1990.

[17] 1932 *Journal*, p. 29.

[18] 1932 *Journal*, p. 36

[19] Downs and Sledge, eds., *Pride of Our Western Prairies*, p. 46.

[20] *Ibid.*, p. 47.

[21] *Ibid.* See also Landreth, *The Missing Book*, pp. 80-81.

[22] Olin W. Nail, ed., *Texas Methodist Centennial Year Book*, p. 744. See also Darris Egger, *Prairie Parsons* (Abilene, Texas: Abilene District of the United Methodist Church, 1990), pp. 67-71.

[23] Landreth, *The Missing Book*, p. 81.

[24] Downs and Sledge, eds., *Pride of Our Western Prairies*, pp. 50-51.

[25] *Journal of the the Northwest Texas Annual Conference: Methodist Episcopal Church, South* (1934), as printed in Olin W. Nail, ed., *Texas Methodist Centennial Yearbook* (Elgin, Texas: Olin W. Nail, 1934), p. 691

[26] Hiram Abiff Boaz, *Eighty-four Golden Years: An Autobiography of Bishop Hiram Abiff Boaz* (Nashville: Parthenon Press, 1951), p. 191.

[27] Ibid.; Landreth, *The Missing Book*, p. 63.

[28] Landreth, *The Missing Book*, p. 62.

[29] *Texas Methodist*, October 1, 1976, p. 1.

[30] *Ibid.,*, December 18, 1976, p. 1.

[31] Vernon N. Henderson, *Fifty-Three rungs up Jacob's Ladder*, p. 10.

[32] *Ibid.*, p. 8.

[33] Haymes, *History*, p. 81; 1930 *Journal*, p. 63.

[34] 1931 *Journal*, p. 75.

[35] See *The Discipline*, 1930, pp. 832, 858, and *The Discipline*, 1934, pp. 832-854.

[36] See Appendix A: Churches of the Northwest Texas Conference, Listed by Founding Date.

[37] *Ibid.*

[38] *Texas Methodist*, April 2, 1976, p. 1.

[39] Appendix B, Northwest Texas Conference Composite Statistical Table, 1910-2008.

[40] See Appendix A.

[41] The 1940 population for the area totaled 702,528, down 3,000 from 1930. Compiled from US Population Tables.

[42] Report of Evangelism Comittee, 1931 *Journal*, p.45.

[43] Report of the Commission on Evangelism, 1939 *Journal*, p. 48.

[44] *Texas Methodist*, September 17, 1976, p. 1.

[45] Sledge, *Hands on the Ark*, p. 195.

[46] *Texas Methodist*, February 27, 1976, p. 1.

[47] *Ibid.*

[48] Hester, "Thirty-Five Years," p.84.

[49] *Ibid.*, p. 87.

[50] 1925 *Journal*, p. 74; Sledge, *Hands on the Ark*, p. 120.)

[51] Haymes, *History*, p. 74.

[52] Sledge, *Hands on the Ark, pp. 228-229;* 1937 *Journal, p. 20.*

[53] 1937 *Journal*, p. 20.

[54] Sledge, *Hands on the Ark*, p. 220.

[55] Haymes, *History*, p. 96.

[56] 1938 *Journal*, p. 20.

[57] 1937 *Journal*, pp. 20-25.

[58] *Ibid.*, pp. 63-64.

[59] Frederick A. Norwood, *The Story of American Methodism* (Nashville: Abingdon Press, 1974), p. 409.

[60] *Daily Christian Advocate*, May 11, 1939, in Papers, J. M. Willson, 1930-1961, Southwest Collection, Texas Tech University. See also Lud H. Estes, ed., *Journal of the Uniting Conference of the Methodist Episcopal Church, Methodist Episcopal Church, South, Methodist Protestant Church, April 26-May 10, 1939* (Nashville: Methodist Publishing House, 1939), p. 398.)

[61] Sledge, *Hands on the Ark*, pp. 234-235.

[62] *Ibid.*

[63] This process took many years. I recall as a boy in the early 1950s that the sign at the Methodist Church in Gruver still bore the ME Church, South, designation.

[64] Vernon, *et.al.. Methodist Excitement*, p. 283.

[65] 1938 *Journal*, p. 12; 1939 *Journal*, p. 13-14.

[66] 1938 *Journal*, p. 11; Haymes, *History*, p. 95.

[67] 1939 *Journal*, p. 46.

[68] Elmer D. Landreth, *The Missing Book: An Autobiography* (Englewood, Colorado: by the author, 1968), p.63.

[69] Haymes, *History*, pp.97- 98.

[70] Lillie Mae Hunter, *A Cloud of Witnesses*, p. 7.

[71] *The Dalhart Texan*, August 5, 1976, as cited in "The United Methodist Church of Clarendon" (Typescript, c. 1976), p. 2, Archives, Northwest Texas Conference, McMurry University.

[72] Hunter, *A Cloud of Witnesses*, p. 7.

[73] Lucy Sperry Wynn, "A History of Methodism in Follett, 1918-1992" (Typescript, 1992), pp. 1-4, Northwest Texas Conference Archives, McMurry University.

[74] Vernon, *et.al., Methodist Excitement*, p. 225..

[75] This information is based on research in Abilene City Directories provided by Joe Specht; see Rob Sledge to David Murrah, email correspondence, June 21, 2007, in possession of author. A Southern Methodist church existed in Abilene for a brief period. In 2007, the Southern Methodist Church's website reported that the denomination had approximately 104 churches and 6,200 members located in 12 southern states, including three located in Texas at Mesquite, Lindale, and Tyler. See the following website: http://www.southernmethodistchurch.org.

[76] 1926 *Journal*, p. 74; J. H. Hamblen, *A Look into Life: An Autobiography* (Abilene, Texas: by the author, 1969), p. 76.

[77] Hamblen, *A Look into Life*, p. 104-105.

[78] *Ibid.*, p. 106. See also Jewell Posey, *Methodist Mosaic: First United Methodist Church, Abilene, 1881-1981,* (unpublished typescript, n.p., n.d), p. 120.
[79] Posey, *First United Methodist Church,* p. 121.
[80] Hamblen, *A Look into Life,* p. 108-109.
[81] 1944 *Journal*, p. 24.
[82] Hamblen, *A Look into Life* p. 111.
[83] *Ibid.*, p. 113.
[84] 1945 *Journal*, p. 20.
[85] Landreth, *The Missing Book,* p. 39.
[86] Edmund W. Robb, *Contending for the Faith: The Ed Robb Story* (Anderson, Indiana: Bristol House, 2002), pp. 58-59.
[87] *Ibid.*, p. 60.
[88] *Ibid.*, p.75.
[89] Rob Sledge to David Murrah, email correspondence, June 21, 2007, in possession of author. See also Vernon, *et. al., Methodist Excitement*, 217-218.
[90] J. Edmund Kirby, "My Memoirs, 1908-1990," (unpublished typescript, 1990), NWT Archives), p. 70.
[91] *Ibid.*, pp. 69-70.
[92] Vernon, *et.al., Methodist Excitement,* p.286; "Texas in World War II" brochure (Austin: Texas Historical Commission, 2005), available at http://www.thc.state.tx.us/publications/brochures/WWIIbrochure05.pdf. For a list of Army Airfield bases in Texas see the National WASP WWII Museum website at http://www.waspwwii.org/museum/texas.htm.
[93] Appendix B, Northwest Texas Conference Composite Statistical Table, 1910-2008.
[94] 1942 *Journal*, p. 36.
[95] Norwood, *The Story of American Methodism*, p. 412.
[96] 1944 *Journal*, Obiturary of Grandma Rogers, p. 66.
[97] Landreth, *The Missing Book*, p. 64. See also Vernon, *et.al., Methodist Excitement*, pp. 155-156.

Chapter 6

[1] 1945 *Journal*, p. 70.
[2] Statistics compiled from statistical tables in the 1940 and 1945 Conference *Journals*.
[3] Vernon, *et.al., Methodist Excitement*, pp. 289-290.
[4] 1946 *Journal*, p. 51; Haymes, *History,* p. 110.
[5] Vernon, *et.al., Methodist Excitement*, p. 290.
[6] 1946 *Journal*, p. 52.
[7] 1946 *Journal*, Statistical Tables.
[8] Louise Allen, *Line of Splendor: History of St. John's Methodist Church/First Quarter Century* (Lubbock: Thatcher Printing, 1965) p. 4.
[9] *Ibid.*, p. 17.
[10] 1947 *Journal*, p. 5; Vernon, *et.al., Methodist Excitement*, p. 309.
[11] 1949 *Journal*, Statistical Tables.
[12] 1942 *Journal*, p. 9.
[13] 1947 *Journal*, p. 1.
[14] 1951 *Journal*, p. 51.
[15] Joseph Weldon Butler, *Called by Grace: The Life and Memories of Joseph Weldon Butler* (n.p.:n.d), p. 71.
[16] Vernon, *et.al., Methodist Excitement*, p. 295.

[17] James E. Kirby, *Brother Will: A Biography of William C. Martin* Nashville: Abingdon Press, 2000), p. 262.

[18] 1951 *Journal,* p. 51, 84.

[19] Graves, *Lubbock: From Town to City,* pp. 10-11.

[20] *Ibid.,* p. 311.

[21] Kirby, *Brother Will,* p. 368.

[22] Haymes, *History,* p. 113.

[23] Kirby, *Brother Will,,* p. 337. See also the United Methodist Church website: http://new.gbgm-umc.org/about/advance/about/?search=advance.

[24] General Board of Global Ministries, *The Advance Overview Booklet* (n.p.: 2008?), p. 3.

[25] 1953 *Journal,* p. 52.

[26] Haymes, *History, p.* 118. See also end maps in Ruth Magee, *A Century of Methodism in the Texas Panhandle.*

[27] 1954 *Journal,* Statistical Tables.

[28] Vernon, *et.al., Methodist Excitement,,* pp. 87-89.

[29] *Ibid.,* p. 255. See also Theodore A. Fuller, "When the Century and I were Young" (typescript, 1979, Corpus Christi Public Library, available online at http://www.ccplarchives.ci.corpus-christi.tx.us/cdm4/document.php?CISOROOT=/odf&CISOPTR=602&CISOSHOW=336&REC=1.

[30] Haymes, *History,* p. 59.

[31] Vernon Henderson, "History of Ceta Canyon Methodist Camp, 1926-1982" (typescript, c. 1994, Northwest Texas Conference Archives), pp. 4-5. A slightly different account is found in Gabie Betts Burton, comp., *History of the Northwest Texas Conference Woman's Missionary Society, Methodist Episcopal Church, South, 1880-1928* (Abilene, Texas: Fisk Publishing Co., 1929), p, 45.

[32] *Texas Methodist*, January 7, 1977, p. 1.

[33] 1923 *Journal,* p. 46; Haymes, *History,* p. 72; Vernon, *et.al., Methodist Excitement*, p. 257.

[34] 1924 *Journal.* p. 43.

[35] Henderson, "Ceta Canyon," p. 9

[36] Marvin L. Boyd interview, as cited in Henderson, "Ceta Canyon," p. 11. See also "Report of the Trustees Methodist Camp Ground, 1927 *Journal*, p. 45.

[37] *Ibid.,* p. 11.

[38] 1927 *Journal,* p. 45.

[39] *Ibid.,* pp.6-7.

[40] 1929 *Journal,* p. 31.

[41] Henderson, "Ceta Canyon," p. 14.

[42] *Ibid.,* p. 27.

[43] Abilene District History Committee, "A History of the Abilene District of the Northwest Texas Conference of the United Methodist Church" (typescript, c. 1984, in Northwest Texas Conference Archives), pp. 34-35.

[44] Henderson, "Ceta Canyon," p. 16; Darris Egger, Sr., compiler, *Butman Methodist Camp in Mulberry Canyon* (Merkel, Texas: Trustees of the Butman Methodist Camp and Retreat Center, 1994), p. 31.

[45] Egger, *Butman Methodist Camp,* pp.7-16.

[46] *Ibid.,* p. 27-28.

[47] Marvin Boyd, as cited in Egger, *Butman Methodist Camp*, pp. 34. It is unclear whether all three men were with Butman, but Darris Egger says that all three played a role in the negotiation at one time or another.

[48] 1953 *Journal,* p. 38.

[49] Egger, *Butman Methodist Camp,* p. 44.

[50] *Ibid.*, p. 47.

[51] S. V. Connor, ed., *Builders of the Southwest* (Southwest Collection, Texas Technological College, 1959), p. 169; Robert Monk to David Murrah, April 9, 2008, in possession of author.

52 Louise Allen and Emil Carmichael, *The First Sixty-two Years: Methodist Hospital, Lubbock, Texas, 1918-1980* (Lubbock, Texas: Methodist Hospital, 1980), p. 28.

[53] 1949 *Journal*, p. 27.

[54] Allen and Carmichael, *Methodist Hospital*, p. 29.

[55] *Ibid.*

[56] *Ibid.*, p. 38.

[57] *Ibid.*, p. 34.

[58] *Ibid.*, p. 37

[59] *Ibid*, pp. 39-40.

[60] J. E. Shewbert, as cited in Allen and Carmichael, *Methodist Hospital*, p. 42.

[61] *Ibid.*, pp. 42-43.

[62] *Ibid.*, p. 42; Barr, Alwyn and Carlson, Paul, *First United Methodist Church of Lubbock: A Centennial Celebration, 1892-1992* (Lubbock, Texas: First United Methodist Church, 1992), p. 33.

[63] Connor, ed., *Builders of the Southwest*, p. 169.

[64] 1954 *Journal*, p. 41.

[65] *Ibid.*, p. 52.

[66] 1955 *Journal*, p. 52.

[67] Ibid.

[68] See Appendix B, Northwest Texas Conference Composite Statistical Table, 1910-2008

[69] 1957 *Journal*, p. 37. Sadly, due to declining membership, the San Jacinto Church sold its large edifice in 2005 and moved into a store front. Rex Mauldin, former pastor of the church, preached the last sermon in the San Jacinto location.

[70] Haymes, *History*, p. 134.

[71] *Ibid.*, p. 235.

[72] Haymes, *History*, p. 113.

[73] Kirby, *Brother Will*, pp. 334, 350.

[74] Haymes, *History*, p. 113.

[75] 1960 *Journal*, p. 118.

[76] Kirby, *Brother Will*, p. 368.

[77] *Ibid.*, p. 411.

[78] *United Methodist Reporter*, September 21, 1984, p. 1.

[79] 1960 *Journal*, p.62.

[80] Haymes, *History*, pp. 134-135.

[81] 1961 *Journal*,. p. 65.

[82] *Ibid.*, p. 126, 133; W. Kenneth Pope, *A Pope at Roam: The Confessions of a Bishop* (Nashville, Parthenon Press, 1976), p. 24.

[83] *Ibid.*

Chapter 7

[1] "United Methodist Membership as Compared to the United States Population Census," from General Conference website online, http://gcah.org/membership.htm, accessed August 15, 2005.

[2] 1960 *Journal*, p. 75.

[3] *General Minutes of the Methodist Church, 1959*, p. 688.

[4] Haymes, *History*, p. 66.

[5] 1921-1929 *Journal*, list of conference officers; "Report of the Sunday School Board," 1929 *Journal*, p. 39.

[6] 1930 *Journal*, p. 54.

[7] 1948 *Journal*, p. 3.

[8] 1952 *Journal*, pp. 88-89.

[9] Haymes, History p. 120.

[10] 1961 *Journal*, p. 42.

[11] 1965 *Journal*, p.75.

[12] *Texas Methodist*, January 18, 1974, p. 1.

[13] See Appendix A: Churches of the Northwest Texas Conference, Listed by Founding Date. One of these churches was Agape in Lubbock in the Redbud neighborhood, established by the City Board of Missions in 1960. It began with 54 families and grew rapidly to have 571 members by the early 1970s. However, membership began to decline as residents of the neighborhood aged. See "A Brief History of Agape United Methodist Church, 1960-1995 (Typescript, 1995, n.p.).

[14] *History of St. Stephen United Methodist Church* (n.p. 1979, pamphlet), pp. 2-16.

[15] Flo Patton, "History of Wesley U.M.C., Andrews, Texas (undated typescript, NWT Archives, McMurry), pp. 1-2.

[16] 1967 *Journal*, Big Spring District, Statistical Table No. 1.

[17] Cooper, *Aspermont*, p. 40.

[18] 1961 *Journal*, p. 68.

[19] Butler, *Called by Grace*, p. 88.

[20] *Texas Methodist*, June 14, 1968.

[21] Henderson, *Fifty-Three Rungs Up Jacob's Ladder*," p. 88.

[22] *Ibid.*, p. 90.

[23] Butler, *Called by Grace*, p. 93.

[24] 1962 *Journal*, p. 65.

[25] 1963 *Journal*, p. 79.

[26] 1965 *Journal*, p. 46, 77.

[27] *Texas Methodist*, May 14, 1965, June 11, 1965; Pampa District, *A Century of Methodism in the Eastern Texas Panhandle*, end cover.

[28] Pampa District, *A Century of Methodism in the Eastern Texas Panhandle*, end cover.

[29] 1965 *Journal*, p. 3. According to the *United Methodist Reporter*, only two bishops were elected on first ballot, Eugene Slater (1960), and Alfred Norris (1992). Both served the Northwest Texas Conference. See *United Methodist Reporter*, March 28, 1997.

[30] 1965 *Journal*, pp. 55, 91.

[31] *Ibid.*, p. 78.

[32] 1963 *Journal*, p. 84.

[33] 1965 *Journal*, p. 91.

[34] District Superintendentd Report, 1966 *Journal*.

[35] Vernon, *et.al*, *Methodist Excitement*, p. 338.

[36] *Texas Methodist*, May 20, 1966.

[37] *Ibid.*, June 3, 1966.

[38] *Texas Methodist*, February 2, 1968, p. 1.

[39] "The Ed Robb Story" (video tape production by James Robb, undated, in possession of Rex Mauldin, Abilene, Texas).

[40] *Texas Methodist*, July 15, 1966, p. 1.

[41] *Ibid.*

[42] 1967 *Journal*, p. 185.

[43] *Texas Methodist*, July 30, 1971, p. 1.

[44] 1967 *Journal*, p. 87.

[45] *Journal of the South Central Jurisdiction of the United Methodist Church* (Vol. 8, 1968), p. 160.

[46] District Superintendent Report, 1968 *Journal*, p. 94.

[47] District Superintendents' Report, 1968 *Journal*, p. 94.

[48] H. L. Ingle and James A. Ward, *American History: A Brief View*. (Boston: Little Brown & Co., 1978), p. 474.

[49] 1967 *Journal*, p. 131.

[50] Norwood, *American Methodism*, p. 429.

[51] District Superintendent's Report, 1969 *Journal*, p. 86; 1965 *Journal*, p. 116; Walter N. Vernon, *et.al., One in the Lord: A history of Ethnic Minorities in the South Central Jurisdiction of the United Methodist Church* (Oklahoma City: Commission on Archives and History, South Central Jurisdiction of the United Methodist Church, 1977), p. 127.

[52] 1970 *Journal*, p. 54. These churches are not to be confused with those of the African Methodist Episcopal denomination, which did not merge with the United Methodist Church. In 2008, the website for the African Methodist Episcopal Church listed AME churches in each of these cities within the bounds of the Northwest Texas Conference: Amarillo, Abilene, Big Spring, Sweetwater, Snyder, Lubbock, Midland, and Vernon. See African Methodist Episcopal Church website, accessed at http://www.ame-church.com/directory/district.php?district=10, August 12, 2008. Another African-American denomination, the Christian Methodist Episcopal Church, lists only one Northwest Texas church, Carter Chapel in Amarillo, on its website. See http://www.c-m-e.org/core/church_list.htm, accessed August 12, 2008.

[53] "A History of Plum Street United Methodist Church" (Typescript, 1997), p. 1, Archives, Northwest Texas Conference, McMurry University.

[54] Grace Sullivan, "The History of Mount Vernon United Methodist Church" (Typescript, undated), p. 1, Archives, Northwest Texas Conference, McMurry University.

[55] "The History of Wyatt Memorial United Methodist Church" (Typescript, undated), p. 1, Archives, Northwest Texas Conference, McMurry University. The original notation indicates that the church was organized in 1946, but a later correction indicates the previous year.

[56] *United Methodist Reporter*, March 28, 1997, p. 1.

[57] *Ibid.*, p. 35; *Journal of the South Central Jurisdictional Conference of the United Methodist Church* (Vol. 8, 1968), p. 136.

[58] *Journal of the South Central Jurisdiction of the United Methodist Church* (vol. 6, 1960), pp. 138-139.

[59] Theodore L. Agnew, *The South Central Jurisdiction, 1939-1972: A Brief History and Interpretation* (Oklahoma City: Commission on Archives and History, South Central Jurisdiction of the United Methodist Church, 1973), pp. 34-35.

[60] Will Steinsick to David Murrah, email correspondence, December 20, 2007, in possession of author; Ava Berry to David Murrah, January 27, 2008, notes in possession of author.

[61] *Texas Methodist*, August 2, 1968, p. 1.

[62] Norwood, *American Methodism*, p. 430.

[63] Vernon, et. al., *Methodist Excitement*, p. 384.

[64] *Ibid.*, p. 365.

[65] *Texas Methodist*, January 10, 1969.

[66] 1968 *Journal*, Statistical Table No. 1, Recapitulation.

[67] 1968 *Journal*, pp. 2, 53; *Texas Methodist*, June 14, 1968, p.1.

[68] S. Duane Bruce, "My Ministerial Journey" (typescript, 1998), p. 23, Northwest Texas Archives.

[69] 1969 *Journal*, p. 60.

[70] 1969 *Journal*, pp. 67, 177-178.

[71] *Ibid.*, p. 67.

[72] *Ibid.*, p. 177.
[73] *Ibid.*, p. 89.
[74] *Ibid.*, p.65.
[75] *Ibid.*, pp. 65, 91.
[76] 1968 *Journal*, pp. 56-57.
[77] 1970 *Journal*, p. 50.
[78] *Ibid.*, p. 52.
[79] Bob Ford, "Ecumenical Life-style," *Northwest Texas Log*, March 1970, pp. 1-2. *The Northwest Texas Log* was edited and published by Ted Dotts from 1968 through 1972. A near-complete run is located in the Northwest Texas Conference Archives.
[80] *Ibid.*, p. 5.
[81] *Texas Methodist*,, May 1, 1970, p. 1.
[82] *Ibid.*, June 19, 1970, p. 1.
[83] 1971 *Journal*, p. 96.
[84] *Ibid.*, p. 66.
[85] Garry Nall to David Murrah, March 18, 2008, email correspondence, in possession of author.
[86] *Texas Methodist*, June 30, 1972, p. 2.
[87] *Ibid.*, p. 91.
[88] *Texas Methodist*, April 28, 1972, p. 3.
[89] *Texas Methodist*, August 11, 1972, p. 2.
[90] *Texas Methodist*, December 17, 1971, p. 1.
[91] *Ibid.*
[92] *Texas Methodist*, April 21, 1966, p. 2. The group formed the Consultation on Church Union, and for forty years, consulted on the concept of merging several denominations. In 2002, the Consultation became the organization, Churches Uniting in Christ (CUIC), which includes African Methodist Episcopal Church, African Methodist Episcopal Zion Church, Christian Church (Disciples of Christ), Christian Methodist Episcopal Church, Episcopal Church, International Council of Community Churches, Presbyterian Church (USA), United Church of Christ and United Methodist Church. See the CUIC website, http://www.cuicinfo.org/history/cocuhistory.html, accessed August 13, 2008.
[93] *Texas Methodist*, July 14, 1972, p. 3.
[94] 1969 *Journal*, pp. 85-86.
[95] "Lubbock District History, 1934," (unpublished typescript, 1934), NWT Archives.
[96] *Texas Methodist*, July 29, 1966, p. 1; October 11, 1974, p. 1.
[97] Judy Edgemon to David Murrah, email correspondence, January 8, 2008, in possession of the author. Judy obtained the information from "Lists of Churches" in the office of the Lubbock Area Baptist Association in Lubbock, where she is employed.
[98] *Texas Methodist*, October 8, 1971, p. 1.
[99] *Texas Methodist*, August 8, 1968, p. 2.
[100] Carlson, *Amarillo*, pp. 178-179.`
[101] Graves, ed., *Lubbock: From Town to City*, p. 12.
[102] Murrah, *The Pitchfork Land and Cattle Company: The First Century* (Guthrie, TX: Pitchfork Land and Cattle Company, 1983), p. 74; "South Plains Rainfall, 1914-1992," on disk in possession of author.
[103] *Texas Almanac, 1980-81* (Dallas: Belo Corporation, 1979), p. 561.
[104] Graves, ed., *Lubbock: From Town to City*, p.16.
[105] *United Methodist Reporter*, August 30, 1985, p. 1.
[106] District Superintendent Report, 1972 *Journal*, p. 59.

[107] *United Methodist Reporter*, August 30, 1985, p. 1.

[108] Terry Matthews, "Lecture 24: The Church in Decline," Wake Forest University website, online Religion 166 course, http://www.wfu.edu/~matthetl/perspectives/twentyfour.html.

[109] Graves, ed., *Lubbock: From Town to City*, p. 321.

[110] *Ibid.*, pp. 431-432.

[111] 1972 *Journal*, p. 59; *Texas Methodist*, September 1, 1972, p. 1.

Chapter 8

[1] *Texas Methodist*, February 14, 1975, p. 3.

[2] 1974 *Journal*, p. 81.

[3] *Ibid.*, p. 3.

[4] Author's note: As a member at the time of what was then Pleasant Ridge Baptist Church in Lubbock, I was a first-hand witness to the beginning of the charismatic takeover, but soon left due to my own discomfort with the change. Within six years of the beginning of the charismatic takeover, the church could no longer service its debt load and allowed the facility to pass to the Lubbock Baptist Association in 1981, which promptly re-established a mission that subsequently became the present-day Redbud Baptist Church.

[5] "History of the Morton United Methodist Church," p. 29.

[6] *Texas Methodist*, September 6, 1974, p. 1.

[7] "David du Plessis," Wikipedia (online encyclopedia), http://en.wikipedia.org/wiki/David_du_Plessis, accessed January 23, 2008.

[8] *Texas Methodist*, October 25, 1974, p. 1.

[9] Vernon, *et.al.*, *Methodist Excitement*, pp. 358-359.

[10] 1968 *Journal*, p. 100.

[11] Eddie Allsup to David Murrah, August 30, 2005, oral history tape, NWT Archives.

[12] Originally printed in *The Christian Advocate*, July 14, 1966 (accessed on the Good News Renewal Website http://www.goodnewsmag.org/renewal/silent_minority.htm, February 2, 2008.

[13] *Texas Methodist*, September 4, 1970, p. 3; *Good News* ((Vol. 4., No. 2, Oct.-Dec. 1970), p. 112.

[14] *Ibid.*

[15] *Ibid.* See also Vernon, et.al., *Methodist Excitement*, p. 365.

[16] *Good News* (Vol. 4, No. 2, Oct-Dec., 1970), p. 112.

[17] 1971 *Journal*, p.91.

[18] Robert Monk to David Murrah, February 9, 2008 (letter in possession of author).

[19] Downs and Sledge, eds., *Pride of our Western Prairies*, p. 159.

[20] Letter to McMurry Board of Trustees, March 2, 1972 (photocopy). Original copy in possession of Johnny Robertson, Childress, Texas.

[21] Johnny Robertson to David Murrah, email correspondence, February 5, 2008, in possession of author.

[22] *Ibid.*

[23] Thomas K. Kim to Members of the Board of Trustees, McMurry College, March 10, 1972, Memorandum (photocopy furnished to the author by Robert Monk; the original is in the McMurry Archives).

[24] *Ibid.*

[25] *Texas Methodist*, May 19, 1972, p. 3.

[26] Darris Egger to David Murrah, February 5, 2005, oral history tape, NWT.

[27] Robb, *Contending for the Faith*, pp. 115-116; "The Ed Robb Story."

[28] Compiled from Statistical Tables No. 1 in 1973-1977 Northwest Texas Conference Journals.

[29] Ava Berry to David Murrah, personal interview, February 4, 2008.

[30] *Texas Methodist,* August 1, 1975, p. 3. The full text of the speech can be found on the Good News Website, Edmund Robb, "The Crisis of Theological Education in the United Methodist Church," http://www.goodnewsmag.org/renewal/robb_speech.htm, accessed February 4, 2008.

[31] *Ibid.*

[32] Robb, "The Crisis of Theological Education."

[33] *Ibid.*

[34] Rex Mauldin to David Murrah, personal correspondence, February 4, 2008, in possession of author.

[35] Robb, "The Crisis of Theological Education."

[36] *Texas Methodist,*August 15, 1975, p. 2.

[37] Albert Outler, "A Fund for 'Evangelical' Scholars," *Christian Century,* February 6-13, 1980, pp. 138-140 (reprinted on the Religion-Online website, http://www.religion-online.org/showarticle.asp?title=1749, accessed February 6, 2008.

[38] Jane Jordan to David Murrah, February 7, 2008, email correspondence in possession of author. Ms. Jordan is an official with the Foundation for Theological Education.

[39] Johnny Robertson to David Murrah, February 5, 2008, email correspondence in possession of author.

[40] 2002 Journal, p. L-4.

[41] Rex Mauldin to David Murrah,

[42] Jim Smith to David Murrah, October 12, 2005, oral history interview, NWT Archives, McMurry University.

[43] 1962 *Journal.*

[44] 1968 *Journal.*

[45] 1966 *Journal,* p. 71.

[46] Jim Smith to David Murrah, October 12, 2005. Robert Coleman enjoyed a long career at Asbury from 1956 to 1983 before moving to Trinity Evangelical Divinity School. He authored 21 books and served as Director of the Billy Graham Institute of Evangelism at Wheaton, Illinois. See Trinity Evangelical Divinity School website, http://www.tiu.edu/divinity/people/coleman, accessed February 8, 2008.

[47] Jim Smith to David Murrah, October 12, 2005.

[48] *Ibid.*

[49] Reprinted from *Lexington Herald Leader*, 1991, The Forerunner website online, http://forerunner.com/forerunner/X0585_Asbury_Revival_1970.html, accessed on July 15, 2005.

[50] 1972 *Journal*, p. 57.

[51] 1974 *Journal,* p. 78.

[52] *Texas Methodist*, March 8, 1974, p. 1; Letter to the McMurry Board of Trustees, March 2, 1972.

[53] *Ibid.*, June 27, 1975.

[54] Robert Kirk, "R. L. Kirk," 2002 *Journal*, p. L-4.

[55] Jim Smith to David Murrah, October 12, 2005.

[56] 1978 *Journal,* p. 162.

[57] 1980 *Journal*, p. 232.

[58] *Texas Methodist*, January 11, 1974; 1974 Journal, p. 2.

[59] Rex Mauldin to David Murrah, February 6, 2005, oral history interview.

[60] 1974 *Journal*, p. 81.

[61] *Ibid.*, p. 82. Kennedy's program emphasized four key points: every Christian is to be a witness; all need to be equipped to witness; on-the-job training is vital;, and training soul winners is most important. See John B. Sorenson, "Vision for our future" (unpublished typescript, 2006), p. 4. Accessed online at http://www.eeinternational.org/vision.pdf on January 24, 2008.

[62] *Texas Methodist*, October 21, 1977, p. 1.
[63] District Superintendent Report, 1975 *Journal*, pp. 95-96.
[64] *Journal of the South Central Jurisdiction of the United Methodist Church* (Vol. 10, 1976, p. 60.
[65] *Ibid.*, December 26, 1975, p. 3.
[66] *Texas Methodist*, May 10, 1974, p. 3.
[67] *Ibid.*, June 20, 1975, p. 1.
[68] 1976 *Journal*, p. 81.
[69] *Ibid.*
[70] *Ibid.*
[71] *Journal of the South Central Jurisdiction of the United Methodist Church* (Vol. 10, 1976), p. 64.
[72] *Ibid.*, pp.67-68.
[73] *Texas Methodist*, June 27, 1975, p. 3.
[74] *Texas Methodist*, September 2, 1977, p. 1.
[75] *Ibid.*, October 7, 1977, p. 1.
[76] *Ibild*, January 21, 1977, p. 3.
[77] Johnny Robertson to David Murrah, February 5, 2008.
[78] *Ibid.*
[79] 1978 *Journal*, p. 204.
[80] Henderson, "History of Ceta Canyon," p. 36.
[81] Egger, *Butman Methodist Camp*,p. 89; 1964 Journal, p.86.
[82] 1964 *Journal*, pp. 86-87.
[83] Henderson, "History of Ceta Canyon," p. 44.
[84] Jim Smith to David Murrah, October 12, 2005.
[85] Jim Smith to David Murrah, February 21, 2008, email correspondence in possession of author.
[86] Jim Smith to David Murrah, email correspondence, February 20, 2008, in possession of author; 1970; *Journal*, p. 86.
[87] 1968 *Journal*, p. 99.
[88] 1971 *Journal*, p. 99.
[89] *Texas Methodist*, July 14, 1972, p. 1; August 17, 1973, p. 1; July 19, 1974, p. 1; Henderson, "History of Ceta Canyon," p. 47-48.
[90] Henderson, "History of Ceta Canyon," p. 48.
[91] Jim Smith to David Murrah, October 12, 2005.
[92] *Texas Methodist*, April 5, 1974, p. 1.
[93] *Ibid.*, January 31, 1975, p. 1.
[94] Jim Smith to David Murrah, October 12, 2005; February 21, 2008.
[95] *Texas Methodist*, January 31, 1975, p. 1.
[96] Jim Smith to David Murrah, October 12, 2005.
[97] Vernon, et.al., *Methodist Excitement*, p. 388.
[98] Jim Smith to David Murrah, October 12, 2005
[99] Jim Smith to David Murrah, February 20, 2008.
[100] *Ibid.*
[101] Minutes of the Conference Camping Commission, October 15, 1977, p. 1, NWT Archives.
[102] *Ibid.*, p. 2; Jim Smith to David Murrah, February 20, 2008.
[103] *Texas Methodist*, June 15, 1979, p. 1.
[104] Minutes, Camps and Conferences Committee, November 10-11, 1978, NWT Archives, p. 1.
[105] *Ibid.*, p. 1.
[106] *Ibid.*, pp. 2-3.

[107] 1979 *Journal*, p. 134.
[108] Egger, *Butman Methodist Camp*, p. 47.
[109] *Ibid.*, p. 54.
[110] *Ibid.*, pp. 54-55.
[111] *Ibid.*, p. 55.
[112] *Ibid.*, p. 59; 1979 Journal, p. 82, 134.
[113] *Ibid.*, p. 66.
[114] 1979 *Journal*, pp. 134-135.
[115] Egger, *Butman Methodist Camp*, p. 67.
[116] 1980 *Journal*, p. 190; Jim Smith to David Murrah, October 12, 2005.
[117] *Ibid.*, pp. 190-194.
[118] 1980 *Journal*, p. 94.
[119] Eddie Allsup to David Murrah, August 30, 2005. Eddie became chair of the Conference Camping Commission in 1981, replacing Albert Lindley.
[120] *Texas Methodist*, June 19, 1981, p. 1.
[121] *Texas Methodist*, August 28, 1981, p. 1. I. See *Texas Methodist*, June 19, 1981, p. 1.
[122] *United Methodist Reporter*, April 9, 1982, p. 1.
[123] 1982 *Journal*, p. 147.
[124] *United Methodist Reporter*, April 27, 1984, p. 1.
[125] *Ibid.*, June 15, 1984, p. 1.
[126] Eddie Allsup to David Murrah, August 30, 2005.
[127] 1978 *Journal*, p. 101.
[128] Downs and Sledge, *Pride of our Western Prairies*, p. 167.
[129] *Texas Methodist*, August 1, 1980, p. 1.
[130] 1984 *Journal*, p. 284.
[131] 1982 *Journal*, p. 306.
[132] *United Methodist Reporter*, June 29, 1984, p. 1.
[133] 1984 *Journal*, p. 111.
[134] *United Methodist Reporter*, June 15, 1984, p. 3.
[135] 1985 *Journal*, compiled from statistical table No. 1,
[136] 1985 *Journal*, p. 146.
[137] *United Methodist Reporter*, June 15, 1984, p. 1.
[138] *Ibid.*

Chapter 9

[1] *United Methodist Reporter*, March 25, 1983, p. 1; 1982 *Journal*, p. 133.
[2] 1983 *Journal*, p. 139.
[3] *Texas Methodist*, September 26, 1980, p. 1; 1982 *Journal*, p. 138; 1983 *Journal*, p. 134.
[4] *United Methodist Reporter*, October 28, 1983, p. 1.
[5] *United Methodist Reporter*, August 30, 1985, p. 3; July 5, 1985, p. 3.
[6] *Ibid.*, July 21, 1989, p. 1.
[7] *Ibid.*, October 28, 1983, p. 3.
[8] *Texas Methodist*, February 4, 1966, p. 1; *United Methodist Reporter*, September 9, 1983, p 1; October 7, 1983, p. 1.
[9] *United Methodist Reporter*, January 1, 1982, p. 1.
[10] *Ibid.*, November 15, 1985, p. 1.

[11] *Ibid.*, October 10, 1986, p. 1; May 1, 1987, p. 1.
[12] *Ibid.*, February 24, 1986, p. 1.
[13] *Ibid.*, February 13, 1987, p. 1.
[14] *Ibid.*, July 25, 1986, p. 1; July 17, 1987, p. 4.
[15] *Ibid.*, February 18, 1987, p. 1.
[16] *Ibid.*, July 21, 1989, p. 1.
[17] *Ibid.*
[18] 1990 *Journal*, pp. 185-286.
[19] *United Methodist Reporter*, May 28, 1982, p. 1.
[20] 1989 *Journal*, p. 189.
[21] *United Methodist Reporter*, June 22, 1990, p. 1.
[22] *Ibid.*, August 24, 1990.
[23] *History of the Seymour District of the Northwest Texas Conference of the United Methodist Church, 1967-1991* (n.p.:n.d.), no page number.
[24] *United Methodist Reporter*, May 3, 1991, p. 1.
[25] Louise Schock to David Murrah, March 28, 2007, oral history interview, Northwest Texas Conference Archives.
[26] Vernon, *et.al., Methodist Excitement*, p. 295.
[27] 1960 *Journal*, p. 69.
[28] Vernon, *et. al., Methodist Excitement*, p. 378; 1962 *Journal, p. 45.*
[29] The last entry for Rev. Apple is in the 1964 *Journal*, p. 142.
[30] *Texas Methodist*, June 30, 1978, p. 1.
[31] Jordan Grooms to David Murrah, October 11, 2005, oral history interview. This account was related to the author after the conclusion of the interview and therefore is not on the oral history tape.
[32] Butler, *Called by Grace,"* p. 111.
[33] Northwest Texas Conference Commission on Status and Role of Women, *50th Anniversary of Full Clergy Rights for Women in the Methodist Church: Women in Ministry who have Served in the Northwest Texas Conference over the Last Fifty Years* (Lubbock: Northwest Texas Annual Conference, 2006), p. 15.
[34] Women's Clergy Service Report, 2007, compiled by Northwest Texas Conference office from Board of Pension and Health Benefits Records. Courtesy Eddie Allsup.
[35] *Ibid.*
[36] *United Methodist Reporter*, June 21, 1991, p. 1.
[37] Jo Carr to David Murrah, March 28, 2007, oral history interview.
[38] Ava Burdine Berry, "Becoming a Clergywoman: The Journey," *Heritage Journal* (Vol. III, 2007), p. 70.
[39] *Ibid.*, pp. 72-73. Rev. Berry became the Plainview District Superintendent in 2002, then moved to the Abilene District in 2005 before being named Conference Director in 2008.
[40] *Texas Methodist*, February 21, 1975.
[41] *The Book of Discipline of the United Methodist Church, 1972*, cited on Religious Tolerance website, http://www.religioustolerance.org/hom_umc6.htm, accessed May 1, 2008.
[42] *Texas Methodist*, August 8, 1971, p. 1.
[43] 1982 *Journal*, p. 315.
[44] *Ibid.*, p. 96.
[45] *Ibid.*, p. 316.
[46] *United Methodist Reporter*, May 18, 1984, p. 1.

[47] Religious Tolerance website, "United Methodist Church and Homosexuality: Conference Decisions," http://www.religioustolerance.org/hom_umc6.htm, accessed May 2, 2008. This site provides an excellent overview of the issue.

[48] Charles Yrigoyen, Jr., John G. McEllhenney, and Kennteth E. Rowe, *United Methodism at Forty* Nashville: Abingdon Press, 2008), p. 59.

[49] Vernon, *et. al., Methodist Excitement*, p. 371.

[50] *Texas Methodist*, May 10, 1974, p. 4.

[51] 1979 *Journal*, p. 261; 1986 *Journal*, pp. 310, 317; 1987 *Journal*, pp. 288-290; Vernon, *et.al., Methodist Excitement*, p.372.

[52] *United Methodist Reporter*, June 30, 1989, p. 1.

[53] *Ibid.*, May 17, 1985, p. 1.

[54] J. Wesley Day, "A Missionary Life," website, http://209.85.165.104/search?q=cache:bwXFFy6fL7MJ:wesleyday.home.comcast.net/~wesleyday/1987trip.htm+faye+armstrong+methodist&hl=en&ct=clnk&cd=1&gl=us, accessed May 6, 2008.

[55] Darris Egger to David Murrah, February 5, 2005, oral history interview, Northwest Texas Conference Archives.

[56] 1983 *Journal*, p. 205; 1992 *Journal*, p. 150.

[57] Gary Mauldin to David Murrah, January 16, 2006, interview, notes in possession of author.

[58] 1995 *Journal*, p. 170; 1996 *Journal*, p. 178.

[59] 1979 *Journal*, p. 83; Ava Berry to David Murrah, July 15, 2008, email correspondence, in possession of author.

[60] 1983 *Journal*, p. 91; 1984 *Journal*, p. 7.

[61] 1987 *Journal*, p. 144.

[62] *United Methodist Reporter*, June 26, 1987, p. 1.

[63] *Ibid.*, June 21, 1991, p. 1.

[64] Jo Carr to David Murrah, March 28, 2007, oral history interview.

[65] 1995 *Journal*, p. 149.

[66] 1999 *Journal*, pp. 114-117; 2003 *Journal*, p. F-3; 2007 *Journal*, p. A-1; *United Methodist Review*, July 4, 2003, p. 1; Robert Monk to David Murrah, August 4, 2008, email correspondence, in possession of author.

[67] Butler, *Called by Grace*, p. 124.

[68] Rex Mauldin to David Murrah, May 6, 2008, email correspondence in possession of author.

[69] 1981 *Journal*, p 89.

[70] *United Methodist Reporter*, July 24, 1992, p. 1.

[71] *Ibid.*

[72] *Ibid.*, September 4, 1992, p. 1.

[73] Alfred Norris to David Murrah, September28, 2007, oral history interview, Northwest Texas Archives.

[74] *Ibid.*

[75] Reconciling Ministries Network website, "A Brief History of the Reconciling Movement," http://www.rmnetwork.org/history.asp, accessed May 7, 2008.

[76] *United Methodist Reporter*, November 8, 1991, p. 1.

[77] *Ibid.*

[78] Judicial Council Decisions, Decision No. 665, *In Re: Par. 906.12 as it Relates to the Decision of the General Commission on Christian Unity and Interreligious Concerns to be a "Reconciling Commission.* Archives Website,United Methodist Church, http://archives.umc.org/interior_judicial.asp?mid=263&JDID=705&JDMOD=VWD&SN=601&EN=700, accessed June 17, 2008.

[79] "The United Methodist Church and Homosexuality," http://www.religioustolerance.org/hom_umc6.htm, accessed May 7, 2008.

[80] *Ibid.*

[81] *United Methodist Reporter*, May 10, 1996, p. 2.

[82] "The United Methodist Church and Homosexuality."

[83] *New York Times,* June 13, 1998, accessed June 13, 2008, at http://query.nytimes.com/gst/fullpage.html?res=9D02E0DD1F30F930A25750C0A96E958260.

[84] Alfred Norris to David Murrah, September28, 2007, oral history interview, Northwest Texas Archives.

[85] 1996 *Journal*, p. 155.

[86] Transforming Congregations website, "Our History," http://www.transformingcong.org/, accessed May 8, 2008.

[87] According to Karen Booth, Executive Director of Transforming Congregations, only three Texas churches "historically partnered with us," and all three were churches in the greater Houston area. Karen Booth to David Murrah, May 9, 2008, email correspondence, in possession of author.

[88] The Confessing Movement Within the United Methodist Church, "Our Story," website, http://confessingumc.org/statement1.htm, accessed August 22, 2005; *United Methodist Reporter*, May 12, 1995, p. 3.

[89] The Confessing Movement, "Our Story."

[90] *Ibid.*

[91] *New York Times,* June 13, 1998, accessed June 13, 2008, at http://query.nytimes.com/gst/fullpage.html?res=9D02E0DD1F30F930A25750C0A96E958260.

[92] "A Petition to the Bishops of the United Methodist Church," (leaflet, April, 1998), in possession of the author. The petition was distributed with a cover letter by Good News in April 1998.

[93] James V. Heidinger II to Dear United Methodist Friend, letter, April 1998, in possession of author.

[94] 1998 *Pre-Conference Journal*, pp. 74-75.

[95] *Ibid.*, p. 86.

[96] Jim Smith, Tom Mills, Bill Couch, and David Ray to All Lay and Clergy Members of the Northwest Texas Annual Conference, Memorandum, May 28, 1998, in possession of author.

[97] *Ibid.*

[98] Thomas N. Mills, K. C. Blackketter, Rick Doyle, and Doug Allen, "A Resolution Toward Charity and Freedom in Ministries," (photocopy), in possession of author.

[99] 1998 *Pre-Conference Journal, Northwest Texas Conference of the United Methodist Church*, p. 77.

[100] 1998 *Journal*, p. 120.

[101] *Ibid.*

[102] Judicial Council Decisions, Decision No. 847, *In Re: Review of Bishop's Decision of Law in the Northwest Texas Annual Conference Related to a Resolution Adopted by the Conference Entitled "A Call to Doctrinal Integrity."* Archives Website, United Methodist Church, http://archives.umc.org/interior_judicial.asp?mid=263&JDID=888&JDMOD=VWD&SN=801&EN=900, accessed June 17, 2008.

[103] *Ibid.*, p. 121.

[104] *Ibid.*, p. 122.

[105] 1998 *Pre-Conference Journal*, pp. 83-84.

[106] 1998 Journal, pp. 123, 271.

[107] *Ibid.*

[108] *Ibid.*

[109] Thom Elliott to David Murah, May 2, 2008, email correspondence, in possession of author.

[110] Darrell and Mary Vines to David Murrah, August 31, 2005, notes in possession of author;

[111] *Ibid.*

[112] *Lubbock Avalanche-Journal*, November 14, 1998, accessed online at http://www.lubbockonline.com/stories/111498/1114980002.shtml, on May 2, 2008.

[113] 1999 *Journal*, p. 299.

[114] 1999 *Journal*, p. 118.

[115] *United Methodist Review*, November 26, 1999, p. 1; Judicial Council Decisions, Decision No. 871, *In Re: Review of Bishop's Decision of Law in the Northwest Texas Annual Conference Requiring Any Church Adopting an Identification Label to Reverse That Action*, Archives Website, United Methodist Church, http://archives.umc.org/interior_judicial.asp?mid=263&JDID=910&JDMOD=VWD&SN=801&EN=900, accessed June 17, 2008.

[116] *United Methodist Review*, November 26, 1999, p. 1.

[117] Alfred Norris to David Murrah, September 28, 2007.

[118] Ava Burdine Berry to David Murrah, July 14, 2008, email correspondence in possession of author.

[119] Complied from 1984 *Journal*, p. 137, and 2006 *Journal*, pp. I-1—I-6.

[120] Statistics supplied by Laura M. Chambers, Office of Analysis and Research, General Council on Fiance and Administration, The United Methodist Church, email correspondence, July 7, 2008, in possession of author.

[121] *United Methodist Review*, July 24, 1998, p. 1.

[122] 2004 *Journal*, Table 1; 2001 *Journal*, p. J41.

[123] Monk and Egger, "The Northwest Texas Annual Conference," p. 8.

[124] Ava Berry to David Murrah, July 14, 2008.

[125] William Wayne Cook, "From Four to Eighty-Four" (unpublished typescript, 1993), p. 294, Northwest Texas Conference Archives.

[126] Methodist Hospital, Lubbock School of Nursing, Announcement, 1955-1957, J. M. Willson Papers, 1900-1961, Southwest Collection, Texas Tech University.

[127] *Texas Methodist*, June 3, 1966, p. 10; *United Methodist Reporter*, February 3, 1984, p. 1.

[128] 1960 *Journal*, p. 79.

[129] *Texas Methodist*, June 3, 1966, p. 10.

[130] 1970 *Journal*, p. 113.

[131] Valerie Ullman-Avery, "Twenty Years Later," Lubbock *Avalanche-Journal*, May 6, 1990, accessed online at http://www.lubbockonline.com/tornado/stories/20Years/014.shtml, on April 25, 2008.

[132] 1974 *Journal*, p. 95; 1975 *Journal*, p. 100.

[133] *United Methodist Reporter*, August 29, 1982, p. 1; April 19, 1984, p. 1.

[134] *Texas Methodist*, August 21, 1981, p. 1.

[135] 1986 *Journal*, p. 227.

[136] *United Methodist Reporter*, April 3, 1987, p. 1.

[137] *United Methodist Reporter*, Supplement, February 7, 1992; Supplement, February 1991, p. 3.

[138] *Ibid.*

[139] Sinay, Ugur Tony, "Pre- and post-merger investigation of hospital mergers," *Eastern Economic Journal*, (Winter 1998), BNET website, http://findarticles.com/p/articles/mi_qa3620/is_/ai_n8761619, accessed April 25, 2008.

[140] 1995 *Journal*, p. 302.

[141] 2002 *Journal*, p. J-47.

[142] *United Methodist Reporter*, February 9, 1996, p. 1; 1972 *Journal*, p. 72; 1998 *Journal*, p.236.

[143] Alfred Norris to David Murrah, September 28.

[144] *United Methodist Reporter*, January 19, 1996.

[145] Alfred Norris to David Murrah, September 28, 2007.

[146] *Lubbock Avalanche-Journal*, January 28, 1996, p. 1.

[147] *Ibid.*

[148] *United Methodist Reporter*, August 2, 1996, insert.

[149] BSA website, http://www.bsahs.org/body.cfm?id=23, accessed April 27, 2008.

[150] 1996 *Journal*, p. 284; 1997 *Journal*, p. 217.

[151] *Lubbock Avalanche-Journal*, January 30, 1996, p. 7A.

[152] 1998 *Journal*, p. 227.

[153] *Ibid.*

[154] 2000 *Journal*, p. 222.

[155] *Ibid.*, p. 223.

[156] 2007 *Journal*, p. J-31.

[157] History, Mission, Vision, Facts and Statistics, Covenant Health System website, http://www.covenanthealth.org/view/AboutUs/history, accessed April 26, 2008.

[158] Alfred Norris to David Murrah, September 28, 2007.

[159] 1993 *Journal*, Statistical, Table 1.

[160] *United Methodist Reporter*, February 5, 1993, p. 1.

[161] 1994 *Journal*, Statistical Table 1.

[162] 1995 *Journal*, p. 190.

[163] *Ibid.*, p. 274.

[164] 2001 *Journal, p. J-79.*

[165] *Texas Methodist, September 10,.1971, p. 1.*

[166] *United Methodist Reporter*, March 28, 1997, p. 1.

[167] *Texas Methodist*, September 12, 1975, p. 1.

[168] *Ibid.* January 2, 1976, p. 4.

[169] *Texas Methodist*, August 17, 1976, p. 1.

[170] *United Methodist Reporter*, August 20, 1993, p. 1.

[171] *Ibid.*, July 31, 1981, p. 1; August 21, 1981, p. 1.

[172] *Ibid.*, Mrch 28, 1997, p. 1.

[173] *United Methodist Reporter*, April 10, 1987.

[174] *United Methodist Reporter*, February 14, 1986, p. 1.

[175] 1988 *Journal*, p. 213.

[176] *United Methodist Reporter*, March 27, 1987, p. 1.

[177] *United Methodist Reporter*, February 5, 1988, p. 1.

[178] 1988 *Journal*, p. 138; *United Methodist Reporter*, May 5, 1989, p. 1.

[179] *United Methodist Reporter*, January 19, 1990, p. 1.

[180] Berneice Mitchell to David Murrah, October 13, 2005, oral history interview, Northwest Texas Conference Archives.

[181] 1991 *Journal*, Statistical Table 1; 2000 *Journal*, Statistical Table 1.

[182] 2005 *Journal*, p. J-30.

[183] 1998 *Journal*, p. 136.

[184] Rio Grande Conference of the United Methodist Church website, http://www.riograndeconference.org/, accessed May 9, 2008.

[185] 2000 *Journal*, Statistical Table 2.

[186] 1999 *Journal*, p. 197.

[187] Alfred Norris to David Murrah, September 28, 2007. In 2003, a Houston church in Bishop Norris's Texas Conference voted to change its name from Parkcrest to Norris Chapel in honor of its new bishop. Norris retired in 2004, but was named in 2006 to the North Texas Conference to complete the term of the late Bishop Rhymes H. Moncure Jr. See *United Methodist Reporter*, January 31, 2003. p. 1; United Methodist Church Website, News Archives, accessed at http://

www.umc.org/site/c.gjJTJbMUIuE/b.2065515/k.ED49/Bishop_Alfred_Norris_to_lead_North_Texas_Conference.htm, on June 23, 2008.

[188] 1998 *Journal*, p. 271.

Chapter 10

[1] *United Methodist Reporter*, February 14, 1992, p. 1.

[2] *Ibid.*, January 31, 1997; 1999 *Journal*, p. 200.

[3] 1999 *Journal*, p. 198.

[4] 2000 *Journal*, p. 267.

[5] 2001 *Journal*, p. J42.

[6] Eddie Allsup to David Murrah, June 21, 2008, email correspondence, in possession of author.

[7] *United Methodist Review*, September 1, 2000, p. 3.

[8] *United Methodist Reporter*, July 21, 2000, p. 3.

[9] Max Whitfield to David Murrah, May 31, 2008, oral history interview, Northwest Texas Archives.

[10] *Ibid.*

[11] *Ibid.*

[12] *Ibid.*

[13] 2003 *Journal*, pp. A1, F3.

[14] 2004 *Journal*, p. J76.

[15] Council of Bishops, United Methodist Church, "Proposed Leadership Strategy, 2005-2008 Quadrennium," accessed online at http://bishops.umc.org//interior.asp?ptid=2&mid=6037, on May 18, 2005.

[16] Max Whitfield to David Murrah, May 31, 2008; Boyce Bowden, "Different Paths to a Common Goal: Healthy, Revitalized Churches Making Disciples," United Methodist Church, Interpreter Program website, accessed at http://www.interpretermagazine.org/interior.asp?ptid=43&mid=11764, on June 24, 2008.

[17] Max Whitfield to David Murrah, May 31, 2008.

[18] 2005 *Journal*, p. J68.

[19] 2005 *Journal*, p. J68.

[20] Dot Harris, video interview, "Important Pre-Conference Information regarding the 2006 Northwest Texas Annual Conference," compact disc (Northwest Texas Conference of the United Methodist Church, 2006),

[21] 2006 *Journal*, p. F4.

[22] Mike Shafer, video interview, "Important Pre-Conference Information regarding the 2006 Northwest Texas Annual Conference."

[23] Max Whitfield to David Murrah, May 31, 2008.

[24] *Ibid.*

[25] *Ibid.*, p. J13.

[26] 2007 *Journal*, pp. J19-J20.

[27] *Ibid.*,pp. F3-F4, F12.

[28] *United Methodist Reporter*, January 25, 2008, p. 1.

[29] Notes taken by author at Conference, June 3, 2008.

[30] D. Max Whitfield, "The Application of Wesley's Approach for Methodism in the United States" (unpublished typescript, 2007), in possession of author, courtesy D. Max Whitfield.

[31] 2001 *Journal*, Table 1; p. J4.

[32] 2002 *Journal*, Table 1; 2003 *Journal*, p. J19.

[33] 2004 *Journal*, Table 1; 2001 *Journal*, p. J41.

[34] *United Methodist Review*, July 16, 2004, p. 1; 2004 *Journal*, p. J27.

[35] Compiled from 2000-2007 *Journals*, Statistical Table One.

[36] 2004 *Journal*, p. F3.

[37] *A Century of Methodism*, inside back cover.

[38] 2005 *Journal*, pp. G3-G4.

[39] *Lubbock Avalanche-Journal*, June 9, 2005, p. A4.

[40] David E. Williams, "Breaking New Ground in Faith: St. Luke's Southwest," in Church History Task Force, *At the Edge of a Dream: The Story of St. Luke's United Methodist Church of Lubbock, Texas* (Lubbock: St. Luke's United Methodist Church, 2005), p. 41.

[41] *Lubbock Avalanche-Journal*, January 12, 2008, accessed at Lubbock Online website, http://www.lubbockonline.com/stories/011208/liv_235996405.shtml, on June 20, 2008.

[42] *Ibid.*

[43] *Amarillo Globe-News*, March 12, 2005, accessed online at http://www.amarillo.com/stories/031205/fai_1469824.shtml, on June 20, 2008.

[44] *United Methodist Reporter*, January 25, 2008, p. 1; 2006 *Journal*, p. F5.

[45] *Blue Skies* (Newsletter of the Methodist Mission Home, San Antonio), Summer, 2008, p. 4.

[46] Methodist Children's Home website, accessed at http://www.methodistchildrenshome.org/history.html, on June 27, 2008.

[47] 2007 *Journal*, p. J365.

[48] *United Methodist Reporter*, July 15, 1994, p. 1.

[49] 2007 *Journal*, p. J233; Lydia Patterson Institute website, accessed at http://www.lydiapattersoninstitute.org/aboutus.php, on June 27, 2008.

[50] 2007 *Journal*, p. J18.

[51] Haymes, *History of the Northwest Texas Conference*, p. 356.

[52] Website, Wesley Community Center, Amarillo, Texas, accessed at http://www.wesleycommunitycenter.com, on August 13, 2008.

[53] *United Methodist Review*, August 31, 2001, pp. 1,3.

[54] 2008 *Pre-Conference Journal*, p. 13.

[55] Haymes, *History of the Northwest Texas Conference*, p. 361.

[56] *Ibid.*, p. 367.

[57] *Ibid.*, p. 363-364.

[58] 1969 *Journal*, p. 67.

[59] 1970 *Journal*, p. 103.

[60] 2003 *Journal*, p. J31.

[61] 2008 *Pre-Conference Journal*, p. 19.

[62] *United Methodist Reporter*, May 23, 2003, p. 1; Northwest Texas Conference of the United Methodist Church website, Summer Camp Brochure, 2008, accessed at http://nwtx.brickriver.com/files/oFiles_Library_XZXLCZ/BCC_Brochure_for_Summer_08_BKXFFUY5.pdf, on June 28, 2008.

[63] Family Camp Weekend brochure, 2008, in possession of author.

[64] 2007 *Journal*, p. J28.

[65] Vernon, *et.al., Methodist Excitement*, p. 301; Downs and Sledge, eds., *Pride of our Western Prairies*, p. 111.

[66] Downs and Sledge, eds., *Pride of our Western Prairies*, p. 151.

[67] *Ibid.*, pp. 167, 179.

[68] 1985 *Journal*, pp. 301-302.

[69] *United Methodist Reporter*, March 6, 1987, p. 1.

[70] *Ibid.*, September 14, 1990, p. 1.

[71] *Ibid.*, April 10, 1992, p. 1.

[72] *Handbook of Texas Online*, s.v. ",", http://www.tshaonline.org/handbook/online/articles/MM/kbm17.html, accessed June 28, 2008; 1999 *Journal*, p. 267.

[73] 1999 *Journal*, p. 267.

[74] 2008 *Pre-Conference Journal*, p. 12.

[75] 2008 *Pre-Conference Journal*, p. 32. http://www.reporternews.com/news/2008/mar/13/mcm-launches-campaign, on June 28, 2008.

[76] *United Methodist Reporter*, February 9, 2007, p. 3B.

[77] *Abilene Reporter-News*, March 13, 2008, online website, accessed at

[78] NCAA Division III Outdoor Track and Field Championship website, accessed at http://www.titans.uwosh.edu/2008NCAATFChampionships/index.html, on June 28, 2008.

[79] 1917 *Journal*, p. 49.

[80] 1925 *Journal*, p. 40; 1927 *Journal*, p. 39.

[81] 1931 *Journal*, p. 46. In the fall of 1931, Texas Tech's enrollment was 4,772 and West Texas's was 870. The "one out of five" statement presumes the Panhandle A&M total enrollment was approximately 400 in 1931. See Ruth Horn Andrews, *Texas Tech: The First Thirty Years* (Lubbock: Texas Tech Press, 1956), p. 35, and J. A. Hill, *More than Brick and Mortar, West Texas State College, 1909-1959* (Canyon, Texas: The West Texas College Ex-Students Association, 1959), p. 91.

[82] 1932 *Journal*, p. 34; 1933 *Journal*, p. 29; Nail, et.al., *Texas Methodist Centennial Yearbook* (1934 *Journal*), p. 723.

[83] Haymes, *History of the Northwest Texas Conference*, pp. 334-335. See also Vernon, *et.al., Methodist Excitement*, p. 263.

[84] 1935 *Journal*, p. 26. According to the Texas Tech Wesley Foundation's website, the Wesley Foundation was founded in 1935. See http://www.ttuwesley.org/about_history.htm, accessed June 29, 2008.

[85] Annette Fetzer to David Murrah, June 30, 2008, telephone conversation. Annette is the associate director of the Wesley Foundation at Texas Tech and said that the building plaque indicates that the building was constructed in 1950. A reference to a 1952 date in Connor, ed., *Builders of the Southwest*, p. 169, is apparently incorrect.

[86] Haymes, *History of the Northwest Texas Conference*, p. 89.

[87] Robert Monk to David Murrah, August 8, 2008, email correspondence, in possession of author.

[88] Roger Loyd to David Murrah, August 12, 2008, oral history interview, Archives, Northwest Texas Conference. Roger Loyd became associate director of the Bridwell Library at SMU in 1980 and later moved to North Carolina to become Theological Librarian for the Duke Divinity School.

[89] Robb, *Contending for the Faith*, p. 122. See also Bill Cox, *At the Edge of a Dream*, p. 10.

[90] Robert Monk to David Murrah, August 8, 2008.

[91] Robert Sledge to David Murrah, August 5, 2008, email correspondence, in possession of author.

[92] Haymes, *History of the Northwest Texas Conference*, p. 351;Gabie Betts Burton, comp., *History of the Northwest Texas Conference Woman's Missionary Society, Methodist Episcopal Church, South, 1880-1928* (Abilene, Texas: Fisk Publishing Co., 1929), p, 47

[93] Monk and Egger, "The Northwest Texas Conference," p. 4.

[94] *Ibid.*, p. 336.

[95] *United Methodist Reporter*, November 17, 1989, p. 1.

[96] Butler, *Called by Grace*, p. 69.

[97] *Ibid.*

[98] 1969 *Journal*, p. 93; Garry Nall to David Murrah, email correspondence, July 1, 2008, in possession of author.

[99] 1996 *Journal*, p. 304.

[100] 1999 *Journal*, pp. 262-263.

[101] 2008 *Pre-Conference Journal*, p. 15.

[102] 2008 *Pre-Conference Journal*, p. 31.

[103] *Ibid.*, p. 32.

[104] Texas Tech Wesley Foundation website, "History," accessed at http://www.ttuwesley.org/about_history.htm, on June 30, 2008.

[105] Africa University website, accessed at http://www.africau.edu/, on June 30, 2008.

[106] General Board of Higher Education and Ministry, United Methodist Church, Black College Fund website, accessed at http://www.gbhem.org/site/c.lsKSL3POLvF/b.3534333/k.4E57/The_UM_Historically_Black_Colleges.htm, on June 30, 2008.

[107] 1970 *Journal*, p. 151; 2008 *Pre-Conference Journal*, p. 12.

[108] Eddie Allsup to David Murrah, June 30, 2008, email correspondence in possession of author.

[109] 1960 *Journal*, pp. 80-87.

[110] 1961 *Journal*, p. 80.

[111] 1962 *Journal*, p. 86.

[112] 1963 *Jurnal*, p. 88.

[113] *Ibid.*

[114] 1967 *Journal*, p. 108; District History Committee, "A History of the Abilene District," p. 38.

[115] District History Committee, "A History of the Abilene District of the Northwest Texas Conference of the United Methodist Church, 1910-1984 (unpublished typescript, 1984), p. 39.

[116] 1985 *Journal*, p. 198; *United Methodist Reporter*, June 8, 1984.

[117] "King's Manor Methodist Home, Inc., Hereford, Texas: A History," Records, King's Manor Methodist home, Inc., Northwest Texas Conference Archives.

[118] 1994 *Journal*, p. 297.

[119] Report, "King's Manor, Inc., undated, Records, King's Manor Records, Northwest Texas Conference Archives; 1997 *Journal*, pp. 211-212.

[120] 1996 *Journal*, p. 270; 1997 *Journal*, pp. 211-212.

[121] 2005 *Journal*, p. J32.

[122] King's Manor website, http://www.kmmrs.com/home.nxg, accessed April 23, 2008.

[123] *United Methodist Reporter*, August 22, 1997, p. 1.

[124] *United Methodist Reporter*, June 27, 1997, p. 1; 1998 *Journal*, p. 233.

[125] *United Methodist Reporter*, April 12, 2002, p. 1; Texas Tech University Health Sciences Center School of Nursing website, http://www.ttuhsc.edu/son/partnerships/garrison.aspx, accessed April 24, 2008.

[126] 2002 *Journal*, p. J-77; 2004 *Journal*, p. J-45; 2005 *Journal*, pp. J38-J39.

[127] 2006 *Journal*, p. J-32; 2007 *Journal*, p. J-38.

[128] Sears Methodist Retirement System Website, http://www.sears-methodist.org/index.php?option=com_content&task=view&id=25&Itemid=81, accessed April 20, 2008.

[129] 2008 *Pre-Conference Journal*, p. 1.

[130] *History of the Crowell Methodist Church*, p. 15.

[131] Haymes, *History of the Northwest Texas Conference*, p. 352. Haymes' 1961 book includes a very fine and detailed history of "Women's Work" in the Northwest Texas Conference, written by Mrs. Marvin Boyd, pp. 343-360. See also 1917 *Journal*, Statistical Table No. 1.

[132] "Mrs. Nat G. Rollins (Lena Elva Hyder: A Woman of Firsts," (unpublished typescript, nd), p. 1, Northwest Texas Archives, McMurry University; Vernon, *et.al.*, *Methodist Excitement*, pp. 229-230.

[133] Haymes, *History of the Northwest Texas Conference*, p. 352.

[134] 1952 *Journal*, Statistical Table No. 1.

[135] 1968 *Journal*, p. 147.

[136] 1973 *Journal*, Statistical Table No. 1.

[137] 1980 *Journal*, Statistical Table No. 1.

[138] 1998 *Journal*, Statistical Table No. 1; 2007 *Journal*, Statistical Table No. 1.

[139] 2008 *Pre-Conference Journal*, p. 42. See also "Our Story, 1982-2000," Vol. II (unpublished typescript, 2000), Northwest Texas Archives, McMurry University.

[140] 1944 *Journal, p. 73.*

[141] Haymes, *History of the Northwest Texas Conference*, p. 346.

[142] 1951 *Journal*, p. 69.

[143] 1955 *Journal*, Statistical Table No. 1.

[144] 1960 *Journal*, Statistical Table No. 1.

[145] *Texas Methodist*, February 4, 1966, p. 1.

[146] *History of the First United Methodist Church, Wellington, Texas*, p. 28.

[147] 1981 *Journal*, 1998 *Journal, 2007 Journal*, Statistical Table No. 1.

[148] *United Methodist Reporter*, July 8, 1983, p. 1.

[149] Ava Burdine Berry to David Murrah, July 2, 2008, email correspondence, in possession of author.

[150] *United Methodist Reporter*, July 19, 1991, p. 1.

[151] *Ibid.*, August 2, 1996; September 13, 1996.

[152] *United Methodist Review*, September 19, 1997, p. 1; September 18, 1998, p. 3.

[153] *United Methodist Reporter*, September 8, 2006, p. 1; September 21, 2007, p. 4.

[154] "Roundup 2008," booklet (n.p.:2008), in possession of author.

[155] 1940 *Journal*, p. 5.

[156] 1959 *Journal*, pp. 31-32.

[157] Landreth, *The Missing Book*, ix.

[158] United Methodist Church General Commission on Archives and History, United Methodist Church Timeline, accessed online at http://www.gcah.org/site/c.ghKJI0PHIoE/b.3504153/k.48DE/United_Methodist_Church_Timeline.htm, on July 2, 2008; *The Book of Discipline* (1984), pp. 372-373.

[159] 1968 *Journal*, p. 101.

[160] Robert Monk to David Murrah, August 4, 2008, email correspondence, in possession of author.

[161] 2000 *Journal*, p. 259.

[162] Based on a compilation of census for the counties in the Northwest Texas Conference, excluding Potter, Randall, Lubbock, Midland, and Taylor counties.

[163] *United Methodist Reporter*, April 20, 2007, p. 7B.

[164] *United Methodist Review*, September 26, 2003, p. 1. See also Tex Sample, *U.S. Lifestyles and Mainline Churches* (Louisville, Kentucky: Westminister/John Knox Press, 1990), pp. 9-17.

[165] Compiled from US Census date, US Census Bureau website, accessed at http://factfinder.census.gov/servlet/QTTable?_bm=y&-geo_id=16000US4845000&-qr_name=DEC_2000_SF1_U_QTP9&-ds_name=DEC_2000_SF1_U&-redoLog=false, on July 12, 2008.

[166] Compiled from population statistics in *Texas Almanac and State Industrial Guide, 1972-1973* (Dallas: A. H. Belo Corporation, 1971), pp.166, 174; U.S. Census Bureau, Population Finder Website, accessed at http://factfinder.census.gov/servlet/SAFFPopulation?_event=ChangeGeoContext&geo_id=16000US4845000&_geoContext=01000US%7C04000US48%7C16000US4803000&_street=&_county=lubbock&_cityTown=lubbock&_state=04000US48&_zip=&_lang=en&_sse=on&ActiveGeoDiv=geoSelect&_useEV=&pctxt=fph&pgsl=010&_submenuId=population_0&ds_name=null&_ci_nbr=null&qr_name=null&reg=null%3Anull&_keyword=&_industry=, on July 12, 2008; 1970 *Journal,* Statistical Table No. 1; 2007 *Journal,* Statistical Table No. 1.

[167] Compiled from 2007 *Journal,* Statistical Table No. 1.

[168] Robert Sledge, "The Rise and Fall of Texas Methodism" (unpublished typescript, 1991), courtesy Robert Sledge. Dr. Sledge presented a portion of this paper to the Texas United Methodist Historical Society in 1991.

[169] Max Whitfield, Sermon preached January 12, 2008 at Called Conference Session, Northwest Texas Conference, meeting at Lubbock, Texas, text courtesy of Max Whitfield.

[170] *United Methodist Reporter*, July 8, 2005, p. 6B.

[171] *Houston Chronicle*, February 24, 2007, p. 5F.

[172] *Corpus Christi Caller-Times*, March 1, 2008, p. 5B; *United Methodist Reporter*, June 27, 2008, p. 6B.

[173] *Wall Street Journal*, February 26, 2008, pp. D1-D2. See also The Pew Forum on Religion and Public Life: U.S. Religious Landscape Survey Website, accessed at http://religions.pewforum.org/, on July 12, 2008.

[174] Sample, *U.S. Lifestyles and Mainline Churches*, pp. 9-17.

[175] Yrigoyen, *et.al.*, *United Methodism at Forty*, p. 77.

[176] Hartford Institute for Religion Research Website, "Megachurch Definition," accessed at http://hirr.hartsem.edu/megachurch/definition.html, on July 12, 2008.

[177] *Houston Chronicle*, July 21, 2007, p. 4F.

[178] Trinity Church, Lubbock, Texas, Website, accessed at http://www.trinitytoday.com/templates/custrinitychurch/details.asp?id=30483&PID=251869, on July 12, 2008.

[179] Hartford Institute Website, Data Sorted by State of Texas, accessed at http://hirr.hartsem.edu/cgi-bin/mega/db.pl?db=default&uid=default&view_records=1&ID=*&sb=4&State=TX, accessed July 12, 2008.

[180] 2007 *Journal*, Statistical Table No. 1.

[181] Jerry Adler, "In Search of the Spiritual," *Newsweek*, September 5, 2005, p.49. For comments on how Methodist churches have been affected by the Hybels model, see Yrigoyen, Jr., *United Methodism at Forty*, pp. 77-78.

[182] *Ibid.*, September 26, 2004, accessed online at http://www.chron.com/CDA/archives/archive.mpl?id=2004_3803820, on June 21, 2008. By 2007, after Lakewood Church moved to the renovated Compaq Center in south Houston, its attendance increased to 47,000. See *The Christian Post*, October 23, 2007, accessed online at http://www.christianpost.com/article/20071003/29559_Top_100_Largest%2C_Fastest-Growing_Churches.htm, on June 21, 2008.

[183] 2004 *Journal*, Recapitulation Table.

[184] *Houston Chronicle*, July 24, 2005, p. 1D.

[185] *Ibid.*

[186] *Forbes.com*, September 17, 2003, accessed online at http://www.forbes.com/2003/09/17/cz_lk_0917megachurch_print.html, on June 21, 2008.

[187] *Houston Chronicle*, September 26, 2004. The article notes that "There are no intellectual interpretations of obscure Bible passages" in Osteen's sermons.

[188] Compiled from statistical tables in the Conference journals from 1910 to 2007.

[189] Nail, *The History of American Methodism*, pp. 498-499. Wright submitted his contribution to the book about 1959 or 1960.

[190] Tim Tanton, "United Methodist Bishops Sharpen Focus on Making Disciples of Christ," News Archives, May 9, 2005, United Methodist Church Website, accessed at http://archives.umc.org/interior.asp?ptid=2&mid=7661, on July 12, 2008.

[191] Gravis, *Twenty-Five Years on the Outside Row*, p. 55.

Index